Understanding
the Representational Mind

LD&CC **Learning, Development, and Conceptual Change**

Lila Gleitman, Susan Carey, Elissa Newport, and Elizabeth Spelke, editors

Names for Things: A Study in Human Learning, John MacNamara, 1982

Conceptual Change in Childhood, Susan Carey, 1985

"Gavagai!" or the Future History of the Animal Language Controversy, David Premack, 1986

Systems That Learn: An Introduction to Learning Theory for Cognitive and Computer Scientists, Daniel N. Osherson, 1986

From Simple Input to Complex Grammar, James L. Morgan, 1986

Concepts, Kinds, and Cognitive Development, Frank C. Keil, 1989

Learnability and Cognition: The Acquisition of Argument Structure, Steven Pinker, 1989

Mind Bugs: The Origins of Procedural Misconception, Kurt VanLehn, 1989

Categorization and Naming in Children: Problems of Induction, Ellen M. Markman, 1989

The Child's Theory of Mind, Henry M. Wellman, 1990

Understanding the Representational Mind, Josef Perner, 1991

Understanding the Representational Mind

Josef Perner

A Bradford Book
The MIT Press
Cambridge, Massachusetts
London, England

First MIT Press paperback edition, 1993
© 1991 Massachusetts Institute of Technology

This book was printed and bound in the United States of America.

Library of Congress Cataloging-in-Publication Data

Perner, Josef, 1948–
    Understanding the representational mind / Josef Perner.
        p. cm. — (Learning, development, and conceptual change)
    "A Bradford book."
    Includes bibliographical references (p.   ) and index.
    ISBN 0-262-16124-9 (HB),   0-262-66082-2 (PB)
        1. Mental representation in children.   2. Philosophy of mind in
    children.   3. Mental representation.   4. Philosophy of mind.
    I. Title.   II. Series.
    BF723.M43P47   1991
    155.4′13—dc20   91-1997
                                                                   CIP

To Cosette, Hannah, and Jacob for their love and incredible patience

To Heinz with his unerring sense for the essential

Contents

Series Foreword

This series in learning, development, and conceptual change will include state-of-the-art reference works, seminal book-length monographs, and texts on the development of concepts and mental structures. It will span learning in all domains of knowledge, from syntax to geometry to the social world, and will be concerned with all phases of development, from infancy through adulthood.

The series intends to engage such fundamental questions as

The nature and limits of learning and maturation: the influence of the environment, of initial structures, and of maturational changes in the nervous system on human development; learnability theory; the problem of induction; domainspecific constraints on development.

The nature of conceptual change: conceptual organization and conceptual change in child development, in the acquisition of expertise, and in the history of science.

Lila Gleitman
Susan Carey
Elissa Newport
Elizabeth Spelke

Acknowledgments

With this book I finally caught up with my past. I remember my early days at university giving presentations in Paul Weingartner's seminars on Brentano's *Psychology* and Hintikka's *Knowledge and Belief* before ever hearing of Jean Piaget, whose theory later became so central to my research interests in children's intellectual development. My appreciation of Piaget's theory, I now realize, was deeply influenced by Dan Berlyne, who also instilled in me a preoccupation with one of the central issues of this book—namely, what makes something a representation. On behalf of the reader I thank Anatol Rapoport for teaching me to stay clear of unnecessary formalization—invaluable advice for the readability of this book.

My developmental research interests would never have been successfully married with my earlier interests in epistemological philosophy had I not cooperated with Heinz Wimmer on children's understanding of deceptive ploys in stories. Fired by David Premack's and Guy Woodruff's "Does the chimpanzee have a theory of mind?" and by several philosophers' illuminating comments on their paper, our project turned quickly into a series of investigations of children's understanding of false belief with the cooperation of Sylvia Gruber, Jürgen Hogrefe and, in particular, Sue Leekam working with me on research grants from the Economic and Social Research Council (grants C00230076 and C00232199) and from the Medical Research Council (G 87 2095 2 N).

My theoretical outlook was shaped by Phil Johnson-Laird's work on mental models in syllogistic reasoning and by helpful discussions with Alan Garnham and Steve Isard on these matters. This led to a resurgence of my interests in semantics and to participation in a three-year discussion group initiated by Alan Frisch around Barwise and Perry's *Situation Semantics*. From there I found my way to Dretske's, Fodor's, Dennett's, and Millikan's more recent ideas about mental representation. With this background I was in a position to critically appreciate Alan

Leslie's analysis of pretend play and to theoretically integrate it with our research on children's understanding of false belief and knowledge.

There was also a substantial and fast-growing body of other related research. This became apparent in two conferences in the Spring of 1986; one organized by David Olson, Janet Astington, Alison Gopnik and Lynd Forguson in Toronto and the other by Paul Harris in Oxford. Two further conferences followed within the next three years, one organized by Chris Moore and Doug Frye at Yale University and the other by Andy Whiten in St. Andrews. I would like to thank the organizers and all contributors to these conferences and to this area at large for their valuable, often infuriating but always stimulating contributions to the field; in particular I would like to add to those already mentioned: Simon Baron-Cohen, Inge Bretherton, Michael Chandler, John Flavell, Uta Frith, Carl Johnson, Bob Lockhart, Jim Russell, Tom Shultz, Beate Sodian, Marjorie Taylor, Henry Wellman, Nicola Yuill, and Debbie Zaitchik.

This book would have never materialized without the necessary reprieve from teaching and administrative duties through a Social Science Research Fellowship from the Nuffield Foundation and a Research Fellowship from The Alexander-von-Humboldt Foundation. I thank Annette Karmiloff-Smith and Peter Bryant for their help in obtaining these fellowships and Franz Weinert for providing such an excellent working environment at the Max-Planck Institute for Psychological Research in Munich, where much of the first draft of this book was composed.

The improvements in the final draft are largely due to the many comments I received on the first. I am much indebted to Sue Carey and John Flavell for feedback on the entire opus and to the following for often very detailed comments on particular chapters: Janet Astington, Merry Bullock, Fabia Franco, Alan Garnham, Frances Green, Paul Harris, Sue Leekam, Gertrud Nunner-Winkler, Beate Sodian, Heinz Wimmer, and Jaan Valsiner. Of particular importance was Amahl Smith's thorough hatchet job ("a philosopher's comments") on my earlier version of chapter 2. Andreas Schmid and Jeremy Maris made it possible for me to produce a camera-ready copy. Ossi Huber and Steve Bell put life and wit into my figures.

Chapter 1

Introduction: Mind × Representation

"Mind is not just an Anglo-Saxon four-letter word."
(George Miller at an APA Convention in the 1960s).

"Mind" was a word in ill repute for many years within scientific psychology of the behaviorist era until "representation" came to its rescue. Rehabilitation began with the early success of cognitive psychology, which described the mind as processing information by transforming mental representations whose form or duration could be specified.[*] This example from the recent history of psychology is just one illustration of the intimate relationship between mind and representation. But it is not an easy liaison.

This book looks at the relationship between mind and representation by investigating how children develop an understanding of the mind as representational. This may seem an unusual angle of attack, but it helps focus attention on a neglected problem in cognitive science:

> The question of what makes a mental entity a representation of something has plagued philosophers but has largely passed psychologists by. ... In consequence, ... psychological theories of meaning have almost invariably failed to deal with reference. ... the question must ultimately have a biological answer: in nature, there is no representation without evolution, and perhaps there is no evolution beyond a certain point without the capacity to represent the world. (Johnson-Laird 1983, 399).

This question of what makes something a representation is not just a hobbyhorse of philosophers. Its answer has tangible developmental implications with respect to how a child's mind unfolds as a representational system and how children's understanding of the representational mind develops. To broach the issue, I contrast the ways in which cognitive psychology and our commonsense theory of mind make use of the notion of representation.

---

[*]What perhaps helped its scientific respectability most was the fact that it could be simulated by computer.

The Problem: Cognitive Psychology versus Common Sense

The hallmark of cognitive psychology is representation (Fodor and Pylyshyn 1988; Olson 1988), and the hallmark of representation is that it stands for something else. Ironically, that defining feature of representation plays no important role in cognitive psychology. Let me make this clearer by example of a typical reaction time experiment.

Anderson and Bower (1974) read their subjects stories in which a sentence like the following might come up:

"The girl was kissed by the boy."

At the end of the story one of the following test sentences was flashed on a display:

(1) "The boy kissed the girl."
(2) "The girl kissed the boy."
(3) "The boy was kissed by the girl."
(4) "The girl was kissed by the boy."

Subjects had to press one of two buttons, the one marked "T" if the test sentence was *true* for the story (sentences (1) and (4)), or the one marked "F" if it was *false*. The reaction time—the interval between the test sentence being flashed on the display and subject's response—was measured. From the fact, for instance, that subjects responded more quickly to sentence (4) than to sentence (1), Anderson and Bower argued that information in the mind preserves the active-passive difference of the story sentence. Furthermore, they were able to show that this was true only for a short time. After about two minutes the pattern of reaction times changed, suggesting that the mental representation had been transformed into a standard "active" sentence form (for instance, "The boy kissed the girl.") regardless of how the information had been given in the story.

I, for one, have always been intrigued by such demonstrations of the particular structure of mental representations. However, these demonstrations do not capitalize on the fact that the mental structures are representations of, for instance, the story events. Although this fact is essential for the mental structures to be representations at all, nothing of theoretical significance depends on it. Its importance is relegated to being a background feature of experimental procedure. It is necessary to make the task meaningful for the subject. There is something outside to which the subject has to respond, but all the interesting predictions about reaction times depend entirely on assumptions about internal processing characteristics. For Anderson and Bower's empirical concerns the question about what the assumed mental processes represent could safely be ignored.

Perhaps this is one reason why these experiments are so intriguing —because commonsense psychology has nothing to say about internal differences with respect to how information is stored in the mind. Commonsense specializes in making distinctions in how the mind is related to what it represents. For instance, if I had been in Anderson and Bower's experiment I might have wondered whether

I *knew* that the boy kissed the girl.

I just *thought* that the boy kissed the girl.

I *remembered* that the boy kissed the girl.

Traditionally, cognitive psychology has contributed little to explaining the difference between knowing, thinking, and remembering. These distinctions concern, what one could call, the semantics of mental states, namely, how the mind is connected to the world it represents. And this is the question that—as Phil Johnson-Laird remarked—has plagued philosophers and that—as my example underlines—has been passed over by cognitive psychology. [**Note 1.1** Semantic concerns in cognitive psychology.]

It is a question of great importance for the developing child. Thinking back, what could have been more important as a youngster than cooking up 50 ways to fool your mother? To make her think it was your brother who kicked you first (when in fact you started the fight), so that she'd blame him? Clearly, the exciting part was to get mother to *mis*represent what happened.

Any good old folk tale has lots of this. German children's stories seem a particularly rich source. Take Wilhelm Busch's story of the seven tricks by rascals Max and Moritz started on the front cover and continued here in figures 1.1 and 1.2. They steal her chickens by angling them through the chimney while Widow Tibbets is in the cellar. As they leave no trace, the poor widow suspects her good old innocent dog Spitz. If thinking is mental representation, then the widow's mistake is a case of misrepresentation.

At the moment down the cellar
(Dreaming not what soon befell her)

Widow Tibbets went for sour
Krout, which she would oft devour
With exceeding great desire
(Warmed a little at the fire).

Up there on the roof, meanwhile,
They are doing things in style.
Max already with forethought
A long fishing-line has brought.

Figure 1.1
Max and Moritz's misdeed number two (by Wilhelm Busch).

Ha! I guess there'll be a humming;
Here's the Widow Tibbets coming!

Rooted stood she to the spot,
When the pan her vision caught.

Gone was every blessed bird!
"Horrid Spitz!" was her first word.

Loud he yells with agony,
For he feels his conscience free.

Max and Moritz, dinner over,
In a hedge, snored under cover;

And of that great hen-feast now
Each has but a leg to show.

Figure 1.2
Max and Moritz's misdeed number two (continued from figure 1.1).

Misrepresentation has become a crucial test case for finding a satisfactory definition of "representation" (Dennett 1987; Dretske 1986b, 1988; Fodor 1987, 1990; Millikan 1984). Consider the theoretical problems Wilhelm Busch has created with his story. If Widow Tibbits thinks *her dog did it*, then what is she mentally representing? Is she representing the fact that *Max and Moritz did it* or is she representing something that never happened, namely, that *her dog did it?* The difficulty in answering this question fuels a deeper skepticism about mental states being representations at all.

To answer questions of this kind, then, it is necessary to get a good understanding of what makes something a representation in the first place. And that is what I set out to do in chapter 2 following recent philosophical writings on the topic. Here is just a brief outline.

Analyzing "Representation"

In his analysis of depiction, Nelson Goodman (1976) distinguishes between *representing* and *representing-as*—a distinction that was made earlier by Gottlob Frege (1892/1960) between *reference* and *sense* in connection with referential descriptions. Goodman points out that pictures always represent something (referent) as being a certain way (sense). He sees this feature as criterial for representation at large, making it impossible to reduce representation to simpler relationships like, for instance, resemblance between picture and depicted.

One interesting question is what makes *something* (particularly mental processes) *represent something else.* Most theorists agree that (at least part of) the answer lies in the causal relationship between the represented world and the representational medium (e.g., mind, photo). For instance, a photograph of a horse represents it as a horse because, as a result of the photographic process, the fact that the object photographed is a horse caused the image on the picture to take on the shape of a horse.

So, for a system to establish what its representational elements mean, it is important to first function in close causal contact with the world to be represented. Following Alan Leslie (1987), I will call representations that serve that function *primary representations.*

As primary representations start establishing their representational relationship to the represented world, things can start to go wrong and *misrepresentation* can occur. Maybe a perceptual error takes place—for instance the internal state represents the external object (referent) *as* a harmless leaf (sense) when in fact it is a dangerous predator.

Misrepresentation occurs when the system is not functioning properly. But shortcomings can be turned into virtues, and intellectually more highly developed organisms use representations of things in the world not to represent how these things are but how they could be. These *secondary representations* are purposely detached or "decoupled" from reality and are at the root of our ability to think of the past, the possible future, and even the nonexisting and to reason hypothetically.

An important point to keep in mind here is that secondary representations are parasitic on the existence of primary representations. Without the causal link to represented reality in primary functioning, internal states would have no representational function. Only after primary functioning has given meaning to internal states can they be "decoupled" from reality and be used as representations in a secondary function.

Another important ability—in particular for social animals—is *metarepresentation*, that is, the ability to represent that something (another organism) is representing something. Since the distinction between *what* is represented (referent) and *as what* it is represented (sense) is central to the concept of representation, metarepresentation requires understanding of this distinction. This distinction can only be understood with secondary representations. Hence, secondary representations are a prerequisite for metarepresentation. This important connection between representational levels can be best explained in the case of misrepresentation where the separation between sense and referent becomes so striking.

To understand misrepresentation, it is necessary to understand that in a specific instance the internal representation that has been created differs from what should have been created given the external (referent) situation. In other words, in order to metarepresent, one must contrast *what happened* with *what should have happened*. This contrast is a clear instance of secondary representation, since it requires representation of the nonexisting, ideal event. And since one can argue that to understand the proper nature of representation one must be able to consider the possibility of misrepresentation, it follows that metarepresentation presupposes secondary representation.

In sum, from the nature of representation and how it needs to be established there follows a necessary sequence. Primary representation has to occur before secondary representation becomes possible, and secondary representation has to develop before the concept of representation can be represented (metarepresentation). This necessary sequence provides the basis for my developmental framework.

Developmental Implications

My strategy is straightforward. From the defining features of representation I have deduced a sequence of three *levels of representation:* primary, secondary, and meta. This sequence has implications for how thinking develops as a representational activity and how children come to think about representation, in particular, about the mind as representational. These consequences are summarized in table 1.1.

The column headings list the three levels of representation. The first row restates these levels in terms of the (mental) models that I use in chapter 2 to give the notion of representation a more concrete form, and the second row gives a rough estimate of when children show the first signs of operating at each particular level.

The third row shows what becomes conceivable at each level of representation, which is the topic of chapter 3. At the primary level during the first year of life children are tied to reality by a single updating model of the currently real situation. At the secondary level, which emerges sometimes during the second year, children have multiple models at their disposal that allow representation of different situations. As a result, the past can be compared with the present and the existing with the nonexisting, hypothetical. Discussion in chapter 3 centers on the argument that pretense is understood as *action in hypothetical situations* (acting-as-if) and is not understood as a *representational activity* as Piaget (1945/1951) suggested. Proper understanding of representation emerges much later, at about 4 years.

The lower part of table 1.1 summarizes the implications of the sequence of representational levels for children's understanding of representation. Chapter 4 covers children's understanding of external representations like language and pictures. In the first year children understand, say, pictures as objects with interesting patterns, and they may recognize the similarity between the pattern and—what we recognize as—the depicted. But they do not yet give the picture an interpretation and see the depicted in the picture. This ability emerges with multiple models in the second year.

For instance, to understand that an image in the mirror is himself, the child needs one model to represent himself in reality and another to represent himself in the mirror. In other words, multiple models allow the child to interpret representations; that is, by looking at the mirror, he recognizes himself and not just somebody who looks like him. However, the ability to interpret representations does not require any understand-

Table 1.1
Representational levels and their developmental implications.

| | Level of representation | | |
	Primary	Secondary	Meta-
Modeling power	Single updating model	Multiple (complex) models	Model of a model
Approximate age of onset	First year	Second year	Around 4 years
What becomes conceivable	Real situation only	Different situations (past–future real–pretend)	Representational medium
Understanding representations		*"Situation theorist"*	*"Representation theorist"*
External (e.g.: picture)	Picture = object resembling depicted	Picture = depicted situation	Picture = marks on paper representing depicted
Mental (e.g.: thought)	External indicators of attention	Thought = situation thought about	Thought = mental state representing what is thought about

ing of the mirror as a representation. The child simply sees himself in the mirror. This is not to say that he confuses his mirror image with himself in reality. He understands that there is a difference between what is in the mirror and what is outside, but he construes this difference as a difference between situations—the real situation as opposed to the mirrored situation—just as he can distinguish the real from a pretend situation or the present from a past situation. I have therefore dubbed children at this age *situation theorists.*

At around 4 years children become proper *representation theorists.* They understand that the picture is an object in itself that represents something else. In other words, children understand that the picture needs to be interpreted. It is at this age that children understand that people can give different interpretations to one and the same picture—for instance, that a turtle drawn lying on its back will be seen as standing on its feet by a person sitting opposite. They start to understand cases of misrepresentation, which is reflected in their ability to distinguish appearance from reality and to remember mistakes. And they begin to understand how the content of a photograph (the situation shown on it) relates to its referent (the situation of which it was taken).

This progression in understanding external means of representation is partially paralleled in children's growing understanding of the mind as outlined in the last row of table 1.1. From early on infants seem aware of the importance of behaviors that we know are indicative of mental processes, such as emotional expression and looking. However, I argue in chapter 6, there is no clear evidence to what degree children actually conceive of the mental states behind these important behavioral indicators. This comes with the acquisition of multiple models which allow children to identify their own emotional experience in others ("If it had happened to me, what would I feel?"), enabling them to have empathic reactions to others' distress. At this age children start talking about mental states—for instance, about what people are thinking. Being situation theorists, however, these young children conceive of thinking not as a representational activity but as a preoccupation with the thought-about situation. An understanding of the mind as representational comes later, which I discuss for three different types of mental states in chapters 7 through 9. For instance, at about 4 years children start to understand cases of mental misrepresentation (false belief).

Since to understand that the mind represents is to understand but one of its aspects, my discussion of children's acquisition of the concept of mind in part II goes beyond that particular issue.

Understanding the Mind: Theory Change

The mind is familiar to us from our commonsense conception of it. Whether the mind is viewed as representational by common sense is far from clear. In chapter 5 I outline three criteria for distinguishing the mental from the physical: one's own mental states are (partly) given in one's *inner experience*; mental states are used as *theoretical constructs* in explaining action; and in the way they are linguistically expressed they are *about* something else *(Intentionality)*.

Using these criteria, I argue in chapter 6 that from the second year on children have some notion of the mental as familiar from their inner experience, which they can use as a theoretical construct in explaining and understanding other people's experiences, thus in turn explaining their actions. From that age on children are well on the way to construct-ing a *mentalistic theory of behavior*. However, there are certain problems with *aboutness* that are difficult to understand without a representational view of mind, in particular, the fact that mental states can misrepresent and that unlike physical relations, they relate only to certain aspects of an object and not to the object as such. These features of mentality are not really understood before the age of about 4 years, underlining my general developmental claim that it is at this age that children acquire an understanding of representation.

A particularly interesting question for developmental theory is how the concept of representation helps children understand the mind. In chapter 10 I argue that representation is not just one aspect among others of the mind, but provides the basis for explaining what the mind is. In other words, by conceptualizing the mind as a system of representations, the child switches from a *mentalistic theory of behavior*, in which mental states serve as concepts for explaining action, to a *representational theory of mind*, in which mental states are understood as serving a representat-ional function. One can think of the concept of "representation" as playing a catalytic role in children's reconceptualization of what the mind is, similar to the catalytic role that important scientific concepts play in the development of new scientific theories.

In chapter 11 I look at the topic of this book in terms of the acquisi-tion of *common sense psychology*. I contrast my view with traditional approaches, notably Piaget's notion of childhood *egocentrism* and the idea that fundamental egocentrism can be overcome by *role taking*. These views are grounded in the intellectual tradition that the mind is transpar-ent to itself, with direct knowledge about its own states. This tradition contrasts with the "theory view," according to which the mind is a theoretical construction for predicting and interpreting other people's as well as one's own feelings and actions.

Synopsis

There are three core ideas to this book. (1) An analysis of the concept "representation" focuses on the question of what makes something (in particular, a mental entity) a representation of something else. This analysis suggests (2) a sequence of three levels of representation with direct developmental consequences for how mental representation develops and how children come to understand what representation is. (3) This understanding of representation helps children form a theory of mind out of their existing mentalistic theory of behavior.

PART I
Representation

Chapter 2

The Concept "Representation"

My aim in this chapter is to explicate the concepts of *representation* and *metarepresentation* (representation of representations) and their different uses. Starting with an intuitive characterization of the notion of representation, I draw attention to the distinction between representational *medium* (e.g., a picture) and representational *content* (the depicted) and point out that the word "representation" should be used unambiguously to refer to the medium (the picture) only and not to its content (the depicted).

I then give a characterization of the *representing relation* that relates a representational medium to its content: representations represent something *as being a certain way*. Further characterizations help evaluate different answers to the question of what turns something into a representation of something else. I briefly discuss the *intentionalist* answer that it is the intentions of the users that confer representational status and the most popular versions of the *naturalist* answer that it is what *causes* a representation and in what *function* it is being used that determine what a representation represents.

Using models as a paradigm example of representations, I illustrate different uses that allow the distinction between *real* and *nonreal*. I emphasize that this distinction is not the same as that between *representation* and *represented*, which can only be made *metarepresentationally* by representing that something is a representation.

These distinctions set the stage for later chapters describing how children progress from being bound to present reality, to being able to think of past, future, and hypothetical events, to eventually think of something as being a representation (metarepresentation).

The Meaning of "Representation"

The notion of *representation* I want to develop here should cover things as diverse as pictures, models, sentences, and mental states. Although these things acquire their representational capacity and are used in quite different ways, they all share one essential feature. They are not just objects in themselves but in their representational capacity always evoke something else. For instance, a *photograph of you* is not just a piece of glossy paper with a certain pattern of color on it; it also has *you* in it——somehow. Although language and mind are quite different from pictures, they nevertheless also exhibit this aboutness: I can *talk* about you and I can *think* about you.

A Bit of Terminology   In all these examples it is fairly clear what we mean by "representation." But in order to be able to talk about it more explicitly, let me call (say) the picture the *representational medium*. What is shown on it—namely, you in all your beauty—I call its *representational content*, and the relation between the picture and you I call the *representing relation*. Putting it all together, we have the following scheme:

Medium ————[Representing Relation]————→ Content
(picture)   (you as shown)

So, to make no mistake, when I use the word "representation," I usually refer to the *representational medium*—that is, the picture. This may all seem terribly obvious, almost trivial, yet even at this point terminological confusion can occur, in particular, when we consider representations of nonexisting entities. In the examples above things seem clear partly because we are representing something real, namely, you. When asked where the representation is, I can point to the picture, and when asked what it represents, I can point to you. And you are obviously not a representation. But now let's exchange your picture for a picture of a unicorn (the philosophers' all-time favorite nonexisting entity). You'll agree that what is in front of you (the picture) is a representation. When asked what that picture represents, you may say, "A unicorn." However, when asked where that unicorn is, you are somewhat at a loss because you can't point anywhere but to the picture again and say, "It's nowhere, really, it just is in that picture; it's just a *representation*." Now, notice that in this case you are using "representation" not to refer to the picture (representational medium) but to refer to the unicorn (its representational content). Your temptation to use "representation" in this way is partly licensed by a certain ambiguity in how we use the word "representation." But failure to clearly register the ambiguity has caused many problems in the philosophy of mind.

Ambiguity of "Representation"   It was David Hume who suggested that what we are thinking of—the content or object of thought—is itself something mental. His contemporary Thomas Reid, however, castigated this view as the result of an ambiguity of representational terms like "conception," "belief," "idea" (and "representation"; see Lehrer 1986). Reid noted that "we use these terms sometimes to refer to the mental *operation or activity* [mental process, or a particular state of the mind as representational medium] and sometimes to the *object or content* of that activity" (cited in Lehrer 1986, 39). When this ambiguity leads to equivocation of the two meanings, a defective argument ensues, leading to Hume's conclusion. To help show where Hume equivocated the different meanings (it occurs in premise 2) I have set in boldface the words that refer to **"mental content"** and underlined references to "mental activity" [state of the medium]. Here, then, is Reid's reconstruction of Hume's argument in Lehrer's modernized version using the word "representation" instead of traditional terms like "ideas" (Lehrer 1986, 40):

(1) If we think of **something**, we must [mentally] represent **it**.

(2) **What** we [mentally] represent is a [mental] **representation**.

(3) A [mental] representation is a mental entity in our own mind.

(4) Therefore, when we think of **something**, **it** is a mental entity in our own mind.

On first sight this seems a perfectly good conclusion since its logical derivation from acceptable-looking premises is valid and since it seems to solve our ontological worries when applied to nonexisting things like unicorns: "If you think of a unicorn, it is a mental entity." That something is not quite right comes to the fore when "I am thinking of **you**," because then "you are just a mental entity." You would object to that, wouldn't you? The problem lies in the ambiguous use of the word "representation."

The first premise is perfectly acceptable to cognitive psychologists who consider "thinking" a representational activity, as long as "represent" and "think" refer to the process of thinking and **"something"** and **"it"** refer to the content of this representational process. The third premise also should be acceptable to cognitive psychologists who consider the mind a collection of representational processes. One could then refer to a particular instance of such a <u>representation</u> (representational process) as a <u>mental entity</u>. But understanding "representation" here as <u>process</u> creates problems for the second premise, because this premise explicitly equates **representation** with the content of representing (i.e., with "**what** we <u>represent</u>"). If "representation" is interpreted as process, then the second premise is obviously false and the whole argument ceases to support the truth of the conclusion. So we see that the alleged truth of (4) rests on equivocating <u>representation</u> as process with **representation** as the content of this process.

I draw so much attention to this equivocation of different meanings of the word "representation" because failure to keep these meanings apart has caused much confusion in recent developmental writings on children's ability to form *metarepresentations* (loosely defined: representations of representations). One can see why. If a unicorn is called a **representation** then a <u>representation</u> (e.g., picture) of a unicorn would be a "<u>representation</u> of a **representation**," hence a "metarepresentation." Similarly, the child's thought (a <u>representational process</u>) of a unicorn would then be a <u>representation</u> of a **representation**, hence a "metarepresentation." Notice that calling a child's thought of a unicorn a "metarepresentation" is only possible by equivocating the two meanings of "representation," and in any case it would mean something quite different than usually envisaged, namely, representation of the representational relation (e.g., Pylyshyn 1978). To avoid the confusions to which such equivocation inevitably leads, I will use the word "representation" to refer to the *representational process* or *medium* only. [**Note 2.1** The effects of the medium-content equivocation on the "metarepresentation" controversy in cognitive development.]

With this terminological clarification we could specify the meaning of "representation" as follows:

A representation is something that stands in a *representing relation* to something else.

This admittedly is not a very insightful definition, but it does straighten out which of the two meanings of the word "representation" we have in mind. To understand better what representation is, we really want some specification of the nature of the "representing relation."

Characterizing the Representing Relation

Representing Something As Something It is common to think that representations simply represent something else. However, with the following example Goodman (1976, 27–31) points out the need to distinguish between *representing* and *representing-as:*

> Everyday usage is often careless about the distinction between representation and representation-as. ... If I tell you I have a certain black horse, and then I produce a snapshot in which he has come out a light speck in the distance, you can hardly convict me of lying; but you may well feel that I misled you. You understandably ... expected the picture ... to be a black-horse-picture [i.e.] that it represents the ... thing in question as a [black] horse. (Goodman 1976, 29)

The problem with Goodman's snapshot is that it doesn't represent his black horse *as a black horse*, which does not mean that it wouldn't represent the horse at all. The lesson of this example is that representations do not just represent something (content) but *represent something as something*. We need to amend the crude definition of representation given above as

> A representation represents something *as something*

or perhaps less tersely as

> A representation represents something *as being a certain way.*

Dretske gives a more elaborate definition along these lines:

> By a representational system I shall mean any system whose function it is to indicate how things stand with respect to some other object, condition, or magnitude. (Dretske 1988, 52)

This distinction between representing and representing-as is not just a feature of photographs but has also been noticed with linguistic expressions.

Sense and Reference Gottlob Frege (1892/1960) noticed that although the expressions "Morning Star" and "Evening Star" refer to one and the same object (namely our planet Venus), their meaning cannot be equated because they differ in how they make reference to Venus. Roughly speaking, they differ because one expression describes Venus as the star visible in the morning, the other as the star visible in the evening. Frege called the part of their meaning that these expressions share their *referent* (Venus) and the part of their meaning in which they differ their *sense*. Following Dretske (1988, 70), I will sometimes use the word "referent" when I want to say *what* a representation represents and the word "sense" when talking about things being represented *as being a certain way.*

Further   The representing relation between medium and content
Characteristics   can be further specified by at least the following four
criteria, which largely follow from the fact that representations represent something as being a certain way.

1. *Asymmetry:* The picture of you represents you but you do *not* represent the picture.
2. *Singularity:* The picture of you only represents you, even if it is indistinguishable from a picture of your identical twin.
3. *Misrepresentation:* For any representation it is possible to misrepresent. For instance, using a flash often produces photos in which people have red eyes. Such a photo would misrepresent your beautiful blue eyes as being red.
4. *Nonexistence:* The object or situation depicted in a picture need not exist, as demonstrated by a picture of a unicorn or a manufactured photograph showing you in an embarrassing situation.

With these characterizations of the representing relation, in particular the fact that representations represent things as being a certain way, we have achieved some means for deciding whether something counts as an instance of representation or not. This will be important in two ways later on. It helps in deciding whether we should call early mental processes mental representations, and in deciding at what age children understand that something is a representation.

Although this issue is not central to concerns in this book, as psychologists we would like to know more about the nature of representation, not just what its logical structure is but also how it comes about.

---

*I should point out that different words have been used by different people to mark this distinction. The *referent* is sometimes called the *object* of representation, *denotation*, or *topic*. *Sense* is sometimes called *meaning* or *comment*.

What Makes One Thing Represent Another

There are two basic answers to the question of what makes something a representation. The *intentionalist* answer is that some things are representations because they are intended and interpreted in that way. As we will see, this can account for representations that are used by people endowed with intentions but not for mental representations since that begs the question of who intends them to be representations. The *naturalist* answer is that some natural process—independent of the human mind—can give representational status. I will briefly discuss three suggestions: resemblance, causality, and function.

User's Intentions   Although Blackburn (1984, 41) traces the idea back to John Locke, more recently Paul Grice (1957) has defined (nonnatural) meaning of symbols and representations in terms of their users' communicative intentions. For instance, the sentence "This is a black horse" means *this is a black horse* because speakers in the linguistic community intend it to mean that and listeners can interpret it this way.

I will not dwell on this proposal but point out that, although it may be useful in explaining the representational qualities of artifacts like language and even pictures, it cannot give a satisfactory account of mental representation since it presupposes the interpretive powers of the mind. If we wanted to use this criterion to explain why a mental state represents something, we would have to take recourse to some other mental state, intending it to have that representational function. Similarly for that second mental state, leading to a third one—and so on ad infinitum. This results in an infinite regress, which renders the *intentionalist* answer unsatisfactory as an explanation of the representational powers of the mind.

However, I mention this approach because understanding that a representation like a picture can be interpreted by the human mind provides a legitimate criterion for deciding whether children have an understanding that something is a representation. If, however, we want to know whether the child's own mind (in early infancy) can be described as representational, we must look elsewhere for help. We need a *naturalist* criterion that does not presuppose the mind as an interpreter of representational states.

Resemblance   It is an old idea that things represent other things because there is *resemblance*. The picture represents the depicted because it "looks like" it. In the case of the mind it was thought—dating back to Aristotle—that the mind represents by forming direct *copies* of external objects, that is, by taking on the same properties as these objects. So, thinking of a round red ball meant entertaining a mental object that is round and red. A weaker form of this view was held by Berkeley and Hume, who assumed thoughts were mental images that (like pictures) resembled the imaged object (see Cummins 1989, chaps. 1 and 3).

This *copy theory of representation* was already criticized by Bishop Berkeley himself, and more recently by Ludwig Wittgenstein and by Nelson Goodman in his analysis of depiction (Goodman, 1976). That resemblance cannot be the same as representation can be seen by checking our criteria.

Asymmetry. Resemblance is a symmetrical relation. For instance, the photograph resembles you as much as you resemble the photograph. Hence, you would represent the photograph as much as the photograph represents you.

Singularity. The photograph taken of you resembles you as much as your identical twin. Hence, it would be not only a representation of you but equally one of your twin.

Misrepresentation. Misrepresentation would be impossible. For instance, the photo that shows you as having red eyes would not misrepresent you but would represent some other person who looks like you but has red eyes.

Nonexistence. Resemblance cannot account for representations of nonexisting entities like unicorns, since there are no unicorns that the picture could resemble.

One reason why resemblance provides such a bad account of representation is its failure to make Goodman's distinction between *what* is represented (referent) and *as what* it is represented (sense). This distinction is impossible because what a picture represents is completely determined by what it looks like. For instance, the photo of Nelson Goodman's horse cannot be a picture of it since it does not resemble it at all. So let us see whether more recent attempts at providing a naturalist account of representation fare better on these criteria.

Causality   More recently—although Cummins (1989) traces the idea back to John Locke—causality has been viewed as the source of representational content for representations in general (e.g., language: Stampe 1979) and mental representations in particular (Dretske 1981; Fodor 1987, 1990). This idea is easiest to understand in the case of photographs or perceptual states of mind.

If we took a proper snapshot of Goodman's black horse, the animal would be causally responsible (through the photographic process) for an image on the eventual color print, and the fact that the animal is a black horse would be responsible for the fact that the image on the print takes on the shape of a horse and the color black. Now we can say that the image represents the particular animal (referent) as a black horse (sense). This we can say, not because the image looks like a black horse, the causal theorist would claim, but because it was the particular animal that caused the image and because it was the animal's properties of being a horse and black that caused the image to be a black horse shape.

This is the basic, bare-bones theory. Even so, it does justice to the *asymmetry* of representations. Since the horse is the causal source of its image on the picture, it is the picture that represents the horse and not the other way round. It also gets around the *singularity* problem. Even if one could not tell by looking at the picture whether it is Goodman's or somebody else's black horse (both would come out looking the same in the picture), the picture still represents Goodman's horse, and only his horse, because it was his horse that caused the image.

However, this basic causal theory cannot account for representation of *nonexisting entities* (Fodor 1984, 238) since a nonexisting entity cannot be the cause of anything. There is also little room for the possibility of *misrepresentation*, which Dretske (1986b, 1988), Dennett (1987), Fodor (1987, 1990), and Millikan (1984) view as a critical feature of representation. To illustrate the problem, let us consider maps of the local environment. By surveying this environment, cartographers can produce marks on a piece of paper, where certain features of these marks reliably covary with features of the environment. For instance, wherever there is a pub, a "PH" (for *public house*) appears on the map. At this stage the meaning of "PH" is completely determined by the causal process of cartography that produces the map. No misrepresentation can occur. For, should a surveyor mistake a church for a pub, with the result that a "PH" is printed where the church is located, the "PH" would simply represent that *church*, since it was the presence of the church that led to the "PH" on the map. To solve this problem, theorists have gone different ways.

Fodor tries to stay true to a pure causal theory and goes counterfactual. Roughly, the idea is this. A fabricated photo showing a horselike creature with a horn on its head represents something as being a unicorn because if such a creature had been standing in front of the camera, the picture would have turned out that way. For his explanation of misrepresentation, see "Asymmetric Dependency" in Fodor 1987, chap. 4 and 1990, chaps. 3 and 4. Dretske (1986a,b, 1988), on the other hand, goes functional.

Representational **Function**   The intuition here is that representations could not just be things that are caused by what they represent because then they would never have developed in the first place. They need to serve some function in some overarching system that uses them. They need to be not only caused by the external world but also "interpreted," which in the case of mental representations needs to be understood nonintentionally as 'causally influencing behavior'. To see this more clearly, let us return to the pubs on our map.

The point of the map is that people can use it to find their way to the pub. Otherwise, maps would have never been invented. Now let us assume that the users have no clue what "PH" stands for. But if all works well and in the vast majority of cases there really is a pub wherever the maps show a "PH," the users will come to rely on this regularity and be guided by the symbol "PH" to those locations where there are pubs. Maps don't have to be perfect. An occasional deviation from this regularity (not yet a misrepresentation) won't matter as long as there are not too many of them to render the maps useless as sensible guides to pubs.

Once the "PH" symbol has taken hold on the users' behavior, its meaning is no longer pinned down by the cartographic process alone but is also determined by its influence on the users. Two important things can happen from here on. It is at this stage that misrepresentation becomes possible. If it now happens that a church is cartographed as "PH," we can say that the "PH" misrepresents the church as a pub because of the map users, since the "PH" will cause them to head toward the church in search of a drink.

The other important development that becomes possible at this stage is that representations can develop *secondary* functions. The *primary* function is to reflect the represented environment faithfully so that the user can learn to use it as a reliable guide. This is primary because it establishes the meaning of representational elements like "PH." But once this meaning has been established, a map of a fictional environment can be generated by combining representational elements established by the primary process. This allows representations to be positively employed to represent hypothetical, nonexisting states of the environment.

Since the acquisition and understanding of different representational functions will be of central importance in the rest of the book. So I want to describe these functions in more detail by using models as concrete illustrations.

Using Representations: "Model Theory"

Establishing
a Model

A good demonstration of a model in action is the sandbox in military headquarters where generals plan their moves on the battlefield. The sand in the box shaped like the battlefield stands for the battlefield, little sticks for the soldiers, furrows in the sand for ditches in the field, blocks of wood for tanks, and the spatial positions of sticks, blocks, and furrows in the sandbox for spatial positions on the battlefield. A simple example is shown in figure 2.1.

The sandbox happens to be an *analogue* model of the battlefield, because the spatial relations between objects on the battlefield are represented by spatial relations between the objects in the sandbox. This should not distract from the fact that the notion of a model can also cover the representational qualities of linguistic expressions (e.g., Dowty, Wall, and Peters 1981). In this case a linguistic symbol is assigned to each relevant object and each spatial relation on the battlefield. For instance, "s" stands for *soldier*, "d" for *ditch*, and "in" for *inside*. Syntactic conventions are necessary to regulate the combination of these different elements. The expression "s-in-d" then represents the fact that *the soldier is inside the ditch* on the battlefield.

Establishing which element in the model represents which element in the world is called an *interpretation* of the model. That is, before the sandbox was interpreted as the battlefield and the twigs as soldiers, the sandbox was just a sandbox and the twigs just pieces of wood. Only when the interpretation as battlefield, soldiers, and so on, has been established can the sandbox be used as a model of the battlefield.

Using
Models

The sandbox can be used as a model in different ways. One important and theoretically primary use is to *inform* about the actual state of the battlefield. If the scout has done a good job, the twigs and furrows in the sandbox will be where the soldiers and ditches are on the battlefield. In this use the model serves to inform the user. It serves the same function as so-called *epistemic* or *cognitive* mental states like *seeing, knowing, believing*—just to mention a few of those states of the mind that reflect or ought to reflect how the world really is.

Another important use of the sandbox is to project future states of the battlefield. Here, the sandbox represents not the actual state of the battle but merely hypothetical situations. Two different uses can be distinguished here. The model can be used to project *desirable situations*, for instance, the enemy cornered in an indefensible position. In this function it is related to so-called *conative* mental states like *wants, desires, goals*. These states represent desirable future situations that govern action provided a possible course of action can be found for achieving those situations.

The other use of the model involving hypothetical situations is to check out the consequences of possible strategic moves: "If we move the tanks over here, then we could ...." Here the model is used in the service of hypothetical *reasoning*, expressed by words like *"think," "assume," "pretend."*

The fact that models and mental states can serve different functions for which they represent different states of the world raises an important question about their representational function. What does a model represent? The answer to this question is clear in the informational case, where the model reflects the actual state of the battlefield. It represents the state of the battle. The answer becomes more controversial in the case of hypothetical situations, since in this case there is no real event or situation out there in the world that could be the thing that is being represented.

Hypothetical Situations Hypothetical situations are a figment of philosophers' imagination, but a useful one. Take the case where the general starts manipulating the model that the scout so carefully constructed to faithfully reflect the current situation on the battlefield: "Now if we move this soldier out of that tank, and then that soldier...." The model still represents! But what? Not the situation on the battlefield, since the tank (block of wood) and the soldier (twig) have been moved. Perhaps its elements still represent but not the combination of elements. But that can't be right either, for the fact that the model tank and soldier were moved to new positions has significance. It's not as if the sticks and blocks had been taken out of the sandbox, retaining significance only as individual elements: *soldier* and *tank*, without spatial

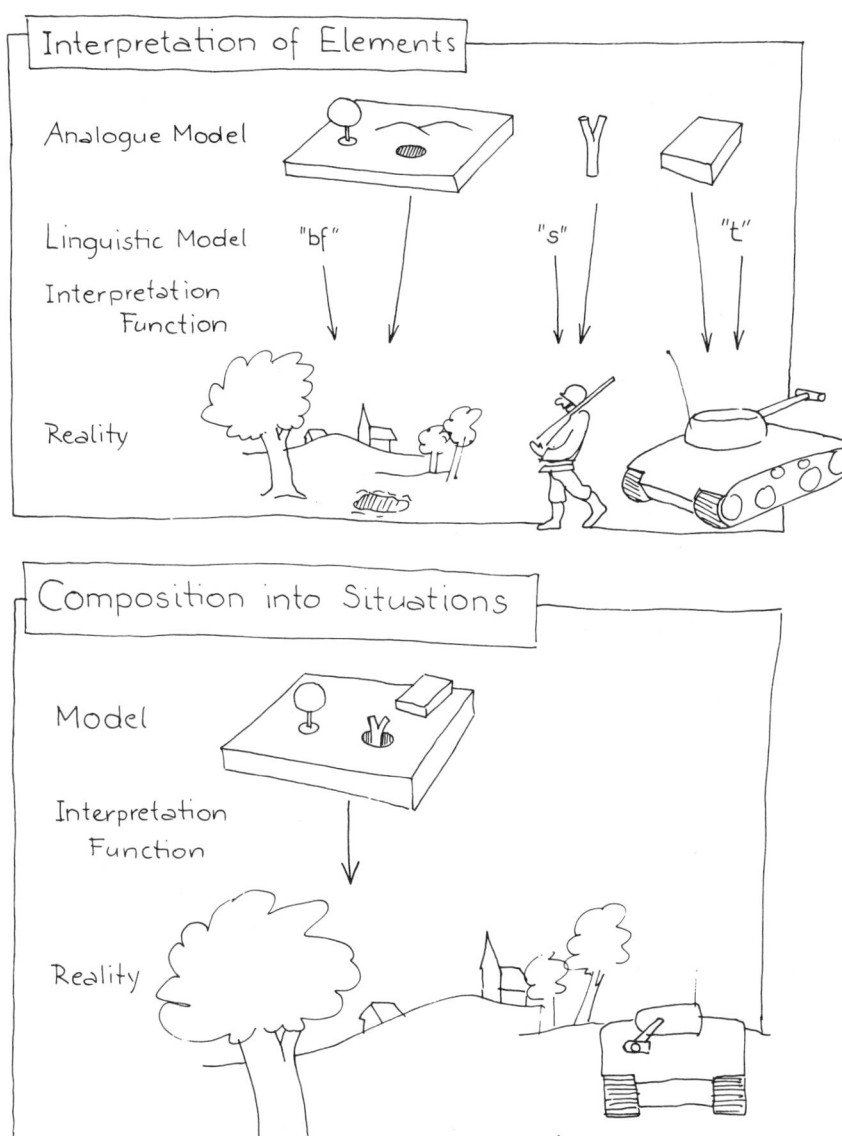

Figure 2.1
Establishing a model.

framework. No, the change of combinations of elements has significance too. It represents a situation, even though not the real one.

Figure 2.2 helps to keep track of what needs to be conceptually distinguished: the situation on the battlefield (reality) where the soldier is sitting on the tank, the sandbox model of that situation with the twig inside the wooden block, the same model after the general has tampered with it and taken the twig out of the block, and finally the object of dispute: the hypothetical situation where the soldier has left his tank as projected by the changed model.

It is only natural to speak of the changed model as representing a hypothetical situation. To deny that the model represents some situation would be utterly strange. Just because the elements are moved around, the model does not cease to represent. But if it still represents, it needs to represent something, and what could that be other than a possible situation? It is the answer to this question about what the changed model represents that requires the invention of hypothetical situations. However, the introduction of hypothetical situations has its philosophical adversaries. No wonder, because it is a serious ontological problem to seemingly posit the existence of something that does not exist. The problem is that we project nonexisting entities and hypothetical situations by using representations, and so the temptation is strong to simply equate hypothetical situations with the representations used to project them.

As noted earlier, the temptation to identify hypothetical situations with representations is fueled by the ambiguity in the word "representation," which although normally used to refer to the representational medium is sometimes also used to refer to **representational content**. And now we can see why equivocation of the different meanings of "representation" is particularly tempting when dealing with representations of nonexisting entities or situations, because it appears to answer the question about what such representations represent. In fact, it would be perfectly legitimate to say that what is represented is merely a "represented situation," meaning that a nonexistent situation is represented that owes its "existence" to being projected by a representation. Such talk of "represented situations" is admissible as long as one is not trapped by it into equivocating "**represented situation**" with the "representation by means of which that represented situation is projected."

My defense of hypothetical situations has provided a tentative answer to the question about what models represent: an informative model represents the actual situation, whereas a model that has been tampered with represents a hypothetical situation. Unfortunately, this answer is too

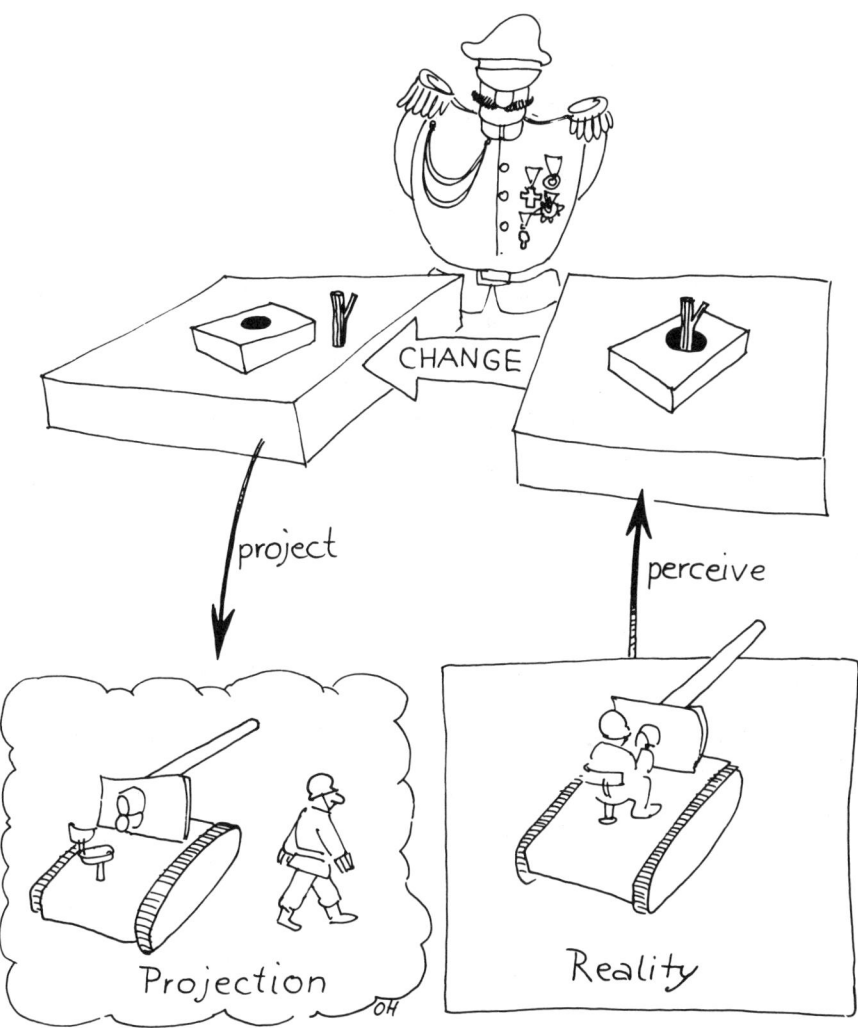

Figure 2.2
Using a model to project a hypothetical situation.

simple to cover cases of misrepresentation. There we need to make
Goodman's distinction between the situation the model represents
(referent) and how the model represents that situation *as being* (sense).

Misrepresentation: The distinction between sense and referent becomes
Sense ≠ Referent   crucial for understanding cases of misrepresentation.
                        To see why, let us go back to the case of our military
model. The scout was supposed to make a replica of the current position
of the battlefield. He worked on the well-founded assumption of absolute
military discipline and put the soldier (twig) into the ditch (furrow) where
he belongs. He did not foresee that this soldier gave in to certain effects
of military cuisine and consequently is spending all day out of his ditch
in the nearby woods.

The generals, not suspecting anything unforeseen, accepted the scout's
model as a representation *of* the battlefield and are basing their plans on
it. That is, for them the model represents the actual situation (where the
soldier is squatting in the woods), although the model (mis)represents
that real situation *as* a different situation (namely the one where the
soldier was dutifully on guard in his ditch). So in some way the model
"represents" both these situations, and it is therefore necessary to
distinguish between them as the situation that is represented (referent)
and the situation *as which* the referent situation is represented (sense),
as shown in figure 2.3.

In the mental realm *false beliefs* correspond to misrepresentation. The
general's belief that the soldier is on duty is a mental model that
misrepresents the real situation in the field, and it, too, is characterized
by the divergence between the real situation it represents (referent) and
how it represents that situation *as being* (sense).

The sense-referent distinction obviously occurs in the case of informative models, where there is something real out there to which the model
(due to its informational role) refers, and the situation projected by the
model's structure. In the case of models whose function is merely to
project possible situations, the distinction between content and referent
becomes less important since there is nothing independent out there to
which the model could refer. So for practical purposes one could get
away with simply identifying what the model represents (referent) with
the situation *as which* the model represents it (sense).

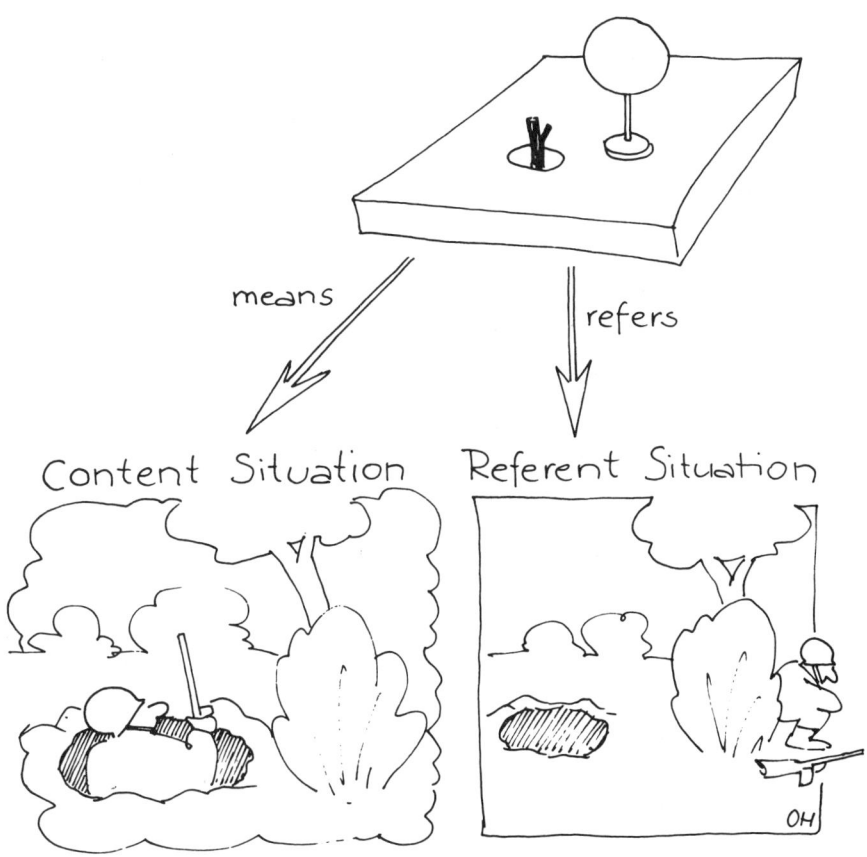

Figure 2.3
Content and referent situation of a "misrepresenting" model.

Mental
Models

Concrete examples such as maps and sandboxes serve a good didactic purpose for introducing problems of representation in a tangible way. However, our ultimate interest lies with these kinds of representations only as a guide to understanding mental representation. I chose the military sandbox as our prime example because, unlike the proverbial "picture in the head," it better captures the point that meaningful elements can be recombined into novel constellations, thereby projecting novel situations or entities. This recombinative ability underlies the mind's flexibility and productivity.*

However, even our sandbox is still vastly different from mental representation. One important difference is that an external representation is always used by somebody with a mind. That is, the generals interpret the constellation in the sandbox by forming mental representations; they *understand* what the elements in the box stand for. In contrast, they do not interpret, and hence do not understand in the same way, their mental models. They simply *use* their mind. So, if we want the sandbox to help us understand mental models, we have to treat it as if it were simply used by the generals and not interpreted. And this brings us to another difference between sandbox and mind. The "mind" represents what is really the case, what was the case, what the future might bring, and so on, all at the same time. The mind must therefore be entertaining several mental models simultaneously.

One thing is clear: if we want to reduce the role of the generals' minds and gradually replace them with sandboxes (the ultimate goal of research in artificial intelligence), we won't get away with just considering a single instance of a model. Although I considered the possibility of using that one sandbox in different ways at different times, I never mentioned the necessity of having several models at the same time. Yet to plan a simple action, one needs to represent the current situation and the desired situation simultaneously. The example of the sandbox did not make this apparent because the needed comparison between situations was carried out by the models in the generals' minds. However, since we want to make the representational states of the mind explicit, we need many sandboxes, and we need to limit the generals' role to being "mindless" model operators.

---

*This is an old empiricist idea. Hume (1748/1962, 34) proposed that complex concepts are created by recombination of primitive concepts that are gained from experience. And this enables us to conceive of nonexisting things like a "golden mountain" by creatively combining existing concepts of "gold" and "mountain."

Multiple Models and Metarepresentation

Multiplicity of models creates new representational problems. The most important issue is that the different models represent different situations, and to avoid confusion each model needs to specify what kind of situation it represents. This is partly taken care of by the internal structure of the model (arrangement of elements specifying the situation as being a certain way). For instance, the model "s-in-d" specifies the situation as one where *the soldier is inside his ditch*, but it leaves open whether this *is* the situation out on the battlefield, whether it *was* the situation there, or whether it is purely hypothetical. In other words, the model's internal structure leaves open what its referent is. However, for correct use of the model this needs to be specified. How can this be done? Focusing only on the difference between *real* and *hypothetical*, I will consider two possibilities: marking the "internal function" of a model and the metarepresentational option of representing that the model is a model of reality. I will show that ultimately only the "internal function" option is suited for marking the referent.

Differentiation by Internal Function   Minimally our generals are faced with two sandboxes, one in the center of the room representing the current defensive situation on the battlefield, the other in the corner representing a hypothetical attack on the enemy. How do the generals know that the center model is the model of the current situation in the field? Well, because that is the role it is supposed to play: it is the model only the scouts are allowed to change, and headquarter colleagues are banned from meddling with it.

A related but different question is whether the center stage model does a good job, that is, whether it models reality accurately. As always, things can go wrong. Some forgetful general did meddle with the center model, or the scout has made an error, or (more sinister), he is a spy who deliberately intends to misinform headquarters. These things do happen, but what defenses do the generals have against them? Only relative ones. They may send out several scouts in the hope that not all commit the same error and that not all are spies; but in the end they have to trust the reliability of some of these scouts. The same holds true for our mind. We typically rely without question on our sense organs. What we see is real! Here again, there is the possibility of illusion or trickery. Fortunately, these occasions are rare, and to uncover the truth we can only look for consistency among other "reliable" sources. For instance, the generals might employ three independently working scouts, each structuring his own model. The generals then can compare all three models. If they all agree, the center model is structured accordingly. If only two scouts agree, the center model takes on their information. Should all three scouts have built different models the generals might send out a fourth scout in the hope that he will agree with at least one of the others.

What the generals are doing is improving their methods for ensuring that their center stage model reflects reality as accurately as possible. What they are not doing is questioning the status of center stage as a model *of* reality. Center stage retains its status purely on the internal grounds that being a model of reality is the role that has been assigned to it. In other words, reality simply "is" that model that integrates the information brought by the scouts who come in from the cold, whereas models that are manipulated by fellow headquarters staff contain merely nonreal situations. And there are rules for using these models: Orders for *serious* action must be based on the center model. The corner model may only be used for play or interesting talk. (Only in peacetime on April 1 may it be used for orders to engage in pretend attacks.)

The main point I want to emphasize is that the distinction between models of reality and models of hypothetical situations is made on purely "internal" grounds. But then one has the feeling that the generals ought to be able to do much better in making this distinction, exactly, by looking outside their headquarters. Or, since our generals are to behave like mental processes that cannot go outside the mind, they should send a scout to investigate whether and how the center stage model is actually linked to the battlefield. The returning scout will bring a report on the other scouts' activity as establishing a link between the battlefield and the center stage model. Notice, however, that for representing the scout's report the generals have to become *metarepresenters*, that is, they have to represent the representational relationship (scouting as part of it) between battlefield and model.

In the next section I first elaborate what metarepresentation involves and then return to the question of whether metarepresentation can give the generals a better criterion for deciding between real and not-real. Perhaps surprisingly, the upshot is that metarepresentation can improve understanding of what role a reality-model should play but that it cannot substitute for internal assignment of that role.

The Meaning of "Metarepresentation"   According to the Shorter Oxford English Dictionary (1973, 1313), one of the chief senses of the prefix "meta-" is "change (of place, order, condition, or nature), corresponding to Latin *trans-*." In this sense "metarepresentational" can apply to anything that occasions a change in the nature of representation. For instance, markings that regulate the "internal" function of a model would qualify, since they modify whether the model represents a *real* or a *hypothetical* situation. I will therefore refer to such markings as "metarepresentational comments."

In the "theory of mind" literature (Leslie 1987, 417; Olson, Astington, and Harris 1988, 1), however, the term "metarepresentation" is commonly given the more specific meaning of *representation of a representation* or, to be precise, *representation of a representation as a representation* (Perner 1988) which captures how Zenon Pylyshyn (1978, 593), one of the first to use the term, implicitly defines it as the "ability to *represent the representational relation itself*" when he speaks of a *"recursive metarepresentational* capacity." This definition is analogous to the use of "metalanguage," which also carries that recursive connotation of "language about language." I reserve the expression "metarepresentation" for this recursive meaning.

It is important to notice that "metarepresentational comments," that is, markings that direct "internal" use and thereby allow differentiation between *real* and *hypothetical*, are not metarepresentations in that recursive sense, since these comments do not represent any representations. Rather, they modify the representational status of representations and hence should be called "metarepresentational" only in the more basic sense of "meta-" as *change in nature*.

These different senses of "metarepresentational" have not been clearly differentiated in the developmental literature, as Johnson (1988, 48) and Perner (1988, 159–162) have pointed out. This has led to contradictory claims about when children acquire the capacity for metarepresentation. [Recall the discussion in Note 2.1 about further confusions concerning "metarepresentation" arising from the equivocation of "representation" as representational medium (process) and **representational content**.]

Metamodels   Our military models also make clear that the distinction between *real* and *hypothetical* does not involve *metarepresentations* in the recursive sense of *representations representing representations*. The generals directing or planning a battle use different models to represent the battlefield as it really is and as it might be. Neither of these

Figure 2.4
A metamodel: modeling the sandbox-battlefield relationship.

models is a metarepresentation, since they are used for representing different states of the battlefield, not for representing representations of the battlefield.

The generals back in the academy make occasional use of metarepresentations or metamodels in their lecture on the use and rationale of models. Figure 2.4 shows what a model that allows explicit depiction of the modeling process has to involve. This model needs to consist of two models: one representing the battlefield, the other representing the sandbox as a model of the battlefield by showing how the sandbox is related to the battlefield. Showing the representational links between the sandbox and the battlefield is necessary, because otherwise the metamodel would not make clear that the sandbox is a model of the battlefield, rather than an interesting object in itself. In figure 2.4 this is indicated by the (model)-scout looking at the (model)-battlefield and changing the (model)-sandbox accordingly.

Clearly, this model that models how the sandbox represents the battlefield constitutes a case of metarepresentation, but is it not overkill? Would it not suffice, as figure 2.5 shows, to make a drawing of, say, Margaret Thatcher on the day of her resignation as prime minister of Great Britain and then make another drawing of that drawing? Would the second drawing not be a case of metarepresentation, that is, a drawing of a drawing? Yes, it would, but only insofar as that metadrawing shows that the depicted drawing is a drawing of Margaret Thatcher.*

Assume the metadrawing is cut so that it still shows Margaret Thatcher but so that one can no longer see that it depicted her as being drawn on a piece of paper. Then the metadrawing reduces to a drawing of Margaret Thatcher, although it has been obtained through a rather indirect process, that is, drawing her after a drawing of Margaret Thatcher rather than after the lady in vivo. But that indirect process of creation does not turn it into a metarepresentation. A drawing of Margaret Thatcher made after a drawing is still a drawing of Margaret Thatcher and not of the drawing. Alternatively, let us obliterate the surface of the metadrawing that shows Margaret Thatcher. Then the

---

*One could object that this falls short of depicting the *representing relation itself*, as required by Pylyshyn's definition of "metarepresentation." However, I would maintain that, although the representing relation is not shown as such—how could one?—it is implied. At least an onlooker who understands the difference between the drawing and the drawing of a drawing must understand that the latter depicts something that is related to something else by being a representation of it.

metadrawing simply shows a piece of paper that does not represent anything. The metadrawing therefore ceases to be *meta-* and becomes a simple drawing of a piece of paper. In summary, only when the meta-drawing explicitly shows that it depicts a drawing of something is it a metadrawing.

When Is Meta-representation Necessary?   At this point it is important to consider which problems require metarepresentation and which do not. I have suggested that metarepresentation would be ideal for distinguishing between the model that represents the real world and other models. This suggestion seems natural, for what better way could there be to make this distinction than to represent that one model represents the real situation whereas the other represents just a fictional situation? Unfortunately this suggestion runs into the problem of an infinite regress, for the following reason. To properly model that a model represents the real situation, one needs a model of the real situation, but for that model the same problem arises, namely, how to mark that it represents the real situation. To answer this question metarepresentation-ally by representing that this model represents the real situation raises the same question yet again, and so on ad infinitum. To mark the difference between real and not-real, then, the metarepresentational approach is not only unnecessary but in fact useless.

The distinction between real and imaginary must therefore be based on a simpler technique. One, if not the only, way to make the distinction is to rely on how evolution has hooked models to the real world. A military apparatus has simply come to rely on certain processes as reliable sources of intelligence. Biological organisms have evolved with perception as the reliable source. Introspectively, we know that what we see *is* real. We do not make that assumption because, having access to a theory of the process of perception, we have decided that this process is reliable and therefore good for composing models of reality. No, we just rely on perception. It imposes itself as reality. In other words, we do not *inspect* our perceptual data base to infer reality but use it—quite transparent-ly—by letting ourselves be guided by it with respect to reality.

Of what use, then, is metarepresentation? To answer this question, it is helpful to first remind ourselves what purpose the formation of a model serves. One decisive advantage of a model is that it can be manipulated, which allows the representational system to break away from reality. It can "think" of alternatives. Thinking of alternatives means "real understanding" of what is going on and forms the prerequisite for

Figure 2.5
Cutting out the "meta-."

finding a way to improve on things, or in any case make them different from what they are now.

Back to metamodels. They allow the generals to represent the relationship between their battlefield-model and the battlefield itself. For instance, they can now model the information-gathering activity of the scout, and if something goes wrong with the scout, they can model alternative possibilities and, therewith, the chance of mending their intelligence problem.

Why, then, did I call metarepresentation useless? My formulation should have been more careful: the metarepresentational option is useless as the ultimate criterion for deciding which model is a model of reality and which models are not. Metarepresentation is in fact indispensable for modeling the information-gathering process and thereby understanding how it works and how one can improve it so that the model of reality reflects reality as accurately as possible—one can carefully vet the scouts, and so on. However, to repeat, metarepresentation cannot substitute for internal role assignment; that is, it cannot substitute for designating which model plays the role of reality model.

The reason for my obsession with showing that metarepresentation is not necessary for making the real-hypothetical distinction will become apparent in the following chapter, where I argue that pretend play indicates sophisticated use of alternative mental models but that such use is different from forming mental metamodels.

Summary

I first made explicit that representation involves a *representational medium* that stands in a *representing relation* to its *representational content*. This explicit terminology enabled me to pinpoint certain ambiguities in the use of the word "representation." To avoid confusion, I restricted my use of the word to refer to instances of the representational medium only, not its content.

I then elaborated the representing relation. Representations do not just represent something but *represent something as being a certain way*. I gave four criteria further specifying the representing relation as *asymmetric, singular,* allowing for *misrepresentation,* and enabling representation of *nonexistent* entities.

I used these criteria to discuss the adequacy of some theories that purport to explain what makes something represent something. This allowed me to exclude the old idea that resemblance accounts for representation. Modern theories that fare much better on these criteria emphasize the causal connection between represented and representation and the functional role within a representation-using system.

Both these theories suggest that representations can only be formed at a *primary* level in close and fairly reliable causal connection with the represented world. Once representations have been formed through this contact with the represented, *secondary* uses can develop in which the causal link to the represented world can be suspended.

I used military models as concrete illustrations of these different uses, which made clear the need for *multiple models*. This raised the question of how the system "knows" what the referent of each model is, in particular, which model stands for reality. I argued that *what* each model represents can only be defined by its internal role, not by metarepresentational reflection, which does help in understanding whether a model serves its function well.

Finally, I explicated the concept of *metarepresentation* as a model that models the representational relationship between a model and the environment (or whatever is being modeled). This concept is particularly important for the topic of chapter 3. The issue there is whether pretense requires the more basic ability to form "metarepresentational comments" in order to differentiate real from hypothetical, or whether it requires the more advanced recursive capacity for metarepresentation to represent symbolic relationships. And in chapter 4 we need to distinguish children's ability to interpret and use representations from their capacity to form metarepresentations in order to understand that something is a representation.

Chapter 3

Toward the Representational Mind

The essential features of the concept of representation having been analyzed in the previous chapter, this chapter provides a bridge to the following one, which deals with children's acquisition of that concept. Understanding the concept of representation is something special if one considers—as cognitive psychologists do—understanding itself to be a representational activity. Understanding representation is then a recursive *metarepresentational* activity since it involves *representing* (the act of understanding) what *representing* is (the concept).

In the present chapter I discuss the development of mental representation as a necessary step toward mental metarepresentation. My proposal is simple: Fairly early in life—if not at birth—babies entertain a *single model* of the world. Then, around 1 to 1½ years, they begin constructing *multiple models*. Even though it is simple, this proposal has interesting implications. As a result of acquiring multiple models children become able to transcend the *present* by representing past events. This shows in their correct search for invisibly displaced objects. Children also become able to break away from present *reality* by representing nonreal alternatives to reality. This is manifested in their pretend play.

There is a reason why I focus on these two developments. Pretend play has often—notably by Piaget—been described as "symbolic." That is, by pretending that something is something else, one "represents" the something else. I argue against the notion that early pretend play is symbolic. Instead, I see early pretense as an instance of (knowingly) *acting as-if* the world were different than it really is. My argument against pretense as symbolic is helped by pointing out the parallel development in understanding temporal change. This developmental parallelism has a plausible conceptual basis because understanding of change over time and understanding of hypothetical alternatives to reality raise similar representational, semantic problems (for instance, the problem of logical opacity). But these problems are not necessarily problems of metarepresentation, since understanding temporal change evidently does not imply that the present needs to be seen as "representing" the past, as an object used in pretense need not "represent" what it is pretended to be.

My arguments against the "symbolic" view of early pretense are useful in setting the stage for my discussion of children's understanding of representation in chapter 4. But first, let me start with the very young infant.

The Origins of Mental Representation in Infancy

A discussion on this topic needs at least a brief comment on how Piaget used the term "mental representation."

"Mental Representation" à la Piaget   Although Piaget saw the newborn endowed with adaptive intelligence, he strictly distinguished infants' mental processes as part of mere "sensorimotor schemes" from the later developing facility for mental representation:

> Representation begins when sensory-motor data are assimilated not to elements that are actually perceptible but to those that are merely evoked. (Piaget 1945/1951, 277).

Piaget's terminological choice contrasts with information processing terminology in cognitive psychology (e.g., Neisser 1967), where representational notions like "ikonic" and "image" are freely applied to even perceptual processes. However, Piaget's use of "mental representation" is not without intuitive backing. Introspectively, we are inclined to use the term "mental representation" when we evoke an image of something in our mind, but not when we straightforwardly perceive something. But then, as the history of introspective psychology has shown, how we perceive ourselves mentally representing need not be the objectively best description of our internal processes. Thus, we need to make this terminological choice on theoretical grounds by applying the defining criteria worked out in chapter 2. An example of a *sensorimotor scheme* may help us.

Take the sucking reflex that is present in neonates (Piaget 1936/1953). As shown by the way they suck, within the first month of life babies differentiate objects for nutritive sucking (the breast) from objects for nonnutritive sucking (pacifier). Presumably, the oral information creates an internal "scheme," which, depending on what goal the baby pursues (eat or merely suck), leads to different kinds of behavior. There seems to be no reason why one could not say that this internal "scheme" represents the object in the mouth (referent) as being "nutritive" (sense). Hence, there is no reason not to call such a "scheme" a "mental representation," especially since Piaget's own terminology of "sensorimotor schemes" is not even mentioned in the Oxford English Dictionary. Thus, it seems better—in line with information processing-terminology—to call all internal processes that are differentiated according to the features of external objects "representations" and then distinguish between different kinds of representations. This is what Leslie (1987) has done in distinguishing between *primary* and *secondary representations* and what I have done in positing the transition from *a single updating model* (tied to reality) to *multiple models* (freed from reality). This transition maps quite closely onto the Piagetian distinction between "sensorimotor schemes" (perceptually evoked) and "mental representation" (internally evoked). However, it puts less of a restriction on the intellectual capabilities of young infants than Piaget's theory and therefore provides a more adequate account for recent experimental evidence of a more competent infant.

A Single Updating Model   For present purposes I restrict myself to simply characterizing young babies from birth to about 1 or 1½ years as entertaining a single updating model of their known environment. This rather bland suggestion does not explain all the interesting developments within that period. It merely provides a framework for what children are and are not able to do. I first discuss a few possibilities in contrast to Piaget's more restrictive view. Then I focus on the restrictions imposed by a single model, which contrast with the advantages of the subsequently emerging multiple models.

Two important features of a single updating model are that it is *not modality specific* and that it is *not limited to representing the presently perceptible*. This renders a single model different from Piaget's sensorimotor schemes. Infants in Piaget's theory have been characterized as "stimulus bound," which has two main consequences.

"Stimulus bound" implies that infants are bound to the (proximal) stimulus. That is, they merely *process stimulation* specific to each modality and do not *process information* about objects. Not until about 1 year (Piaget 1936/1953: coordination of secondary circular reactions) are inputs from different modalities integrated as a precondition for *representing* the objects from which the stimulation emanates. However, evidence reported by Meltzoff and Moore (1977) that even 1-hour-old neonates engage in facial imitation (by now a well-replicated phenomenon: Meltzoff and Gopnik 1989, 35) challenges this view. Imitation of another person's face requires integration of at least two different modalities. The infant obtains visual information about the adult's face and has to translate that into movements of her own face for which there is no visible but only proprioceptive feedback. The evidently early ability to make this transmodal match suggests that infants are innately endowed with a modality-free representation of facial features. Early facial imitation is possible with a single model of reality as long as the representational vocabulary contains expressions for facial features of the imitated person and the infant's own face.

"Stimulus bound" also implies that the infant is tied to the immediate environmental stimulation—as the saying goes, "Out of sight, out of mind." Again, Meltzoff and Moore have shown that facial imitation also occurs even when delayed. That means that the representation of the face to be imitated cannot vanish with the perceptual stimulation but must persist for at least a few seconds. Apart from this special skill at imitating faces, there is also good evidence from Renée Baillargeon's (1987) laboratory that by 3½ to 4½ months infants are to some degree aware of the existence of an object that has been obscured by a moving screen. They are therefore surprised when this screen apparently moves through the space taken up by the obscured object without encountering any noticeable resistance. A single model of reality is compatible with this finding, since models are built gradually by integrating sensory information over time. For instance, when the infant sees the block being put down, an expression stating the new location of the block is inserted in the model. When the stimulation ceases (the infant looks elsewhere), that expression does not extinguish with it but persists, thus integrating information over time. The expression is changed or erased either through forgetting or when the model needs to be updated as new, incompatible information is received—for instance, the infant sees the block being removed.

All this is not to say that infants' understanding of object permanence, and of where objects can be found, does not improve within the first year. In fact, as several decades of Piaget-inspired research has demonstrated, there is tremendous intellectual change during exactly that period. But on my account this change would be due to improving spatial concepts used to build the single model of reality. An idea by Bower and Wishart (1972; see Bremner 1988, chap. 4 for recent research on this) may help illustrate my point. They observed that 6-month-old infants were quite able to search for an object that had disappeared *behind* a screen or reach for an object that had gone out of sight because the light was switched off (Hood and Willats 1986). Yet these same children failed to search for the object in the more traditional Piagetian task where it was put *under* a cloth or *inside* a cup. Bower and Wishart argued that the younger children know about the permanence of objects but have difficulty conceiving of the object being *inside* something else (e.g., the cup). Before they understand "inside," it may appear to infants that the cup has replaced the original object. What develops, then, is a better understanding of when an object remains in its place and when it is being displaced. But all these are improvements within the representational means of a single model.

However, a single model also has severe limitations, which become apparent when incompatible facts need to be recorded. Incompatibility of new information with the existing state of the model is typically used to update the model. The old information is erased and supplanted by the new. Systematic understanding of temporal change is therefore not possible with a single updating model. A second model is needed to preserve a record of past states. Such a record is needed in Piaget's more advanced tests of object permanence, tasks involving invisible displacement. And these tasks are typically not mastered until well into the second year of life.

Emergence of Multiple Models

Somewhere around 1½ years—the first signs occur as early as 1 year —infants acquire a series of skills that require facility with multiple mental models. They come to understand means-ends relationships (Piaget 1937/1954), which require multiple models to project the desired state and the necessary steps to get there. They can infer the location of an invisibly displaced object, which requires extra models for representing past points in the course of displacement. They start to engage in pretend play, which requires an extra model representing the world as different from the way it really is. They learn to interpret representational media, like pictures, language, and mirror images, which require models for representing the information conveyed in these media.

In chapter 4 I will return to children's use of representational media. For the time being I concentrate on infants' understanding of invisible displacement as a worked example of how multiple models make it possible to understand temporal change, that is, for representing *past* alternatives to *present* reality. In the following section I apply a parallel analysis to infants' pretense which requires multiple models for representing *hypothetical* alternatives to present *reality*.

Understanding Temporal Change: Invisible Displacement   A systematic understanding of change over time requires several models. One model has to show how the world is now and others are needed to represent how the world used to be at previous points in time. This is not necessary in a simple search task where the object simply disappears behind an occluding screen or inside some container. To find the object again in this kind of task, the infant has to be able to interpret the visual disappearance information (to infer from the kind of disappearance where the object is after it has gone out of sight). This information can be stored in a single model of reality, and it stays there until new information about the object's whereabouts is received (or it falls prey to forgetting).

In invisible displacement tasks this method of storing and updating information about the object's current location is not sufficient. For instance, Piaget (1937/1954, 75–76) observed his daughter Jacqueline at 1 year and 6 months in the following situation:

> Jacqueline is sitting on a green rug and playing with a potato which interests her very much (...). She ... amuses herself by putting it into an empty box and taking it out again. ... I then take the potato and put it in the box while Jacqueline watches. Then I place the box under the rug and turn it upside down thus leaving the object hidden by the rug without letting the child see my maneuver, and I bring out the empty box. I say to Jacqueline, who has not stopped looking at the rug and who has realized that I was doing something under it: "Give papa the potato." She searches for the object in the box, looks at me, again looks at the box minutely, looks at the rug, etc., but it does not occur to her to raise the rug in order to find the potato underneath.

That Jacqueline is at her wit's end can be explained by the limitations of a single, updating model. To begin with, her model shows

"Potato inside the box in front of me."

Then she sees the box with the potato inside being moved under the rug. She updates her model:

"Potato inside the box under the rug."

If she were to search for the potato now, she would know where to look: under the rug. But the displacements continue. She sees the box reemerge and updates her model the same way an older child would:

"Potato inside the box in front of me."

And now she is allowed to look for the potato. Like any older child she looks in the box, finds it empty, and updates her model again:

"Box empty."

But where is the potato? Her nicely up-to-date model doesn't give a clue. It is at this point that older children can do better. They update their model of current reality just like Jacqueline updated hers, but when they discover that they have gone wrong they can—unlike Jacqueline—think back to where the potato had been before. And they can use that knowledge to make an educated guess about where the potato might have been left. For this guess, however, at least one additional model is necessary, which preserves the record of the last position of the potato:

Model 1
[past: "Potato inside the box under the rug."]

Model 2
[present: "Box empty. Potato -?-"]

Having access to the information about the potato's last location before the final displacement of the box would have allowed Jacqueline to correct her current model retroactively:

Model 2
[present: "Box empty. Potato might be under the rug."]

In fact, a few weeks after the last observation Jacqueline seems to have acquired this representational skill, though in the context of a key being hidden in her father's fist and then invisibly transferred into his beret:

In order to check on the firmness of the recent acquisitions I take a key in my fist, place my fist in a beret, leave the key in the beret and finally throw it on the floor at the end of the room. Jacqueline runs toward the beret but as I say, "Key, key, look for key," she turns around, looks at me laughingly, looks at my hands which are open and, resuming her idea, goes toward the beret. She picks it up and without hesitation puts in her hand and removes the key. (Piaget 1937/1954, 82)

In a tightly controlled experimental investigation of invisible displacement Haake and Somerville (1985) used two spatially separated cloths as covers. A small target object was put on the experimenter's palm. He then closed his hand around the object and put his hand under the first cover. After about 2 seconds the hand emerged, still closed. It then stopped between covers, opened for 2 seconds, closed again, and disappeared under the second cover, where it stayed again for 2 seconds before it emerged and was opened to show that it was empty. In one condition the hand was already empty when it opened between cloths. The correct response in this condition was to search for the object under the first cloth. In the other condition the object was still inside the hand between cloths and the correct response was to search under the second cloth.

Haake and Somerville's procedure controlled for the possibility that infants might search correctly without real understanding, being guided by some spurious associations with the correct location. Systematically correct decisions about which cloth to lift could only be made if the child remembered where the hand with the object was before it was shown to be empty. At 12 months infants showed no clear preference for searching under either of the two cloths (about 52% correct; an average over three conditions reported in their table 1). At 15 months the first clear sign of correct search emerged. Children lifted the correct cloth about 67% of the time, and this percentage rose to about 80% at 18 months.

I conclude from this that around 15 months infants become able to use multiple (at least two) models to free themselves from being tied to current reality by a single updating model. They become free to contemplate the past.* This emergence of multiple models—I argue— enables another kind of liberation, the freedom to go beyond reality by conceiving of the hypothetical.

---

*This freedom may be rather limited, of course, as reported by Somerville and Haake (1985) in a search task with four locations where the hand passed under two cloths before it opened. Children were quite good at limiting their search to one of these; but when the object was not there, they did not opt for the other logical possibility but searched at random under any of the other locations. It seems as though children are restricted to only one model of the past until they are 3 or 4 years old.

Breaking Away from Reality: Pretense

> In play, things lose their determining force. *The child sees one thing but acts differently in relation to what he sees. Thus, a condition is reached in which the child begins to act independently of what he sees.* (Vygotsky 1966/1978, 96-97).

Piaget (1945/1951, 96) observed his daughter Jacqueline at 1 year and 3 months in the following circumstances:

> She saw a cloth whose fringed edges vaguely recalled those of her pillow; she seized it, held a fold of it in her right hand, sucked the thumb of the same hand and lay down on her side, laughing hard. She kept her eyes open, but blinked from time to time as if she were alluding to closed eyes. Finally, laughing more and more, she cried "Nene" (Nono).

Jacqueline's apparent delight in her atypical use of that piece of cloth and her verbal comment "no-no" were a telling sign that she was not just making a mistake but fully appreciated the discrepancy between the reality of the object being a piece of cloth and her pretense of treating that object like her pillow. This kind of play becomes more frequent and universal in the middle of the second year (for reviews see Fein 1981; McCune-Nicholich 1981; Bretherton 1984) and takes on quite intricate forms in the third year, particularly when the infant is playing with an older sibling (Dunn and Dale 1984).

Different Interpretations of Play   This playful activity has been variably described as "pretend play," "make-believe," "fantasy play," "symbolic play," and "acting-as-if." These terms suggest quite different interpretations of the child's activity. For instance, "make-believe," interpreted literally, carries a deceptive connotation: "She *makes* her father *believe* she is sleeping." "Fantasy" suggests detachment from reality: "She *imagines* herself sleeping." "Symbolic" suggests a representational function: "She *represents* herself as sleeping." "Acting-as-if" suggests, "Although she is awake, she *acts as if* she were asleep."

A common denominator of these different interpretations of play is that they suggest a certain deviation from normality, and one could agree with Vygotsky (1966/1978, 93)

> In establishing criteria for distinguishing a child's play from other forms of activity, we conclude that in play a child creates an imaginary situation.

One thing is clear. This deviation from normality into an imaginary situation indicates nothing particularly interesting about the child's intellectual development *unless* the child is to some degree *aware* of this discrepancy and of the fact that the situation is imaginary. If it is only the adult onlooker who puts this interpretation on the child's activity, then the child is engaging in mere "functional play" or is making a mistake. As Huttenlocher and Higgins (1978) have pointed out, there is a difficult methodological problem in deciding whether a child engages in functional play or pretense. Faith that it is more than mere functional play comes from children's apparent delight (a "knowing smile") and their explicit comments on the discrepancy, like Jacqueline's "no-no." But, even if we ignore this basic methodological problem and dismiss functional play as one interpretation, we are still left with four other interpretations of the child's play activity.

To reduce the number of possibilities, we can discount "fantasy" as a good description of play. Although fantasy involves the creation of an imaginary situation, it is typically passive. Fantasy, or pure imagination, implies only mental evocation of the imagined situation without any activity in the real world so characteristic of play. The remaining three interpretations can all be covered by the term "pretend," which does capture this element of active distortion of reality in play. Therefore, "pretend play" seems an appropriate terminological choice, with the additional advantage that it has been widely adopted as the generic label for this kind of play (Fein 1981).

This terminological choice also has its dangers, precisely because its connotations cover different aspects. Calling this type of play "pretense" implies that all these different aspects are part of the young child's play. But in the everyday use of "pretend" these different aspects can be clearly separated. For instance, "pretend" can be used with a definite deceptive component, as in "I pretend to be sick [to get a day off work]"—though no major theorist, I think, has tried to read such a deceptive intention into early pretend play.* But "pretense" still covers at least two more distinguishably different aspects that have been used as interpretations of early play.

"Pretend" can refer to two different kinds of substitutions. It can mean a *symbolic* (or representational) substitution, for instance, when a general

---

*Piaget does refer to pretend play quite frequently as "make-believe." Interpreted literally, this expression suggests a deceptive intention, for one can ask "Who does the pretending child try to make believe something?" However, Piaget seems to be using that expression in a different way, namely, to indicate that the pretending child herself does not seriously believe in her pretense (Piaget 1945/1962, 167 distinguishes "make-believe" from "belief").

pretends that the sticks in the sandbox are his soldiers. It can also be used to refer to a substitution of a *hypothetical* (imaginary, nonreal) situation for reality, for instance, when I act on Monday as-if it were Sunday (knowingly and with joy). [See **Note 3.1** for making this distinction with military precision.]

Back to children's pretend play. It is not clear which substitution Jacqueline intended when her father observed her treating a piece of cloth as her pillow. Did she mean to behave "as if it were" her pillow, or did she want to use the cloth "as a symbol" for her pillow? One thing is clear, though: the two substitutions are not the same, since *acting as-if something were something else* is different from *using one thing to represent another*. Or for short: Possibility is not representation!

My argument is that acting-as-if provides an adequate interpretation of early pretend play. To this end I provide an analysis of the cognitive mechanism (mental models) necessary to sustain acting-as-if and show that the required mechanism is the same as the one needed for understanding temporal change in invisible displacement tasks. In the following section I argue that it is unnecessary to attribute "symbolic" intentions or the capacity for metarepresentation to the young pretender.

Pretense:
Acting As-If
Pretense has been described by psychologists as "behavior in an 'as-if' mode" (Bretherton 1984; Fein 1981, 1096). Going back to Piaget's observation about his daughter, we could say that Jacqueline acted as-if she were sleeping and as-if the piece of cloth were her pillow. Unless Jacqueline just mistook the cloth for her pillow, or simply wanted to put her head to rest on the cloth (functional play), then she must have been able to entertain two mental models. This is necessary under the assumption that the content of mental models governs action jointly with current desires. Let us assume that Jacqueline has the desire to *put her head on her pillow*. Then the cloth in front of her will not elicit the observed behavior, since her mental model

"This object in front of me is a soft piece of cloth."

does not direct her to show it, unless she is plainly *mistaken* about reality and her model specifies

"This object in front of me is my pillow."

In this case, however, she is making a mistake and not pretending. Assume, now, that Jacqueline has the desire to *put her head on something soft*. Then the veridical model would elicit the observed behavior, but not because she is pretending. Jacqueline would be engaging in "functional play." In both these cases the unusual character or deviance of Jacqueline's behavior is being recognized only by the observer, not by Jacqueline herself. Yet exactly this recognition is essential for her actions to qualify as pretense, and she can come to this recognition only if she has two models:

Reality Model
[for real: "This object is a piece of cloth."]

As-If Model
[for fun: "This object is my pillow."]

To execute the pretense, Jacqueline has to switch action control from the reality model to the as-if model. This ability to switch between reality and pretense is a minimally necessary condition for being "aware" or "being in control" of the distinction and not being merely mistaken.

The theoretically important question is what the relationship between these two models has to be. My answer to this question is that the two models simply represent two different situations: the *real situation* and a *hypothetical situation*. And so pretend play involves an intellectual skill similar to the one needed for understanding temporal change, where again two distinct situations need to be represented: the *present situation* and a *past situation*.

Comparing Search with Pretense   Of course, there is a difference between search and pretense. The model governing the as-if action of pretense represents a hypothetical situation (more often than not a counterfactual situation) that may not be and probably never was real, whereas the model of a past situation encodes something that was real. Despite that obvious difference, however, their underlying logic is similar.*

For demonstrating the similarity between representing temporal change and representing pretense I again use Piaget's invisible displacement task where he hid a key from his daughter Jacqueline in his fist, put his fist

---

*The logical similarity between time and "factuality" (whether something is real or hypothetical) is underlined by how tense and expressions of possibility are treated in possible-world semantics (e.g., Dowty, Wall, and Peters 1981). Time and possibility are just two different kinds of indices that range over different instances of time and different possible worlds, respectively.

inside his beret, invisibly deposited the key, and withdrew his closed hand. I pointed out that since Jacqueline was able to figure out where the key was after finding the hand empty, she must have been storing information in two models: one containing information about the past location of the hand when the key was still in it ("key in the hand inside the beret") and another showing the key's suspected current location ("key in Daddy's hand"). When she discovered that the current model was wrong (the key wasn't in the hand), she could consult the model of the past for relevant information about the key's potential whereabouts.

To facilitate comparison with pretense, I have listed three critical features of these two temporal models:

1. The information about present and past must be stored in *different models*; otherwise, the child would simply be confused about where the object was and where it is now.
2. The models must be *labeled* in a way that enables the mental management system to use the right one when looking for missing information about the present.
3. In order to find the needed information, the model of the past must be *about* the same entities as the present. This is ensured by the fact that the tokens "key," "hand," "beret," "inside," and so on, in the two mental models represent the same entities and relations.

The same three features must be met by the model used for pretense:

1. The representation controlling play action must be contained in a *different model* than information about the real world controlling serious action; otherwise, the child would be confused about what is real and what is pretend.
2. The models must be *labeled* in a way that enables the mental management system to pick the right one for playful enjoyment and for serious action.
3. In order that the pretend model can govern pretend action in the real world, the two models must be *about* the same entities. This is again ensured by the fact that expressions "this object," "is," "piece of cloth," "my pillow," and so on, in the two mental models represent the same entities and relations.*

---

*Notice an important point for the discussion about metarepresentation to follow soon: the constituent expressions in both models mean the same. The necessary distinction between the different bits of information is ensured by their being in different models, and there is no need to distinguish them further by giving the elements of each model different meaning as, for instance, Leslie (1987) does. In his account of pretense mental writing about reality ("primary representations") refers to external objects and relations whereas mental writing about pretend scenarios ("secondary representation") refers to representations of those external objects and relations.

The critical aspect of my analysis of pretense is that the representation of reality and the representation of the pretend scenario are just representations of different situations or contexts. This feature makes it radically different from Piaget's proposal that pretense is symbolic or Leslie's (1987, 417) suggestion that pretense involves mental metarepresentation in the recursive sense of *representations of representations*. Pretense as symbolic or metarepresentational in this recursive sense requires a more complicated mental mechanism than just models of different situations. What would be necessary are models of models that model the representational relationship between pretense and reality. This additional complexity is unnecessary for interpreting children's early pretend play.

Against Pretense as Symbolic Action

> I believe that play is not symbolic action in the proper sense of the term,... (Vygotsky 1966/1978, 94)

Piaget's View   Piaget (1945/1962) sees the major importance of pretend play as fostering the child's symbolic functioning ("semiotic function"). The story goes something like this (pp. 277–284). To start with, it must be remembered that Piaget does not consider sensorimotor intelligence mental representation. Mental representation derives from internalized imitation. Presumably, imitation represents the imitated because of its similarity.* However, if representation (the symbolic function) were based on similarity, then how could the child ever understand a symbolic system like language, where there is no resemblance between the linguistic symbol and what it symbolizes? Piaget's answer to this puzzle is that the child learns the arbitrariness of the symbolic function through pretend play. By pretending that the piece of cloth is her pillow, young Jacqueline comes to understand that anything (cloth) can stand for anything (her pillow) if so designated.

Piaget clearly interprets his daughter's pretense as symbolic play:

---

*I have always had difficulty appreciating Piaget's reasons for insisting that mental representation is internalized imitation. Why imitation? I think I now understand his deeper motivation: an ingrained copy theory of representation. Indeed, if resemblance were the essence of representation, then imitation would provide a good start because its prime point is to produce resemblance with the imitated. But resemblance in itself does not make for representation. Although a comedian may symbolically evoke a person by imitation, I would not call my attempts to play better tennis by imitating John McEnroe a symbolic act.

> As early as the VIth stage [about 8–12 months], the scheme of going to sleep is already giving rise to ludic ritualizations, since [Jacqueline] reproduces it at the sight of her pillow. But there is then neither symbol nor consciousness of make-believe, since the child merely applies her usual movements to the pillow itself, i.e., to the normal stimulus of behavior. There certainly is play, in so far as the scheme is only used for pleasure, but there is no symbolism. On the contrary, in [the observation cited above] J. mimes sleep while she is holding a cloth ... instead of a pillow, ... It can therefore no longer be said that the scheme has been evoked by its usual stimulus, and we are forced to recognize that these objects merely serve as substitutes for the pillow, substitutes which become symbolic through the actions simulating sleep. (Piaget 1945/1962, 97)

This passage makes two things clear about how Piaget views pretend play. With her pretend activity the infant turns something (the piece of cloth) into a symbol for something else (the absent pillow), and she is to some degree aware of this symbolic substitution (otherwise, the play is just nonsymbolic, ludic ritualization).

If this interpretation of infants' play were right, the pretending child would have to engage in metarepresentation. For instance, Jacqueline would have to *mentally represent* (as understood in information-processing psychology to cover the necessary "awareness") that the cloth *represents* (symbolizes) her pillow. What is the evidence that the child does take that view? On the face of it, it's not particularly plausible.

Acting-As-If
≠
Symbolizing
If the cloth were understood as a representation of the pillow, then why would the infant act as if it were a pillow? If I look at a map of the Mediterranean, I am not even tempted to dive into it (the map, that is). Maybe that's because I'm older. There is evidence that infants do treat pictures of objects as if they were indeed the depicted objects, and it has been reported that before the age of about 18 months infants treat their own mirror image as if it were another person (Amsterdam 1972). Amsterdam had each infant's mother put a red dot on his or her forehead (the control group got a colorless dot in a replication described in Lewis and Brooks-Gunn 1979) and then set the infant in front of a mirror. Infants younger than about 1½ years tended to touch the red dot on the image in the mirror, like monkeys in Gallup's (1968) original study. Older infants, like Gallup's apes, spontaneously touched their own forehead upon seeing their face in the mirror.

Notice that the younger infants treated the mirror image as-if it were a person, but that behavior is not interpreted as a sign of understanding the representational quality of the mirror image. Rather, it tends to be interpreted as plain confusion between picture and reality. One could argue, rightly, that this behavior is also not interpreted as pretense, since there is no sign that the child is aware of any discrepancy. However, the older infants, who do understand to some degree that the mirror image reflects something about themselves, stop acting as-if it were a person, not even with a knowing smile. It seems that representations, once infants know to use them as such, stop eliciting pretend behavior. So why should acting toward one object (e.g., cloth) in a way that is appropriate for another object (the pillow) be a sign that the first object is used and understood as a representation of the second?

Also, it is unlikely that pretense could be a necessary playground for practicing the arbitrariness of representation as Piaget's theory demands. This is because children start to use words—the paradigm of an arbitrary symbol system—at the same time or even earlier than they start to pretend on a large scale.

Substitution
≠
Symbolization
It is easy to deny pretend play any representational function, but then why have so many theorists seen it as symbolic?* A possible answer might be found in the traditional definition of representation as something that *stands for* something else, where "stands for" is being equated with "standing in for," that is, substituting. In many pretend scenarios it seems clearly appropriate to say that, for instance, Jacqueline used the cloth as a *stand-in (substitute) for* her pillow. If *use as substitute* constituted *representation*, then indeed, Jacqueline could be said to have intended the cloth to *represent* her pillow. However, this is clearly not the case since substitutes do not represent what they substitute for *as being a certain way*, as required by Goodman's criteria for representation listed in chapter 2.

In sum, although I tend to agree with Piaget's more general idea that pretense serves an important function in the formation of mental representation—namely, mental representation that breaks away from being shaped by perceived reality and can be internally evoked—I see no

---

*Here I am applying Perner's Principle of Understanding: "Nevver think you've understood something unless you've also got a good explanation for why others before you kept getting it wrong!"

good reason for considering pretend play a symbolic activity in the sense that some substitute object represents what it has been substituted for. [**Note 3.2** Other voices against interpreting play as symbolic.]

This, however, is not the end of the argument. In a recent analysis of pretend play Alan Leslie arrived at a conclusion similar to Piaget's that pretense requires the capacity for metarepresentation (understanding symbolization), even though Leslie started his analysis from different premises about mental representation than did Piaget. I now take a closer look at Leslie's arguments.

Against "Metarepresentation" in Early Pretense

Alan Leslie (1987) cogently points out that if the sole function of mental representation (as conceived of in the information-processing tradition) were to reflect reality, then pretense creates a problem because it distorts reality. Lest pretense result in mental chaos, then a special "cognitive mechanism" is required. I am largely in agreement with Leslie's diagnostics of the representational problems created by pretense and about what that cognitive mechanism has to achieve. Disagreement starts with his claim that this mechanism must be metarepresentational.

Which Meta-? I argue that multiple models for representing different situations provide an adequate mechanism for pretense to occur. As noted in chapter 2, this requires that the different situations be marked with respect to whether they are "real" or "hypothetical," "past" or "present," and so on. Now these markers could be called "metarepresentational" because they are not representations like the rest of the model but they change what the rest refers to, that is, whether the model describes the real or a hypothetical situation. Thus, pretense does require a metarepresentational skill in this sense. However, Leslie goes further. He claims that metarepresentation in its recursive meaning is involved:

> Pretend representations ... are in effect not representations of the world but representations of representations. For this reason I shall call them second order or, borrowing a term from Pylyshyn (1978), *metarepresentations*. (Leslie 1987, 417)

In contrast, I would prefer to say

> Pretend representations are not representations of the world as it is but of the world as it might be.

In any case Leslie's suggestion raises a question that he does not answer: What representation does a pretend representation represent?

One possible reason why Leslie claims pretend representations to be metarepresentations may be that he is tacitly committing Hume's error of equivocating two distinct meanings of "representation." To equivocate representation (the mental process) with **representation** (its representational content) is particularly tempting when the content does not exist, as, for instance, in the case of a unicorn or a pretend scenario. By committing this equivocation (one of philosophy's mortal sins), one could call any thought (or other representation) about something nonreal a "metarepresentation" in the pseudorecursive sense of "a mental representation of a **representation**."

If this is what Leslie means by "metarepresentation," then we are engaging here in a purely terminological squabble. However, this meaning of "metarepresentation" is not the recursive meaning Pylyshyn (from whom Leslie borrowed the term) had in mind, since he defined it as "representing the representing relation itself" (1978, 593), which is how I use the term. In this usage Leslie's characterization of pretend representations as metarepresentations goes beyond a mere terminological difference. It has tangible empirical implications.

For instance, my analysis puts pretense on a par with understanding temporal change, whereas Leslie's proposal puts it into the camp of understanding representations (as process) and mental states (construed as mental processes that represent). Therefore, I want to demonstrate that all of Leslie's valid diagnostic points about the emergence of pretense can be fully accommodated by the acquisition of multiple models without the capability of metarepresentation. Let me show this for several properties that Leslie has identified in his analysis of pretense.

Quarantining   The necessity for some special cognitive mechanism is clear. If the system mixes representation of reality (say, "This is a banana") with representation of pretense ("This [banana] is a telephone"), the result is confusion about reality. To avoid this mental muddle, the representation of pretense needs to be "quarantined," cordoned off as "secondary" from the "primary representations" of reality. The question is how this quarantine can be achieved. My answer lies in constructing *multiple models* (or contexts).

The same need for quarantining exists when information about different times is to be stored. It won't do to mix "I am 2 years old" with "I am 3 years old." To avoid confusion about one's age, one must mark one of these representations as "past" or the other as "future." Analogously, my suggestion for pretense is to mark off the pretend scenario as "nonreal" or "hypothetical." So, although the need for quarantine is clear, it is not clear why quarantining requires metarepresentation.* The need for quarantine is served adequately by multiple models representing different situations.

Let us check whether any of the other features of pretense in Leslie's analysis provide a better case for the necessity of metarepresentation.

Opacity   Another important pillar in Leslie's analysis is that pretense needs a special mechanism because it displays special logical properties, which logicians have identified in so-called *opaque contexts*. [Note 3.3 Background on opacity.] One of these logical properties is *referential opacity*, which Leslie (1987, 416) illustrates with the following somewhat nationalist version of Frege's original cosmic example of the Morning and Evening Star.

> For example, "the prime minister of Britain" and "Mrs. Thatcher" refer at the time of this writing to the same person. Therefore, anything asserted about the prime minister of Britain, if true, must be true of Mrs. Thatcher as well (and, likewise, false for one, false for the other). If it is true that the prime minister of Britain lives at No. 10 Downing Street, then it must be true that Mrs. Thatcher lives at No. 10 Downing Street. But put this proposition in the context of a mental state term and this no longer holds. Thus, "Sarah-Jane believes that the prime minister of Britain lives at No. 10 Downing Street" in no way entails the truth (or falsehood) of "Sarah-Jane believes Mrs. Thatcher lives at No. 10 Downing Street."

Unfortunately, Leslie goes no farther than this (by now familiar) demonstration of opacity in belief contexts. He does not attempt to show what is so central to his claim: that the same logical problems occur in pretense and, crucially, to what degree they are understood by the pretending child as Leslie claims they are: "Pretend representations, ..., are *opaque*, even to the organism who entertains them" (Leslie 1987, 417). So let me attempt it here.

---

*In fact, in the context of my military sandbox models in chapter 2, I argued that the metarepresentational option of representing which models get reliable input from reality cannot provide the ultimate criterion for distinguishing reality from mere hypothetical considerations. This distinction can only be based on the function each model has been internally assigned.

What needs to be shown is that Sarah-Jane understands that one description can be substituted for another without loss of truth in transparent contexts but not in opaque pretend contexts. Let us assume that Sarah-Jane is holding a banana that she knows is *Daddy's dinner for tonight* (in analogy to *Mrs. Thatcher being prime minister* at the time of writing). In this scenario "this banana" and "Daddy's dinner" both refer to the object in Sarah-Jane's hands, and so she may substitute one description for the other without loss of truth. That is, if *"this banana* is yellow" is true, then *"Daddy's dinner* is yellow" must be true, too. Sarah-Jane's understanding of this logical implication might be tested by asking her about the color of Daddy's dinner. If she answers, "yellow," she at least uses the rule in her own reasoning.

This substitution becomes illegitimate, however, when Sarah-Jane *pretends that the banana is a telephone* (in analogy to *thinking the prime minister lives at No. 10 Downing Street*). To assess Sarah-Jane's understanding of this limit to the rule, one might try to ask her whether she was pretending that Daddy was having a telephone for dinner. Her probable denial (when knowing that the banana featuring in her pretend play was for Daddy's dinner) will indicate awareness of the logical limitation created by pretense.

My hunch is—though we really need some data—that fairly young children will respond as I assume Sarah-Jane would. On this assumption I agree with Leslie that children who pretend are aware of the opacity of their pretense. What I do not agree with is that this shows that there is "an isomorphism between mental state expressions and pretense" (Leslie 1987, 416), which, I suspect, is another reason why Leslie was led to claim that pretense involves metarepresentation. [**Note 3.4** Problems with Leslie's isomorphism of opacity between pretense and mental state reports.]

Opacity and Metarepresentation   Reports on mental states—in particular, beliefs (as I will argue in chapter 5)—are *metarepresentations* since they are reports (representations) of mental representations. But why should pretense therefore be metarepresentational? What mental representation does it report (represent)? The agreed fact that pretense raises some of the same problems of opacity raised by mental state reports does not make pretense like mental state reports in every respect. What Leslie overlooks is that problems of opacity are also raised by temporal contexts, by statements about necessity and possibility (Carnap 1947; Dowty, Wall, and Peters 1981) and even by discourse about spatial contexts (Fauconnier 1983/1985) which are also not metarepresentational because they do not report on (mental) representations.

How these contexts raise the same problems of opacity as pretense can be illustrated with a situation where Sarah-Jane is talking about different times. The point about pretense was that, although "this banana" and "Daddy's dinner" refer to the same entity within the transparent context of current reality, one cannot be substituted for the other within Sarah-Jane's pretend play without affecting truth. The same danger exists when substitution occurs across different temporal contexts. If *yesterday* Daddy had spinach for dinner, the true sentence "Yesterday, *Daddy's dinner* was green" becomes false by substituting "Yesterday, this banana was green," even though *this banana* is *Daddy's dinner* today.

Generally speaking, the classical problems of opacity arise whenever different contexts (of time, possibility, space, etc.) are evoked. As a consequence, opacity occurs in pretense because pretense evokes a possibility different from reality, and opacity occurs in belief reports because people can think of different times and possibilities. But there is no reason to think that the metarepresentational quality of belief reports must therefore be shared by pretense, since there is no reason that reports about different times are metarepresentational.

In sum, although I agree with Leslie that pretense raises the logical problems of opacity, I can see no reason why this fact should require metarepresentation. The mechanism of multiple models can deal with these problems adequately. Let us check one other aspect of pretense from Leslie's analysis to see whether it supports his claims about metarepresentation.

Decoupling   Another critical feature of pretense in Leslie's analysis is that pretend representations are secondary representations *decoupled* from reality:

> A basic feature of my model is the creation of a pretense by the copying of a primary expression into a metarepresentational context. This second-order context in effect gives a report or quotation of the first-order expression. (Leslie 1987, 417)

Again, although I agree that pretense involves decoupled representations that originate as copies of primary representations, I cannot understand why copies should be metarepresentational, that is, why they should be giving a report of the original, primary representation. The fact that they are copies cannot explain this. This point can be brought home more forcefully by looking at the picture in figure 3.1. This picture shows Heinz Wimmer, Henry Wellman, Alan Leslie, and myself—apparently debating representational problems of overhead projection—at a conference organized by Paul Harris in Oxford, June 1986. It is of admittedly inferior quality, but for good reasons. It is a copy of a negative that our photographer took of John Flavell's original print, which itself was a copy of the film in his camera at the time he took this snapshot. Despite being a degraded product of multiple copying, it still is just a simple *picture of us*. If copying created metarepresentations, then we would have to face the absurd consequence that this innocent-looking picture of us is really a *meta-meta-metapicture*: depicting our photographer's negative depicting John Flavell's print depicting his film depicting us. It plainly does not represent any of these representational relationships and thus, by Pylyshyn's (1978) definition of metarepresentation, it is not a metarepresentation at all, just a plain picture of us. [**Note 3.5** Copying a representation does not create a metarepresentation.]

So, here too, I can fully endorse Leslie's insight that pretense requires secondary representations, which are not, like primary representations,

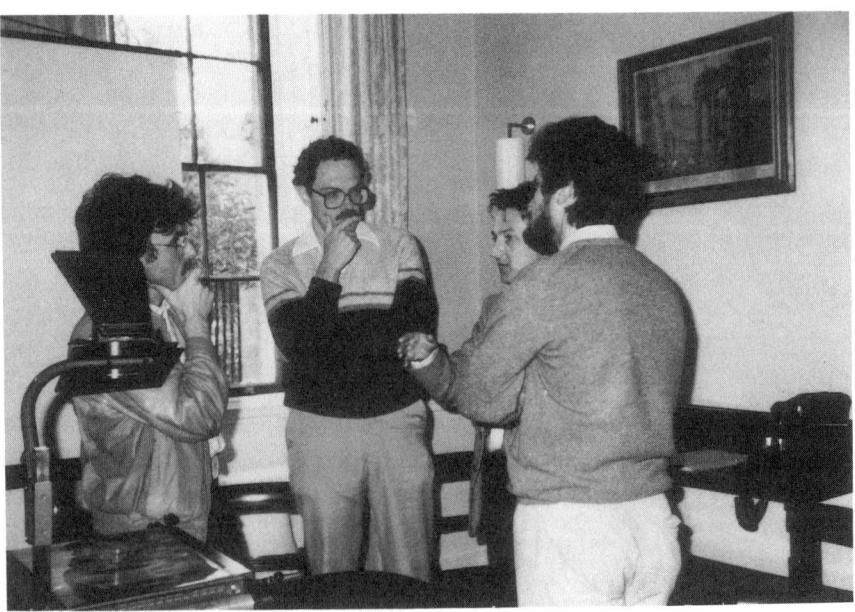

Figure 3.1
A picture, not a meta-...metapicture!

direct copies of what they represent but copies of primary representations. This is exactly how multiple models originate from the primary one. Yet there is no need to assume that these secondary models would therefore be metarepresentations.

In sum, despite my agreement with Alan Leslie on several points about the features of mental representations required by pretense—quarantine, opacity, decoupling—I can see no need for metarepresentation. In my analysis pretense requires only multiple models for representing different contexts. The developmental fact that children in the second year start to pretend at the same time as they understand temporal change goes well with this contention. And as we will see in chapter 4 and in part II, there is good evidence that children are not able to metarepresent until much later.

Contextualization: Implicit – Explicit

Before leaving the topics of this chapter, I need to point out a crucial shortcoming in my treatment of how temporal change and pretense are represented by mental models. So far I have suggested only that different mental models be used to represent different contexts, so that events at different times are not confused with the present and pretense is not confused with reality. For instance, I suggested that Jacqueline represented the sequence of invisible displacements in the following two models,

Model 1
[past: "Potato inside the box under the rug."]

Model 2
[present: "Box empty. Potato under the rug."]

where the expressions inside quotation marks constitute the representational content of each model and the expressions outside quotation marks are markers that guide how each model is used by the system. In this example these markers could have originated from the fact that the model marked "past" was formed *before* the one marked "present." And these markers serve a useful purpose if they direct the child's action in such a way that actual search for the potato is governed by the model whose content situation is marked "present," whereas the model marked "past" is used for looking up missing information about the present situation.

However, viewing "past" and "present" as implicit codes guiding the use of models provides an adequate account only as long as children merely use these models correctly. But children soon do more. For instance, Gopnik and Meltzoff (1984) suggest that as soon as infants reach a certain sophistication in their search for invisibly displaced objects, they start to explicitly comment on the disappearance of the object by saying, "All gone." It is tempting to see such a comment as an indication that the infant is aware of the temporal relationship between the immediate past, when the object was visible, and the present, when it has disappeared. If that is right, then children as young as 1½ years must be doing more than just using models correctly. The labels "past" and "present" must be represented explicitly, that is, they must be part of the representational content of a model.

Explicit modeling of the temporal relationship can be achieved by merging the hitherto separate models into one complex model containing different situations or *contexts*:

Complex Temporal Model
["past: [Potato inside the box under the rug.]
  present: [Box empty. Potato under the rug.]"]

Children show not only awareness of temporal distinctions but also awareness that their pretense is different from reality. Again, the distinction must be represented more explicitly than by mere guidelines of how to use models. Jacqueline, whose apparent delight ("knowing smile") indicated such awareness, must have been able to form the following complex model:

Pretend – Reality Model
["real: [This object in front of me is a piece of cloth.]
  pretend: [This object in front of me is my pillow.]"]

Not much has really changed by integrating different models into a single complex model, except that temporal and pretend-real markers are now part of the representational content of the model (within the quotation marks). Past, present, real and pretend are now *explicitly* represented. But what is the significance of this representational change?

Implicit versus Explicit   The significance of representing context markers explicitly is best explained by outlining the function of explicit representation in general. One important difference between *implicit* and *explicit* representation is reflected in the difference between primary representations (single updating model tied to reality) and secondary representations (multiple models detached from reality). Primary representations are determined by perceived reality. The perceiver has no option of representing anything but current reality. This changes once reality is explicitly modeled. Alternative models to reality can be created by forming novel combinations of elements. For instance, acquisition of multiple models allowed Jacqueline to represent not just what is true

"This object is a piece of cloth."

but also an alternative to this true description:

"This object is my pillow."

This is possible because the elements "this object," "my pillow" are *explicitly* represented and so can be combined at will.

Similarly, as long as context markers are *implicit*, they become automatically attached to representations of situations. What Jacqueline could not do at this stage was to rearrange the combination of situations and markers. For instance, she could not change

past: ["The potato is inside the box under the rug"]

to:

present: ["The potato is inside the box under the rug"]

The combination of marker and content would be fixed. Until the child can make the temporal markers explicit, then she remains limited in two important respects:

1. Conceivability of alternatives
2. Linguistic accessibility.

That is, she cannot contemplate the possibility of the observed displacement occurring in the opposite direction, that instead of being moved from inside the box under the rug, the potato could have been moved from under the rug into the box.

Furthermore, when the child makes a statement like "I just pretend," she is contrasting the play scenario with reality. Jacqueline's "knowing smile" and "no-no" at 1½ years may just have been a very rudimentary sign that she was aware of that contrast. But soon, as they enter their third year of life children explicitly talk about pretense, as this youngster does at 29 months: "Mommy you (pre)tend to cry!" (Wolf and Gardner 1979). And around that age children explicitly reject false statements with a firm "No" (McNeill and McNeill 1968; Pea 1980). Such explicit rejection could not occur if children did not have an explicit representation of the contextual relationship between real and not-real. I will take a closer look at this development in the next chapter.

Summary

In this chapter I made two main points:

I started by making a rough and ready suggestion of how infants develop mental representation. From early on they are equipped with a *single, updating model* of the world (primary representation). A single model has many features in common with Piaget's "sensorimotor intelligence," but it puts fewer restrictions on early competence in tune with recent experimental evidence. The great intellectual advance that occurs during the first year I attribute to improvements in the concepts used to state the content of that single model. In contrast, the watershed noted by Piaget at about 1½ years, which marks the end of his "sensorimotor period" and the onset of "true mental representation," I see as the result of the emergence of *multiple models* (secondary representation). I illustrated the intellectual consequences of acquiring multiple models with infants' newly found ability to retrieve invisibly displaced objects, where at least two models are required, one to represent the current location and another to represent a previous location of the displaced object.

The emergence of *pretend play* at about the same age can also be explained by the emergence of multiple models, since such models are necessary for children to stay aware of the fact that the world is different from how they pretend it to be. This explanation is based on interpreting pretend play strictly as *acting as-if something were something else*, which is different from *using something to represent (symbolize) something else*, as Piaget interpreted early pretend play. I argued against Piaget's (1945/1951) view of pretense as a symbolic activity and against Leslie's (1987) claim that pretense requires mental metarepresentation, because in the next chapter I present evidence from different quarters that children do not start to mentally represent symbolic or representational relationships until much later.

Chapter 4

Understanding Representations and Appearances

In this chapter I investigate children's grasp of symbolic and representational means such as language and pictures. I will cover a wide range of their level of understanding: from the ability to interpret and use a symbolic medium (as in "I can *understand* French") to the metarepresentational ability of understanding *that* something has a representational function. I start by looking at the emergence of the ability to interpret pictures and language and emphasize that such *use* of representations does not require the *concept* of representation. I then mention some studies on children's understanding of correspondence, which is a prerequisite for my final topic, the ability to *metarepresent* that something is a representation. Minimally, this requires an understanding of *interpretation* and *reference*, since these two aspects differentiate representation from close relatives like correspondence. This developmental step is discussed in the context of children's realization that a picture can have different interpretations depending on the interpreter's point of view, that visual appearance or linguistic expressions can misrepresent reality, and how the content of a photograph can be inferred from its referent.

Interpreting and Using Symbolic Means

Before I launch into children's use of symbolic media, a few words about the functional differences between different media like language and pictures are necessary. The literature is replete with contrasts between these two types of representation. My focus is only on how they differ in their representational function, and I want to contrast both of them in this respect with perception.

Perception, Pictures, and Language   Perception is not commonly thought of as involving a representational medium. In fact, James Gibson (1950, 1960) argues that perception provides *direct* contact with the perceived environment. Interestingly, he therefore plays down the role of perceptual illusions. He emphasizes that illusions are extremely rare and usually due to unnatural restrictions on normal perceptual exploration. In contrast, modern cognitive psychology treats perception as a process of representational stages. These schools of thought highlight the possibility of regarding *perceptual illusion* as indicative of the representational nature of perception, following Helmholtz (1896), who spoke of visual perception as involving *unconscious inference*.

To speak of "inference" may be going too far, but I see no reason why one should not consider perceptual input as serving a representational function. What is important is to see which particular type of representational function perception is to serve. Its sole function is to produce a faithful representation of what one is looking at. In other words, a perceptual representation should always represent its referent as it really is. For instance, if my eyes tell me that what is going on outside our window (referent) is that there is a car parked in front of our house (sense) then—unless I am hallucinating—there really is a car parked outside and I can use this visual information to update my model of the world.

Contrast this with linguistic information. When my big sister says "Look! There is a helicopter outside the house," then there is, more often than not, no helicopter in front of our house. Obviously, I shouldn't rely on my sister for updating my model of reality, though sometimes she does provide useful information: "Gosh, Mommy has brought some candy from the shop." And that is the difference. Language can be used to inform (sometimes misinform) about reality, or it can be used to just describe a possibility. Pictures are hardly ever used to represent current reality (mirror images and live video pictures are the exception). Photos do depict real events, but events that happened in the past. This makes it clear that language and pictures cannot be used like perception as an uncritical guide for updating one's model of reality. For interpreting symbolic media, *multiple models* are required.

The Need for Multiple Models   Multiple models become necessary for different reasons in different uses of symbolic media. If the symbolic input describes a nonreal situation, then an additional model is needed to represent that hypothetical situation. If, however, the symbolically presented information is supposed to inform about reality, then an additional model is needed to first interpret the input and check its consistency with what is already known before using the information to update one's knowledge base. The information may be wrong or may have been misunderstood.

The need for multiple models to deal with symbolically presented information suggests that it is not pure coincidence that children start to appreciate pictures and language as they enter their second year of life. For this is the age at which they show other signs of multiple model use, like search for invisibly displaced objects and the emergence of pretense.

One point I have tried to make, then, is that infants in their first year cannot properly appreciate symbolic means because they entertain only a single, updating model of reality. If symbolic input were fed into this mental model—as perceptual input is—then the infant would be severely confused about reality. The other point that follows from this is that proper appreciation of symbolic input needs multiple models to prevent interference with the mental representation of reality.

The next question is what kinds of symbolic input can be understood on the basis of multiple models. In the following sections I argue that multiple models allow a great deal of understanding. They enable children to understand representations as a special kind of *represented situation** in which the same people, objects, and relations occur as in real life but in which they behave and exist in a quite different, "nonreal" way. So I have dubbed children at this age *situation theorists*.

By being able to draw the difference between real and nonreal situations, children can capture quite important aspects and characteristics of the situations projected by representations without a proper concept of representation. That is, the young situation theorists do not yet understand that such a projection takes place. They merely interpret the symbolic input as a peculiar kind of situation.

---

*When using the expression "represented situations" it is essential to be aware that it is we who gave them that name—we who understand that they are nonreal situations that have to be projected by representations. Young children need not be aware of that reason for giving these situations that name. For them "represented" simply serves the purpose of classifying a certain type of situation that is not real.

Infants as young as 5 months recognize the similarity between a picture of a person and the person. Dirks and Gibson (1977) demonstrated that infants habituate to a person's appearance by repeated exposure to the person's photograph. That is, after the infants had been repeatedly shown the photograph of a particular person, they looked less intently at that person than at another person whose photo they had not seen. However, this habituation to the person's picture does not demonstrate that infants *interpreted* the picture as showing the person. For them the picture may simply be an object that shares salient features with the depicted person; that is, the overall shape (the outline of the face) and the constellation of round (eyes), vertical (nose), and horizontal (mouth) elements are similar.

It is also interesting that infants in their first year show no particular interest in pictures; they treat pictures with indifference, as boring pieces of paper. This attitude changes drastically in their second year, when it becomes nearly impossible to keep them away from pictures even if one tries (Hochberg and Brooks 1962).

Perhaps the best experimental evidence for children's ability to interpret visual media is the fact that around 15 to 18 months they learn to interpret their own mirror image. Using a test developed by Gallup (1968), Amsterdam (1972) and Lewis and Brooks-Gunn (1979) observed infants with a bright red spot painted on their foreheads standing in front of a mirror. Whereas the younger infants investigated the red spot on the person in the mirror or looked for a person behind the mirror, the older children immediately touched their own foreheads.

It seems clear that by around 1½ years children can interpret pictures and mirror images, and they understand that the people and objects depicted are those that exist in the real world: self, mommy, and so on. They also understand that the people in the picture are not doppelgängers of the real people, and they understand that objects have quite different properties in a picture than in reality: 1½-year-olds do not seriously try to bite into the picture of an apple, and that's not because children don't like apples at that age.

Clearly, then, in the second year children come to understand representations. But at what level? My answer is that children have only an implicit understanding of representations, in that they can *use them as representations*—in particular, they can interpret them. Their understanding of representation is not explicit in the sense that they could model the representational relationship between picture and depicted or model the fact that a picture needs to be interpreted.

Situation Theory of Pictures   Interpreting a picture means to form a mental model of the depicted situation. For instance, a child is sitting with his dad at the table looking at family photos. They come across one taken last winter, with Daddy skiing down the hill just outside the window. Interpreting that picture, the child forms a mental model of daddy on skis. However, the child also sees his dad sitting on a chair next to him, which requires a mental model of Daddy sitting on the chair. To avoid confusion about what Daddy is actually doing, the child must have a complex model differentiating two contexts:

Viewing Picture Model
["In the flesh: [Daddy on chair]
In the picture: [Daddy on skis]"].

The important point about this proposal is that there is no mental model representing the picture as a physical object representing, for instance, Daddy. Daddy simply appears in two different contexts: real and pictorial. This makes the understanding of pictures (as depicted situations) essentially the same as the understanding of other contexts, for instance, the child *remembering* last winter's events

Remembering Model
["Here and now: [Daddy on chair]
Last winter: [Daddy on skis]"].

or the child *imagining the possibility* of his dad on skis:

Imagining Possibility Model
["Really: [Daddy on chair]
Could be: [Daddy on skis]"].

In all these cases the expressions inside the embedded brackets specify situations. The underlined expressions outside these brackets differentiate contexts: real – possible, now – past, real – picture. The critical feature of the expressions inside embedded brackets describing situations is that the tokens within these expressions have the same meaning regardless of context. For instance, the token "Daddy" refers to the same daddy whether the token is used in the "here-and-now" context or in the context of what took place last year. [**Note 4.1** The difference between mental tokens and definite descriptions.]

The fact that "Daddy" refers to the same person in every context within the model is presumably least controversial in the case of present and past. Although each model shows Daddy doing different things, sitting on a chair and standing on skis, it is one and the same daddy doing these things. There are not two dads involved, *this year's dad* and *last year's dad*. The same holds true for the example of an imagined possibility, since it is the real dad the child is thinking of. However, since we are dealing with a situation that does not (and never did) exist, some theoreticians might be tempted to say that in this case "Daddy" refers to a sort of *mental daddy*. But that, surely, is not what the child is thinking of. The child is not considering the possibility of a *mental daddy* skiing. The same considerations hold for the picture. When the child interprets it, then the mental token "Daddy" stands for his daddy and not a pictorial daddy, since the child sees *his daddy* in the picture and not a *pictorial daddy*.

In other words, what is "mental," "pictorial," and "last year's" is not Daddy but the characterizations of the respective contexts. And it is important to remember that by calling a context "mental" and "pictorial," we use the means by which these contexts are projected for identification. We do not mean that the projected situation itself is mental or pictorial. To suggest otherwise would be confusing the *real − nonreal* distinction with the distinction between *representational medium* and *(represented) content*.

Pictures may be particularly confusing in this respect because there is always the physical presence of the picture to contend with, that is, the pattern of colors on the paper that represents Daddy. But certainly, the color on the paper is not what the mental token "Daddy" refers to, even when we are speaking about the picture. "Daddy" refers to *Daddy*. And the child sees Daddy both in real life and in the picture and knows that *in the picture* he behaves differently and has to be treated differently than *in real life*.

Thus, we say that there is only one Daddy but that he figures in different situations. By attributing the right qualities to the respective situations, the child has gained a quite powerful distinction between reality and depicted situations.

Power and Limitation   The child has to learn by experience what each type of situation affords. For instance, the child has to discover that in the picture Daddy can't move, just as he has to discover what real situations afford, for instance, that after a ski accident Daddy in his cast cannot move.

When children make their first knowing encounters with pictures, they may treat them as largely identical to real objects. We once observed Jacob at the age of 1 year and 4 months (just after he showed his first interest in pictures at all) looking at a picture of a shoe, similar to his own shoes and about the same size. He then stepped onto the picture "as-if" he wanted to put on the shoe and was "surprised" that it didn't work. Similar observations have been reported by Murphy (1978, 379), Ninio and Bruner (1978, 5) and Church (1961, 10, 16).

Very gradually children sort out what pictures do and do not afford. Even from 3 to 5 years children studied by Pearlman (1989) showed a significant reduction in confusions about which properties of the depicted are carried by the picture itself. For instance, the younger children were more likely than the older to expect a picture of a flower to smell like the flower, or a picture of an ice cream cone to feel cold.

My concern here is to emphasize that these improvements in distinguishing pictures from reality can be explained within the framework of a *situation theory*. Hence, it is worth pointing out that existing empirical investigations into children's ability to distinguish pictures from reality do not get at the question whether children are *situation* or *representation theorists*. Both "theorists" have to learn by experience which properties of the depicted real object are reflected in the picture. Even the representation theorist cannot know this on a priori grounds. For instance, we used to think—on grounds of past experience—that pictures reflect visual properties only. But times have changed. There are congratulation cards depicting bouquets that smell of roses, and picture books with cats and dogs that feel furry. Recent speech technology makes it possible to buy personalized party invitations decorated with an image that not only looks like you but talks in your voice when the card is opened. In short, investigating children's ability to predict which features of real objects are reflected in pictures does not tell us what kind of theorist the child is. It only tells us how much experience the child has had with a particular representational medium.

It is legitimate to ask, what differentiates the situation theorist from the representation theorist? My answer is that without a proper concept of representation the young situation theorist cannot understand that a picture can be given *different interpretations*, that a picture can have a *sense* and a *referent*, and that pictures can therefore *misrepresent*. Before turning to these issues, I want to look at children's ability to interpret verbal expressions, since linguistic communication exemplifies a quite different use of symbolic media than pictures.

Using Verbal Information   An important function of verbal communication is to inform about current reality. Language can be used with a clear claim to truth. However, sometimes it is not. Whether it purports to contain true information or not we judge by various pragmatic cues like assertiveness, conversational context, and choice of words. Children learn to make this distinction very early. For instance, "Look! There's a helicopter parked on our front lawn!" will make them run to the front window, whereas, a calm "Let's assume there is a helicopter ..." will leave them sitting attentively at your side. Their different responses indicate practical understanding of the difference between the statement's *sense* ("a helicopter is parked on our front lawn") and its *referent* (the actual situation outside the front window).

Relating what is represented (referent) to how it is represented as being (sense) is most clearly exercised in rejecting a false statement. The theoretically important question is whether such rejection must be based on a *metarepresentational* understanding of statements as having *sense* and *reference* or whether—as I try to argue—correct *use* of the statement in these respects is sufficient.

Rejecting False Statements   Pea (1980) observed that negation in the form of the word "no" appears in children's earliest utterances. This word has many different uses. Of special interest here is its *truth-functional* use, to deny the application of a predicate. Even that use occurs quite early (McNeill and McNeill 1968; Antes 1989). Let's take a simple example reported by Pea. He asked a child at 2 years and 1 month about an apple: "Is that a biscuit?" The child replied, "No, apple." What does the child have to understand about the question to be able to make this denial?

From our point of view the following metarepresentational analysis applies: The interrogator put forward a description, "This is a biscuit," where it is clear from the discourse situation that "this" refers to that object (which is an apple), and he raised the question whether the description "is a biscuit" applies to or is *true* of that object. To judge truth, we first have to find the interpretation of the sentence "This is a biscuit," which is the situation *that object is a biscuit.* Finally we need to find the truth-value of this interpretation. This is done by comparing the *described* situation, *the object is a biscuit,* with the *perceived* situation in front of our eyes, *the object is an apple*. Since the described situation does not match the perceived situation, the questioned statement is false and the answer has to be "No."*

This analysis is clearly metarepresentational, since it refers to the statement as a representational entity with an interpretation (sense) and to the necessity of comparing this interpretation with the real situation (because the real situation is the referent of the statement). Once the purpose of these two situations is clear, then the actual comparison process—whether the interpretation matches reality—is not metarepresentational anymore. It is simply a comparison of two situations.

My contention is that young children are not aware of (do not model) the fact that the statement has an interpretation and a referent. All they know is how to treat a yes-no question, namely, by comparing the described situation with reality. The question "Is this a biscuit?" is short for saying, "Tell me whether the situation I am describing here is the same as what you see out there!"—a comparison that is well within the capabilities of a situation theorist.

There is another, even simpler possibility. The child's "No" may be a judgment that what the experimenter said was *incorrect* or *inappropriate.* Incorrectness is not a semantic function, but a comparison between what has been done and what should have been done. That is, the child knows how to play the "naming game": that when pointing to this particular object, one should say, "Apple." Hearing the experimenter say, "This is a biscuit," the child says, "no," because what the experimenter did was not what one should do in front of an apple.

From the child's point of view the situation is similar to observing another person trying to put a square peg in a round hole. Here, too, the child might say, "No," and point to the square hole as a helpful clue about what would be right. Words, from the child's point of view, are primarily something to do something with and do it correctly. They are not seen as expressing something true. This use of words can also be illustrated by standard formulae of greeting. When someone says "Good morning" in midafternoon, then he deserves a "No, it's already afternoon." However, the objection is not that he said something *false* but merely that he said something *inappropriate* for this time of day.

---

*I have tried to model this analysis on situation semantics. In particular, I followed Barwise and Perry's (1983, 6) suggestion of a two-step process from meaning to truth: first determine the interpretation (i.e., a situation) and then determine the truth-value of the interpretation.

These examples are intended to demonstrate that the child need not understand her "No" answer as a metarepresentational judgment of truth on a false statement. From her point of view the "No" simply marks disagreement between the situation described by the statement and the perceived situation. Therefore, in order to reject false statements, the child does not necessarily need to possess the metarepresentational ability to represent the relationship between a statement and what it is about. [Note 4.2 Do early assertions imply a concept of truth?]

Now let me turn to children's acquisition of important prerequisites for their metarepresentational ability to mentally represent the representational relationship between symbolic medium and represented.

Understanding Correspondence

Understanding the use of representations to truthfully inform about the represented world requires understanding of correspondence. That is, one has to understand, for instance, that the horse shape in a picture signalling that something is a horse must correspond to the fact that the depicted object is indeed a horse. Correspondence in itself, as we will see, does not constitute representation. It is but an essential component of it. Nevertheless, for this reason it is interesting to know when children begin to understand correspondence and to take advantage of it. A recent series of experiments by Judy DeLoache on how children come to use 3-dimensional models speaks to this issue.

Using 3-D Models   DeLoache (1987, 1989a) reports a drastic change within half a year in children's use of three-dimensional models. Children from 2 years 6 months to 3 years 2 months were first familiarized with a small laboratory room furnished like a typical living room (couch, coffee table, armchair, etc.), and were told that this was Daddy Snoopy's room. Then they were shown a miniature plywood replica of this room and were told that this replica was Baby Snoopy's room. It was pointed out to them, piece by piece, that Baby Snoopy and Daddy Snoopy had exactly the same kinds of furniture in corresponding places in their respective rooms. They were also told that "Baby Snoopy and Daddy Snoopy like to do the same things. When Daddy Snoopy sits in his chair [and the big toy beagle was put into the large armchair in his room], then Baby Snoopy also sits in his small chair [and the child was shown how the small toy beagle was seated in the miniature room]." After some more demonstrations of this kind the experimenter placed Daddy Snoopy inside a particular piece of furniture in his big room and asked the child to put

Baby Snoopy in the same place in his little room. If necessary, the child was prompted: "Remember, Daddy Snoopy is in the cupboard, so where's Baby Snoopy?" After this thorough familiarization the experimental trials commenced.

In the experimental search task the child was first shown where Daddy Snoopy was hiding in his large room and was then told that the other experimenter would now hide Baby Snoopy in the same place in his small replica, which was kept in an adjacent room of the laboratory. Upon the other experimenter's return the child was to search for Baby Snoopy in his room. In the oldest group the children instantly went for the corresponding location, but in the youngest group very few did so. The percentage of successful children for the three age groups is represented by the steeply ascending dark bars in figure 4.1. The large majority of 2½-year-olds simply did not know where to look. Their helplessness could have been due to their failure to remember Daddy Snoopy's hiding place. To check this possibility, all children were asked at the end of the trial to look for Daddy Snoopy. Children of all three age groups did quite well on this memory control, as indicated by the hatched bars in figure 4.1.

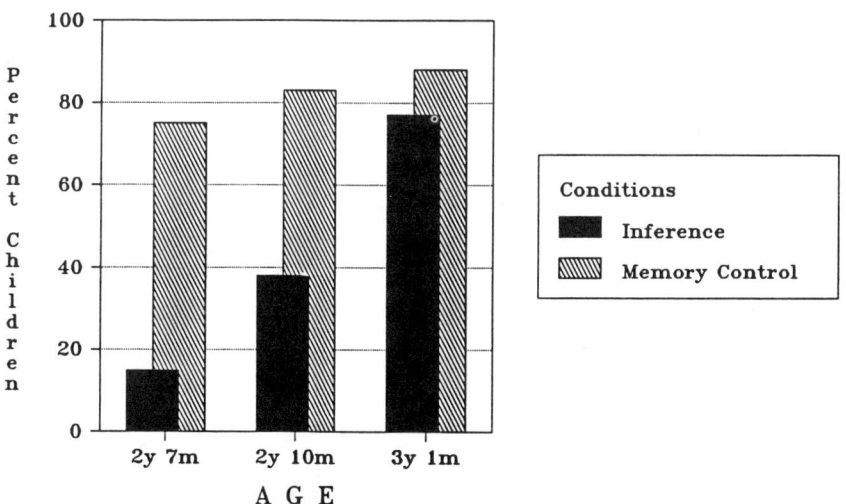

Figure 4.1
Correct search in corresponding/original room.
Data from DeLoache 1987, experiment 1 and 1989b, experiment 1, combined.

The steep developmental gradient on the experimental task indicates that something important is happening between the ages of 2½ and 3 years. Something clicks in children's minds, but what? To answer this question, we need to explain both the younger children's difficulty and the older children's competence.

Failure to see Correspondence The younger children's problem may stem from various sources. They may be incapable of understanding the correspondence between pieces of furniture in the two rooms. They may understand the correspondence of items but not understand the correspondence of events (the two Snoopies' behavior) in the two rooms. Or they may have no problem with either kind of correspondence but be incapable of taking advantage of the correspondence in their search. DeLoache (1989b, experiment 2) looked into this issue and concluded that understanding the correspondence between rooms is the critical factor. Children who failed the search task also had severe difficulty in imitating the experimenter's placement of Daddy Snoopy in the large room by placing Baby Snoopy in the corresponding location in the small room.

So it seems that the developmental curve of dark bars in figure 4.1 marks the emergence of understanding correspondence and of the ability to draw inferences from the state of one system (Daddy Snoopy's location in the large room) about the state of another system (Baby Snoopy's location in the small room). DeLoache summarizes her results in a similar vein:

> The older children ... used their memory representation of the location of one hidden object to draw an *inference* about where a different object could be found. They were so adept at making this *inference* that their success in finding the object they had witnessed being put in its hiding place was virtually identical to their success at retrieving the toy they had not seen being hidden. Undoubtedly these children understood the *relation* between the two spaces. (DeLoache, 1989a, 10, italics mine)

However, she gives the same results a different interpretation in describing their wider significance:

> The 3-year-old understands both that the model *represents* the large-scale room and that his or her memory representation of the original hiding event in the room can be used to figure out where the miniature toy is hidden in the model. (1989a, 2, italics mine) Results ... reveal the sudden achievement, in a group of children between 2.5 and 3 years of age, of an important developmental milestone: the

realization that an object can be understood both as a thing itself and as a *symbol* of something else. (1987, 1556)

What has been described in the first passage as *"understanding the relation between two spaces"* (correspondence) and as the *"ability to infer"* is equated in the second passage with the *"ability to understand represen-tation and symbolism."* Although I once interpreted DeLoache's results in a similar way (Perner, 1988), I want to emphasize here that correspon-dence and inference should not be equated with representation or symbolism.

Correspondence + Inference ≠ Representation   In chapter 2 I reviewed some of the standard argu-ments against equating *representation* with *resem-blance*. Correspondence shares the same problems as resemblance in this respect. It cannot differentiate *what* (referent) is represented from how it is represented *as being* (sense). Two things either correspond or they don't. There is no room for the analogous case of *misrepresentation*.

That correspondence cannot be equated with representation in DeLoache's task can easily be seen from the following counterexample. In England houses of same size built in the same period are almost identical in their layout. As you enter one of the same period as your own, you know immediately where the loo is to be found. Yet I have never thought of English houses as *representing* one other.

This example, of course, only concerns correspondence between elements in the rooms. The other important kind of correspondence in DeLoache's task is the one between states of affairs in the two rooms: whenever *Daddy Snoopy hides under his big couch*, then *Baby Snoopy crawls under his little couch*. It is this parallelism of canine behavior that makes it possible to infer from Daddy Snoopy's location where Baby Snoopy can be found. But that parallelism cannot account for representa-tion either, as another counterexample shows. In professional ski races in North America two identical slalom courses are staked out next to each other and two racers are released simultaneously, one onto each course. Since top competitors achieve almost identical times, they are in corresponding slalom gates at the same time. So by just looking at one skier, you can infer where the other one is. But again, one skier does not represent the other skier, and one slalom course does not represent the other slalom course.

These examples are very similar to the situation in DeLoache's experiment, but it is obvious that they are not cases of representation.

Yet in the case of the two Snoopies' rooms there is some sense in which one might want to talk of representation. What that sense is becomes clearer when we compare the experimental setup with our slalom courses. The reason why the two skiers behave similarly is quite different from the reason why Baby Snoopy does the same things as Daddy Snoopy. The skiers quite independently try to negotiate their respective courses as fast as possible. It is the two skiers' similarity in skill, the identical structure of the slalom courses, the common force of gravity, and the identical starting time that produce a nearly identical timing throughout the course. In the case of the Snoopies it is the experimenter's intention that makes Baby Snoopy do the same things as Daddy Snoopy in a corresponding room so that the child can use knowledge of Daddy Snoopy's location as a guide searching for Baby Snoopy. Without being designed or used for this purpose, one room could not count as a model (representation) of the other room.

Now, if this is the distinguishing characteristic, then children can be said to "understand ... that the *model represents* the large-scale room" only if they understand at least some aspect of this distinguishing feature. There is, however, no indication in the data that they do understand the experimenter's *purpose* in making the rooms correspond and making one Snoopy do whatever the other does. [**Note 4.3** Four points about DeLoache's paradigm and data.]

To get at children's understanding of representation, it is not sufficient to demonstrate that they understand correspondence between two systems (rooms) and that they can infer events in one system (hiding place) from observing events in the other. What needs to be assessed is children's awareness of the critical elements of representation, for instance, the need for interpretation and the difference between reference and sense. Understanding these criterial features of representation requires the ability to form metarepresentations, and (as we will see) this ability at best *starts* to emerge at the age of 3 years.

Metarepresentation

The prefix "meta-" is here again used to give "-representation" Pylyshyn's (1978) recursive connotation to mark the child's ability to mentally represent the representing relation itself. In chapter 2 I have spelled out what metarepresentation involves in the case of models, namely, a model that shows how a model (military sandbox) relates to what is being modeled (battlefield). And in the case of pictures, a metapicture has to depict a picture showing its pictorial qualities. By analogy, a child capable of mental metarepresentation who, for instance, represents that a picture is a representation needs to construct a mental model containing two substructures and their relationship. One structure has to represent the picture (as a physical entity) and the other what the picture depicts (its interpretation), and, very importantly, the model has to include links between these two structures representing how the picture relates to the depicted. Without these links the model would not be a metamodel. It would be merely a model of a piece of paper (picture) and of a hypothetical situation without making clear that the hypothetical situation is the interpretation of the picture.

To better explain what metarepresentation implies, let me compare the young situation theorist, who is able to interpret pictures and who has come to understand correspondence in DeLoache's task, with the child capable of metarepresentation. The left-hand observer in figure 4.2 illustrates what might be going on in the mind of a situation theorist in a setup inspired by DeLoache's experimental procedure but with only a single Snoopy who is hiding inside his cupboard and a picture showing Snoopy sitting there. The child encodes the presence of *Snoopy* with the mental token [Snoopy], the presence of the *bed* with [bed], and so on, and combines these tokens in the way she sees them combined in the room: [Snoopy inside cupboard].

Knowing how to interpret a picture consists in being able to form a mental model of it by using the same tokens that are used for the objects depicted. That is, interpreting the picture of Snoopy in his cupboard requires a model using tokens [Snoopy], [cupboard], and so on, and combining these elements as they are in the picture: [Snoopy inside cupboard].

This creates the problem emphasized by Leslie (1987) of confusing the depicted with reality. This problem can be solved by enshrining the mental representation of the pictorial content within a separate (spatial) context labeled "picture," yielding the following complex model:

Pictorial-Situation Model
["Picture: [Snoopy inside cupboard]
  to the left, in front of
  Room: [Snoopy inside cupboard]"]

This kind of mental model equips young situation theorists with considerable power for understanding the nature of pictures but leaves them restricted in certain ways:

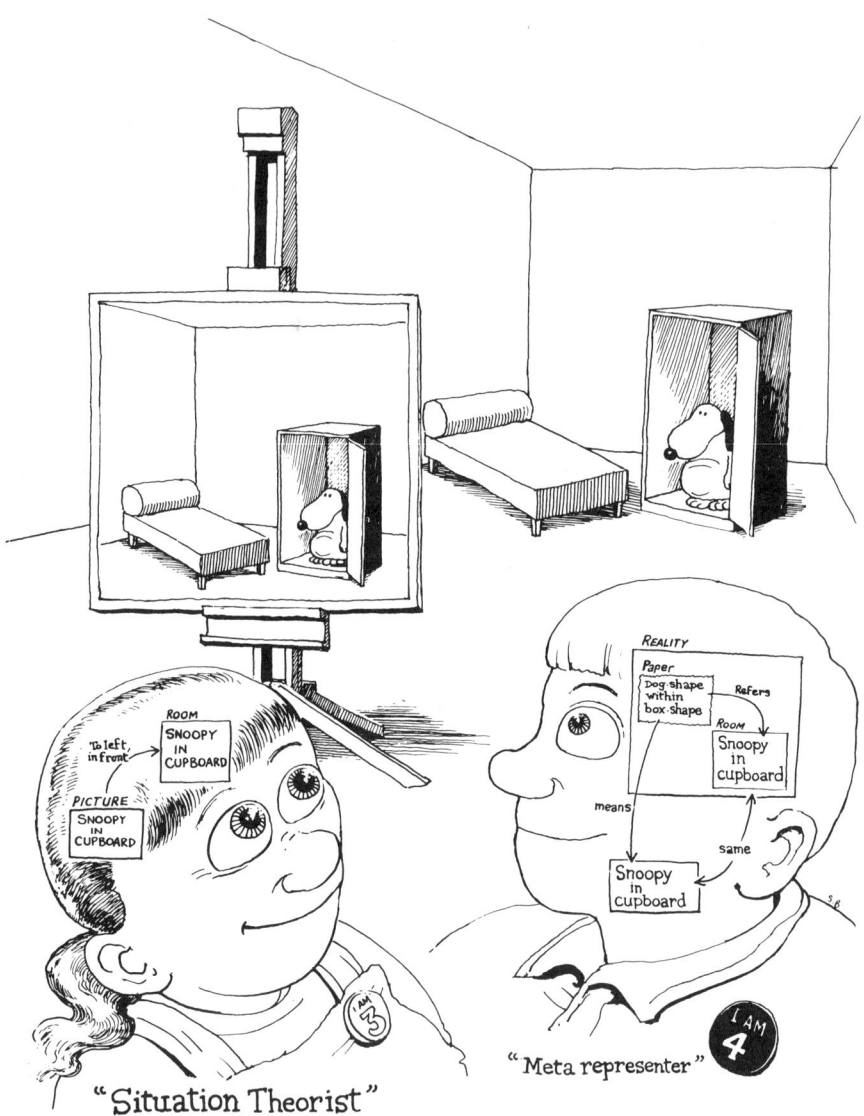

Figure 4.2
Different mental models of a picture and the depicted.

The Situation Theorist's Power

1. By interpreting the picture, the child encodes it with the same mental tokens as reality; that is, the child sees *Snoopy* in the picture, not a dog shape. Hence, interpretation establishes automatic reference between the recognizable parts of the picture and real individuals and objects. Notice, however, that although this referential relationship is implicit in how the child mentally encodes the picture, it is not explicitly *represented* by the child.

2. The child can compare the situation in the picture with that in the room and judge whether they are the same or different. Also, the child can come to expect the situation in the room to be the same as in the picture and so successfully search for Snoopy after having been shown the picture.

3. Because the pictorial content is contained in a different context labeled "picture," it is not confused with reality in the room.

4. Since the picture has a spatial location in the real situation, the child can locate the depicted situation in space and answer questions like "Where is Snoopy in the picture?" by pointing to the appropriate region of the picture.

5. Depending on how much the child knows about "pictorial situations," the child may be aware that in the picture Snoopy does not move, cannot be stroked very rewardingly, does not snap, and so on. This awareness, however, does not show that the child is also aware of the representational relationship between the picture and the real scene. Snoopy is there twice, once in reality and again in the picture.

Restrictions on the Situation Theorist

1. The child cannot think of the possibility that the picture could be interpreted differently since the notion of "interpretation" is not yet modeled (explicitly represented) and so the child cannot form an alternative model showing this possibility.

2. Although interpretation establishes reference for recognizable elements, it does not establish reference for the picture as a whole for the simple reason that the referent situation (e.g., current reality, past reality, hypothetical possibility) is not "visible" in the picture. What the referent situation is needs to be established metarepresentationally by representing that pictures have referents and by a theory of what that referent is (e.g., the scene in front of the camera when the photo was taken).

Before looking at a metarepresentational mental model that will overcome these restrictions, let me first look at the mental model of a child capable of understanding correspondence in DeLoache's task. Here the child faces two similar-looking rooms: one large, one small. Unlike in the case of a picture, the child has not learned to *interpret* the small room as a representation of the large room. They are just two different rooms. *Daddy Snoopy* is mentally encoded as [Daddy Snoopy], *Baby*

Snoopy is encoded as [Baby Snoopy], the *bed* in the large room is encoded as [big bed], and the *bed* in the small room is encoded as [little bed]. Unlike looking at the picture, then, just looking at the small room, does not evoke a mental representation of the large room.

Now the correspondence between the two rooms is pointed out to the child. This might result in the following complex model:

Correspondence Model

["Small room: [Baby Snoopy inside little cupboard]
  Large room: [Daddy Snoopy ?]
  Correspondence rules: [Daddy Snoopy --corresponds-- Baby Snoopy
                         big bed --corresponds-- little bed
                         big cupboard --corresponds-- little cupboard]"]

The knowledge that Baby Snoopy likes to hide in the same places as Daddy Snoopy can be represented by the mental rule

[If Baby Snoopy hides in X, then Daddy Snoopy hides in whatever *corresponds* to X].

The two examples of mental models I have just given serve to highlight that the situation theorist can interpret pictures (in terms of real entities) and understand the correspondence between the two rooms in De-Loache's experiment without being able to form a metarepresentation, that is, a mental model that represents the representational relationships (interpretation and reference) between picture and room. Let us now look at the mental model the "metarepresentational" child might construct.

In a way, one could say that the metarepresentational children combine the ability to *interpret* a picture and the ability to *compare situations* with what they have demonstrated in DeLoache's task—namely the ability to represent that there can be correspondence between two systems, in this case the picture as a physical object and the real room. This is illustrated by the mind of the right-hand observer in figure 4.2. That child observer represents three essential relationships. He represents that the picture as a physical entity and as part of reality has an *interpretation* (what the picture "means") in terms of something else. By noticing that the interpretation of the picture has the *same objects* in it as the room (for instance, *Snoopy*), he can see that elements in the picture (say the dog-shape), *correspond* to elements in the room (Snoopy). Since this correspondence is not something that can be observed in the external world but something that needs to be established "internally" by noting the identity between the picture's interpretation and the external situation,

I labeled this correspondence "refers" in figure 4.2. A less picturesque way of summarizing the metarepresentational child's model is as follows:

Metamodel

["In reality: [Snoopy in cupboard and there is a piece of paper
                   with: [dog-shape within box-shape]], which **means**:
 In picture: [Snoopy inside cupboard]
 Reference links:[dog-shaped area --corresponds-- Snoopy
                  box-shaped area --corresponds-- cupboard]"]

What has changed? Whereas before the picture and reality were related only because the child described them by using the same mental tokens, this relationship is now explicitly represented.

The critical question arising from this is, of course, what the child actually gains from this new metarepresentational ability. At least two kinds of abilities can now emerge. The child can understand that different interpretations are possible and can build a theory about the reference. I start by presenting evidence for children's understanding of alternative interpretations.

Conceiving of Alternative Interpretations Once children start to represent (model) that a representation has an interpretation, then they can become able to conceive of alternative interpretations, because the ability to conceive of alternatives is the hallmark of modeling. Research from John Flavell's laboratory on visual perspective taking indicates that this ability emerges after the age of 3 years.

Masangkay et al. (1974) and Flavell et al. (1981) showed young children drawings, for instance, of a turtle and asked them whether the turtle was *standing on its feet* or whether it was *lying on its back*. Children were able to make the standard interpretations. If the picture placed flat on the table was oriented so that the turtle's feet pointed toward the child, then the answer was that the turtle was standing on its feet; when the picture was rotated by 180°, the answer was that it was lying on its back. As the hatched bars in figure 4.3 show, even the youngest 3-year-olds had little difficulty with this part of the task. This shows that 3-year-olds have no problem *using* pictorial conventions and interpret one and the same picture differently depending on what vantage point they are viewing it from. However, this does not imply that these children understand *that* they are applying different interpretations. For them it is as if the turtle is changing positions as the picture is being rotated.

This practical ability to give different interpretations, however, will not allow the child to understand that another person viewing the picture from a different vantage point will give it a different interpretation. To be able to do this, children need to model the fact that the picture is being interpreted so that (by forming an alternative model) they can conceive of the possibility of different interpretations. And with that task young children do have great difficulty. As the dark bars in figure 4.3 indicate, only very few 3-year-olds understood that when they saw the turtle lying on its back, the experimenter sitting opposite would see it differently, namely, as standing on its feet. Their typical error was to attribute the same interpretation to the experimenter as they themselves were giving to the picture at the time. By 4 years, however, very few children committed this error.

The 3-year-old's difficulty cannot be explained by Piaget's theory of *spatial egocentrism*, according to which the young child is unable to differentiate between her own view and other people's (Piaget 1959, 267, fn. 1). This theory cannot account for the data because, as Masangkay et al. (1974) and Lempers, Flavell, and Flavell (1977) have demonstrated,

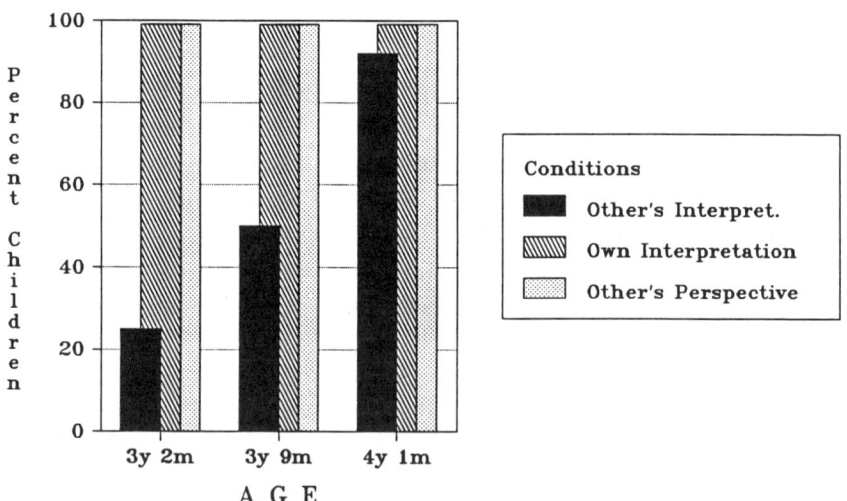

Figure 4.3
Correct construal of interpretation and perspective.
Data from Masangkay et al. 1974, experiment 2. Percentages shown are of children who answered 5 out of 6 questions correctly.

even children younger than 3 years understand differences in what people can and cannot see. For instance, Flavell et al. (1981) showed children the drawing of the turtle bisected by an upright screen so that the child could see only the tail end while the experimenter could see only the front end. Masangkay et al. (1974) used a piece of cardboard with a dog drawn on one side and a cat on the other. The dotted bars in figure 4.3 show that 3-year-olds had no difficulty understanding that the experimenter seated opposite would see something different from what they themselves were seeing. These were the same children who could not understand that the experimenter could give the drawing of the turtle a different *interpretation*.

So, although 3-year-olds are aware that other people have a different view when looking from a different vantage point, they do not understand that people looking at the same picture from a different angle may give it a different interpretation. Conceiving of alternative interpretations requires metarepresentational abilities because the relationship between a representation (picture) and what it represents (the turtle's position) has to be mentally modeled. This same ability is also required for understanding cases of misrepresentation; and the evidence for when that understanding emerges points toward the same age period.

Understanding Misrepresentation: Separating Sense from Reference

Understanding cases of misrepresentation requires the ability to metarepresent because the child has to mentally represent that, say, a false statement about reality has an interpretation (described situation) that is at odds with reality (its referent situation). This understanding is implicit in children's earlier *use* of statements. For instance, as early as 2 years children use statements as sources of information about reality and even reject them with a firm "No" when their interpretation does not match up with reality. However, as I have argued, rejection of false statements does not show that children mentally represent what they are doing. To demonstrate that 3-year-olds still have problems understanding that a statement misrepresents, Heinz Wimmer and I looked at children's difficulty in remembering their own mistakes committed out of ignorance.

Memory for **False Statements**   The logic of our investigation rests on the observation that things we say for no good reason, or for which we do not understand the reason, are more difficult to remember than things we meant to say. Furthermore, since memory tends to be reconstructive, we remember only the gist of what was said and therefore can only reconstruct what was actually said from the gist we remember (Bartlett 1932; Sachs 1967). Thus, if young children have no conception that a statement can misrepresent reality, then they should be bad at reconstructing a mistaken claim about reality. This idea can be made clearer with reference to our experimental procedure.

In the experimental situations children were confronted with a typical container that was familiar to all of them—for instance, a box of chocolates . Then Kasperl was announced, a well-known character of Austrian puppet shows with a reputation for being curious and a penchant for the obvious. He asked the child, "Hello! What a beautiful box you've got. What is in it?", and all children dutifully replied, "Chocolate." Kasperl then opened the box, and to his and the child's surprise he found no trace of any chocolate but instead a toy car. The child was asked to confirm that there was really a car in the box instead of chocolate, and the crucial *memory question* was asked: "When Kasperl asked you what is in the box, what did you say was in it?" The dark bars in figure 4.4 show that very few 3-year olds were able to answer that question correctly, whereas practically all 4-year-olds could do so.

The majority of 3-year-olds did not just fail to remember their mistaken answer, "Chocolates." In fact, they *misremembered* having said, "car," the actual content of the box. That is what one would expect if these children cannot differentiate between sense (interpretation) and referent of their mistaken claim. Since the point of their original answer was to *say what is in the box*, they can only reconstruct their answer as having said what was in the box, namely, "The car." They cannot reconstruct it as "Chocolate" because they would need the metarepresentational ability to separate *what* they described (the referent) from what they described it *as being* (sense).

Of course, this interpretation of results is only warranted in view of children's good memory for their wrong answer in a control condition. Instead of being tricked into saying something false by mistake, they were induced to make a jokingly wrong statement. This condition differed from the one already described only in that the children knew that there was a toy car in the chocolate box before making the statement. Upon the imminent arrival of curious Kasperl they were instructed to tell him something silly, namely, that there was chocolate in the box. Unfortunately, since 7 of the 22 3-year-olds and 1 of the 12 4-year-olds could not be persuaded to play along and told Kasperl what was really in the box, the graphs in Figure 4.4 had to be based on only those children who did play

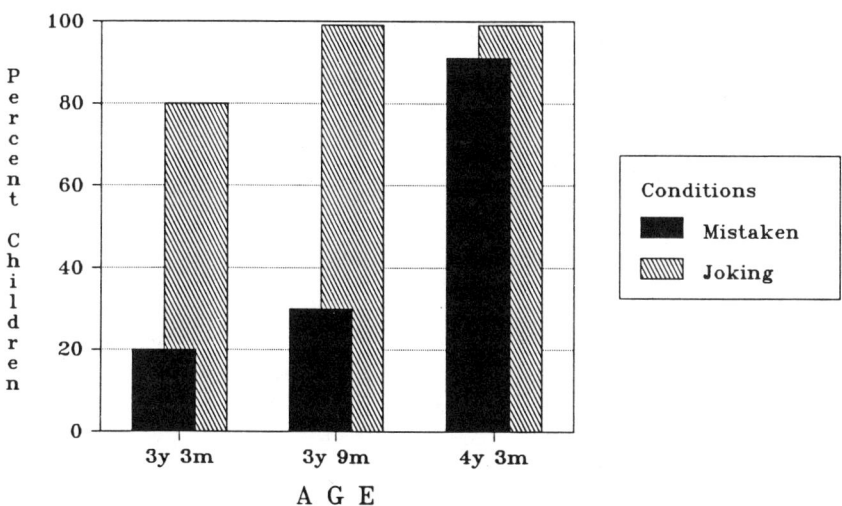

Figure 4.4
Memory for false statements.
Data from research by Wimmer and Perner (1990). Percentages shown are of those children willing to give jestingly wrong answers.

along.[*] As the striped bars in the figure show, even most 3-year-olds were perfectly able to remember their silly answers but not their mistaken answers (dark bars). Why is that?

Unlike the first condition, where the children were genuinely mistaken and experienced their answers to Kasperl as *describing the actual content of the box*, the children in the second condition know that they are not describing the real content. So, from their point of view they are describing a different situation from the real one. As I have argued in chapter 3, creating a difference between reality and some hypothetical situation is the hallmark of pretense and is therefore well within the conceptual capabilities of 3-year-olds and even much younger children. In this case 3-year-olds could make sense of their silly, "false" statements,

---

[*]Subject numbers are therefore somewhat small. So it is comforting to know that this experiment was already a replication of a study by Martin Schreibmüller (1989). In his study very few children refused to play silly and tell Kasperl something wrong. Yet the difference in memory for jestingly false and mistakenly false statements was as massive as in our replication.

and consequently their memory for what they had said was fairly good. [**Note 4.4** Ruling out embarrassment as a cause of children's refusal to remember their own mistake.]

The contrast between the two conditions of this experiment illustrates very well the theoretically important point that 3-year-olds have no conception of *misrepresentation*. They have no notion that a statement can *describe* the real situation (referent) and yet *(mis)describe* it *as* a quite different situation (sense). They can just use statements in different ways. When they use a statement knowingly to describe, in jest, a situation that differs from reality, they can remember what situation they described. But when they use it to *describe* the real situation (experience it as information about reality), then they can remember it only as describing that reality. Only 4-year-old *metarepresenters* can remember that they *misdescribed* the real situation *as* different from what it really is.

Our experiment demonstrated young children's difficulty with understanding misrepresentation in the case of verbal statements about reality, but the same difficulty exists in other domains. One domain that has received much attention recently is children's understanding of *visual misinformation*.

Distinguishing Appearance from Reality   Sensory information is about reality. It informs the perceiver how the real world is. Unlike language and pictures, which depict objects in past or hypothetical situations, perception specifies reality here and now. Yet occasionally it may *misspecify* it. And only in these rare cases of serious visual illusion do we become aware of the fact that perception is not a direct, infallible imprint of reality but that it has representational qualities. It specifies reality *as* something—and when things go wrong, it specifies reality *as* something *else*.

Flavell, Flavell, and Green (1983) investigated children's understanding of deceptive appearances. For instance, the child was shown a piece of sponge that looked just like granite. When they first saw it, virtually all children said that it was some kind of rock. Then the experimenter gave it a good squeeze and the child was allowed to do the same and experienced its spongy qualities. The child was then asked two questions:

Reality Question
"What is this *really, really*? Is it *really, really* a rock or *really, really* a piece of sponge?"

Appearance Question

"When you *look* at this with your *eyes* right now, does it *look* like a rock or does it *look* like a piece of sponge?"

Only 5 of 20 3-year-olds gave the correct answers: that it is really a piece of sponge but looks like a rock. The other 15 children tended to give *realist* answers to both questions, namely, that the object really is and also looks like a piece of sponge. In contrast, 17 of 20 4-year-olds differentiated correctly.

If my characterization of 3-year-olds is correct—they are able to *use* visual information but lack the *metarepresentational* ability of understanding its representational nature—then they cannot conceive of the possibility of perception as *misrepresenting* and therefore cannot distinguish appearance from reality. To understand why this is so and why children commit the particular "realist" errors on the "What does it look like?" question it is helpful to look at the use of perceptual information in this particular task.

The only role of visual perception is to inform about reality. But it does so very adaptively. The viewer may be fooled the first time he looks at that sponge that resembles granite and he *sees* a rock. But once he has explored the object more fully with his hand, he knows that it is a piece of sponge. And this knowledge stays and influences what he sees from then on. Even after he has released the object from his hands, he still sees it as a piece of sponge (the one that looks unusual). He does not revert to seeing a rock.

That is how children use their visual sense. But what do 3-year-olds understand about this use? Without a concept of misrepresentation all they can understand is its main function, namely, that looking at something "tells" you what that object is. Children therefore cannot fully appreciate the expression "look like" in the test question "When you look at this right now, does it *look like* a rock or does it *look like* a piece of sponge?" The best 3-year-olds can do is to gloss this question as "When you look at this right now, are you looking at a rock or are you looking at a piece of sponge?" The answer to this question is the "realist" response of the young child: "A piece of sponge."

In contrast, once children (at about 4 years) have a notion of misrepresentation, they can understand "look like" as referring to how vision (without the benefit of tactile exploration) misspecifies the looked-at sponge *as* a rock. In other words, 4-year-olds can understand that visual input has a representational *content* that, in the case of deceptive appearance, makes its *sense* deviate from its *referent*.

I think Flavell, Flavell, and Green's rock-sponge task assesses this ability very well because the child's responses to the deceptive material demonstrate that the following two conditions are met:

(1) The object's visual appearance has the desired misleading effect
    (child thinks it is a rock)
(2) The child eventually discovers the object's real identity
    (child knows it is a piece of sponge)

If these conditions were not met, even an adult could not give correct answers to the test questions. If the object's visual appearance had no misleading effect, one could not say that it looked like a rock. One would give a "realist" answer to the appearance question. Similarly, if one never found out that it is really a piece of sponge, one could not answer the reality question correctly but would give a "phenomenist" response. The child's initial response, "It's a rock," makes it clear that condition (1) is met, and since practically every child (in experiment 1) said that it was really a piece of sponge, condition (2) is met. Hence, we can conclude that the younger children's inability to answer the appearance question correctly indicates their difficulty in differentiating appearance from reality. This conclusion cannot be drawn if condition (2) is not met.

From Appearance to Reality   There is a large range of tasks in which children tend to make "phenomenist" errors; that is, they answer the reality question "What is it really?" with the object's appearance. What I would like to make clear is that this error occurs because condition (2) is not met. The child simply does not know what the object really is. These tasks, therefore, are not suitable tests for demonstrating children's difficulty in distinguishing appearance from reality (since under such conditions even adults could not give the expected correct answers). These tasks test something different, namely, children's ability to infer reality from the perceptual information (appearances) available.

A rather crude case in point is a task used by Flavell, Flavell, and Green (1983, experiment 3). Children were handed an imitation fried egg made of rubber. Many subjects spontaneously said that it was an egg (we don't know what the rest thought). Not surprisingly, then, the majority of subjects later committed "phenomenist" errors when asked, "What is this really?" They said it was an egg rather than a piece of rubber. Why did children give that answer? Presumably because they did not yet know enough, or did not have the right "theory" about fried eggs that allowed them to distinguish fake ones from real ones.

In most tasks of this kind children can readily determine an object's real nature. However, the problem of determining what an object really is becomes much more difficult when the object changes its appearance. This leads to "phenomenist" errors since the change in appearance is mistaken as a corresponding change in the object's identity or properties. For instance, DeVries (1969) used a trained cat by the name of Maynard who did not object to wearing a quite realistic-looking dog's mask. The majority of 3-year-old children in DeVries's study tended to say that the cat wearing the mask "was really a dog." Keil (1989, chap. 9) told children stories illustrated by pictures about a more drastic change in the appearance of a raccoon whose fur was shaved off and dyed so that it looked just like a skunk. At the end children were asked what the animal really was after its beauty operation. At 5½ years most and even at 7½ many children tended to give "phenomenist" answers, saying that the animal was now a skunk.

Another group of tasks involves changes in the appearance of an object's property like color, size, or shape. For instance, Flavell, Flavell, and Green (1983) had children observe a white index card being moved behind a pink piece of glass so that the card looked pink. Children were asked whether the card was really, really pink or really, really white, and "When you look at this with your eyes right now, what color does it *look* like?" Children who answered wrong tended to respond to the reality question in terms of the object's apparent color: "It is really pink." This task is in fact quite similar to Piaget's well-known conservation tasks, as Braine and Shanks (1965; Russell and Mitchell 1985) realized. There, too, children have to learn (develop a *theory*, or, in Piagetian terms develop *operational thought*) that neither the quantity, weight, nor volume of a clay ball changes in the face of evident changes in its visible dimensions when it is rolled out into a sausage. Before children have acquired the necessary understanding of these phenomena, they can but assume that the property under consideration changes as its appearance changes. [**Note 4.5** Evidence that children assume that an object changes color when moved behind a color filter.]

Development of this understanding depends on the particular task. On most of the tasks used in Flavell's laboratory 4-year-olds started to give correct answers. Piaget's conservation tasks are mastered at different ages depending on the particular concept under scrutiny (Piaget and Inhelder 1941/1974), a finding for which the term "horizontal décalage" was coined. And correct answers may not appear within a lifetime on some tasks involving seductive appearances. To put it crudely: if one had asked people some centuries ago whether the sun really moves or really stays still (and the earth moves), even the most erudite would have given the "phenomenist" answer: "The sun moves across the sky." Indeed, without the prerequisite theory it would have been foolish to answer otherwise.

Two Problems: Ontology – Epistemology   My point here is that when we speak of appearance and reality, two distinct problems are involved. There is the problem of knowing on the basis of available information (appearance) what is *really the case* (problem of ontology). Another problem is to understand that there is a distinction between appearance and reality and that we *get to know* (problem of epistemology) reality through its appearances, which can, therefore, fool us. The age at which the ontological problem is solved differs for each problem domain (for some domains scientific progress is needed). Understanding of the epistemological aspect that there is a distinction between appearance and reality can only be demonstrated in a domain for which the ontological problem has been solved, that is, a domain in which the child is susceptible to misleading appearance but knows what is really the case. The rock-sponge task used by Flavell, Flavell, and Green (1983, and several other of their tasks leading to a "realist" error pattern) meets this requirement. Errors on these tasks therefore tell us something about the child's problem in distinguishing appearance from reality (the epistemological problem) and the data suggest that before the age of 4 years children cannot make this distinction in terms of appearance representing reality. [**Note 4.6** Controlling for performance difficulties on the appearance-reality task: temperature sensation.]

I have discussed the 3-year-olds' problem with misrepresentation in two distinct domains. We saw that they have difficulty remembering false affirmative statements and differentiating between an object's real nature and what it appears to be according to its visual appearance. According to theory, 3-year-olds were expected to encounter these difficulties because they cannot understand that a statement or visual appearance misspecifies reality. They cannot understand this because they cannot differentiate between the sense and the referent of a representation. And this limitation, in turn, follows from the central assumption that children younger than about 4 years do not have the ability to metarepresent.

Cases of misrepresentation are not the only problems that require the distinction between sense and referent. Understanding that a photograph provides evidence for some past event poses a similar difficulty because the young child has to *coordinate* sense and referent to understand that there must have been a past situation (referent) that corresponded to the situation shown in the picture (sense). Experimental evidence indicates that this understanding is also difficult for 3-year-olds.

Understanding Photographic Evidence: Coordinating Sense with Reference

Understanding photographic evidence requires coordination of a photograph's content and referent since the child has to understand that the situation shown in a photograph (content) reflects a real situation of the past (referent). The developmental emergence of this ability has been experimentally investigated by Deborah Zaitchik (1990).

Predicting What a Photo Shows   Zaitchik taught 3- and 4-year-old children how to work a Polaroid camera. She first let them play with a toy camera for taking pretend pictures of various objects. They understood that to take a picture of an object, one has to point the camera at the object so that one can see it through the viewer. Then the children managed to take a picture of a designated object with the Polaroid. After this initiation period a sketch was enacted in which the well-known *Sesame Street* character Ernie took a Polaroid picture of his friend *Bert lying on a mat* in the sun. While the picture was developing (it takes about 2 minutes), Bert decided it was too hot in the sun and both friends went inside, leaving the camera pointed at the mat. After the two friends left, Big Bird passed by and lay down on the mat. At this point the color started to appear on the developing picture. Children's attention was drawn to the emerging photograph, but before they could look at the picture, they were asked, "In the picture, who is lying on the mat?"

Children were given two skits of this kind. Only 25% of the 3-year-olds in the study answered correctly that Bert (not Big Bird) was lying on the mat *in the picture*. At 4 years 63% were able to give a correct answer. In other versions of this experiment Zaitchik confirmed that children gave a wrong answer even though they could remember who had been sitting on the mat when the "picture was being taken" (experiment 2). Difficulties persisted even when children were asked at the time the picture was being taken, "Who will be lying on the mat in the picture?" and they answered correctly, "Bert" (experiment 5).

Why do 3-year-olds have such difficulty with such a simple task? One answer could be that the task is not really simple since the causal mechanism that leads to the formation of the picture is complicated and 3-year-olds simply don't understand it. However, as Zaitchik points out, sophisticated understanding of the mechanics of photography is not really required for her task, since many adults have practically no understanding of these principles and because it is unlikely that 4-year-olds, who perform much better on the task, would have a significantly better understanding of them than 3-year-olds.

Probably, all that technically naive adults understand is that when the camera "clicks," a pattern of colors is transmitted (whatever the technical implementation) from the scene in the viewer onto the film, so that one can recognize the scene from the photo. The 3-year-old, who is not yet able to metarepresent, cannot think in terms of the photograph as a physical entity that is made to correspond to some real scene and that has an interpretation in terms of that scene. And so one would expect children at this age to have difficulty with Zaitchik's tasks.

Color Transmission Control   To test whether it is indeed representational factors that make the photo task difficult for children, Sue Leekam and I—with financial assistance from the Medical Research Council—invested in a Polaroid camera. For our *photo condition* we changed Zaitchik's setting to one with Judy, a doll dressed in yellow. The camera was described as a machine with a piece of paper in it, which, when the button is pressed, goes "click" and makes a *picture of Judy wearing this color.* While waiting for the picture to develop, Judy felt the urge to change into a blue dress. After that change in clothes children were alerted to the developing photo and asked, "In the picture, what color is Judy?"

Children from 3½ to almost 5 years found this question difficult to answer, and most either opted wrongly for "Blue" (the color of Judy's current dress) or said they didn't know and then—about half and half—guessed the right or wrong color. Only a minority of the 32 3-year-olds and 35 4-year-olds gave the correct answer, "Yellow," as the dark bars in figure 4.5 show. These results closely replicate (45% correct answers) Zaitchik's finding (experiment 1, 3- and 4-year-olds combined: 44% correct).

The important innovation of our study was the *color transmission control.* In this task the camera was facing a screen covered with a yellow cloth. Children were given exactly the same instructions as in the photo condition, except that they were told that when the button was pressed, the machine *makes the piece of paper inside the same color as the cloth outside.* Again, while the photographic paper was developing the cloth was changed to blue. Before they could see the color of the paper the children were asked, "In my hand, what color is the paper?"

Notice that this task is almost identical to the original photo task. The same photographic mechanism was involved, the same memory problems were raised, and almost identical questions about the same colors were asked. The only difference was that whereas in the *photo condition* the piece of paper was described in *representational* terms as depicting Judy in her dress, in the *color transmission control* the piece of paper was described *nonrepresentationally* as merely taking on the same color as the screen outside (or: made to *correspond* in terms of color). Despite this similarity in tasks children found the color transmission condition easier than the photo task. This is reflected in the difference between hatched bars and dark bars in figure 4.5. In fact, 19 children had no problems on the control task but gave wrong or uncertain answers on the photo task,

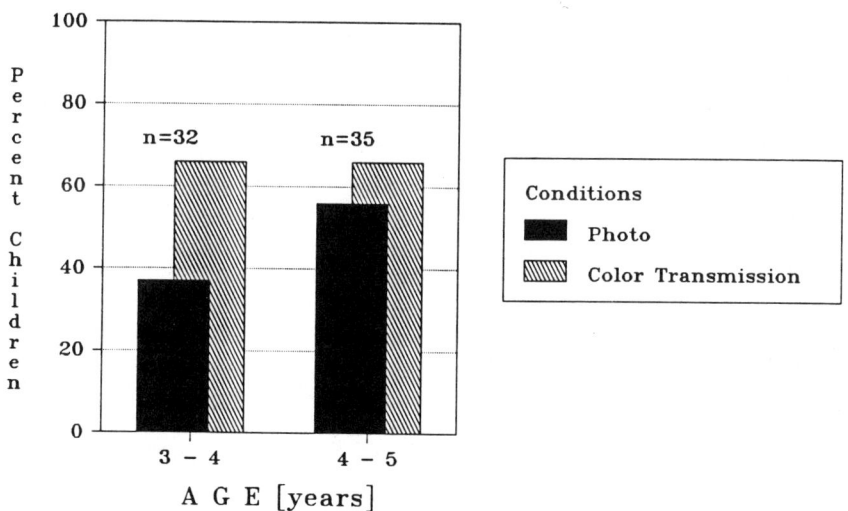

Figure 4.5
Predicting correct color of paper or of person in photograph.
Data from research by Perner and Leekam (1990) comparing understanding of photography with understanding of color transmission.

whereas only 5 children did better on the photo task than on the control task.*

The bars in figure 4.5 make two things clear. The fact that performance on the color transmission control was far below perfection indicates that the task setup itself created difficulties (partly attributable to problems remembering the old color). However, the fact that performance on the photo task was even below that on the control task does indicate that children (in particular, 3-year-olds) have a specific problem with the representational aspect in the photo task. My explanation for this difficulty is that young children cannot *metarepresent*, hence cannot understand the photo *as* a representation representing *something* (referent) *as something* (sense). Without this understanding they cannot understand the task in the same way as adults do.

However, there remains one problem with this explanation. Although 3-year-olds' inability to metarepresent explains why they cannot reason in the same way as adults do about this task, it does not explain why they gave the specific kind of wrong answer they did. Their wrong answers become particularly puzzling when one considers their good memory for *true statements* about a past situation in a control condition used by Wimmer and Hartl (in press). This control condition and the photo task are remarkably similar. In the memory-for-true-statements task children observe another person *making a statement* about the contents of a box, whereas in the photo task children observe a person *making a photo* of a person on a mat. Then they observe how the contents of the box change or how the person on the mat changes, and in both cases they faithfully remember the previous contents of the box or occupant of the mat. Despite these close similarities the difference in children's performance is striking. Although 3-year-olds can reconstruct *what the person had said was in the box*, they, and even many 4-year-olds, cannot tell *who the picture shows was on the mat*.

The difference can be explained by how the young child *uses* statements and photographs. Three-year-olds can reconstruct a past statement about a past situation because they can *use* statements to describe past situations. So when asked in Wimmer and Hartl's experiment what the other person had said was in the box, they simply described what was in

---

*McNemar's $\chi^2(1, N = 24) = 8.16$, $p < 0.01$. The order of tasks was counterbalanced within age groups.

the box at the time (and they went wrong when that statement mis-described the true contents of the box).

In contrast, photographs are not used to make statements. All that children typically know to do with photos is to interpret them. They know that some of the same objects and people appear in photos as in the real world. In Zaitchik's warm-up phase they also learned how to get people into the picture by catching them with the viewer and pressing the button. However, beyond the fact that the same people and objects occur in depicted situations and in reality there is typically—particularly when looking at old family pictures—no obvious relationship between where these people and objects are in the picture and where they are in the real world. In short, from normal use of pictures the child simply cannot predict where people are in a picture. The nearest answer to the experimenter's question, "..., who *is* on the mat?", is to consult reality. In fact, the present tense form of the test question may increase the tendency to answer with the present occupant of the mat.

Clearly, more research is needed to determine what factors lead 3-year-olds in Zaitchik's experiment to give the particular wrong answer they did give. But the fact that they have such great difficulty with a seemingly easy task demonstrates yet again their inability to metarepresent, since they cannot coordinate the content of a photograph with the situation at the time when the photograph was being taken (its referent situation).

Summary

In this chapter I discussed children's growing understanding of how symbolic means relate to the world. I began with the early ability to interpret representations like language and pictures. This becomes possible through the acquisition of multiple models so that the child can separate reality from what is said and from what is in a picture.

When interpreting, the child needs to explicitly model the content situation of the representation. In order to take informational advantage of a statement, the child needs to have available a procedure to compare situations. The child needs to check the compatibility of the statement's interpretation with what is already known and to incorporate useful additional information as new knowledge. But this procedure need not be modeled itself.

I presented DeLoache's finding that just prior to their third birthday children start using information about the location of an object in one room to find a corresponding object in a corresponding room. I concluded that children at this age start to understand correspondence between one structure and another and that they become capable of exploiting the informational value of that correspondence. I argued against its being evidence of an explicit understanding of representation.

Explicit understanding of representation (mentally modeling the representational relationship = metarepresentation) is required, for instance, for understanding that one and the same representation can have different interpretations. Evidence from John Flavell's research on visual perspective taking indicates that this ability emerges between 3 and 4 years.

Metarepresentational facility is also necessary to understand the distinction between sense and reference, which is necessary for understanding cases of misrepresentation. Developmental data from my collaborative efforts with Heinz Wimmer and his research group on children's memory for false statements and John Flavell's research on children's distinction between appearance and reality indicate that children start to understand cases of misrepresentation not much before the age of 4 years.

It is not only in the case of misrepresentation that children below the age of 4 years have difficulty understanding what is represented (referent) in relation to how it is represented as being (sense). Results from Deborah Zaitchik's photo experiment and our color transmission control indicate that children have at least equal difficulty figuring out the content of a picture if they have to infer it from the referent situation.

PART II
Mind

Chapter 5

Characterizing "The Mental"

In this chapter I introduce the study of children's growing understanding of the mind by outlining the view children come to acquire: namely, our commonsense view of the mind. As a first step I characterize the mind by distinguishing *the mental* from *the physical* according to three criteria:

1. Inner Experience
2. Theoretical Constructs in Explanations of Behavior
3. Aboutness (Intentional Inexistence)

These criteria are useful for deciding when children understand inner states like emotion *as mental* states, as discussed in chapter 6 on early understanding.

I then raise the question to what degree our commonsense psychology conceives of the mind as *representational*. My answer is that common sense (like much of the philosophy of mind) tries to get away without representation. But certain mental phenomena do require a representational theory of mind. This provides the basis for my developmental claim that children do not understand these aspects of the mind before they are about 4 years when they start to acquire a proper notion of representation. This development is the focus in the three chapters on children's understanding of the central mental concepts *knowledge, belief,* and *desire*.

Distinguishing "Mental" from "Physical"

A rough and ready answer to the question of what the mind is can be given by pointing to the expressions in our language by which we talk about the mind: *"knowing," "thinking," "wanting," "feeling,"* and so on. Table 5.1 gives several examples, which are classified in two ways. Reading down, mental states are grouped in terms of the role they serve in the information-processing interchange with the world. Perceptions and cognitions take information from the external world and store, transform, or even distort it. Feelings and emotions can be seen as effects of evaluating the received information in view of what is expected and desired. Finally, desires and intentions are those mental states that specify how the world *should* be changed and that effect these changes.

Reading across, mental states are classified with respect to their *aboutness* (Intentionality), a feature of mentality to be discussed in detail later. Following McGinn (1982), they are grouped into *sensations* and *attitudes*, the latter being further differentiated with respect to whether they are directed toward an object or toward a proposition (*propositional attitudes*). This classification will be helpful in discussing the applicability of different criteria of mentality.

Defining the mental by example gives us some grounds for communication, but it is not a satisfactory answer to the question of what the mind is. One reason why it is unsatisfactory is that it does not help us decide borderline cases. Should we include "looking" or "pushing" in our list? What we need are explicit criteria. In the following subsections I outline three different criteria that I gleaned from Churchland's (1984) very readable introduction to the philosophy of mind.

Inner Experience   The commonsense definition of the mental has its philosophical roots in Descartes's writings. *Mental states are what we observe in our inner conscious awareness.* We know what knowledge or pain is because we have experienced it. This also answers the question of what our everyday mental terms mean. They denote those internal states that form our experience (definition by *inner ostension*).

This view of the mind does justice to how we intuitively feel what the mind is. However, it has its problems, in particular, it creates the *problem of other minds*. If mental states are defined by what we see in ourselves, then since we cannot experience other people's inner states, how can we know that other people have such states, too?

I think there is a link among this tradition in the philosophy of mind, Piaget's (1959; Piaget and Inhelder 1948/1956) notion of *childhood egocentrism*, and the idea that this egocentrism is overcome by means of *role* or *perspective taking** (e.g., Feffer 1959; Flavell et al., 1968; Chandler

---

*I use the notions of role and perspective taking synonymously, as in much of the developmental literature. However, a meaningful and precise distinction can and should be drawn, as Newman (1986) has pointed out.

Table 5.1
Classification of mental states.

| Sensations | Attitudes | |
	Toward object	Toward proposition
Perception and cognition: (Getting it in)		
She is thinking.	She knows him. She thinks of him.	She knows he is dancing. She thinks he is dancing.
Feelings and emotions: (Internal evaluation)		
I feel pain. He is happy. He is anxious.	He is happy with it. He is afraid of the dog.	He is happy about getting it. He is afraid of the dog biting him.
Desires and intentions: (Getting it out)		
	Maxi wants candy.	Maxi wants to put the candy away. Ann intends to get the candy.

1977a,b). [**Note 5.1** George Herbert Mead's notion of role taking.] I will return to this issue more fully in chapter 11, but the main idea can easily be seen. According to Piaget and Inhelder (1948/1956), when asked about what another person sees who is standing at a different vantage point, young children tend to answer by describing their own view. This tendency can easily be understood on the assumption that for these young children "what a person sees" is defined in terms of their own visual experience. Therefore, the primary developmental problem is not to understand what mental expressions mean but to bridge from an existing understanding of these expressions in terms of one's own experience to other minds.

Role or perspective taking is seen as the solution to this problem of other minds, putting an end to egocentrism. For instance, to figure out what another person sees or knows, one has to imagine oneself being in the other's position ("putting oneself in the other person's shoes") and asking what one would see or know in that situation.

Although certainly useful, awareness of inner experiences cannot be *the* primary source of our understanding of the mind. Even the mechanism of role or perspective taking would not work if mental states were understood purely by internal observation. For role taking to work, mental states need to be systematically linked to externally observable events. Only if there is a systematic relationship between where I stand

and what I see can I figure out what I would see if I stood where the other person stands. And this requirement brings us to another way of specifying the meaning of mental terms.

Theoretical Constructs   The essence of this view is that mental states serve an explanatory role in our *commonsense psychology of behavior*. The idea goes back to Aristotle and his *practical syllogism*. Here is an example taken from one of our experiments with children:

A Practical Syllogism

Desire premise:	John *wants* to be where the ice-cream van is.
Belief premise:	John knows the ice-cream van is in the park.
Behavioral conclusion:	John will go to the park.

This practical syllogism makes explicit just one aspect of how, say, knowledge relates to observable behavior. Knowledge also relates in specific ways to informational conditions. John can know where the ice-cream van is only if he had information about it (saw it, was told, etc.).

Philosophical behaviorism tried to use this dependency between mental terms and observable behavior to define the mental as complex combinations of behavior and situational stimulation. But direct definition ties the mental too closely to observable events, creating insurmountable problems of infinite lists of exceptions (Churchland 1984, 24, 25). For instance, in the example of the practical syllogism above one could not use the predicted behavior as part of a definition of knowledge since the prediction only works if no unusual circumstances intervene. Despite his knowledge and desire John will not go to the park if he is prevented by some more urgent business or is physically restricted by some external obstacle.* However, when no such ifs and whens are raised, we do expect John to go to where he knows the ice-cream van is stationed, or else he must be well beyond the reach of common-sense psychology or rationality.

The *theory view of mind* gives mental states needed flexibility by treating them as *theoretical constructs*. Theoretical constructs get their meaning not by definition but from the role they serve in explaining and

---

*Fodor (1987) emphasizes that such hedges about the generality of "laws" are not peculiar to our commonsense psychology. Even respectable sciences like geology need such ceteris paribus clauses when explaining a real geological event.

predicting observable phenomena. They are part of every science. A classical example is the concept of gravity in physics. That there is gravity cannot be observed. Its existence is nevertheless assumed because without it we would not have a consistent theory explaining such disparate facts as the planets' orbit and apples' falling off trees.

The unobservability of mental states and their use as theoretical constructs in predicting and explaining behavior motivated Premack and Woodruff (1978) to suggest that we employ a *"theory of mind"* when we impute mental states to others. This catchphrase was quickly adopted by developmental psychologists as a label for the study of children's understanding of the mind (Astington, Harris and Olson 1988; Bretherton, McNew, and Beeghly-Smith 1981; Baron-Cohen, Leslie, and Frith 1985; Wellman 1985, 1990).

Perhaps one should not call it a "theory," since this evokes overly strong pretensions about its being like theories in science. However, there are some good reasons for using this portentous label to emphasize that each particular mental concept gets its meaning not in isolation but only as an element within an *explanatory network of concepts*, that is, a theory (Murphy and Medin 1985; Keil 1989; Wellman, 1990, chap. 5).

In any case, with the view of mental states as theoretical constructs, the mental ceases to be the precinct of inner experience. It becomes, as Daniel Dennett (1978) has suggested, our best way of explaining the behavior of any really complex system. It enables us to talk meaningfully about mental states in animals and even in computers. For instance, Dennett argues that the best way to describe what a chess-playing computer is up to is to impute intentional states to it—say, that it *knows* it is in danger of being checkmated, that it *wants* to escape the trap, and so on.

In sum, my second criterion of mentality is that mental states are *theoretical constructs* that are necessary for explaining the behavior of very complex information-processing systems. And these systems also display a feature that philosophers have called "aboutness" or "Intentionality," my third criterion of mentality.

Aboutness or Intentional Inexistence   Besides being internally experienced and playing a role as theoretical constructs in a "folk theory of behavior," mental states are characterized by *aboutness*, or what Franz von Brentano (1874/1955) called *intentional inexistence of objects*. Brentano suggested that this is what distinguishes the mental from the physical (Brentano's thesis):

Every mental phenomenon is characterized by what the medieval scholastics called the intentional (sometimes also mental) inexistence of an object, and what we would call ... relating to a content, direction toward an object, or the immanent objectness. Each [mental phenomenon] contains something as an object, though not every one in the same way. In the imagination something is imagined, in judgment something is accepted or rejected, in love something is loved, in hatred something is hated, in desire something is desired, and so on.

This intentional inexistence is exclusively a property of mental phenomena. No physical phenomenon shows anything similar. (Brentano 1874/1955, 124–125 [my translation])

Intentional inexistence characterizes the way in which mental objects or mental content "exists." The mind is therefore called an "intentional system" (Dennett 1978); alternatively, we could say that the mind is "intentionally directed," or that it has "Intentionality"* or "aboutness."

How intentional inexistence helps differentiate the mental from the physical can best be explained by example of a mental attitude like thinking. Take for instance the statement

"Wilhelm is *thinking* of the apple on his son's head."

The described process of thinking is not just an internal process but a mental activity that is *about* an object. Or one could say that it *aims* at the object (Latin *intendere* = aiming at; hence, *intentional object* = the object the mind *aims at*). Yet if that were all, then why is the mental so different from the physical? Why is *mental aiming* different from *physical aiming*, as when Wilhelm points his crossbow at the apple on his son's head? To answer this question, I work out three criteria by which mental aiming at *mentally inexisting* objects differs from physical aiming at *really existing* objects: *nonexistence, aspectuality,* and *misrepresentation.* [**Note 5.2** Intentionality of sensations.]

Nonexistence   One difference between physical and mental aiming is that physically the crossbow can be pointed at the apple only if that apple actually exists. In contrast, Wilhelm's thought can aim at an apple even if that apple does not exist—by imagination.

---

*Although this is the most commonly used term, I tend to avoid it since it is easily confused with the common usage of "intentional" in its meaning "on purpose."

This difference can be further characterized by saying that talk about "thinking" creates a logically opaque context, which invalidates certain inferences otherwise logically valid within the transparent context of marksmanship. For instance:

"Wilhelm *points* his crossbow at an apple on his son's head."
It follows: "There is an apple on his son's head."

The same conclusion does not logically follow from a report about Wilhelm taking mental aim at an apple:

"Wilhelm *thinks* about an apple on his son's head."
It doesn't follow: "There is an apple on his son's head."

Aspectuality   Even if a mental act aims at something that really exists as in the case of knowledge, mental aboutness still differs from a physical relationship. Although knowledge—like a physical act—aims at an existing object, it does so—unlike a physical act—only with respect to certain *aspects* of that object. A physical relationship involves the object as such, in all its aspects. [**Note 5.3** The intensionality of causality.] Again, this can be made salient by a difference in logical properties between sentences about the mental and sentences about the physical. In descriptions of physically existing states of affairs it is possible to substitute one true description of an object for another without negatively affecting the truth of the sentence (Leibniz's law of the substitutability of identicals). That this holds in the case of physically taking aim we can see from the following inference:

"Wilhelm *points* his crossbow at the apple on the boy's head."
"The apple on the boy's head is a crabapple."
It follows: "Wilhelm *points* his crossbow at a crabapple."

This is a valid inference according to Leibniz's law since the expressions "apple on the boy's head" and "crabapple" both describe the same object. But as Frege noted (see chapter 3, in particular note 3.3), this law is violated in the opaque context created by a statement about knowledge:

"Wilhelm *knows* he has to hit the apple on the boy's head."
"The apple on the boy's head is a crabapple."
It doesn't follow: "Wilhelm *knows* he has to hit a crabapple."

This conclusion cannot be drawn because Wilhelm may not know that the apple on the boy's head is a crabapple. He only *knows* the object he has to split under the *aspect* of being *an apple on the boy's head*, not under the aspect of being *a crabapple*.

Misrepresentation   A third mark of intentional inexistence is *misrepresentation*. The apple exists. It is a crabapple, but Wilhelm thinks it is a Swiss Golden Delicious. Like his physical action of taking aim, his thought is *directed at* a really existing apple. The difference is that his thought misrepresents this apple as being a different kind than it really is. The physical action of aiming cannot achieve this. When physically pointing his crossbow at the apple, which is a crabapple, he simply is not pointing it at a Golden Delicious.

Brentano has put forward intentional inexistence as the mark of the mental because we experience our mental states and talk about them as being about some intentional object or content. But this raises the question about the nature of mind that makes this phenomenon of intentional inexistence possible. One popular opinion in the philosophy of cognitive science is that mental aboutness is a result of the mind's being a *representational information-processing system* (e.g., Dennett 1978; Dretske 1981; Fodor 1985).

There are two sides to this claim. One is that the mind—as scientifically studied—is a representational system; the other is that commonsense psychology—as revealed in our talk about the mind—conceives of the mind as a representational system. My concern is with the latter claim, since the study of how children acquire an understanding of the mind is the study of how they acquire our commonsense view of the mind and not the study of how they become cognitive scientists. The claim that our conception of mind is based on a representational view of the mind is, however, controversial.

Is the Mind Representational?

The precise question is whether our common sense conceives of the mind as a representational medium. This is an important question for present concerns since if our conception of mind is representational, then children should not be able to acquire our commonsense view before they have a proper understanding of representation. On the other hand, if it is not representational, children can acquire our commonsense theory of mind earlier.

Unfortunately, the answer to the question is far from clear. Take a mental state like pain. When I am in pain (or feel pain), what am I representing? When I am happy, am I representing anything? At least in the case of *sensations*, then, it seems that our commonsense conception of mind does not imply the mind to be representing anything.

On the other hand, a plausible case for a representational view of mind can be made with mental *attitudes*—in particular, *propositional attitudes*, since they create the more intricate problems of intentional inexistence of mental content. Yet even there the case is far from obvious and needs careful argument. Two different uses of the word "see" illustrate the subtle shades of what our talk about the mind implies and does not imply.

Seeing: epistemic – nonepistemic   Fred Dretske (1969) has pointed out that English distinguishes between—what he calls—*epistemic* and *nonepistemic seeing* by means of the sentential constructions in which the word "seeing" is used. For instance, I can report a certain event in American history in these two different ways (Barwise and Perry 1983, 179):

(1) "Nixon *saw that* Rosemary Woods erased the Watergate tape."
(2) "Nixon *saw* Rosemary Woods erase the Watergate tape."

The construction with "that" in report (1) carries the epistemic implication that President Nixon realized the significance of the event; that is, he realized that it was *the Watergate tape* that his secretary was erasing. This implication is clear from the fact that I could not add "...but he didn't realize that it was the Watergate tape."

The "naked infinitive" construction in report (2) does not have this implication. What is reported is that Nixon was looking at the event of his secretary erasing the Watergate tape, but the report is *epistemically neutral* about what aspects of that situation he did take in. For this reason it is legitimate to add the disclaimer "...but he didn't realize that it was the Watergate tape."

Strictly speaking, only epistemically realized aspects of an observed event can have psychological significance. For instance, Nixon will have warned Rosemary not to tell the FBI *only* if he realized that it was the Watergate tape that he saw her erasing. Although our language provides us with that sophisticated distinction, common sense, I suspect, largely ignores it. I can use the epistemically neutral form to imply psychological significance: Why did Nixon tell his secretary not to tell the FBI what she

Figure 5.1
Common sense: Desire as a relationship to a nonexisting situation.

was doing? Because he *saw* her erase the Watergate tape.

I take it that unless these finer points about "seeing" become a crucial issue—in court, for instance, where Nixon might have pleaded not guilty because he was not aware of the significance of his secretary's actions—we ignore these subtleties. We treat "seeing" as a relationship between a person and the seen event, without concern for what aspects of the seen event are being cognitively represented.

And so I think that children can learn much about the psychological significance of seeing long before they can understand it as an act that leads to mental representations. But, one could argue, this is possible only in the case of *seeing*, because it is always directed at real events. A representational view could not be avoided with mental attitudes that involve nonexisting events. However, this is not so, as we can see in the case of *wanting*.

"Wanting":
Nonrepresentational

A prototypical mental attitude that involves a nonexisting situation is desire ("want"), because we typically desire what we do not have. But even here it is far from clear that when we talk about someone's desire, we impute a mental representation to that person. For instance, when I say,

"Sue *wants* to be in Australia."

I express that Sue aims at the (nonexisting) situation where she is in Australia. I do not—it seems to me—imply that Sue aims at that situation by *representing* herself being in Australia. In other words, we express Sue's desire as a relation between her and what she desires. No representation on Sue's part is involved.

This, one might object, cannot be right (e.g., Forguson 1990, chap. 4). How could we do without representation, since the situation of Sue being in Australia does not (yet) exist? We must first represent that situation before we can represent that it is what Sue desires. That is correct. But the need for representation in this sense also arises in the case of attitudes toward existing situations. For instance, to express that Sue feels happy about her *presently* being in England, we still need to represent the fact of her being in England in order to represent that Sue is happy about it.

What creates confusion here is an important distinction, namely, *who is doing the representing*. As cognitive psychologists—I presume—we are all agreed that the person (commonsense psychologist) must be doing some representing—for instance, representing the nonexisting situation— when reporting on Sue's desire. What is at issue is whether that commonsense psychologist is imputing any mental representations *to Sue* when reporting on her desires.

Figure 5.1 illustrates the simpler option. A commonsense psychologist is shown as representing the nonexisting situation and representing that Sue desires that situation. Notice that what is missing is a *metarepresentation* of Sue representing the situation that she desires.

This characterization of Sue's desire need not be devoid of psychological significance. It gets its psychological meaning from our knowing the relevant implications of wanting something (and these implications need to be spelled out even when Sue's desire is seen as a representational state). For instance, commonsense knowledge of desire includes the rule that people wanting something will take the necessary steps to get what they want. With that knowledge I can use information about Sue's desire to be in Australia to predict that she will do something to get there. (Right I was: She is now living in Australia.)

I can thus use "wanting" as a theoretical construct in explaining Sue's future actions. In this sense (criterion 2) I attributed a mental state to Sue. I may also be aware that Sue's desire is the same kind of state that I experience when wanting to be in Australia (criterion 1). Furthermore, it is a state that is directed at a hypothetical, nonexistent situation. It therefore must be characterized by some form of intentional inexistence of that nonexisting situation (criterion 3). Clearly, then, I am imputing a mental state to Sue, and yet I did not construe Sue's desire as a *representational* state.

It is important to realize that this is commonsense psychology. From a scientific point of view my explanation would be quite unsatisfactory, because how could a person be related to a nonexisting situation? [**Note 5.4** Relating people to nonexisting situations as a scientific problem.]

"Wanting": Cognitive psychology posited mental representations to **In Cognitive** account for the aboutness of mental states in a (hopefully) **Psychology** scientifically satisfactory way. Figure 5.2 gives the cognitive psychologist's view of Sue's desire to be in Australia. An internal representation is posited in Sue's mind, which represents the nonexisting situation that she desires. Positing a representation in Sue's mind solves the problem in a scientifically satisfactory way because of the dual nature of representations. As an existing brain state (medium) the mental representation can exert its influence on Sue; and by representing Sue's

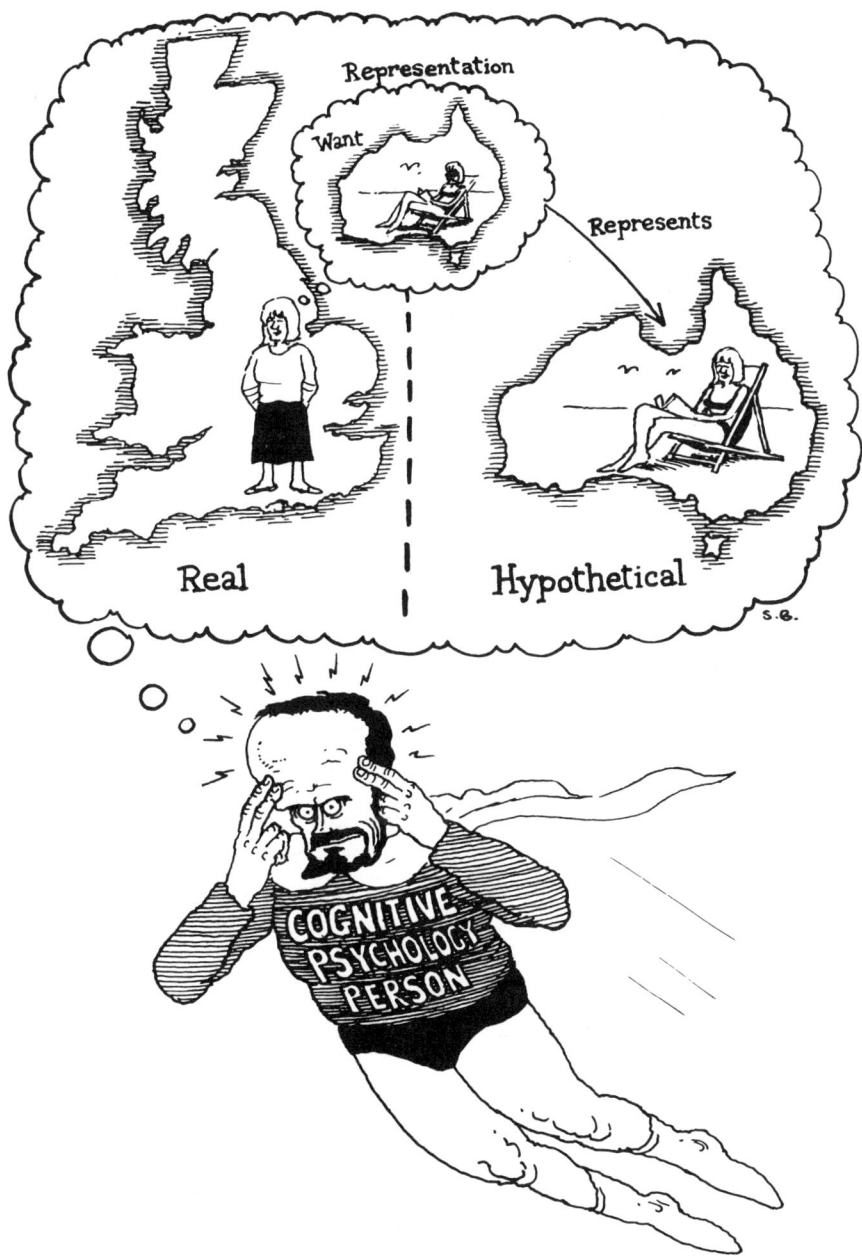

Figure 5.2
Cognitive psychology: Representing desire as a representational state.

desired situation ("representational content" explicated as a scientifically admissible functional concept), it relates Sue to something nonexisting.

Clearly, the cognitive psychologist is engaging in an act of metarepresentation, since he mentally represents that Sue mentally represents the nonexisting situation that she desires. But is that complexity in figure 5.2 really necessary? In particular, is it necessary to represent not only Sue's mental state as a representation but also the hypothetical situation of her being in Australia that her mental state represents? Aren't these two things—the psychologist's representation of Sue's mental representation of her desired situation and the psychologist's representation of the desired situation—the same? The answer is that these cannot be the same, lest the psychologist lose his ability to distinguish the following two sentences:

"Sue wants to be in Australia."
"Sue wants to represent being in Australia."

And these two statements differ vastly. According to the second Sue would be instantly satisfied, since she already has her representation, whereas in the first case she has to be patient and assiduously work her way toward Australia. In other words, it is essential to distinguish between Sue's causally effective mental processes (representational medium) and the representational content of her mental processes (the desired, not yet existing state of the world).

Back to common sense. Since common sense does not have to be scientific, it can take the simpler option and conceive of desires as a direct relationship between person and desired situation without the intervention of mental representation. The explanatory and predictive power of commonsense desire psychology remains the same whether we view people as attracted by desired situations or whether this attraction is mediated by a mental representation of that situation.

An important developmental consequence of these considerations is that children can understand much of the psychology of desire before they have an understanding of representation. There are limits, however, since parts of our commonsense psychology do take a representational view of the mind.

Seeing in Perspective: Aspectuality   One case where commonsense psychology cannot ignore the representational side of the mind involves problems of visual perspective. The representational view becomes necessary there because a difference in visual perspective is not a problem of being related to different situations but a problem of being related to one and the same situation in different ways. The problem can be made clearer by comparing a difference in desire with a difference in point of view.

As an example, let us take two people sitting in front of the model of three Swiss mountains that Piaget and Inhelder (1948/1956, 211) used for studying children's understanding of visual perspective. First the difference in desire. A toy hiker is to be put on one of the mountains. Jean wants him on the summit of the tall mountain, whereas Bärbel wants him next to the hut. We therefore have two hypothetical situations to contend with:

Situation 1
"Hiker at the summit."

Situation 2
"Hiker next to hut."

The one situation is what Jean desires and the other what Bärbel desires. Knowing this, we can venture a commonsense prediction about what Jean—when left to his own devices—will do and what Bärbel—when left to her own devices—will do. He'll move the hiker up to the summit and she'll move him up to the hut.

Now let us switch to differences in perspective. Bärbel, sitting on one side of the mountain, sees the tall mountain behind the mountain with the hut. Jean, sitting opposite, sees the tall mountain in front of the one with the hut. That is, they give different descriptions of the relative position of the mountains. However, these descriptions describe not different situations but different views of one and the same situation:

View 1
"The tall mountain is *behind* the one with the hut."

View 2
"The tall mountain is *in front* of the one with the hut."

What is involved in understanding these differences in perspective is a genuinely representational problem because the two views pertain to one and the same currently existing situation but describe that situation in different ways. It is therefore not possible to talk about different situations. One needs to talk about different representations of a given situation. The two representations (visual percepts) have the same referent (that is, the situation in front of Jean and Bärbel), but the visual percepts represent that situation by specifying different, viewer-specific aspects of that situation.

False Beliefs: Misrepresentation   False beliefs are another typical case where common-sense psychology has to evoke a representational view of the mind. For example, Bärbel had to leave the scene and so Jean got his way and moved the hiker up to the summit. But to please Bärbel, he told her later that he had put the hiker next to the hut. Bärbel now *thinks that* the hiker is next to the hut when in fact he is standing on the summit. Here two situations are involved: the real one and the one that Bärbel thinks is the case. But more is involved than just two alternative situations. The fact is that Bärbel is not just *thinking of* the hiker being next to the hut, but *thinks that* he is next to the hut.

To capture the difference between *thinking of* and *thinking that*, one must make explicit that Bärbel is representing. In case of *thinking that* Bärbel represents the real situation (referent: The hiker is on the summit) *as* some quite different situation (sense: The hiker is next to the hut). Hence, this is a genuine case of misrepresentation. In the case of *thinking of* Bärbel is not misrepresenting anything; she is just entertaining a representation of a situation that differs from reality—namely the hiker being next to the hut (thought-of situation)—without referring to the real situation.

Therefore, if common sense wants to get away without representation, it can capture the difference between reality and thought as a difference between situations (the real and the thought-of situation), but it cannot differentiate between *thinking of* and *thinking that*. But that distinction is important. Only when Bärbel *thinks that* Jean has put the hiker next to the hut will she be pleased with Jean.

I have tried to argue on commonsense grounds that our common sense is capable of taking a representational view of the mind but that, unless really necessary, it tries to get by without it. So it is interesting that a similar dispute arises in formal semantics about whether mental state reports express direct relations to propositions (possible-worlds semantics; e.g., Dowty, Wall, and Peters 1981) or whether they imply a relationship to representations (Carnap 1947). Barwise and Perry (1983, chaps. 9 and 10) make that distinction explicitly. They argue that mental state reports cannot be interpreted as relations to situations when, for instance, differences in visual perspective are involved or cases of misrepresentation are reported. [**Note 5.5** The representational view of mental state reports in situation semantics.]

Summary and Developmental Implications

One purpose of my three criteria of mentality is to help decide when children construe the states they impute to people as *mental*. Since this sets much of the agenda for chapters 6–9, I use this summary to point out its relevance for those chapters.

Theoretical Constructs   To show how the three criteria of mentality should be applied to children's imputations of "mental" states, it is useful to say something about the relative importance of these criteria. The weakest criterion is the second: *theoretical construct in a theory of behavior*. The problem with relying solely on this criterion is that, as Davidson (1963; Brand 1984) has pointed out, behavior cannot be clearly differentiated from mere physical movement without recourse to the mental states causing behavior. As a consequence, we cannot define *mentality* in terms of a *theory of behavior*, if we need mentality to define behavior. To see this problem more clearly, consider an infant who knows about the permanence of objects. This infant will assume that a person who has disappeared behind a bush will continue to exist there. This continued existence is a theoretical construct. Since it is not directly perceptible, it has to be inferred, and this gives the infant greater power for predicting that person's future movement (or behavior?). If we were to call the person's reappearance "behavior," then continued existence would qualify as a mental state, and by Premack and Woodruff's (1978) criteria the infant would be endowed with a "theory of mind" simply because she knows about the permanence of objects—a somewhat unwelcome consequence. Being a theoretical construct in a theory of behavior will therefore not do as a sole criterion for mentality.

In chapter 6 I raise a developmental issue: whether infants as they start to engage in social interaction must attribute the same or similar mental states as adults do when engaged in that kind of interaction. The issue typically hinges on the question of whether mental states are necessary theoretical constructs for understanding complex interaction. Two lines of counterargument are possible. One is to doubt whether social interaction—of the sort infants engage in—actually requires theoretical constructs of the same sort as the mental states adults would attribute in similar social interaction. The other is that even if infants were to use theoretical constructs serving a similar predictive role as the psychological states that adults impute (e.g., visual attention), the question remains whether infants recognize these states *as mental states*.

As I have just argued, the fact that they are used as theoretical constructs is not sufficient.

Inner Experience   *Inner experience* (criterion 1) might suffice as a criterion of mentality, but only if interpreted strictly as *conscious awareness of having an experience*. That is, the child has to be *aware of having an experience of happiness*, rather than just being *aware of being happy*. Now try to have a clear discussion about that with an adult. So to establish the necessary awareness of inner experiences in young children or even preverbal infants poses an insurmountable methodological problem. Looser application of this criterion is meaningful, however, when used in conjunction with criterion 2. In chapter 6 I illustrate how this conjunction of criteria can be used in the context of infants' *empathic* reactions to another person's distress. The argument is that empathy is based on identifying another person's inner state as an emotion one is familiar with from one's own inner experience of being in that state. Empathic reactions are possible because infants project that familiar state as a *theoretical construct* onto the other person in order to understand what is going on inside her and how to alleviate her distress.

Aboutness   Probably the strictest criterion for mentality is *aboutness*, differentiated from physical relations by the three features of *nonexistence, aspectuality, and misrepresentation.* An important question in scientific psychology is what makes aboutness possible. The solution taken in cognitive psychology is to view the mind as a *representational system*. As commonsense psychologists we tend to avoid that view for everyday explanation, but we can shift to a representational view when needed. And it is needed for understanding aspectuality and misrepresentation.

The requirement of a representational view for understanding these features of the mind but not others has important developmental consequences. It leaves open the possibility that children from an early age are able to understand mental states directed at nonexisting entities and states of affairs. It excludes the possibility that they are able to understand *aspectuality and misrepresentation* before the age of about 4 years, when—as I have argued in part I—they acquire the proper concept of representation. In chapter 6 I illustrate this transition with the example of children understanding *looking* and *seeing*. Even very young infants understand the psychological importance of looking for social interaction, and young children are able to differentiate what a person

Table 5.2
Relating representational levels to understanding of mind.

Representational level	Criterion of mentality	Description and examples
Primary: Single model [first year]	Theoretical construct/ (Inner experience)	May form theoretical constructs (e.g., attention) that adults identify as *mental* but that the infant does not distinguish from physical constructs.
Secondary: Multiple models [second year]	Theoretical construct + Inner experience	Can link theoretical constructs for explanation of behavior to inner experiences; hence, theoretical constructs become specifically *mental*.
	Aboutness: Nonexistence	Can understand mind as relating to nonexisting objects and situations. Captures much of desire psychology as goal-directed action.
Meta: Modeling models [~4 years]	Aboutness: Aspectuality Misrepresentation	Can understand visual perspective, aspectuality of knowledge, false belief.

can and cannot see. Nevertheless, understanding that one and the same scene can be seen under different aspects or perspectives does not emerge until about 4 years. In the three subsequent chapters I present wider evidence for this transition from children's understanding of knowledge (chapter 7), belief and thinking (chapter 8), and desire (chapter 9).

Table 5.2 summarizes the relationship between representational levels in development and children's growing understanding of the mind. At the primary level of single mental models the infant may be able to form theoretical constructs such as *visual attention* that correspond to what we identify as mental states. However, from the child's point of view these hypothetical mental states may not be systematically different from physical constructs like *continued existence* behind a screen.

Formation of multiple models in the second year gives infants the necessary hypothetical reasoning power to ask, "what would I experience (feel) if I were in the other person's position?" and thereby to integrate their own inner experience within the framework of theoretical constructs for explaining observable behavior. By integrating inner experience with theoretical constructs, these constructs obtain an identifiably *mental* character.

Multiple models also allow the infant to represent nonexisting objects and situations. The infant can start to grasp one facet of mental aboutness—namely, that the mind, unlike physical action, can aim at the nonexisting. Thus, from that early age the child can start to acquire a good portion of our commonsense psychology.

At the secondary representational level the infant's potential for understanding the mind remains restricted insofar as the mind cannot be construed as *representational*. This becomes possible at about the age of 4 years, at which point children can acquire notions of aspectuality and misrepresentation, as evidenced by their understanding of visual perspective and false belief.

Theory Change   An important argument is associated with the transition from a nonrepresentational view to a representational view of mind.

Children do not just acquire more knowledge about the mind. Rather, this transition constitutes a "theory change" in children's commonsense psychology—that is, a change from using mental states as theoretical constructs in a *theory of behavior* to understanding the representational information-processing basis of the mind in (what one could call) a *theory of mind*.

The difference lies in the theoretical role played by mental states. At first children use mental states to bring some order into their observations about how people behave in different situations. This is similar to the use of the concept "gravity" in classical physics. Newton introduced it as a particular force in his explanation of the motion of bodies. Much became known about it, for instance, its precise value on our planet ($g = 9.81$). Yet Newton's theory is not specifically a *theory of gravity*, but is known as *"classical mechanics"* (that is, a *theory of bodily motion*). My argument—most strongly put in chapter 10—is that children at first come to understand mental states as theoretical constructs within a *theory of behavior*, just as gravity is used as a theoretical construct in Newton's theory of motion.

Modern particle physics has given us a *theory of gravity*, that is, an explanation of why celestial (or any other) bodies exert a force on other bodies. My claim is that a representational view of the mind serves a similar role in the child's understanding of mental states and for that reason might be called a *theory of mind*. Evidence for this theoretical shift will be at the heart of chapters 7 through 9, and in chapters 10 and 11 I explore the wider implications of viewing children's acquisition of commonsense psychology as the acquisition of a "theory."

Chapter 6

Early Understanding: Emotion and Seeing

In this chapter I raise two questions about children's early understanding of the mind. The first concerns the claim that early social interaction implies that infants have an—at least implicit—theory of mind. To evaluate this claim, I ask whether the infant's mind must contain some structure corresponding to (implicit knowledge of) a mental state in the mind of the person with whom the infant is interacting, without which the interaction would be impossible.

This strategy may remind some of Occam's razor. Lloyd Morgan (1894/1977, 53) reformulated this principle in his "canon of interpretation" as a help for deciding when we should attribute higher faculties of mentality to animals: Only when no simpler (behaviorist) account of observed behavior can be given. Similarly—but one step up, as it were—we could stipulate: Don't endow infants with an understanding of mind unless no simpler level of understanding will suffice to account for existing data. But this is *not* my strategy. As Jonathan Bennett (in press) has pointed out, parsimony for its own sake is not necessarily a good method. I do not begrudge infants their intellectual capacities.

The real issue here is not parsimony but the question why infants—despite all their social sophistication—are still different from older children in their understanding of social phenomena. Giving in to our temptation to endow infants with a "theory of mind" raises the danger of losing sight of theoretically interesting differences between infants and older members of our species.

The second question I raise in this chapter is closely related to the first. Once we agree about when children impute inner psychological states, the question arises whether they understand these states *as mental*. My answer makes use of the three criteria of mentality worked out in chapter 5: *inner experience, theoretical constructs,* and *aboutness*. With *empathy* as an example I argue that when children become able to entertain multiple (complex) mental models at around 1½ years, they can understand emotion as something familiar from their *inner experience* and use it as a *theoretical construct* in understanding another person's behavior. I use the example of children's understanding of *looking* and *seeing* to argue that around 4 years they develop a fuller understanding of mental states as *intentionally directed* (aboutness). And in the following chapters I substantiate the claim that a full understanding of aboutness emerges out of children's acquisition of a *representational theory of mind*.

Early Social Interaction: An Implicit Theory of Mind?

Research in early infancy shows that babies are predisposed for social interaction (Trevarthen 1979; Stern 1977; Schaffer 1984). From birth they prefer to look at stimuli resembling the human face (Fantz 1961), and soon afterward they show sensitivity to the intricate contingencies of human interaction. For instance, Murray and Trevarthen (1985) studied 6- to 12-week-old infants looking at their mothers on a video screen. In one condition mother and baby were interacting in a live interchange on video, and each one's facial expressions and behavior were thus contingent on the facial expression and behavior of the other. In the control condition the baby was looking at a recording of the mother made during the earlier live interaction. So the baby got exactly the same visual input as before, but the contingency of the mother's behavior on the baby's current behavior had vanished. Even at the young age of about 2 months babies looked more at their mother on screen and frowned less during the interactive session than during the replay.

By the age of 9 to 12 months infants' social awareness virtually starts to bloom (Trevarthen 1979: secondary intersubjectivity), which has led Inge Bretherton and her colleagues to say that infants possess a "theory of interfacible minds" or an "implicit theory of mind" (Bretherton, McNew, and Beeghly-Smith 1981, 340, 341). They elucidated the meaning of this expression by means of an analogy.

> Let us make this clear by way of an analogy: When at around age 2, babies begin to use syntax in the construction of utterances, their knowledge of syntactic rules is only implicit. Late in the third year of life, however, some young children start correcting the speech of younger siblings and even come up with simple etymological explanations... They have become aware of some of the rules underlying language. (Bretherton, McNew, and Beeghly-Smith 1981, 340)

This analogy suggests the following: As we can infer from children's correct syntactic constructions that they must have *implicit knowledge of syntactic rules* (presumably an "implicit theory of syntax"), we should be able to infer from infants' appropriate social interactions that they have *implicit knowledge of mental states* (an "implicit theory of mind"). In other words, there must be some mental process governing infants' social interaction that corresponds to (implicitly represents) participants' mental states. I explore whether this claim can be sustained on the basis of two experimentally well documented social abilities in 1-year-old infants: their ability to interpret expressions of emotion and to understand the importance of their mother's gaze.

Emotions: Social Referencing   Some of the experimentally best documented evidence of early meaningful social interaction is what Campos and Stenberg (1981) have called *social referencing*. It occurs when infants in an ambiguous situation, where they don't know what to do, consult their mother's face for "advice." This situation arises, for instance, on the "visual cliff" that was used by Walk and Gibson (1961) to assess infants' depth perception. It consists of a large table with a glass surface. Beneath the glass is a pattern that makes it appear that part of the table is safe ground for crawling but that halfway to the other side there is a sheer drop. When infants are separated from their mother—infant seated on the shallow side of the table and mother standing on the other side—they have a strong urge to crawl over to her. However, from about 6 months on most infants nevertheless refuse to cross the visual cliff.

Sorce et al. (1985) made this visual drop less pronounced so that 12-month-old infants weren't quite sure whether it would be dangerous or safe to cross. When they reached the visual drop, they therefore looked at (referenced) their mother. Of 17 infants whose mother was instructed to look fearful, not one dared to cross, whereas 14 of 19 whose mother showed a happy face did venture across the somewhat perilous-looking drop. When there was no "cliff" at all, just two shallow sides separated by a noticeable strip, hardly any infants even bothered to check their mother's face. However, 4 of those children whose mother was instructed to look fearful did check her face and, interestingly, all 4 of them proceeded to cross the strip despite her fearful expression. Evidently, infants are not just deterred by their mother's expression of fear but interpret it in relation to their decision problem. A fearful face *means* that one should not cross the cliff.

Paul Harris (1989a, 22, 23) has concluded from this evidence that 1-year-old children treat their mother's emotional expression as a comment on the object that is under mutual attention, that is, the dubious surface of the table. This interpretation is further strengthened in the finding by Hornik, Risenhoover, and Gunnar (1987) that 1-year-olds started to specifically avoid toys toward which, when they first encountered them, their mother showed signs of disgust.

Now let us investigate whether this kind of evidence could be used to support the claim by Bretherton, McNew, and Beeghly-Smith (1981) that young infants have an "implicit theory of mind," which in this case would be more specifically an "implicit theory of emotion." In my fairly lenient reading of the expression "implicit theory" we could agree with this claim if we could conclude from infants' appropriate reaction to their mother's fearful face that infants must have some implicit mental representation of the fact that their mothers fearful face is an expression or the result of *fear*. I don't think even that conclusion is warranted.

An Implicit Theory of Emotion?   It is undeniably true that the children's reaction to their mother's facial expression makes sense only because (normally) when a mother sees her infant approach a dangerous cliff, she experiences fear, and that fear automatically shows in her face. For that reason a fearful face *means* "danger" (or: "avoid!"). However, infants can react appropriately to the fearful face without understanding the deeper mental reason why a mother shows a fearful face when her baby is in danger. All infants need to have implicitly represented is the *environmental meaning* of their mother's fearful face—for instance, according to the behavioral rule that "When you see something dubious and your mother is watching you and shows a fearful face, then avoid that object or area."

On the face of it, then, an "implicit theory of emotion" is not necessary for children to *interpret* their mother's expression in social referencing studies. But perhaps one could argue that the infant needs implicit knowledge of emotion for "finding the interpretation." To evaluate this claim, we need to know more about how children acquire this interpretation.

One possibility (following Darwin, a particularly plausible one from the point of view of survival) is that infants are equipped with *innate recognition* of the environmental meaning of emotional expression to allow an early and quick response to danger. If recognition is innate, then there is no need for implicit knowledge of the mental-emotional mechanism underlying the relationship between facial expression and its environmental meaning.

Another possibility is that the interpretation of emotional expression is acquired through learning. The infant experiences the consequences of ignoring his mother's fearful face and of carrying out the intended action. The negative consequences teach the infant that situations in which his mother shows a fearful face are dangerous. In this case, too, the child need not understand the deeper emotional reasons for his mother's fearful face since he experiences the meaningful connection between facial expression and danger directly. [**Note 6.1** Learning the meaning of emotional expressions by imitation.]

In summary, it is far from clear whether one could use infants' ability to interpret facial expressions of emotion in social referencing experiments as evidence for an "implicit theory of mind (emotion)." Let us now look at infants' understanding of looking and pointing and consider whether that could count as an indication of an "implicit theory of mind," that is, an indication that they have at least some notion of *mutual attention* as a mental state.

Checking Mother's Gaze   Another experimentally well documented social skill is infants' ability to follow another person's direction of gaze. As early as 2 months (Scaife and Bruner 1975) infants adjust their own gaze contingent on a change in an adult's visual focus. George Butterworth (in press) and his associates have conducted a more extensive investigation of children aged 6 to 18 months in a situation where infants are facing their mother. At 6 months infants follow their mother's gaze reliably to the same side of the room she is looking at but do not focus on the same object as she does. By 12 months infants can localize an individual target object correctly as long as it is within their visual field. They do not yet turn around when their mother is fixating an object behind their back. As children learn to follow another person's gaze, they also start to follow with their gaze another person's pointing gesture.

Between 9 and 14 months children themselves start to point in a clearly distinguishable way (Murphy 1978; Murphy and Messer 1977; Bruner 1983). Furthermore, Franco and Butterworth (1989; Butterworth, in press) found that at around 12 to 16 months children not only point but also check the gaze of the adult whose attention they are trying to direct. They do that in two different ways. Before pointing, they check whether the adult is looking at them; and as they point, they check whether the adult is looking at the indicated object. The fact that infants do not just try to manipulate the other person's gaze but also check on it indicates that they are aware of its importance.

The infant's checking makes sense because a person's gaze indicates where that person's *attention* rests. That, in turn, is important to know because a person's focus of attention predisposes that person to act in relation to the object in focus. For instance, if the child wants another person to hand him an object, it is advantageous to direct the person's attention to that object. What the 14-month-old has apparently learned is that the relevant steps in that process are (1) get the caretaker's attention on himself (so that she can see what he is doing), (2) point to the desired object to get the caretaker's attention focused on it, and (3) determine whether he was successful by checking that the caretaker is, indeed, now looking at the target object.

One might be tempted to argue that children must have a notion of *(shared) attention* (hence part of an "implicit theory of mind") since their efforts to direct the other person's gaze would make no sense if the person's attention were not manipulated thereby. But, again, the question is whether infants need any implicit knowledge of the fact that their actions are directing *attention* rather than just influencing *looking*. In other words, infants need not recognize (implicitly or explicitly) the internal (mental) mechanism of attention as the underlying reason why their mother's looking predisposes her to act in the appropriate way.

Attention as Mental?   In any case, even if infants do have an implicit notion of the mediating internal processes (attention), the next question is to what degree and by what criterion they conceive of these processes as mental states. Conceiving of attention as a theoretical construct for explaining their mother's behavior is not sufficient in itself. To establish that infants understand attention as something specifically mental, more is needed, since we do not know whether infants understand their mother's attention as a specifically mental construct distinct from, say, physical constructs governing her behavior.

Our third criterion, intentional inexistence, might help settle this issue. However, that may be setting standards too high, since there is no indication that infants at this age understand the object their mother is looking at as *intentionally inexisting* in her mind. We would need evidence of infants' understanding that their mother attends only to certain aspects of the object (or attends to something nonexisting, or misrepresents the perceived object). But we cannot infer such understanding from infants' behavior.

Our first criterion may provide a better chance for detecting early understanding of mentality. By this criterion the infant should understand that when his mother is looking at the object, she has the same experience as the infant himself when looking at the object (shared experience). In fact, it has been suggested that this is exactly what infants want to do when they start pointing things out to others: they have the goal of *sharing experiences*, and not merely that of *influencing behavior* (Bates 1979; Hobson 1990). But what in the available observations suggests that the infant has that goal?

It is thought that instrumental or "protoimperative" pointing (Bates, Camaioni, and Volterra 1975)—namely, pointing to get one's mother to pick something up—is less convincing evidence for this hypothesis than "protodeclarative" pointing, which seems to serve no other purpose than to direct her attention (e.g., Baron-Cohen 1989a, in press). In the case of instrumental pointing it is plausible that the infant is merely manipulating his mother's gaze as a means of getting her to act appropriately. In the case of "protodeclarative" pointing, however, the infant is seeking no action on his mother's part. So, it is thought, the only goal the infant could possibly have is a desire to share his experience with his mother.

I think this interpretation appeals to our adult intuition because we feel that this is the reason why we would point in that situation. Yet it is not clear to me that the infant is really aiming at manipulating *attention* to produce a *shared experience*. Given that infants (perhaps innately) find their mother's eyes and gaze so fascinating, I think it equally plausible that infants engage in "protodeclarative" pointing and check their effect on their mother's eyes because they enjoy their mastery over her eyes. And there is a boost in those mastery activities around 1 year because at this age, as Piaget (1936/1953) observed in his children's interactions with inanimate objects, they are able to combine sensorimotor schemes and start to systematically explore novel effects (tertiary circular reactions). Thus, even from "protodeclarative" pointing we cannot conclude that 1-year-old infants have a concept of *attention* and that they understand *attention as a mental state.*

In the following sections I argue that in the second year infants do start to understand other people's inner states *as mental.* I use evidence of *empathic behavior* to show that they understand emotion as mental. The case rests on the argument that empathic reactions involve an understanding of the other person's emotional expression as a result of a *theoretically constructed* inner state that infants recognize as something familiar from their own *inner experience.*

Empathy: Emotion as Inner Experience and Theoretical Construct

That children understand what another person is feeling is indicated by their empathic reactions to another person's distress. Following Bischof-Köhler (1988, 149), I characterize *empathy* phenomenally as the experience of participating in or sharing another person's emotional state and thereby understanding what that state is. However—and this is critical, in order to differentiate empathy from emotional contagion—in empathizing with another person one remains aware that it is the other person's emotional state that one is sharing.

Emotional contagion occurs practically from birth. One- and 2-day-old infants will cry in response to the sound of another infant's cry (Hoffman 1977). But this does not show that the neonate is aware of the other infant's emotions, or her own, for that matter. Understanding of another person's emotional state is better indicated in the empathic concern expressed in the second year of life. Yarrow and Waxler (1975; Dunn 1987) report that, as early as the second year, children show remarkable sensitivity to affective states of other people. They show distress in response to parental disputes, even trying to intervene by (punitively) kicking the one perceived as the guilty party or trying to comfort a parent who is emotionally hurt. The fact that children not only participate in the emotional distress but also take appropriate comforting action toward the distressed person suggests that they do understand the other person's emotional state by analogy to their own experience of distress.

In order to show empathic responses, children need some minimal role-taking skills. They have to be able to ask themselves two questions—"What would I feel if I were in that situation?" and "What would soften my distress?"—and then apply the answers to these questions to the other person. This requires some *hypothetical thinking* by imagining oneself in the other person's situation. Thinking of hypothetical situations requires the ability to construct multiple models. Consequently, clear empathic reactions should emerge during the second year when so many other abilities based on multiple mental models emerge. One of these abilities is the ability to recognize oneself in the mirror.

As I argued in chapter 4, the reason why self-recognition in a mirror requires the use of multiple mental models is not that this skill marks the onset of a concept of self (e.g., Lewis and Brooks-Gunn 1979; see Neisser 1988 for a critical view of this interpretation), but that it requires an understanding of alternative situations. In order to understand that the person in the mirror is myself, I have to be able to construct two models, one in which I figure as myself in reality and another in which I figure as myself in the situation reflected in the mirror.

Thus, empathic responses and self-recognition in the mirror both require the ability to think in multiple situations. In the case of the mirror children have to be able to represent reality vis-à-vis the situation reflected in the mirror.* In the case of empathy children have to represent the real situation that is distressing to the other person vis-à-vis the hypothetical situation of themselves being in the other's situation.

Empathy + Self-recognition   Doris Bischof-Köhler (1988) studied the emergence of self-recognition in the mirror and of empathic reactions in 16- to 24-month-old infants. For the *empathy* test infants joined a familiar experimenter in play with the experimenter's teddy bear. After about 20 minutes the teddy's arm fell off, whereupon the experimenter turned very sad, started crying and lamented, "My teddy bear is broken." Unless the child intervened, the experimenter kept up her distress for about 2½ minutes. Children's reactions to the experimenter's distress fell into four categories in order of decreasing empathy:

Types of Empathizers

1. The *helpers* were touched and engaged in prosocial intervention (trying to calm the experimenter, fix the teddy bear, or console the teddy bear).
2. The *blocked* were clearly touched by the experimenter's distress but did not take any relevant action during the experimenter's distress. However, they did do something afterward or directed their mother's attention to the experimenter's plight.
3. The *confused* were obviously touched without any relevant reaction. They remained transfixed by the experimenter's plight without seemingly "understanding its nature."
4. The *unconcerned* just briefly noticed the event and then returned to business as usual, ignoring the experimenter in their subsequent play activities.

To assess *self-recognition in the mirror*, infants were given the "rouge test" developed by Gallup (1968) for chimpanzees and adapted by Amsterdam (1972) for children. After 1 minute of play in front of a large mirror the child's mother pretended to wipe some dirt off her child's cheek and thereby left a blue spot. Then the child was left for another

---

*Of course, the mirror image is the same situation as the real one; it's just a representation of it. However, my hypothesis (chapter 4) is that young infants cannot understand it *as* a representation. The young situation theorists can only understand the mirror image as a different though structurally identical situation.

3 minutes in front of the mirror. On the basis of their behavior during these 3 minutes children could be classified into three levels of ability:

Types of Self-Recognizers

1. The *self-recognizers* immediately touched their own cheek when they saw the blue spot on their cheek in the mirror. They also tended to *experiment* with the mirror image, trying out particular movements or grimaces in order to observe them in the mirror.

2. The *transitionals* behaved coyly in front of the mirror, which is a typical phase in development before self-recognition occurs (Dixon 1957; Lewis and Brooks-Gunn 1979, 23). Some of these children did touch their own cheek eventually, but they also tended to treat the mirror image like a playmate rather than an image of themselves—for example, they offered something to the mirror image, or looked behind the mirror to find the person, or threw a ball at the image.

3. The *non-recognizers* did not touch their own cheek and did not show any coyness. Many of them tended to treat the image like a playmate.

As figure 6.1 shows, there was a strong correlation between level of empathic behavior and self-recognition (r = 0.80). All "helpers" and most "blocked" empathizers recognized themselves in the mirror, whereas most children who were "confused" in the empathy test were transitionals in

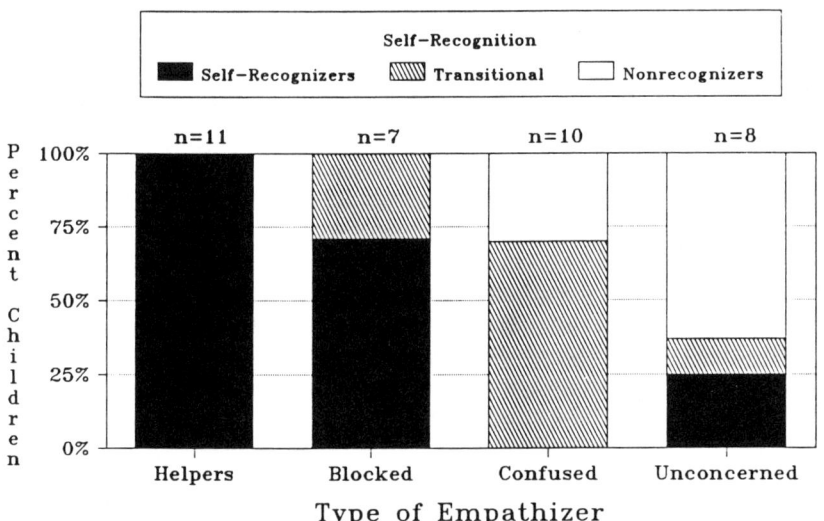

Figure 6.1
Self-recognition and empathy.
Data from Bischof-Köhler 1988.

the mirror situation and most emotionally "unconcerned" children did not show any sign of self-recognition.

Importantly, although self-recognition and empathy correlated with age ($r = 0.63$ and $r = 0.59$), there was a substantial correlation between self-recognition and empathic behavior after age was partialled out: $r = 0.68$, which shows that the close correspondence between the two abilities is not due to a common improvement with age but must be due to some more specific developmental factor. I claim that this factor is the emerging ability to construct multiple models.

Emotion: Theoretical Construct + Inner Experience The claim that this kind of empathic behavior reflects understanding of emotion as an internally experienced state rests on the fact that children are touched by the other's plight *and* try to help. If children were merely touched by the event, one could explain it away as a case of emotional contagion. But if it were purely contagion, then children would simply be distressed themselves but not think of helping the other person. If children simply helped without showing signs of being emotionally touched, then it might be nothing more than a learned response to people in distress. But the sequence of first being emotionally touched by the other's distress and then trying to figure out how to help suggests that children are basing their response on their own experience of distress.

If children are basing their empathic reaction on an understanding of their own experience of distress, then they must be imputing a state of distress as a hypothetical construct to the other person. That is, children are not operating on the principle of making the other person stop crying but are trying to alleviate the other's *sadness*. This state is not directly observable in the other but is a *hypothetically constructed* (criterion 2) state that is assumed to be analogous to the children's own *inner experience* (criterion 1) of sadness and that creates the necessary connection between the distressful event, outer signs of distress, and the children's own inner experience.

That children understand emotions as theoretical constructs and go beyond the external signs of emotions is also supported by the flexibility of their understanding of emotional terms and the fact that they start talking about emotions quite frequently from about the age of 1½ years (Bretherton, McNew, and Beeghly-Smith 1981; Bretherton and Beeghly 1982; Dunn, Bretherton, and Munn 1987).

Understanding the Intentional Directedness of Emotion

By the third criterion of mentality, children should understand that emotions are characterized by intentional inexistence. How emotions have that characteristic has been the subject of some dispute among philosophers of mind.

Emotion and Intentional Inexistence   For Descartes emotions were the "feelings" associated with physiological states *caused* by external events. This view has also become dominant in empirical psychology with the formulation of the James-Lange theory of emotion (James and Lange 1885/1922; see Calhoun and Solomon 1984). The older Aristotelian position was made popular within philosophy by Brentano (1874/1955, 126–127) and more recently by natural language philosophers Anthony Kenny (1963) and Errol Bedford (1957/1984). In this view emotions are *about* other objects or events. The philosophers' view on emotion is probably a better reflection of our commonsense view than the scientific approach taken by psychology, since philosophers analyze how we—as commonsense psychologists—talk about emotion. In particular, the claim that emotions are characterized by aboutness takes its support from the fact the same syntactic constructions are used both for talking about emotions and for expressing aboutness of mental states like "know," for instance. And in the case of "know" it is clear that aboutness is expressed and not causality, since it would be absurd to rephrase a sentence about *what* a person knows as a sentence giving a reason for *why* a person knows:

"Heidi *knows that* the teddy has lost its arm."
"Heidi *knows because* the teddy has lost its arm." (absurd paraphrase)

Now, although we can talk about emotions in the same way we talk about knowledge, namely, as being *about* some event, a rephrasing of emotional aboutness in terms of causality does not seem out of the question:

"Heidi is *sad that* the teddy has lost its arm."
"Heidi is *sad because* the teddy has lost its arm." (reasonable paraphrase)

Since it appears to be impossible to disentangle what we, as sophisticated commonsense psychologists, have in mind when talking about emotions, it seems hopeless to try to decide whether empathic reaction to Heidi's plight by a 1½-year-old infant expresses an understanding of "sadness *about* the event" or "sadness *because* of the event."* In any case, an understanding of emotions as internal states that are caused by certain events gives a powerful understanding of emotions. It seems unnecessary to assume that the infant has an understanding of the "intentional directedness" of emotions, and consequently it seems superfluous to assume that the infant has a *representational theory of emotion.*

If infants do not conceive of emotions as being "intentionally directed," the question arises when—if ever—they develop such an understanding. John Searle (1983, 29-36) argues that emotions inherit their aboutness from their dependence on other mental states. For instance, an event makes a person sad only if the person did not *want* that event to happen and if the person was *aware that* it did happen. That is, if the experimenter in Bischof-Köhler's study either wanted to break her teddy or was not aware that it broke, then she would not be sad.

Children's Cognitive Theory of Emotion   Children's understanding of how emotion depends on other mental states—which are clearly characterized by intentional inexistence—has been investigated in a few recent studies. Results show that understanding of this dependency emerges as—or lags somewhat behind the time that—children come to understand the respective mental state. Nicola Yuill (1984) assessed children's understanding of how *happiness* (being "pleased") depends on the match or mismatch between what a person *wants* (desires) and what that person *gets*. For instance, a boy with a ball wants to throw it to a girl in the distance. In one version of the story the girl does catch the ball; in the other version it is a boy standing next to her who catches it. Even at 3 years children quite reliably rated the ball thrower as more "pleased" when, as intended, the girl caught the ball and less "pleased" when against his wishes the other boy caught it. Wellman and Woolley (1990) reported that even at 2½ years children can understand this dependency of happiness on wish fulfillment.

---

*This distinction can be easily overlooked, as for instance in Peter Hobson's argument about early evidence for understanding *mentality* and *intentionality*: " 'Feelings' have significance not just for their pivotal role in processes of intersubjectivity, but also by virtue of their intentionality. Infants come to perceive the focussed outer-directedness of the emotional states of other people, what others are frightened of, angry with, and so on, a phenomenon most clearly evident in social referencing" (Hobson 1990, 117). What gives the mind intentionality is not its being directed at objects or scenes in the outer world but its ability to make intentional inexistence of objects possible.

However, these young children's good understanding of *happiness* as a function of what people *want* and what they *get* stands in contrast to children's ability to understand *surprise* as a function of what people *believe* and what is *really* the case. Julie Hadwin (Hadwin and Perner, in press, experiment 1) assessed understanding of surprise in two stories that paralleled those in Yuill's study. The protagonist in Hadwin's stories, who was separated from the two other characters by a high wall, was described as *thinking* that the girl was holding the ball. In one story, when the protagonist looked behind the wall, he found that this was indeed the case. In the other story he discovered that the boy was holding the ball. Children had to judge in each story how "surprised" the protagonist would be. Not until 5 or even 6 years did children reliably answer that the protagonist would be surprised only when he discovered the unexpected (that the boy held the ball) and not when his expectation (that the girl held the ball) was plainly confirmed.

Finding that there is a vast gap between children as young as 3 years understanding that happiness depends on what a person *wants* and children not understanding until 5 years or older that surprise depends on what a person *thinks*, we checked the reliability of our surprise results. However, they proved quite resistant to various attempts to make the stories clearer and more obvious.

We wondered whether children would find judgment of other emotions equally difficult when based on belief. To test this, we (Hadwin and Perner, in press, experiment 4) used a paradigm developed by Paul Harris and his collaborators (Harris, et al. 1989). In these stories the protagonist is described as, say, liking Coke but hating milk. Later he is presented with a Coke can that has been surreptitiously emptied and filled with milk. Children in the study knew about the switch and knew that the protagonist did not know about it. Thus, most 4-year-olds and older children understood that the protagonist *thought* that he was being given Coke. Nevertheless, when asked how the protagonist felt about what he was being given—at the point where he was still mistaken about the can's true contents, that is, before he had a chance to sample its contents—these children ignored the protagonist's mistaken belief and said that he would feel "sad," just as if he already knew the disappointing truth. Only by 5 or 6 years did children understand that he would feel "happy," since he (mistakenly) expected the can to contain his much-liked Coke.

Similarly, it was at about the same age that children understood that later, when the protagonist sampled the contents of the can, he would be "surprised" only when he did not expect it to contain milk and that he would not be surprised when it contained Coke as expected. Therefore, these results confirm that the understanding of aboutness that emotion inherits from belief develops rather late, at about 5 to 6 years, whereas aboutness inherited from desire (want) is understood at an earlier age.

In summary, *emotion* is understood *as mental* sometime during the second year, as suggested by the emergence of empathic reactions. At this age children use their understanding of their own *inner emotional experience* (criterion 1) as a *theoretical construct* for understanding another person's distress (criterion 2). Understanding of emotions as *intentionally directed* (criterion 3) emerges as children understand the dependence of emotions on other mental states from which they inherit their aboutness. Understanding of these mental states and the specific ways in which they make intentional inexistence possible (nonexistence, aspectuality, and misrepresentation) develops at different ages, as the next three chapters will show.

From Looking to Seeing

As we have seen, even around the age of 1 year children are quite sophisticated in their knowledge about the importance of looking for successful social interaction. Children understand that getting their mother to *look* at something is a useful prerequisite for getting her to act appropriately. The question is whether they understand anything about her that goes beyond the looking. Do they understand that she also has to *see* something when looking? "Looking" describes the physical act of directing one's eyes in the right direction, whereas "seeing" describes the mental effect of that action. When do children understand seeing as a mental activity? This question is difficult to answer with respect to young children, but let me speculate on it by describing their advances in responding to requests "to show."

Showing   Lempers, Flavell, and Flavell (1977) asked children from 1 to 3 years *to show* a toy or a picture to another person facing them. When the object was a picture, it was glued either onto a piece of cardboard, or onto one face of a wooden block, or onto the inside bottom of a cup (hollow cube). Even at 1 year most children *showed* the toy rather than *giving* it to the other person, but they had little idea what to do with the picture.

At 1½ years children started showing the picture in a very interesting way. The majority did not hold the picture vertically and turn it toward the other person; rather, they held it horizontally so that they themselves could see it at the same time as the adult. The desire to have the picture simultaneously in one's own view and the other person's was difficult to achieve for the picture inside the cup. So some children held the cup rather low and tilted its opening back and forth to allow themselves and the other person alternating glimpses of the picture inside.

By 2 years children showed the picture upright facing the other person without being able to see it themselves at the same time. And many took the effort to turn the picture on the card right side up. Getting the orientation right for the picture on the cube was not perfected until 3 years, and even then the orientation of the picture inside the cup remained a problem.

Another interesting finding was that when the other person covered her eyes, most children as young as 1½ moved her hands away from her eyes before showing the picture. However, when the other person simply had her eyelids shut, only some 2-year-olds took action to make her open her eyes.

These observations suggest that as early as 1 year children understand that "showing" means getting an object close to the other person's eyes or face. By 1½ they already understand that the line (of sight) between eyes and object must remain unobstructed and so they bother to move the other person's hands away from her eyes. But why do they show the picture in such a way that they themselves can see it at the same time? An interesting possibility is that they understand from their own experience when being shown something that showing must lead to an *inner experience* of seeing. Since they cannot have the other person's experience, the only way of ensuring that this critical part is not missing is to produce the experience in themselves. This, of course, can only be achieved by looking at the picture simultaneously with the other.

By 2 years most children have dropped the need to have their own inner experience when showing something to someone else. They probably understand that the other person has her own inner experience. But the important question is how children conceive of this *inner visual experience*. An interesting speculation is that children understand visual experience as they may understand emotional states like *happiness*. Happiness can be understood quite adequately as a nonpropositional state, that is, as just "feeling happy." Its propositional content, "what one feels happy *about*," is understood as the event *causing* that (propositionally undifferentiated) state of happiness. In a similar vein, children may think of visual experience as a propositionally undifferentiated state (difficult for us to conceive), and they may bring in its usual propositional content as "that which one is *looking at*," or "the scene that is *causing* the visual experience." In other words, the *directedness* of seeing is not yet *intentional* but is tied to the *physical* relation of *looking at*. [Note 6.2 Children's projections of their own visual experience onto others.]

The adult concept of visual experience is different. We differentiate what we are *looking at* from the *visual percept*. In other words, the looked-at object or scene "intentionally inexists" in the visual experience.

Intentional Directedness of Visual Experience   Once children can construe the propositional content of visual experience independently from the physically existing scene, they have the conceptual prerequisite for understanding that visual perspectives of one and the same physical situation can differ. John Flavell (1974, 96) dubs this understanding "level 2 knowledge of visual perception." As I argued earlier, differences in visual perspective are beyond the young situation theorist's intellectual capabilities, since the different perspectives are not different situations but different views of one and the same situation. To understand difference in views, the child therefore needs a concept of representation; that is, the child needs to understand that different views of a particular situation are different *representations* of this situation.

Certain words in English are used to describe aspects of visual scenes that are specific to the speaker's view of the scene, like "in front" and "behind." Correct use of these terms therefore provides a potentially useful indicator of children's understanding of visual perspective, since children who did not yet have a notion of perspective would have a hard time sorting out the correct linguistic usage.

"In Front" and "Behind"   The expressions "in front" and "behind" look fairly innocuous, but upon closer examination (Bierwisch 1967) it turns out that their use is governed by quite intricate rules. Imagine yourself as a participant in the experiment by Kuczaj and Maratsos (1975) testing your understanding of the meaning of "in front of" and "in back of." You are handed a doll and asked to place it "in front of you" (or "in back of you"). That's pretty easy; even children younger than 3 years can make those placements fairly accurately, as the blank bars in the background of figure 6.2 show. Even at this age they understand that there is a difference between "in front" and "in back."

Now the problem gets a bit more difficult. A hippopotamus is placed in front of you, and you are asked to place the doll "in front of the hippopotamus." A hippo is known in the trade as a "fronted object"; that is, it has a *front* (where its head is), a *back* (where its tail is), and two *sides*. Your most natural response will be to put the doll in front of the hippo's head. The real difficulty becomes apparent in the next version of the task, when instead of the hippo you are faced a with "nonfronted object" like a plain old drinking glass and are asked to "Put the doll in front of the glass." Now what do you do, since the glass has no front? You have to switch to a different frame of reference. Instead of interpreting "in front" as "where the front of the reference object is" (the glass doesn't have one), you have to understand it "egocentrically" as "so that *I see* the doll *in front* of the glass."

As an adult, you won't find this too difficult. But now imagine a child who has no concept of specific viewpoints. The child lacks the "egocentric" interpretation frame for placement in relation to nonfronted objects. So the child cannot systematically switch frames of interpretation, and it will be difficult to figure out from adult use what spatial relation these terms describe. The child's natural tendency as a situation theorist will

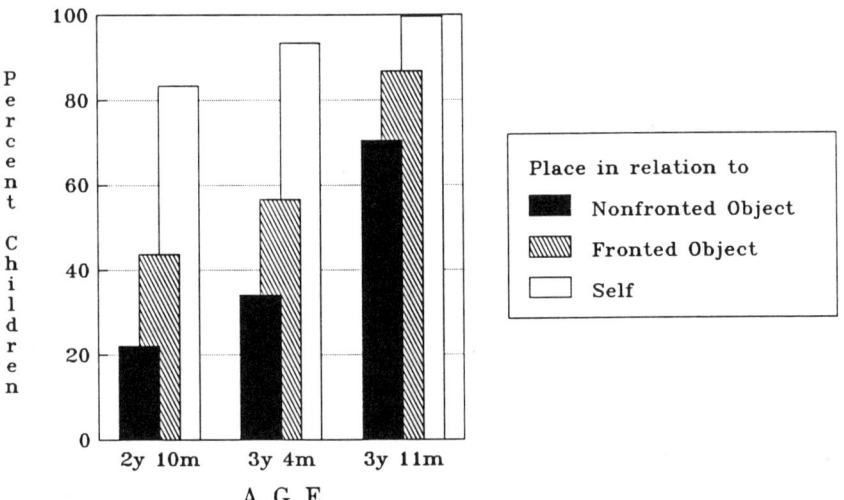

Figure 6.2
Correct placements in response to "in front of" and "in back of".
Data from Kuczaj and Maratsos 1975.

be to interpret the expressions as describing a particular situation. This is possible for fronted objects. And as the hatched bars in figure 6.2 show, placement around a fronted object is indeed easier than placement around a nonfronted object (dark bars). However, the whole terminology of placement relative to another object is confusing for younger children. Only as they approach the age of 4 years does performance go up to acceptable levels, indicating some systematic understanding.

That egocentric placement becomes systematic by about 4 years of age was also confirmed in a similar study by Tanz (1980, 26, table 3). Of the younger two groups in this study, ranging in age from 2½ years to just under 4 years, only 20% made consistently correct placement "in front of" and "in back of" nonfronted objects. The percentage of consistently correct children rose dramatically to 66% among younger and to 90% among older 4-year-olds.

It is plausible to assume that children master the different reference frames once they can understand difference in viewpoints. It is therefore remarkable that this understanding emerges around the age of 4 years when there are many other indications that children develop an understanding of representation (chapter 4). [**Note 6.3** Understanding other deictic expressions.]

The fact that they also become able to understand view-specific spatial descriptions at this age suggests that they start to conceptualize the mind as a representational system. This interpretation would be even better supported by evidence that children can judge how another person would see the same scene (e.g., "doll in *front* of the glass") when seated at a different vantage point than they themselves (e.g., "doll in *back* of the glass"), as Masangkay et al. (1974) have shown for 4-year-old's understanding of view-dependent differences in picture interpretation (see chapter 4).[*]

In the following three chapters I present much additional evidence for how the emergent understanding of representation revolutionizes children's understanding of mental states.

---

[*]Maureen Cox pointed out to me that Bill Ives (1983) used a task like this but with older children. He tested them on a version of Piaget and Inhelder's (1948/1956) scene of three model mountains: the mountains were painted different colors, and a camera was pointing at the scene from an angle different from the child's own point of view. Children had to describe the camera's view as, for example, "the yellow mountain *in front of* the red one." The youngest group of 5½-year-old kindergarten children gave correct descriptions 64% of the time.

Summary

In this chapter I have argued three points.

I argued that social interaction by young infants does not make it necessary to assume that they have an "implicit theory" about the mental states that govern this interaction. My argument for imputing as little as possible to young infants is not born out of *parsimony* but constitutes an attempt to preserve claims about developmental differences that are as theoretically strong as possible, and yet compatible with empirical evidence.

Young children's *empathic reactions* to another person's distress served as a paradigm case to argue that by 1½ years children become able to identify their own *inner emotional experiences* in others and use them as *theoretical constructs* for understanding another's plight and for taking appropriately helpful action. The theoretical claim is that this ability emerges *at this age* because children become able to entertain *multiple mental models*. For this reason it was instructive to see that empathic reactions emerge at the same time as children's ability to recognize themselves in a mirror, since self-recognition requires two models: one to represent oneself in reality and another to represent oneself in the mirror.

I reviewed some of the developmental changes in children's understanding of *looking, showing,* and *seeing* to argue that children first develop a fairly sophisticated understanding of the physical relationship of looking and its *psychological importance* for behavior. Only later do they understand seeing as an *intentionally directed* mental act. This understanding emerges at about 4 years, and I argue in the following chapters that it is occasioned by the development of a *concept of representation*. This concept revolutionizes children's existing understanding of mental states as theoretical concepts in a *theory of behavior* by enabling them to develop a *representational theory of mind*. With that they understand the representational underpinnings of mental states, which helps explain how these states are formed and how they govern behavior.

Chapter 7

Acquiring a Theory of Knowledge

In this chapter I investigate how children come to understand knowledge. The main evidence is based on how children use and comprehend the word "know." Quite plausibly, children learn their use of this word from observing that of adults. What children can glean from adults' use depends on how they approach their task. My claim is that at first children work within a *theory of behavior.* They pick up the basic rule that the best way of telling whether a person knows something is to check whether that person can give correct answers or act successfully. Later, at about 4 years, children's understanding of knowledge changes with their newly gained understanding of representation. Within an emerging *representational theory of mind* knowledge becomes *a properly caused mental representation* of the known fact. This change in the concept of knowledge triggers a "theoretically" (or conceptually) motivated shift in judging a person's knowledge. The heavy reliance on success as a best indicator for "knowing" gives way to understanding that access to sufficient and reliable information is a necessary prerequisite for knowing.

This change in children's thinking about knowledge can be observed in natural play activities like hide and seek. It is also apparent in their acquisition of specific linguistic distinctions, and it has been experimentally documented in their emerging ability to differentiate knowledge from lucky guesses and to understand that different sense modalities are needed for getting to know different aspects of an object.

Furthermore, the changes in children's concept of knowledge has an important impact on their own memory performance. By encoding how they came to know about an event, they achieve long-lasting memories of life events. The lack of such encoding in early childhood explains the phenomenon of *childhood amnesia,* that is, the fact that adults cannot remember events that occurred before they were 3 to 4 years old.

Before getting too deeply immersed in the topic of how children acquire the adult concept of knowledge, it is useful to remind ourselves what that concept actually involves. Again, philosophers of mind have led the way in making this concept explicit. [**Note 7.1** Remarks on the concept of knowledge in philosophy.]

The Concept "Knowledge"   What is the adult concept that the child has to acquire? By elaborating Dretske's (1981, 86) information-theoretic definition, our commonsense concept of "knowledge" can be characterized by the role correct mental representation plays in our information-processing activities:

> Access to reliable information about a fact (e.g., seeing, being told by a reliable informant) creates a correct mental representation of that fact, which in turn enables correct action relating to that fact (e.g., informing someone else correctly, finding something).

This formulation of our commonsense theory of knowledge has three critical aspects:

1. Truth (correct representation of facts)
2. Access to relevant information
3. Successful action.

These three aspects are reflected in different commonsense uses of the word "know."[*] Interestingly, however, everyday usage and information theory put different emphasis on these aspects. Take our implicit information theory first. Access to information is most important. It is a *necessary* condition for the existence of knowledge, whereas successful action is a useful but optional benefit of knowledge. In other words, one can know something and choose not to use that knowledge, but one *cannot* know without proper information.

This contrasts with how we talk about knowledge. Access to information does not get the attention it deserves when measured by its theoretical importance. It is hardly mentioned. We emphasize the power gained by what we know rather than how we acquired that knowledge.

---

[*]Richards (1982, 388) lists the following three corresponding common uses of the word "*know*": "By telling someone we 'know' something, we persuade that person to believe the statement is true. . . . A second commonly intended sense of *know* is that of acquaintance or familiarity [previous encounter]. . . . A third frequently intended sense of *know* explicitly equates knowing with being correct, . . ."

This is particularly true in our conversations with children. Just imagine looking at a picture book with a toddler. Almost every other question is "Do you know what this is?", which is nothing more than a request to name the indicated picture correctly.

If children learn about knowledge by observing how we as adults use the word "know," then their understanding should reflect the biases in our use of that word. Furthermore, having knowledge is desirable. It confers status and is something to boast about. Consequently, for the young child a major concern must be the diagnostic problem of how to decide whether a person's claim to knowledge is justified or not.

All these considerations about the commonsense use of "know" suggest that for the young child the relative importance of the different aspects of knowledge ranges from successful action (the most important), down to access to information (the least useful diagnostic criterion). The plausibility of this rank ordering can be seen by the following examples:

Three Aspects of Knowledge in Order of Diagnostic Importance
1. Successful action
    Example 1: "He knows how to put on his socks."
        Test: "Can he in fact do it?"
    Example 2: "He knows where the socks are."
        Test: "Can he find them?"
2. Correspondence with facts
    Example: "He knows the socks are in the drawer."
        Test: "Are the socks in fact in there?"
3. Access to relevant information
    Example: "He knows the socks are in the drawer."
        Test: "How did he find out? Did he see them, was he told, etc.?"

Indeed, if Johnny claims to know where the socks are, the best way to show him up is to ask him to look for the socks. It is of little use trying to find out whether he could have seen someone put the socks away or heard someone tell him where they are.

Evidence on how children come to appreciate the different aspects of knowledge suggests that, in fact, children's earliest use of "know" emphasizes its link to successful action and that their understanding of the importance of informational access develops relatively late.

Early Understanding and Difficulties

Our main and most obvious gateway to children's understanding of the mind is how they use our mentalistic terminology. Young children use the word "know" mostly in connection with their ability to get things right. Not until about 4 years do they start to talk about reasons for knowing (by other people and themselves). Let me start by describing some early psycholinguistic observations.

Using the Word "Know"   Inge Bretherton and her colleagues studied toddlers' early use of mental terms and listed the following occurrences of "know" by children aged between 15 months and 3 years (Bretherton, McNew, and Beeghly-Smith 1981, 369):

> J at 15 months: "I don't know." (said while gesturing with hands turned up when asked, "Where is X?")
> Tr at 20 months: "I don't know." (when asked for something and she cannot find it)
> Cathy at 26 months: "I know how to turn it on." (said about faucet)

These examples show that from an early age children use the word "know" to express ability or inability to inform or act correctly. Shatz, Wellman, and Silber (1983) also report that in their study "know" was the most frequently used mental word between 2 and 3 years and that the majority of these instances were uses of the idiomatic negative expression "don't know," which probably served to deny the ability or willingness to comply with a request or answer a question. "Know" is also often used to emphasize correspondence with facts. Shatz, Wellman, and Silber report that 12% of occurrences of "know" in their study were used to underline the correctness of an assertion: for instance, "I know this fits too." (after being challenged).

In contrast to this early linguistic evidence of understanding that knowledge relates to success or correctness, it is difficult to find evidence that children understand the importance of informational access in knowledge formation.* For instance, Hood and Bloom (1979), who studied the early occurrence of causal justifications, found that very young

---

*One could argue that there are some signs of understanding that "know" is being related to information. Shatz, Wellman, and Silber reported that 24% of uses fell into their category "directing interaction," under which they classed (among others) expressions used to introduce or get information: for instance, "Know what?" said to get another person's attention in order to tell that person something. However, it is not at all clear from this use of "know" that children really understand what they are doing.

children frequently use mental states in their justifications. For instance, one child justified her inability to do something with her lack of knowledge:

> Mariana (at 2 years 11 months) bringing a book to adult: "Could you read this to me cause I don't know how." (Hood & Bloom 1979, 6)

However, these authors do not report any instances of children giving a justification for their knowledge. Again, this underlines that what young children understand about knowledge is its impact on correct action (or lack of knowledge to explain the need for help) but not the necessity of access to information for acquiring knowledge. Lack of this understanding is also suggested by linguistic data from Turkish children, whose language requires grammatical marking of the evidential source for one's claims about past events.

Turkish Evidentials: -DI & -mIş   In Turkish, if you want to report a past event (for instance, "The red balloon popped"), then you have to inflect the verb "pop" ("patla" in Turkish) with the ending "-di" if you were an eyewitness to the event ("Kirmizi balon patla*di*"), or with "-miş" if you were told about it or had to infer it from just observing the final state of the popped balloon ("Kirmizi balon patla*miş*").

Aksu-Koç (1988) investigated the acquisition of these inflectional markers by Turkish children. In her chapter 6 she reports showing children from 3 years up either illustrated stories in which events like the popping of a balloon were explicitly shown or a kind of puppet show in which the event of the balloon's popping was screened from the child but could be inferred from the perceived outcome of the story, the popped balloon. When asked to relate the story, even the youngest group of children, age 3 years to 3 years and 8 months, showed some sign of using the ending "-di" when the popping was shown in a picture and "-miş" when it had to be inferred. Right after 3 years and 8 months the reliability of correct use of these evidential markers improved markedly to a level that was not exceeded by the oldest children in the study (just over 6 years of age).

To see whether children do not just *use* these evidential markers but have some awareness of their meaning, Aksu-Koç (1988, chap. 8) let children judge whether a doll who reported an event with the "-di" or "-miş" ending had seen the event or was told about it. There was a sharp developmental improvement just after the age of 4 years. Only 3 of 24 children younger than 4 years and 3 months could make that judgment, whereas all but one of the 36 older children could correctly judge the speaking doll's evidential base.

In summary, at the age of 3 years Turkish children can use the endings "-di" and "-miş" to mark the difference in evidentiality, but their use is very unreliable and they seem not to be aware of what they are doing. By 4 years, in contrast, children rapidly develop some explicit understanding that these endings indicate the speaker's source of evidence. A very similar developmental progression emerged from recent experimental studies on children's understanding of how seeing relates to knowing.

Associating Seeing with Knowing   Three-year-old children know something about the fact that knowledge and perceptual activities, especially seeing, go together. When asked about two people (or dolls), one of whom has looked inside a box and one of whom hasn't, which one *knows* what is in the box, a majority of children between 3 and 4 years opt for the person who has looked (Hogrefe, Wimmer, and Perner 1986, experiment 5: 70% correct by an Austrian sample; Pratt and Bryant 1990: over 77% correct by a British sample; also see Pillow 1989 for success in a slightly different experimental paradigm). [**Note 7.2** The possibility that correct responses on know-see tasks are due to common association with success.]

However, children's ability to judge what somebody knows or doesn't know by that person's informational access is not well established at this age. The percentage of 3-year-olds who answer on the basis of informational access differs widely, from over 75% in studies by Pratt and Bryant (1990) and Pillow (1989) to less than 15% in studies by Marvin, Greenberg, and Mossler (1976), Mossler, Marvin, and Greenberg (1976), Perner and Ogden (1988), and Wimmer, Hogrefe, and Perner (1988). There has been some speculation (Wimmer, Hogrefe, and Perner 1988) about what factors might contribute to this variation, and Pratt and Bryant (1990) have shown the form of the test question to have some effect. A more important factor leading to such differences across experiments may be the degree to which the experimental procedure highlights informational access as a salient criterion. In any case, the fact that 3-year-old children tend to rely only occasionally on informational access in their attribution of knowledge suggests that, although they associate informational access with knowledge, they are not fully aware of its real importance.

**Knowing
Why
You Know** The impression that 3-year-olds have no firm understanding of the importance of informational access is strengthened by the observation that they cannot answer explicit questions about why a person knows or doesn't know something. Wimmer, Hogrefe, and Perner (1988) showed that this was a problem for 3-year-olds even when they were asked about their own knowledge. For instance, when shown or told what was put inside a box these children answered correctly that they knew what was in the box. Similarly, they answered correctly that they did not know when they were given no information. However, when asked, "How do you know that?" (or "Why don't you know that?"), only 3 of 12 3-year-olds gave adequate answers.*
In contrast, almost all 4-year-olds were able to answer this question correctly.

This is a rather surprising but important finding, because it suggests that although 3-year-old children may associate seeing or being told with knowing, they do not fully understand the causal basis of this association. Unfortunately, there is an obvious concern about drawing this conclusion from 3-year-olds' failure to answer a "why"-question. At this age children may not answer "why"-questions of this kind at all.

These concerns can be allayed, to some degree, by the finding that children of that age are perfectly able to answer an open-ended "why"-question about another person's hunger—"Why is the boy hungry?"—quite happily with "Because he hasn't eaten." Yet they have serious difficulty with a rather similar question about knowledge. When asked, "Why does the boy know what's in the box?", they fail to answer, "Because he's looked inside" (Perner and Ogden 1988).

Another attempt to demonstrate more convincingly that young children do have serious problems justifying their own knowledge is to replace the open-ended "why"-question by a forced choice between relevant alternatives. Alison Gopnik and Peter Graf (1988) and Sarah Poole (1988) and I followed up the original study by Wimmer, Hogrefe, and Perner (1988) along these lines. For instance, in our study the experimenter picked out one item from a set of familiar objects and either showed it to the child, told the child what it was, or let the child feel it under a piece of cloth. On each trial two objects were put into a box in such a way, so that the child received different kinds of information about the identity of each

---

*Also, Pillow (1989), who emphasizes 3-year-olds' proficiency in judging knowledge on the basis of the presence or absence of informational access, reports that only 3 of 12 3-year-olds produced justifications for their judgments.

object. For instance, the child might first *see* a toy car being put inside the box. Then something else hidden in the experimenter's hand was put inside so that the child could not identify it, but the child was *told* that it was a marble. Although children had little difficulty remembering the two objects in the box, few could answer the question "How do you know that there is a marble in the box?" by answering, "Because you told me." When an explicit choice was given—"Did you know it because I showed you or because I told you?"—our 3-year-olds performed better than chance (66.7% correct) but far worse than on a control condition in which there were three different ways of putting objects into the box. An object was put inside the box either by the experimenter, by the child, or by being slid through a tube, and children were asked about each object how it got into the box. If they did not answer, they were given an explicit choice, for instance, "Because I put it in there or because you put it in there?" Here children almost always gave correct answers (92.7%).

This difference between conditions again confirms the original contention that 3-year-old children have difficulty understanding the reasons why they know things. Their difficulty is all the more remarkable because explicit alternatives may have made their task unduly easy. The test was supposed to get at children's understanding that *they knew that there was a spoon in the box because they had seen it being put into the box.* Unfortunately, it is quite plausible that children may have given the correct answer for a much simpler reason. They may have opted for "Because I've seen it" simply because *they had seen the spoon*, not because they understood that *they knew there was a spoon inside because they had seen it.* For this reason the original open-ended "why"-question was a better indicator of children's understanding of the causal link between seeing and knowing, and there is little evidence that many children younger than 4 years answer such questions correctly.

By the age of 4 years children's performance on these kinds of tasks becomes quite good and consistent. They can attribute knowledge to another person on the basis of whether or not that person has access to relevant information, and they can explicitly justify their attributions of knowledge—to others and to themselves—by reference to the availability of information. That something important is acquired around this age is also supported by children's behavior in hide-and-seek play.

Hide and Seek Well before they are 3 years old, children love to play hide and seek. They hide behind a curtain, say, and enjoy it tremendously when their partner in play—usually an adult—goes through much searching and many melodious repetitions of the question "Where are you?" Although these children are quite proficient at getting *out of sight*, they seem not to appreciate that the point of it all is to get *out of knowledge*. This lack of appreciation is well illustrated by the following anecdote recorded by Heinz Wimmer, concerning his son Theo at 3 years and 5 months:

> Heinz is hiding in the pantry. After some searching Theo finds him. Heinz asks, "How did you know I was in here?", to which Theo answers, "Because I opened the door." Then it is Theo's turn to hide. Right in front of Heinz (!) he "hides" in the pantry. Heinz plays along and calls out, "Where are you?" Theo giggles and answers, "In the pantry." Again it is Theo's turn to hide. He chooses the pantry yet again, where Heinz finds him in due course after the obligatory process of a mock search and Theo comments, "But now I've made it difficult,"* saying it as he is still crouching there with his hands over his eyes.

Such failure to keep the other person genuinely in the dark by getting oneself or an object out of sight is not unusual at this age. Gratch (1964) studied young children's behavior in the hand-guessing game. The objective is to hide a marble behind your back in one of your fists and then let the other person guess where the marble is in the hope that he won't find it. Of 30 children between 2 and just under 4 years 10 could not be brought to hide the marble at all. Sixteen hid the marble in their fist; but as soon as the experimenter set out to guess, they showed him where the marble was. Only 4 children kept the marble hidden. In contrast, 31 of 34 4- to 5-year-olds kept the marble properly hidden.

When it was the child's turn to guess, the experimenter had a marble hidden in both hands in order to see how children would react on the second trial after a successful first one. It was thought that children who do not understand that the point of the game is to keep the guesser in the dark would simply be conditioned by a successful response and repeat their choice of hand on the second trial. In contrast, it was thought that older children who understand that the other player will try to make it difficult to find the marble might anticipate a switch of hands. Indeed, of

---

*This is my unimaginative translation of Theo's comment in German: "Jetzt hab ich mich aber schwierig versteckt." I find it impossible to give a more accurate translation.

the 34 children between 4 and 5 years, 30 chose the other hand on the second trial, whereas only 10 of the 30 children under 4 years did so.*

Similar age trends on this game were also reported by DeVries (1970) and Shultz and Cloghesy (1981). And the 3-year-old's difficulty with this task was brought home to me when I watched Hannah at 6 years trying to teach this game to her brother Jacob at 3 years and 4 months. She could easily get him to make proper fists so that one could not tell in which hand the small object was hidden. But she could not get him to hide it unpredictably. At one point she put it in one of his hands and he formed a fist. Then she clenched her eyes shut and told him, "Now hide it!", but he just sat there keeping his fists tightly closed. When Hannah opened her eyes, she was hoping that her brother had made the minimal effort of shifting the object to his other hand, but she discovered in frustration that it was still where she had put it.

There is, then, quite varied evidence that around the age of 4 years children acquire a better understanding of the conditions that aid or prevent knowledge acquisition. My argument, however, is that one should not think of this development as gradual accumulation of more and more rules about how knowledge relates to other activities, since such cumulative improvement will not yield our adult concept of knowledge. A deeper, conceptual-theoretical change is required.

From Diagnostic Rules to Information Theory

The young child comes to understand knowledge by learning the rules of when the word "know" can justifiably be applied. The frequently mentioned and diagnostically more prevalent aspect that knowledge manifests itself in successful or correct action is understood first. Later, children include informational access in their judgment. From this developmental sequence one might conclude that with age the child gradually learns about less conspicuous aspects of knowledge. However, acquisition of ever more detailed and finer rules for diagnosing the

---

*On game-theoretic grounds one could argue that the younger children came pretty close to the rationally optimal strategy of choosing either hand with a 50-50 probability. However, that would not explain why the older children resorted to a less sophisticated strategy. It seems more plausible to follow Gratch's interpretation that the younger children simply tended to repeat their previously successful choice whereas the older children anticipated a strategic move on their opponent's part, albeit at a game-theoretically naive level.

presence of knowledge will not lead to our adult understanding of it. The reason is simple. Access to information is not merely a less emphasized and more subtle aspect of knowledge than success. Rather, informational access is a necessary condition for the existence of knowledge, whereas success is only something made possible by knowledge. Therefore, what the child has to understand is not that access to information is *also* important, but that it is *necessary* and more central to the existence of knowledge than success.

To understand the real importance of informational access, the child has to gain a new *conceptual* or *theoretical* understanding of knowledge. This new understanding arrives with an information-processing view in which knowledge is seen as a mental representation whose function it is to reflect facts correctly. As I have argued in part I, at the age of about 4 years the child acquires the necessary concept of representation for such a view. At this age representation can be understood as a medium representing something (referent) as being a certain way (sense). And this conceptual framework provides the basis for understanding that such a medium can be a true representation of the external referent situation only if there exists some reliable, causal mechanism that ensures that the medium is set into correspondence with that external situation.

Seeing what is in the box and being told what is in the box are both good candidates for such an information mechanism since these activities are couched as *propositional attitudes*. That is, they pertain to the target fact, the content of the box: "He saw that *there is a flower in the box*" and "She was told that *there is a flower in the box*" specify a link between the person and the target fact that *there is a flower in the box*. In contrast, a person's age which is also a useful diagnostic for whether or not a person knows facts in general, is not a good diagnostic for whether or not a person knows a specific fact, since a person's age does not specify a linkage between the person and the target fact.

Understanding mental states as representations also allows the 4-year-old to understand that knowledge can be used to guide action in the world. If knowledge is a correct representation of the world, then action guided by it will tend to be correct. Having acquired the concept of representation, then, the child can interpret "knowledge" as a correct mental representation. Armed with this new interpretation, the child can understand the relative importance of informational access over success and, in general, start asking the right questions about what is important for gaining knowledge. These achievements are apparent in the child's development from 4 years on and mark the acquisition of a *representational-informational theory of knowledge.*

Distinguishing "Know" from "Guess"   If our objective is not to determine when children start to use informational access as another diagnostic factor for having knowledge but when they appreciate its essential role in knowledge formation, then a good strategy is to play one diagnostic factor against another—in particular, *success* against *informational access.* The critical case is that of a *lucky guess*, for instance, when subjects find something right away even though they did not see where it was put. Since successful action is the dominant diagnostic criterion, young children should say that they *knew* that the object was in that location, whereas older children with an informational theory of knowledge should be aware that in the absence of any relevant information success must have been due to a lucky guess rather than to knowledge.

To assess children's understanding of the importance of informational access for the formation of knowledge, we tested children in three conditions. For instance, a piece of candy was placed in one of two boxes.

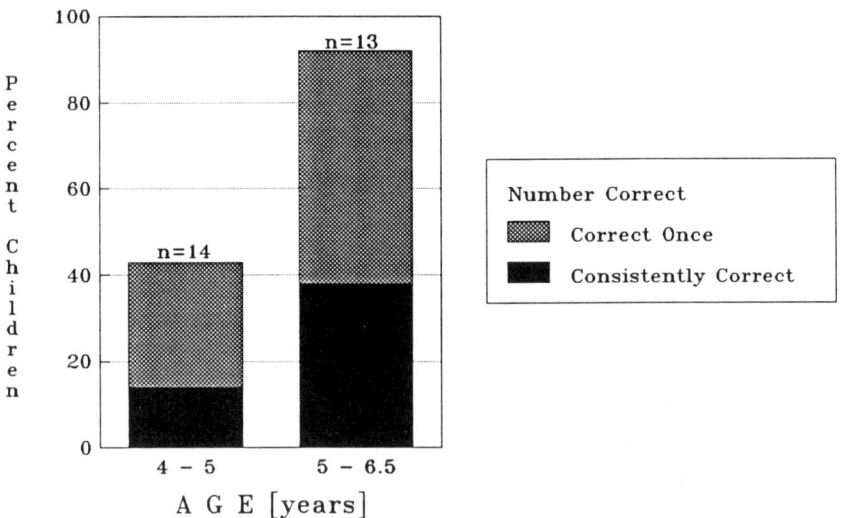

Figure 7.1
Distinguishing "know" from "guess"/"think."
Data from ongoing research.

In the *know* condition the child saw that it was placed in the blue box. Then the boxes were moved about (to make the subsequent question a bit more meaningful), and the child was asked, "Where is the candy?" In practically all cases the child pointed to the blue box; the box was then opened and the candy put on top of its lid. The child was then asked the critical question: "Did you really know that the candy was in there or did you just guess?."*

In the *guess-correct* condition a screen was set up between the child and the boxes while the candy was placed in one of them. (In order to ensure a correct guess, the experimenter actually put candies in both boxes, taking care that the child did not find out.) Then the screen was removed and the child had to guess where the candy was. The indicated box was opened, the candy was taken out, and the critical question was asked. In the *guess-wrong* condition the procedure was the same, except that both boxes were actually empty. The experimenter opened the box the child had pointed to and commented that the candy was not in there. The experimenter then opened the other box, took out the candy (which she had hidden in her hand), put it on top of the box, and asked the same critical question as in the other conditions.† On another day children were again given the same three tasks, but this time the question was phrased as a choice between *knowing* and *thinking*: "Did you really *know* that the candy was in this box or did you just *think* so?"

At the time of writing we had tested 27 children between 4 and 6½ years. Only 2 4-year-olds and 1 5-year-old consistently failed to distinguish between "know" and "guess"/"think" in the obvious cases: the know and guess-wrong conditions. The vast majority of errors were as predicted: children judged in the guess-correct condition that they had "really known" where the candy was. The dark portion of the bars in figure 7.1 shows the percentage of children who gave the correct responses on all three tasks in both sessions (in other words, who differentiated "know" from "guess" and "think" reliably). The cross-

---

*The question in German was "Hast Du wirklich gewußt, daß das Bonbon da drin war, oder hast Du nur geraten?" On this occasion I would like to thank Sabine Simon and Sabine Knoll for their help with data collection.

†Admittedly, in this condition the critical question was somewhat awkward. However, since the purpose of this condition was to demonstrate that children do give the answer "guessed" in response to our test question, we had to use the same question asked in the other conditions at the cost of a few perhaps otherwise unnecessary wrong responses, increasing experimental noise.

hatched portions show the percentage of children who differentiated correctly on only one session (in other words, who showed some but less reliable understanding of the difference).*

Figure 7.1 makes clear that between 4 and 5 years most children come to understand the relative importance of information access over successful action in the application of the term "knowledge." [Note 7.3 Early studies of the know-guess distinction.] That this understanding emerges at this age supports the view that from about 4 years on children develop an *information theory of knowledge*. And there are other signs that around this age children come to appreciate the importance of information for knowledge.

Spontaneous Inquiry into Reasons for Knowing   Another important indicator that children have acquired an *information theory of knowledge*, rather than using knowledge to explain behavior, is their spontaneous desire to explain where knowledge comes from. As we have seen from the work by Hood and Bloom (1979), starting at an early age children use knowledge to justify their action but there are no reports of young children justifying their knowledge. Heinz Wimmer, who has kept track of his son's concern about how people know something, recorded that Theo's first inquiry came at 3 years and 8½ months:

Heinz: "Today will be nice."

Theo: "Where do you know that from?"†

And at 3 years and 9 months:

Theo: "From where do you know that drinking soapy water makes you sick? Have you tried it yourself?"

Somewhat later these concerns can become a veritable obsession, as the following anecdote shows.

---

*There was no systematic difference between children's ability to differentiate "know" from "guess" and their ability to differentiate "know" from "think."

†This somewhat peculiar formulation is my attempt to capture the original German question, "Woher weißt Du...?"

Sybille at 5 years and 1 month was visited for the first time by Judith (a friend from kindergarten) and her mother, who live in a distant village.* After the visit Sybille asked her father:

Sybille:	"How did they know where I live?"
Father:	"Maybe they asked in the kindergarten."
Sybille:	"But Sigrid [the kindergarten teacher] doesn't know where I live."
Father:	"Maybe Judith's mother looked up our address in the phone book."
Sybille:	"But how did they know the way?"
......	
Sybille:	"From where did they know which door we live at?" (in a house with three families and three separate entrances)
Father:	"They could have looked at the nameplate, where it says 'Spangler.'"
Sybille:	"Does it just say 'Spangler' there? Then how did they know that Sybille also lives there?"

and so on

Another example of a somewhat less persistent inquiry I observed with my daughter Hannah. It took place in the evening of December 5 in Austria. Both time and place are important, because in Austria the evening of December 5 is when St. Nicholas goes from house to house in his red bishop's suit, carrying a big bag of goodies and a large book. With the whole family assembled he calls up each child and reads from his book all the child's misdeeds and good deeds (for which the child, in the end, receives a bag of nuts, fruit, and other assorted delicacies). Later on this particular evening we asked Hannah (6 years minus 2 months) what she remembered of St. Nicholas's admonitions. After a brief résumé her concern quickly switched to how St. Nicholas could have known about all her misdeeds without ever having seen her. I said that this was written in his book. "But how did it get in there?" she insisted, and then answered herself: "Maybe there are lots of fairies around who watch us and who help him."

I find this anecdote interesting for two reasons. Not only does it show Hannah's concern about how someone without any conceivable access to relevant information could know something, it also indicates what kind of answer is deemed satisfactory. Hannah's own answer solved only the *theoretical problem* in a sort of hypothetical fashion. If indeed there

---

*This anecdote was collected by Dr. Spangler at the University of Regensburg after a colloquium by Heinz Wimmer on this topic.

were fairies around, then they could provide St. Nicholas with the required information. But at a factual level this explanation remains utterly unsatisfactory, for I am sure Hannah clearly had never met a fairy. In other words, she accepted an explanation involving some fictional characters, who were intangible to her experience but who satisfied the theoretical requirement of being potential carriers of information.

These anecdotes illustrate how children after the age of 4 years cannot let go of a case of knowledge with unexplained origins. This urge to find an explanation—at least one of principle—underlines the earlier finding that at the same age they can distinguish a lucky guess from genuine knowledge. All these findings attest to the fact that at this age children are in the grip of an information theory of knowledge.

My wider claim is that the acquisition of such a theory of knowledge depends on the emergence of the concept of representation (metarepresentation), which (as we have seen by the quite independent evidence cited in chapter 4) also emerges at about the age of 4 years. To substantiate this dependence, we should look at features of knowledge that cannot be understood without a representational view of mind. As I argued in chapter 5, *aspectuality* of knowledge (an important feature of "intentional inexistence," a hallmark of mentality) is difficult to grasp without an understanding of representation.

Aspectuality of Knowledge   Without a representational view of mind it is difficult to understand that, for instance, seeing informs only about certain *aspects* of an object. If *seeing* is treated by the young child *nonepistemically*—that is, not as a mental (intentional) activity but more like the physical relationship of *looking at*—then it is difficult for the child to understand, for instance, that by looking at an object a person comes to know its color but not its weight. This is so, because the physical relationship of *looking at* (or *nonepistemic* seeing) is indifferent to aspect. If the object you are looking at (or that you are *seeing*) is heavy, then you are looking at (seeing) a heavy object, but—and this is what is difficult to appreciate without a representational view—you are *not seeing that* it is heavy, and consequently you *won't know that* it is heavy.

Daniela O'Neill and Janet Astington (1989) investigated children's ability to understand this difference in a task of intriguing simplicity. Their basic piece of apparatus was a tunnel. Children could either lift the tunnel to see what was hidden underneath or put a hand in to feel what was inside, but not both. Children practiced this with balls of different colors or different textures. Then they were introduced to the critical test objects, which came in pairs. For instance, there was a pair of identical-looking piggybanks—one filled with pennies, the other empty. One of them was put inside the tunnel, without the children knowing which one, and they were asked, "Now, to find out for sure which piggybank is under the tunnel, what would you have to do?" Children who did not answer were given a forced choice: "Do you have to *see* the piggybank or *feel* the piggybank?" The correct answer, of course, was to say that one needed to "feel" the piggybank. For another pair of critical objects (for instance, two toy footballs of the same size and shape but different colors) the correct answer was that one needed to "see" which one was inside.

Children were given four tasks of this kind, two with "see" and two with "feel" as the correct response. The dark portions of the bars in figure 7.2 show the proportion of children who gave correct answers on all four tasks. The cross-hatched portions represent the children who gave 3 correct answers, which can be interpreted as a sign of understanding among the oldest group, since there were no children who gave 3 wrong answers. The developmental trend in this figure confirms that the

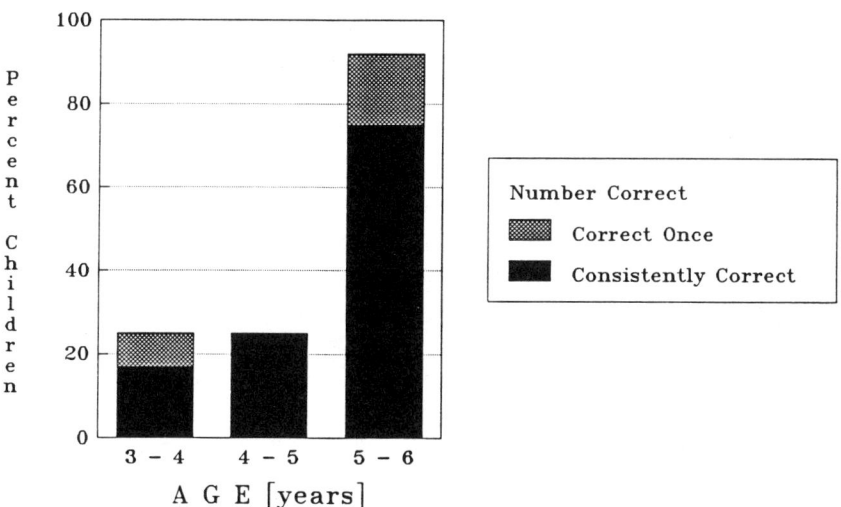

Figure 7.2
Correct choice between "see" and "feel."
Data from O'Neill and Astington 1989.

majority of children come to understand the aspectuality of knowledge between 4 and 5 years.

The inability of the younger children to master this simple task is underlined by the following anecdotal evidence. On the last trial 12 of the 3- and 4-year-olds were challenged to demonstrate the validity of their mistaken claims. Eight of these 12 children just gave a blank stare, seemingly unable to comprehend why they could not tell whether it was the full or empty piggy bank even though they were *looking* at it, or why they could not tell which color football it was even though they were *feeling* it with their hands inside the tunnel.

The finding that the aspectuality of knowledge is understood between 4 and 5 years is also compatible with earlier data reported by Beate Sodian (1986, experiment 5). She tested whether children understood that looking at a picture of a dog informs about its visible attributes but not its name. A majority of 4-year-olds committed the error on at least 2 of 3 trials of thinking that a doll would know the dog's name from looking at its picture, whereas all but 1 of 14 6-year-olds understood that the doll would not know the dog's name. [**Note 7.4** Substitutability of co-referential expressions as a test of understanding aspectuality.]

In sum, I have argued that around 4 years children acquire a *representation-information theory of knowledge,* and I have discussed evidence for three consequences of this claim. One is that until 4 years of age children are not able to understand the true importance of *informational access* in the formation of knowledge. Children may be able to associate "seeing" or "being told" with "knowing," but they do not appreciate that informational access is a necessary condition for knowing and more important than successful action in judging a person's knowledge. The data I have presented indicate that this appreciation emerges between 4 and 5 years.

This change in the understanding of knowledge is also reflected in the fact that younger children, although they use knowledge in explaining action or justifying requests for help, do not seem to be concerned about explaining the existence or absence of knowledge. Anecdotal evidence suggests that *spontaneous inquiry into the origin* of knowledge develops at around 4 years of age and soon turns into a major concern.

Another consequence of my claim is that without a representational theory of knowledge children find it difficult to understand *aspectuality of knowledge*, for instance, that a particular sensory modality informs only about certain aspects of objects. Available data indicate that this understanding, too, emerges between 4 and 5 years.

Furthermore, acquisition of a representational theory of knowledge has other more surprising consequences, for instance, a change in how children encode experienced events.

Episodic Memory Traces and Childhood Amnesia

Endel Tulving (1985) argues that there are three types of memory—procedural, semantic, and episodic—which are related to three levels of consciousness—anoetic (unconscious), noetic (conscious), and autonoetic (self-conscious). The distinction that concerns us here is the one between semantic and episodic memory. Here is a brief account of the relevant parts of Tulving's idea.

What we remember of, say, a list of words we have seen is determined by two types of information: *semantic cue information* and *episodic trace information*. Semantic cue information is something like information in a semantic net. For instance, the item "pear" on the list is embedded in various associations: "denotes a fruit," "name starts with 'p,' " and so on. Retrieval of the item "pear" via semantic cue information tends to be facilitated when the experimenter provides helpful cues: "Wasn't there a fruit on the list?" This is called *cued recall*. In *free recall* no such cues are given: "Tell me what was on the list!" Recall of items is therefore typically worse in this condition. And it would be worse still if we did not have access to what Tulving calls *episodic trace information*.

Episodic Traces   According to my (Perner 1990) elaboration of Tulving's ideas, episodic trace information, is a *metarepresentational comment* on how information was obtained. For instance:

> "I have information that 'pear' was on the list, and I have this information because I have seen 'pear' on the list."

This is clearly metarepresentational (and autonoetic in the profound sense of being self-conscious as a knowing subject) since the mind is talking about its own information and where that information came from. It is the kind of metacomment that saves free recall from being as bad as it would be if only semantic cue information were available.

To prevent a common misunderstanding, it helps to realize that *episodic traces* should not be equated with *episodic memory* in its everyday meaning: "ability to recall an episode of the past." As Tulving explicitly states,

People can have and can express knowledge about things that have happened to them even if they can rely only on their semantic memory. (Tulving 1985, 6)

There is of course a strong correlation between the ability to recall episodes and recovery of information via episodic traces. Since personal episodes are typically not part of a rich semantic net, one needs episodic trace information to retrieve them.

There is another important distinction that goes hand in hand with semantic cues and episodic traces. Semantically recovered information is *phenomenally experienced* as simply *known*, whereas information recovered through episodic traces is experienced as *remembered*. Tulving (1985) reports data showing that items recovered in free recall were subjectively judged as "properly remembered" and subjects had no doubts that these items had been on the list, whereas items that could be produced only with the help of semantic cues were judged as "just known" or "not really remembered" and subjects were less certain that they had really been on the list. (See Gardiner 1988 for other experimental demonstrations of this distinction.)

Now comes my part of the argument. If everything is as Tulving says, then before the age of about 4 years children should not be able to form episodic traces. They do not have the necessary metarepresentational facility. But notice that an inability to form episodic traces does not mean an inability to relate past episodes because, as Tulving says,

Even when a person does not remember an event, she may know something about it. (Tulving 1985, 6)

And there is increasing evidence that children from a very early age are in fact able to relate interesting episodes (e.g., Fivush, Gray, and Fromhoff 1987). However, an inability to form episodic traces does imply—as Tulving argued—a relative impairment in free recall as compared to cued recall.

Concept of Knowledge and Free Recall The theory is that formation of episodic traces depends on children developing a representational theory of mind, because only then can they understand the origins of their knowledge in their perceptual experience (Perner 1990: "Experiential Awareness"). To test this, I correlated measures that index children's understanding of the origin of their knowledge with their free recall in relation to cued recall, as one of the indices of episodic trace information pointed out by Tulving (1985).

To assess children's relative proficiency in free recall, they were given two trials of free and two of cued recall. Each trial involved 12 pictures of things that fell into 3 common categories, for instance, 4 animals, 4 pieces of furniture, 4 kinds of fruit. About 2 minutes after presentation of all 12 pictures children were asked, in the free recall trials, "I showed you some pictures. What was on them?" and, in the cued recall trials, "I showed you some pictures. There were some animals on these pictures. What were they?" The dependent measure was the difference between the number of items recalled under free recall and the number of items recalled under cued recall.

To assess emerging understanding that knowledge originates through information, I tried two different measures. The obvious method, originally employed by Wimmer, Hogrefe, and Perner (1988), was to ask children, "How do you know?" There were three trials in which an object was put inside a box. On one trial the children *saw* what was put inside, on another they did not see but *were told*, and on a third they were *not given any information*. Almost all children correctly said that they knew what was inside the box and could name the object in the first two conditions and said that they did not know what was inside in the third condition. However, when asked why they knew or didn't know what was in the box few of the younger children gave all correct answers. Their scores ranged from 0 to 3 correct.

I also used another measure because I had argued that even correct responses to these "why-do-you-know" questions might not reflect a proper understanding of the real role of information in the formation of knowledge as a mental representation. To get at proper understanding, one should trade off *successful action*, a most powerful indicator of knowledge in normal circumstances, against *informational access*, a necessary condition from a theoretical point of view. As a consequence, I ended up using the three tasks in which children had to judge whether they really knew where something was or whether they had just guessed. The critical one was the "lucky guess" condition in which children did not have information about where something was but retrieved it successfully by sheer (manipulated) luck. This condition sorts out the children who appreciate the crucial importance of informational access from those who do not, because it tempts the latter into saying they knew where the object was on the basis of having been successful in retrieving it. Children were scored as *correct* ("experientially aware") if they gave correct answers to all three tasks, as *incorrect* otherwise.

Table 7.1
Stepwise regression on free recall – cued recall difference.

Factor partialed out	Experiential awareness measure	Partial correlation	F-value	Level of significance
	Know-guess	.46	15.8	p < .001
	How-do-you-know	.16	1.4	n.s.
Age	Know-guess	.46	14.6	p < .001
Age + cued recall	Know-guess	.45	13.7	p < .001

To see which of the two measures was better in explaining children's free recall, a stepwise regression was carried out with the difference between free and cued recall as the dependent measure indicative of episodic trace formation. The first two rows in table 7.1 show how well each of the two measures predicts the difference between cued and free recall. The know-guess test is a statistically highly reliable predictor and its correlation is quite good. In contrast, the "how-do-you-know" question has a much smaller correlation not significantly (n.s.) different from zero. This result confirms my argument that the know-guess test gets at the more important changes in children's understanding of the origin of knowledge better than the "how-do-you-know" question.

As it stands, the correlation between recall and the ability to make the know-guess distinction may not be all that interesting. One could argue that the changes in both tasks simply reflect improvement with age. As children get older, they get better at drawing the know-guess distinction and the gap between free and cued recall narrows. Therefore, to see whether the correlation goes beyond a common change with age, I partialed out age and looked at the correlation again. As shown in the third row of table 7.1, the correlation between making the know-guess distinction and the free recall – cued recall difference stays as large as it was before.

Figure 7.3 gives an impression of how well the ability to distinguish "know" from "guess" predicted the difference between free and cued recall. The dark line is the best fit regression line to all data points along age. Its gentle slope indicates that as children get older, their free recall performance tends to catch up with their cued recall performance and the free recall – cued recall difference approaches zero. Just how well the ability to distinguish "know" from "guess" predicts relative memory performance can be seen from the fact that 2 of the 16 filled stars (data from those children who succeeded on the know-guess test) lie below the regression line, whereas 2/3 of the open circles (children who failed) lie below that line.

Still, another argument can be raised against my interpretation of these data. The same kind of argument that the observed correlation is just a common product of increasing age can also be made for memory capacity. There are some children who are just brighter and can remember more. These children are better at understanding know-guess tasks, and since their cued recall performance is already high, their free recall has to be closer to their cued recall because of a ceiling effect. Fortunately, this argument is implausible because even these children's performance on cued recall was far below ceiling (on average 6.3 items of a possible 12 per task). Moreover, it correlated negatively with the dependent measure (r = −.62) meaning that free recall became increasingly worse than cued recall as children remembered more items rather than the opposite. In any case, the bottom part of table 7.1 shows that the important correlation between know-guess performance and the dependent measure remains undiminished even when performance on cued recall is partialed out in addition to age.

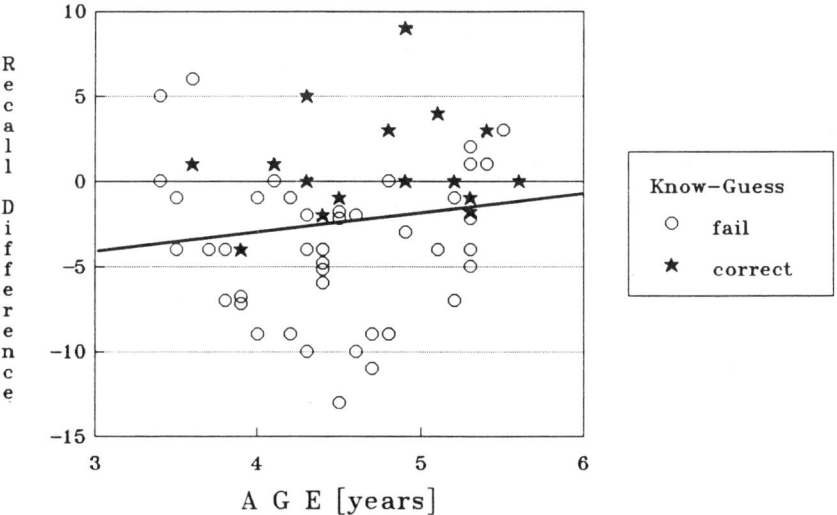

Figure 7.3
Distinguishing "know" from "guess" and free recall – cued recall.
Data from ongoing research.

Now the support for the theory from this experiment looks fairly impressive. There is evidence for a specific relationship between understanding the importance of informational access in knowledge formation (know-guess test) and the ability to form episodic traces (relative performance on free recall) that goes above and beyond common changes with age and memory capacity. This finding is particularly important since it provides the basis for a new theory of *childhood amnesia.*

Childhood   The phenomenon of childhood amnesia was first described
Amnesia   by Sigmund Freud (White and Pillemer 1979). He noticed
                 that many of his neurotic patients had difficulty remember-
ing early childhood events:

> What I have in mind is the peculiar amnesia which, in the case of most people,
> though by no means all, hides the earliest beginnings of their childhood up to their
> sixth or eighth year. (Freud 1905/1953, 174)

Freud's observation engendered several questionnaire studies of early childhood recollections, of which the one by Waldvogel (1948) is the largest, involving 124 adults. The noticeable result was that on average, these people could remember less than one event that had happened before the age of 3 years, whereas they could remember almost three events that had happened between 3 and 4 years. And the number of events remembered for each consecutive year increased rapidly.

More recently Sheingold and Tenney (1982) took a more experimental approach. They constructed 20 questions about events during and around the birth of a younger sibling—for instance, "Who told you that Mother was leaving to go to the hospital?"—and checked the correctness of their subjects' answers with the subjects' parents. None of the 26 college students interviewed could verifiably remember any event that happened before the age of 3 years. Memory for events that happened between 3 and 5 years was markedly better; students could answer about half of the questions correctly if they pertained to events that happened between those ages.

These studies tend to indicate that around the age of 4 years children become rapidly better at long-term memory for life experiences. That this ability sets in at that age goes remarkably well with the idea that life events can only be retrieved after a long period if they have been encoded with an episodic trace. And as the experimental data suggest, this ability is acquired and improved from the age of about 4 years onward.

Apart from providing a new explanation for childhood amnesia, the results from my experimental study are also interesting for my general theoretical claim that children develop a representational theory of mind from about the age of 4 years. By showing that understanding of the know-guess distinction specifically relates to free recall, the study supports two independent parts of the theoretical argument: (1) that the ability to make the know-guess distinction is an indicator that children are starting to conceptualize knowledge as a representational state of the mind, and (2) that understanding of knowledge as a mental representation is necessary for forming episodic traces, which are metarepresentational comments on why information is in the mind.

Summary

Acquisition of the concept of knowledge proceeds in two stages. Children start by using knowledge as a theoretical construct within a *theory of behavior* that explains success and failure. Later, as children acquire the concept of representation at about 4 years, they reconceptualize what they know about knowledge within a *representational theory of mind*.

(Mentalist) Theory of Behavior. The explanatory role of knowledge at this stage is shaped by how the word "know" is used in everyday conversation. The emphasis is on correct action and success, which remains the dominant criterion for judging a person's knowledge. Informational access is used as a criterion only when made salient as the only option. In justifications "know" is used to explain successful action (by the presence of knowledge) or to explain failure (by the absence of knowledge).

Representational-Informational Theory of Knowledge. With the acquisition of the concept of representation, knowledge can be understood as part of an information-processing system, which provides insight in how knowledge is formed and how it governs behavior. The following observations are symptomatic of this change in theory:

The *importance of informational access* is fully appreciated, relegating successful action to its place as a "mere" consequence of knowledge. Children stop judging successful guesses as indicators of knowledge.

Knowledge is understood as *aspect specific* and seeing (that) as modality specific. For instance, children understand that by looking at an object, they come to know only its visible aspects, not others.

Spontaneous inquiries into the reasons for knowing become frequent. This is a sign that children have a theory of knowledge concerned with how knowledge is formed and that they do not just use knowledge in a theory of behavior.

The formation of *episodic traces* becomes possible, leading to better performance in free recall and putting an end to childhood amnesia.

Chapter 8

Understanding Thinking and Belief

The topic of the last chapter was children's understanding of knowledge, whose function it is to correspond faithfully to reality. The human mind, however, has a special reputation for its ability to transcend reality and represent things as they are not. Children's understanding of mental states serving this "devious" function are the topic of the present chapter. These mental states are characterized by terms like "thinking," "imagining," "dreaming," "believing," "assuming," and intentional manipulation of such states in others gives rise to *deception, lying*, and other unsavory practices. Of these mental terms, the word "think" is the most basic, flexible, and widely used and will serve as my paradigmatic case.

To understand the representational functions of these states, we have to ask how the mental representations engendered by these mental states relate to what they represent. And there are differences. Some states imply that the person has a (mis)conception about reality (e.g., belief), whereas others indicate that the person is merely entertaining possibilities without claiming that they reflect reality (e.g., mere thoughts). These differences are also reflected in different uses of the word "think."

"Thinking of" When "think" is used with the conjunction "that," it **and** enforces a claim about reality, which is not entailed by **"Thinking that"** the use of the prepositions "of" or "about." My favorite hedonic examples for illustrating this difference are these (Perner, in press):

(1) "You think *of* me lying on a Mediterranean beach."
(2) "You think *that* I am lying on a Mediterranean beach."

The difference between these two sentences is important. The first describes a (for me) nice thought of yours, but the second shows your serious misconception about my life-style (when I am sitting at my desk working hard on this passage). The difference arises because "think of" reports a mere *thought*, with no claim about reality, whereas "think that" reports a *belief* about my real activities. [**Note 8.1** On thinking influencing action and feeling.]

"Thinking of" can be used in different ways. It can describe a pure thought, as in the above example, or it can imply interest or even outright preference. For instance, if we are trying to decide where to go for dinner and you are not quite happy with my suggestion to go to the Italian place, you might say, "I was rather *thinking of* having Peking duck."

Another important distinction is between two uses of "thinking that." When used in first person present tense, "I think that...," it is used to make a direct statement about reality without expressing any conception or misconception about reality. For instance, confronted with the fake rock that John Flavell and his colleagues used for their appearance-reality test, you notice that it seems a bit strange and you say, "I *think* it's a rock." Your statement does not, I think, entail something like "I have a mental description of this object as being a rock but this description is possibly false." Rather, your statement describes reality but marks it as uncertain, merely probable. This interpretation is supported by the fact that you could equally well have said, "It's *probably* a rock."

The use of "think" for marking possibility can be modified in opposite directions depending on context. It can be used to emphasize one's own uncertainty: for instance, "I'm not sure, but I *think* it's a rock" [emphasis on "think"]. It can also be used to state one's opinion verging on certainty: "He thinks it's a sponge. Ridiculous! *I* think it's a rock" [emphasis on "I"].

In contrast, imagine that you have been handed the "rock" and have discovered that it is actually a rock-like piece of sponge. You exclaim, "Ah, it's a piece of sponge and I *thought* it was a rock." Now your sentence clearly states your former *misconception* about the object's true identity. That is, you are saying something like, "I represented this object mentally *as* being a rock, even though it is really a piece of sponge." In any case, you are not stating a possibility, since your exclamation cannot be paraphrased as "Ah, it's a piece of sponge but it probably was a rock."

For the sake of completeness, note that "thinking" can also be used as a description of an activity without propositional complement—for instance, one can say, "He is thinking," when looking at Rodin's sculpture of a sitting man resting his chin on his hand. Including this nonpropositional use, my analysis suggested the following five different uses of the word "think":

Five Uses of "Think"
1. Mental activity: "He is thinking." (nonpropositional)
2. Entertaining a thought: "He is thinking of Santa Claus getting his reindeer out."
3. Stating a possibility: "I think it's a rock."
4. Stating a preference: "He is thinking of eating Chinese."
5. Reporting a misconception about reality: "I thought that it was a rock."

The theoretically important implication of this analysis is that only for the fifth use, when someone's misconception is reported, do we need to interpret that person's mental activity as a mental *representation*. This is necessary here because we need to express the dual relationship of that person's mental state as relating to the real situation as its referent and to some hypothetical situation as its sense. In all the other uses of "think" our language seems to refer not to representations but only to hypothetical situations (2), marked with respect to their likelihood (3) or likeability (4). The developmental implication is that children younger than 4 years can understand the first four uses but not the fifth, since that use requires the ability to metarepresent. In the following section I examine children's spontaneous use of the word "think" and their understanding it (and of the words "imagine," "dream," and so on.) in experimental situations.

Children's Use and Understanding of "Think"

Children Using "Think"   "Think" is among the cognitive words that are used with some frequency by very young children. Bretherton and Beeghly (1982) report that in their study 33% of children between 10 months and 2 years and 4 months used the word at least once. The example that they cite is one where "think" is (probably) used to state a possibility or disagreement: "I think mommy is beautiful." Theo Wimmer, in his first recorded utterance of "think" at 2 years and 2 months, used it to surmise what person was hiding in his father's bed:

Theo: "Mummy I think is in there."

Most uses cited by Bretherton, McNew, and Beeghly-Smith (1981) fall into this category—for instance, these two (and four of their other six examples):

> Cathy (at 26 months):   "I think I can't." (Mother asked her to get blanket, but the bedroom door, which she can't open yet was shut)
>
> Alison (at 33 months):   "I think he'll play with the truck." (about baby to whom she had given a truck to play with)

Also, Bloom, et al. (1989, 117–118) summarize their results by saying that 2- to 3-year-old children use "think" to "qualify the degree of 'certainty/uncertainty' of the complement propositions in their sentences." Shatz, Wellman, and Silber (1983) point out that the most frequent uses of mental verbs (basically "know" and "think") in their sample of 30 children observed from 2 years to 3 years were expressions of uncertainty (*modulations of assertions*) and opinions on what would have been desirable: "I *thoughted* we'd eat some cake" (classified as "directing the interaction").

Few cases have been reported where young children make a clear reference to "thinking" as a misconception of reality. [**Note 8.2** Anecdotal evidence for early reference to belief as misrepresentation.] This is also supported by experimental evidence. In contrast, there is good evidence that most 3-year-olds do understand other uses of "think" that do not imply an understanding of belief as a mental (mis)conception of reality.

Talk of "Inner Worlds"   In a series of experiments Henry Wellman and David Estes (1986) demonstrated that children as young as 3 years old have a good grasp of the difference between the "inner, mental world of thinking" and reality. For instance, Estes, Wellman, and Woolley (1989) told children about a boy who either (a) *thought* of, or (b) *dreamt* of, or (c) *remembered* a bicycle, or (d) *possessed* one in reality. They then asked the children in each case whether the boy could (1) *see* the bicycle, (2) *touch* it, or (3) *hide* it under his bed. Even 3-year-olds judged 79% of the time that the boy who had a real bike could touch it, whereas they judged 62% of the time that if the boy only thought of, dreamt of, or remembered a bike, then he could not touch it. Furthermore, when asked why he could or could not see or touch the bike, about 30% of the 3-year-olds also gave a mentalistic explanation: ",Cause it's his imagination," "Because he is just remembering it in his brain," and the like.

Estes, Wellman, and Woolley (1989) also showed that children understand not only the limitations of the mental world but also its possibilities. They asked children to form a mental image of various objects, one of which was a cup. Children were then asked about the cup itself when (a) *visible*, (b) *hidden*, or (c) in a *mental image*. In each case four questions were asked: (1) whether *they could see* the cup with their eyes, (2) whether *they could touch* it with their hands, (3) whether *someone else could see* it, and (4) whether *they could transform* it—for instance, "Just by thinking real hard, without moving your hands, can you make it turn upside down?" Three-year-olds differentiated practically as well as 4- and 5-year-olds what one can do with an object when it is visible, when it is hidden, and when it appears in a mental image. They understood that when the object is present, one can see and touch it, whereas when it is hidden, one cannot see or touch it. They also understood that one cannot transform the object whether present or hidden by just thinking, whereas one can do that with the object in one's mental image even though one cannot see (with one's eyes) or touch the object in the mental image.

Wellman and Estes (1986) interpreted these kinds of results as showing that children understand the mental-real distinction. I agree on that point. The best evidence, I think, comes from the image transformation study where children were able to follow instructions to form an image and talk about it. Children's responses also demonstrate that they attribute the right sort of qualities to imagined situations: they cannot be seen (with one's real eyes) or touched; access to them is private, not public; and their existence is under mental control (as soon as one stops imagining, the situation vanishes).

I want to point out, though, that all these distinctions are perfectly possible if children understand the content of their images (thoughts, memory, etc.) as "imagined situations," that is, as real or counterfactual situations. There is nothing in the data that suggests that children understand their mental images *as representations*. But Wellman and Estes (1986, 912) claim exactly this:

> Thus, young children behaviorally distinguish mind and external reality—they do not behave toward a mental image of a fire like they do toward a real fire. What is at issue is their ability to conceive of and represent this distinction, a metarepresentational task in Pylyshyn's (1978) terms.

As I have discussed in chapter 2, the markers that are necessary to distinguish real from hypothetical (imagined) situations can be called "metarepresentational" in the sense that these markers are not part of the represented situations but are outside comments on the status of these situations. However, these markers are not "metarepresentational" in the recursive sense defined by Pylyshyn in the paper cited by Wellman and Estes:

> His ability to represent the *representational relation itself* ... this kind of metarepresentational ability ... the recursive meta-representational capacity... (Pylyshyn 1978, 593)

The important point here is that the evidence reported by Wellman and Estes and Woolley is compatible with my claim that the 3-year-old child is a situation theorist. By analogy to my analysis of children's understanding of pictures at this age, children differentiate between *mental* and *real*, between *depicted* and *real*, purely at the level of situations. This is similar to the way we construe the difference between *hypothetical* and *real*, or between *yesterday* and *now*. For instance, children understand that the imagined bike cannot be touched because they understand what limited possibilities imagined situations afford, just as they understand the limitations of real and hypothetical situations. When the bike is (if the bike were) behind shop windows, one can (could) not touch it either.

Three-year-olds not only understand that thought-of, imagined situations are different from reality but also understand that thinking influences people's action. But this, too, is within the intellectual reach of the young situation theorist.

Thinking Affects Action Wellman and Bartsch (1988) told 3- and 4-year-old children very brief stories. Children were told in which of two locations the protagonist thought a desired kind of object was, and they were asked where the protagonist would look for that kind of object. For instance:

Discrepant Belief Story
"Look there are bananas in the cupboard and bananas in the refrigerator. Jane wants a banana. Jane thinks there are only bananas in the cupboard: she doesn't think there are bananas in the refrigerator. Where will Jane look for bananas?"

Even from 3 years and 2 months to 4 years 82% of children answered that Jane would look in the cupboard. But what else should they say? Although Wellman and Bartsch (1988) insist that the adequate response would be to say, "Jane will look in both locations," this cannot be expected from young children since it violates basic conventions of conversation. There is an implicit understanding that the question is whether Jane will look for one set of bananas OR for the other; and where there is such a choice, the natural convention is to opt for one but not both.* The only information in the story that points to one rather than the other location is contained in the "think" sentences. And it seems that from early on children can take this cue. [**Note 8.3** Basic problems with Wellman and Bartsch's study.]

Although Wellman and Bartsch designed the study to test understanding of belief, children's correct responses may be due to a simple rule that "thinking" predisposes people to act in relation to the thought-about object (see Note 8.1). And they can pick up that rule from any of the different uses of "think." For instance, if I state, "I am thinking of eating Chinese tonight," then one can reasonably predict that I will be heading for the restaurant that serves Chinese food rather than the one that specializes in Italian cuisine. No understanding of "thinking" as *belief* is required.

We have here a situation similar to the case of knowledge, where, under well-controlled experimental conditions, 3-year-olds understand that seeing leads to knowing without understanding knowledge as an information-carrying representational state of the mind. To get at children's representational "theory" of knowledge, I suggested looking at their understanding of the relative importance of *informational access* over other diagnostic criteria like *successful action*. The empirical test satisfying these criteria involves judgments of whether a person knew or guessed where something was when that person had no information but nevertheless happened to find the object (lucky guess).

"Think" poses a similar methodological problem. Letting children indicate in which of two locations a person will look for an object, when the only basis for their choice is information about what the person is thinking, may be a sensitive test to determine whether children understand that thinking influences action. But it is not a convincing test to determine whether children conceive of thinking as a representational activity, since their correct predictions do not allow us to decide whether they interpret "think" as indicating belief or one of the other uses of that word. As in the case of knowledge, a better task for making this decision is one where the action predicted on the basis of belief differs from the action predicted on the basis of other well-established rules of how people act. This is a better test because vague dependence of action on

---

*Piaget's class inclusion question "Are there more poppies or more flowers?" has been criticized on these grounds (e.g., Donaldson 1978, 43–44; Ford 1976).

"thinking" would not be enough to override these established rules. Only the emergence of a representational theory of belief then explains why children violate their previously used rules of prediction, because a representational theory makes clear that action always depends on belief. Such a task is provided by the *false belief test* (Wimmer and Perner 1983).

The Representational View: Understanding Belief

My argument is that with the ability to interpret certain thinking activities as mental *representation* the child gains new insight into aspects of mental functioning that are nearly impossible to comprehend without a representational theory. One such case is *mistaken action*, that is, action based on a *misconception* of the world or *false belief*. Such cases are difficult to understand without a representational view of mind because false beliefs are mental misrepresentations of reality requiring a clear distinction between *sense* and *reference*, since they guide action in the real situation (referent) as if it were a different situation (sense).

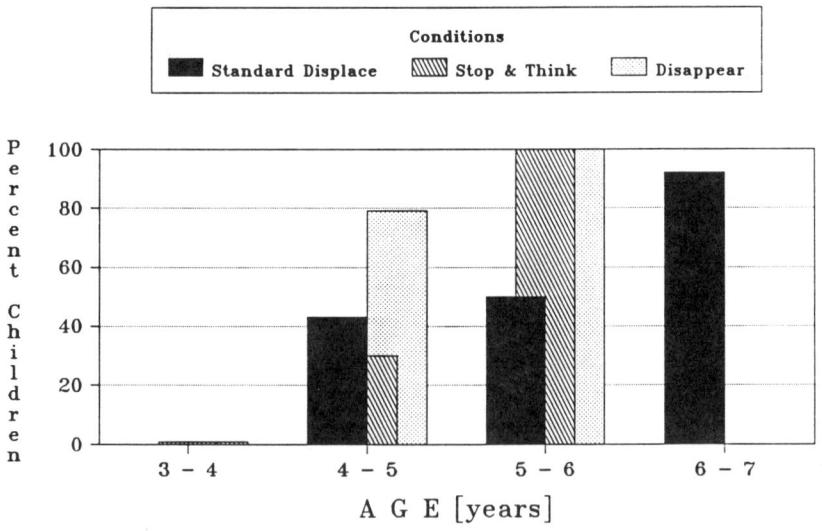

Figure 8.1
Correct answers to belief question.
Data from Wimmer and Perner (1983, experiment 2, with data for 6-year-olds from experiment 1).

Understanding   Heinz Wimmer and I (1983), with the assistance of
False Belief   Sylvia Gruber, carried out the first systematic experimental investigation into children's understanding of how a
person develops a false belief about some everyday fact and how such a
belief affects that person's action.* We tested this by enacting some
simple, concrete stories. For instance, there was "Maxi and the chocolate." Small dolls symbolized Maxi and his mother, and a cardboard stage
symbolized their living room, with three different-colored boxes on the
wall as cupboards. The enacted story was as follows (e.g., experiment 2,
abbreviated rendition):

"Maxi and the Chocolate"

Maxi is helping his mother to unpack the shopping bag. He puts the chocolate into
the GREEN cupboard. Maxi remembers exactly where he put the chocolate so that
he can come back later and get some. Then he leaves for the playground. In his
absence his mother needs some chocolate. She takes the chocolate out of the
GREEN cupboard and uses some of it for her cake. Then she puts it back not into
the GREEN but into the BLUE cupboard. She leaves to get some eggs and Maxi
returns from the playground, hungry.

Test Question: "Where will Maxi look for the chocolate?"

Children were told another similar story with the corresponding test
question at the end.

The dark bars in figure 8.1 show how many children gave correct
answers to this question on both stories (very few gave a correct answer
on only one story), that is, saying that Maxi will look for the chocolate in
the GREEN cupboard. The developmental progression shown by these
bars indicates that children develop an understanding of belief as a
representational state of the mind at around 4 or 5 years. This accords
well with the acquisition of a representational theory of knowledge
discussed in chapter 6.

However, the findings of these first experiments on false belief raise
two important methodological questions: Do the data *overestimate*
children's understanding of belief as a misrepresentation of reality? and
Do the data actually *underestimate* children's understanding of belief?

---

*Our study focused on the mental processes (models) necessary to represent belief,
whereas an earlier study by Johnson and Maratsos (1977) focused on children's
understanding of mental verbs "think" and "know" and their implicatures, in the tradition
of Macnamara, Baker, and Olson (1976).

Overestimation?
"False
Positives"
Our investigation originated in the research tradition of showing that children acquire intellectual capacities at an earlier age than Piagetian theory would predict. [**Note 8.4** The research tradition of "Piaget Bashing".] We therefore took precautions that correct predictions of where Maxi will look for his chocolate could not easily be cast aside as a methodological artifact. One such argument against our data could have been that children make the correct prediction that Maxi will look in the empty cupboard simply because they have forgotten themselves where the chocolate really was. This possibility can be safely excluded, however, since all children who made correct predictions also remembered where the chocolate really was.

Originally we were content to argue on the basis of these data that young children have a better understanding of other people's minds than hitherto thought. I now want to make a much more specific claim on the basis of these data, namely, that they document children's acquisition of a representational theory of mind. To sustain that claim, I have to exclude the possibility that children gave correct answers on the basis of a sophisticated but nonrepresentational view of the mind. In fact, Paul Harris (in press) has recently argued this possibility by turning one of my arguments against me. I originally focused on convincing cognitive psychologists that young children's competence in understanding "mental" phenomena does not mean that they understand representation. I did not expend much argument on what most people were inclined to accept anyway, namely, that the older child, who can understand false belief, does take a representational view of mind. Having accepted my arguments about younger children, Harris now asks whether older children, too, could get by without a representational view. [**Note 8.5** Paul Harris's proposal that the false-belief task can be solved without understanding representation.]

A Nonrepresentational
Simulation of Belief
The difficult question here is whether children need to understand Maxi's belief as a mental representation or whether they can get by treating it as a hypothetical "inner world" that takes a hold on Maxi's external behavior. To answer this question, I need to discuss again what it means to predict a person's action by imputing a mental representation to that person as opposed to making the prediction as-if that person were in a hypothetical situation (as in pretense). In both cases the person's action is predicted on the basis of the nonexistent (past) situation (e.g.,

"chocolate in the GREEN cupboard"). The difference is that in the as-if case the person is also aiming to act according to that situation, whereas in the case of false belief she is not. She is aiming to act according to the real situation but still acts as though he were in a different situation. I once termed this the *puzzle of false belief* (Perner 1988, 157).

The representational view of mind solves this puzzle in an elegant way. For instance, in our experiments the child can understand that Maxi experiencing himself putting the chocolate inside the green cupboard forms a representation of the chocolate as being there. Then the chocolate is moved without Maxi being informed about it. Lacking information about its new location, Maxi keeps representing the chocolate as being in its original location. When Maxi looks for the chocolate, the representational view implies that when he is aiming at acting according to the real situation, he will be guided by his *representation of the real situation* and not by the real situation directly. But Maxi's mental representation misrepresents the real situation as a different situation ("Chocolate still in GREEN cupboard"), which explains why he acts as-if the real situation were a different one despite his aiming at the real situation.

For the nonrepresentational view the puzzle of false belief remains puzzling. However, that does not mean that younger children, limited to a nonrepresentational view of mind, could not give the correct answer about where Maxi will look. They could do so *if* the story led them to assume that Maxi was aiming at acting according to the past situation, in other words, if the story led children to assume that they are required to predict what Maxi would do if he were acting as-if (pretending) the chocolate were still in its old place.

That children "solved" our experimental tasks in this way—without any notion of belief as representational—is a real possibility. But is it likely? Intuitively, it seems rather far fetched. What in the story might have given children the idea that Maxi would act as-if the chocolate were in its old location? He is *really* hungry and he *really* wants some chocolate. So he will go where it *really* is.

I see no obvious way that our original procedure might have suggested to subjects that they were expected to predict what Maxi would do "if the chocolate were still in its old place." However, when discussing modifications of the false belief test, designed to make the test easier, we may have to contend with this possibility.

So far my critical evaluation of our data has been confined to considering the dangers of overestimating children's understanding of the mind. This concern arose from our original objective of demonstrating earlier competence than allowed for by Piagetian theory. However, we soon realized—as we told nonpsychologists about our results—that the intuitively more surprising aspect of our data was not that 4-year-olds could understand another person's different view of the world but, rather, that 3-year-olds failed to understand such a trivial aspect of mental life. Our days of Piaget bashing were over. We suddenly found ourselves on the receiving end, defending a claim about young children's limited competence. As a consequence, the methodological focus shifted to guarding against the dangers of *underestimating* children's intellectual abilities.

Underestimation? "False Negatives"   There are many reasons why the dark bars in figure 8.1 may underestimate children's true competence in understanding belief. For instance, in our first experiment we noticed that the young children, when asked where Maxi would look for the chocolate, pointed automatically—without any sign of reflection—to the chocolate's current location. So we introduced a *stop-&-think* condition in which children were simply asked to stop and think before answering the test question. The hatched bars in figure 8.1 show that this reminder eliminated all errors from the responses by 5-year-old children but had no effect on younger children. I am inclined to think that the hatched bars in figure 8.1 therefore reflect children's true competence in understanding belief better than the dark bars.

In this experiment we also used another technique to suppress children's automatic responses to the chocolate's actual location by simply providing no such location. This was achieved in a *disappear* condition. Instead of the chocolate being transferred from one cupboard to another, it was all used up in a cake that Maxi's mother made and then gave away (the cake was taken off stage). The dotted bars in figure 8.1 show that this change now brought even 4-year-olds close to perfection. Remarkably, however, these changes had no effect whatsoever on the 3-year-olds. They kept pointing to the chocolate's actual location even when it was ground up in a cake behind the scenes.

In subsequent research we controlled for further possible ways in which we might have underestimated the 3-year-old child's competence. For instance, the youngest children may have had difficulty following and remembering our stories. Alerted to this possibility by Peter Bryant and

Tom Trabasso's (1981) critique of Piagetian studies on logical reasoning, we asked children at the end about various events in the story. They had little difficulty remembering (Wimmer and Perner 1983). However, we had forgotten to check memory for one very important nonevent, namely, that *Maxi had not seen where his mother had put the chocolate*. If children did not take in this fact, then they would be quite justified in predicting that Maxi would look for the chocolate where it really was. And this worry was not without substance, since children did find the question "Did Maxi see where his mother put the chocolate?" quite a challenge.[*] To make sure that even this fact was registered, we emphasized Maxi's absence at the time of transfer, and before the crucial test question was asked we reminded children of it (Perner, Leekam, and Wimmer 1987, experiment 1):

> "Maxi is still on the playground. He *couldn't see* where his mother put the chocolate. When Maxi comes home, where will he look for his chocolate?"

With this method we got correct responses even from several 3-year-olds, but, as figure 8.2 shows, only from older 3-year-olds. Below 3½ years very few children answered correctly. Also, whereas children older than 3½ improved on a second story, of the many younger children in great need of such improvement, only one was able to take advantage of the repeated exposure to the same story pattern. And young children's persistent failure to predict that Maxi would look in the empty cupboard could not be due to memory failure, since 12 of the 16 younger 3-year-olds who gave consistently wrong answers could remember Maxi's lack of information and several other story events.

These data show that although some children may understand belief as early as 3 years, there are very few of them. But it is these children who may account for the rare examples of elaborate talk about belief at an early age (for instance, Abe's precocious remarks reported by Shatz, Wellman, and Silber 1983). At 3½ years a noticeable number of children gave correct answers in this last experiment. However, to conclude that these children did, therefore, really understand belief, we have to rule out that the modifications to our original belief task did not elicit "false positives." And, indeed, this possibility is difficult to discount.

---

[*]One could argue that this fact in itself—that children did not spontaneously pay attention to the protagonist's informational gap—attests to their lack of an "informational-representational theory of mind."

The Over-/Under-Estimation Gap   With our efforts to take any unnecessary difficulties out of our task in order to avoid underestimation of children's true competence, we may have raised the dangers of overestimation. For instance, because we made Maxi's chocolate disappear (ground up in a cake removed from the scene), some 4-year-olds may have realized that the chocolate that Maxi is looking for does not exist any more (at least not in an acceptable state or not within reasonable limits of search). So there is no sensible realistic answer to the question where he will look for it. "Nowhere!" As a next best choice these children may have translated the question "Where will Maxi look?" into "Where would Maxi look if the chocolate still existed within attainable limits?" The best answer to this hypothetical scenario is "In the GREEN cupboard," where the chocolate used to be before it was ground up and taken away. Notice that children who engaged in some such hypothetical reasoning would have given the correct answer without really understanding Maxi's belief as misrepresenting the chocolate's actual location.

Similarly, the heavy emphasis on Maxi's not having seen his mother transfer the chocolate to the new location may have induced a sense that Maxi would therefore not look in the right location. And this is not implausible since, as pointed out in chapter 6, even infants understand something about the connection between "looking" or "seeing" and "getting it right." Again, this makes it not implausible that correct answers were given without proper understanding of belief. [**Note 8.6** Three-year-old children's belief explanations of mistaken action.]

It is remarkable that despite these possible ways in which children may have been unduly helped in giving the correct answers, at 3 years extremely few were able to answer correctly. No other study has succeeded in demonstrating understanding of belief at the age of 3 years by a convincing majority of children.

We can summarize one side of the story, then, by saying that children acquire an understanding of belief not much before the age of 4 years. And on the basis of the original, more conservative procedure we can summarize the other side by saying that from 4 years up a substantial proportion of children and from 5 years up most children understand belief as a mental representation of reality. These age boundaries go remarkably well with the evidence cited in chapter 6 about children's acquisition of a representational theory of knowledge and the evidence cited in chapter 4 about understanding external representations *as* representations.

What's So Difficult About False Belief? Having satisfied ourselves that young children do not just flounder on our experimental procedures but have genuine difficulty in understanding belief, we can now ask the more substantial question regarding the source of this difficulty. Two general kinds of explanation have been put forward:

1. Failure to understand causal connections: In this class of explanation it is assumed that children understand (can mentally represent) that someone has a false belief, but they fail to understand what role beliefs can play in the *causal fabric of real events*. For instance, children's difficulty with Maxi resides in understanding that a sequence of real events—Maxi sees where the chocolate is stored and then he is absent when the chocolate is moved—leads to Maxi's belief that the chocolate is still in its original place. Heinz Wimmer formulates this hypothesis specifically as a difficulty in understanding of how beliefs are formed (Wimmer, Hogrefe, and Sodian 1988). Alan Leslie (1988) intends it more generally. That is, even when children were told where Maxi believed the chocolate was, they could not understand the causal effect

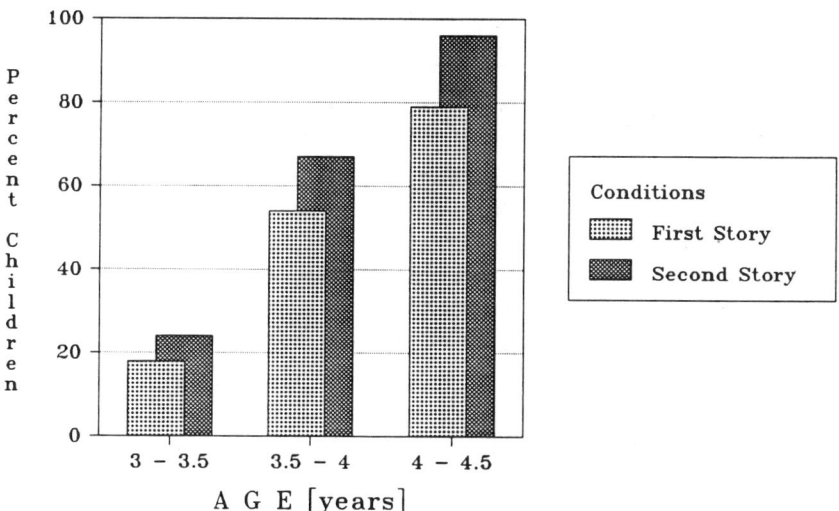

Figure 8.2
Correct answers to belief question.
Data from Perner, Leekam, and Wimmer 1987, experiment 1.

of Maxi's belief on his action, hence could not predict where Maxi would look.

2. Metarepresentational deficit: In this class of explanation it is assumed that children fail to understand belief because they have difficulty understanding that something represents; that is, they cannot *represent* that something is a *representation*. This is the position I have been taking in this chapter (also in Perner 1988). Similar proposals include those by John Flavell (1988), Lynd Forguson and Alison Gopnik (1988),* and David Olson (1988).

An elegant test of these two classes of hypothesis has been provided by Alison Gopnik and Janet Astington (1988). Instead of asking children about another person's false belief, they investigated whether children could understand changes in their own beliefs, that is, remember that they had earlier held a false belief. If changes in their own beliefs are as difficult for children to understand as beliefs in others, then understanding the causal origin of belief cannot be the critical factor, since children can internally experience their own beliefs without having to understand how they are formed. However, if children have no difficulty remembering what they thought in contrast to what they now know, then they have the metarepresentational ability to represent their own belief. In that case their difficulty with the traditional belief task must be due to failure in understanding how beliefs are formed in others.

The new test was carried out with a somewhat different, more elegant method. In this test children are shown a typical container—for instance, a tube of Smarties (confectionery well known to all British and Canadian youngsters, which is similar in content but not in packaging to M&Ms in the United States of America) and they are asked what is in that tube. All children answer "Smarties." They are then shown that they are mistaken. There are no Smarties inside—just a boring pencil. When this method was originally devised (Hogrefe, Wimmer, and Perner 1986; Perner, Leekam, and Wimmer 1987), it was used to ask children what another child (who had not seen the tube before) would think it contained when shown it, just as they themselves had been shown it a minute ago. Gopnik and Astington's important change consisted in asking the children what they themselves had thought was in the tube when they were first shown it. Results spoke quite clearly in favor of a *metarepresen-*

---

*I have discussed elsewhere my difficulties in interpreting their position (Perner 1988, 161–162).

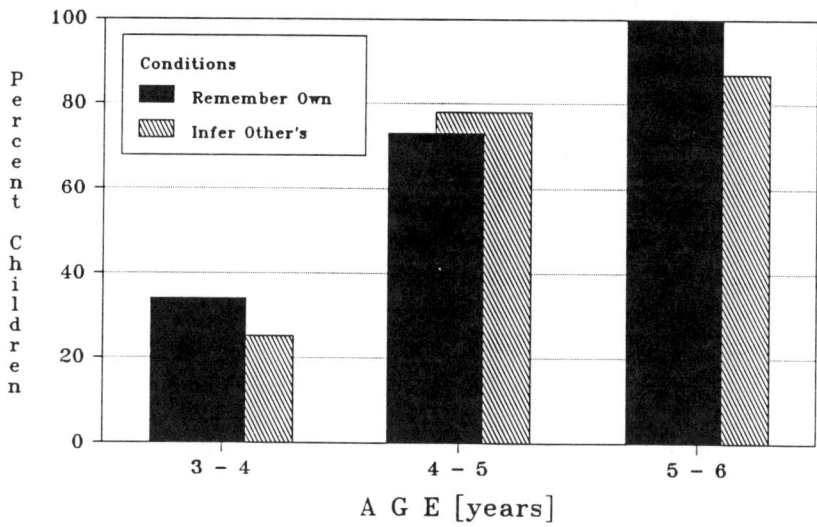

Figure 8.3
Understanding own and other's belief.
Data from Wimmer and Hartl, in press, experiment 1.

tational deficit. Children found it as difficult—if not even more so—to remember their own false belief as to predict what another child would think.

Heinz Wimmer realized the dangerous implications for his theory (Wimmer, Hogrefe, and Sodian 1988) and embarked on a larger replication effort in the hope of proving Gopnik and Astington's finding to be a procedural artifact (Wimmer and Hartl, in press). But his hopes were thwarted.[*] As figure 8.3 shows, children's memory for their own false belief (dark bars) was as bad as their ability to predict another child's belief (hatched bars).

Wimmer and Hartl were also able to show that children were not just reluctant to admit their own mistake. This was tested by seating the child right next to another person and showing both of them the deceptive container (a typical matchbox containing chocolate). Both the child and

---

[*]At Heinz Wimmer's request I add that he consoled himself very quickly by realizing what good company he was in, since these data also pose a problem for the view of mind espoused by René Descartes. I discuss the implications of these results for Descartes's philosophy of mind in chapter 11.

the experimenter's confederate stated audibly that they thought there were matches in the box. After their mistake was revealed, children were just as unable to recall what the person next to them had said he'd thought (hatched bar in figure 8.4, right panel: "experiment 3") as they were to recall their own mistake (dark bars). Since children are usually not reluctant to gloat over others' mistakes and since the other person's belief was made explicit in his mistaken statement, children's inability to recall another person's mistake confirms again that they find it difficult to *represent* belief and not just to infer it from the informational conditions that led to it.

Importantly, children's difficulty in remembering their own and another person's false belief cannot be attributed to problems of memory for past thoughts. In a control condition the matchbox was filled with matches and children's initial predictions were thus correct. The matches were then removed and replaced by chocolate. So at this point the situation was the same as in the other conditions (chocolate in the matchbox), but children had little difficulty remembering that they had (correctly) thought there had been matches in the box when first shown (dotted bar in figure 8.4, left panel: "experiment 2").

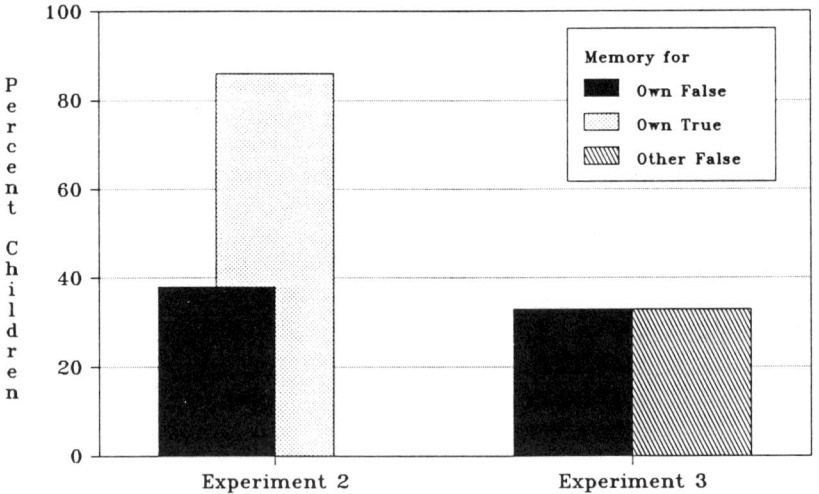

Figure 8.4
Memory for beliefs.
Data from Wimmer and Hartl, in press, experiments 2 and 3.

Success on this control condition also makes clear that the difficulty with belief goes beyond a mere linguistic difficulty—in particular, difficulty getting the intended temporal reference straight, as Lewis and Osborne (1990) have argued. Children might wrongly answer with the box's true contents because they construe the experimenter's question as referring to the time *after* the true contents had been revealed instead of to the point in time *before* that revelation. If that were the difficulty, then one would expect children to encounter similar difficulty interpreting the same question in the control condition as referring to the point in time *before* the change in content rather than the point in time *after* that change. The good performance in the control condition, however, makes this hypothesis implausible.

These results thus confirm that children before the age of about 4 years have a deep seated difficulty with belief. My argument is that this difficulty stems from having to understand belief as a misconception of reality. This understanding is necessary because a clear differentiation between the belief's referent (reality) and its sense (what reality is represented as) is required. And so these data confirm my overall claim that children acquire the metarepresentational ability to mentally represent that something is a representation (or misrepresentation) around 4 years. In the following section I look at children's ability to use their understanding of belief to their advantage by manipulating another person's beliefs in acts of deception.

Deception and Lying

Deception involves manipulation of others' behavior by manipulating their information so as to induce a false belief about reality. Hence, acts of deception are potentially useful indicators of the deceiver's understanding of belief and thus of a representational-informational conception of mind. Furthermore, since deception is a practical, real-life action of practical significance and emotional involvement, it seems the perfect way to study children's ability to attribute beliefs to other people, just as it has been one of the main methods for studying the "theory of mind" in chimpanzees and other apes (Goodall 1968; Woodruff and Premack 1979; deWaal 1982; Byrne and Whiten 1988).

When we, in human company, accuse each other of having committed an act of deception, we imply that the act was *conceived as deception*, that is, as an act intended to manipulate the victim's belief. And that intention is responsible for the great moral upset about deception. However, not every act that happens to work by deceiving someone was necessarily conceived as an act of deception. Only acts that were planned as acts of deception are based on an understanding of belief constituting genuine deception (see Mitchell 1986 for several grades of deception). Distinguishing genuine from fortuitous acts of deception poses a difficult methodological problem.

Deception by Animals   Even plants and insects manipulate their predators' information and belief by mimicry and camouflage within their surrounding environment. But who wants to say that they do so by understanding the effect of their mimicry on the beliefs of their predators? The standard intuition is that evolution, by trial and error, preprogrammed these strategies of mimicry. Because mimicry is preprogrammed, it is automatic. The mimic's color adapts to its surroundings regardless of whether a predator is nearby or not.

Birds like the plover are capable of much more sophisticated acts of deception. For instance, the plover flies from her nest and feigns a broken wing when a predator approaches, to lead the intruder away from her young. Moreover, Carolyn Ristau (in press) has shown that the bird can adjust quite flexibly to the intruder. For instance, she may ignore an intruder who merely passes by or is not looking at the nest, reserving her distractive action only for the serious intruder who is heading for or looking at the nest. Despite this flexibility with respect to when the feigning act is triggered, David Premack (1988, 161, 162) argues that it is still unlikely that this act is based on an understanding of belief manipulation. A concept of informational manipulation would enable the bird to employ a similar strategy for a variety of ends, like luring competitors away from the food supply or a receptive mate. However, the bird's "deception" occurs quite rigidly, only in the service of protecting her offspring.

Other acts that work by deception (but are not genuine cases of deception) and that are not preprogrammed by evolution have anecdotally been reported of dogs. Here is the story of Ashley's dog, as related by Daniel Dennett (1978, 274–275):

One evening I was sitting in a chair at my home, the *only* chair my dog is allowed to sleep in. The dog was lying in front of me, whimpering. She was getting nowhere in her trying to "convince" me to give up the chair to her. Her next move is the most interesting, nay, the *only* interesting part of the story. She stood up, and went to the front door where I could still easily see her. She scratched the door, giving me the impression that she had given up trying to get the chair and had decided to go out.

However as soon as I reached the door to let her out, she ran back across the room and climbed into her chair, the chair she had "forced" me to leave.

As in the case of the feigning plover, the dog's ploy worked by deception. Yet in contrast to the bird's feigning reflex to approaching intruders, dogs do not have an innate mechanism to scratch the door when their master is occupying their chair. And since the dog's behavior seemed quite novel for the occasion, it attests to a remarkable feat of creative reasoning on her part. However, the question remains whether it was genuine deception. Did the dog aim to manipulate her master's belief in order to make him get up? Or did she aim at getting her master out of the chair by using a routine she knew had worked before? Difficult to decide. But the case gives us a better understanding of what possibilities we need to rule out before we can interpret the act as one of genuine deception.

Criteria for Genuine Deception   Analysis of genuinely deceptive acts and fortuitous cases of deception provides the following critical variables. In a given environmental *setting* the deceiver carries out the *critical act*, which affects the opponent's *belief* in such a way that the *opponent's action* results in an expedient outcome for the deceiver. To identify genuine cases of deception, then, one has to be able to rule out two important possibilities.

Criteria for genuine deception by eliminating the possibility
(1) that there is an innate tendency to carry out the *critical act* in the particular *setting*, as for instance in the plover's feigning action, and
(2) that the *critical act* is not known by experience to elicit the *opponent's action* in the current *setting*, as for instance in Ashley's anecdote about his dog.

Since these possibilities are difficult to rule out for animal anecdotes, the discussion continues whether animals are able to impute beliefs and other mental states (e.g., Whiten and Byrne 1988) or not (Premack 1988). Now let us see how the ability to deceive develops in children and at what age their actions are geared to manipulating belief.

Early Deception and "Pseudo-Lies"   From early on children intentionally act in a "deceptive" way. The question, however, is what part of that action they intended. It seems clear that they intend the effect of their action, as is suggested by the following observation by Piaget on his 16½-month-old daughter Jacqueline:

Jacqueline has just been wrested from a game she wants to continue and placed in her playpen from which she wants to get out. She calls, but in vain. Then she clearly expresses a certain need, although the events of the last ten minutes prove that she no longer experiences it. No sooner has she left the playpen than she indicates the game she wishes to resume! (Piaget 1937/1954, 297)

This observation is very suggestive of the fact that Jacqueline intended to be taken out of the playpen by "expressing a certain need." However, her expression of this need does not allow us to conclude that she was genuinely trying to deceive her mother, since we cannot rule out (criterion 2) the rather plausible possibility that Jacqueline knew that "expression of her need" would result in her being taken out of her playpen. Although this is an impressive feat of creative reasoning, it does not imply that Jacqueline was intentionally manipulating her mother's belief.

Clara and William Stern (1909/1931), who were among the first to systematically study children's lies from observing their own children and from reports of other parents, noted that many of the early apparent cases of lying were not genuine acts of deception; to refer to these cases, they coined the term "pseudo-lies" (my translation of "Scheinlügen"). A particular interesting class are what the Sterns called "provoked pseudo-lies." These pseudo-lies occur when children are confronted with something embarrassing. For instance, when asked, "Did you hurt your brother?", they answer, "No." However, as the Sterns pointed out, with this "no" children often do not express a claim to the contrary ("I did not do it") but instead express a desire to avoid being reminded of the embarrassing fact.

Lewis, Stanger, and Sullivan (1989) confronted children with an embarrassing fact under laboratory conditions. Thirty-three children aged 2 years and 9 months to 3 years and 1 month were seated with their back to a table on which the experimenter put out a surprise, a toy zoo. Children were instructed not to peek while the experimenter was out of the room and were told that they could play with the toy when the experimenter returned. The experimenter then left the room and returned after 5 minutes or as soon as the child did peek. Only 4 children did not peek. When asked whether they had peeked, these children said, "No." Of the 29 peekers, 11 said "yes," 11 said "no," and 7 did not give any answer.

Keeping in mind Clara and William Stern's admonition about how to interpret such "no"s, one should not conclude from these data that 3-year old children engage in genuine deception. In the first place, their "no" may not have been a denial of the fact that they had peeked but instead may have been an avoidance reaction. And even if they meant "No, I didn't look," we cannot be sure whether they *intended* to make the experimenter *believe* they hadn't peeked or whether they just used denials as a well worn strategy for avoiding reproach.

Stern and Stern (p. 222) also note that children have standard formulae for avoiding the unpalatable, citing the example of one child who pretended to be in pain ("Hurt, hurt") whenever he was asked to do something he did not like to do. I remember Jacob at 3½ saying "I am soo tired" as a standard ploy for getting his way. This seemed sometimes extremely appropriate (for instance, when he wanted to be carried on a mountain hike), but sometimes patently out of place (for instance, when he was trying to escape bedtime). It is exactly the rigidity with which these early "lies" are used that reveals them as no more than previously successful strategies for avoiding the undesirable, rather than genuine cases of deception designed to manipulate the other person's belief.

Genuine Deception by Children   Joan Peskin (1989) tested children's ability to hide their own intention in a simulation of quite natural situations where another person wants exactly the same thing the child wants. For this purpose sets of four stickers were used. All children tended to prefer a particular sticker. Each child was told that she could have that sticker, *but* that two puppets would each be allowed to choose a sticker first. They were also told that the puppet in the dark dress never wanted to choose the sticker that the child liked best, but that the puppet in the light dress always wanted the sticker that the child was after (an all too familiar situation among siblings and peers). First the (friendly) puppet in the dark dress came to choose a sticker. It asked the child beforehand which sticker she herself was going to pick. Practically all children pointed truthfully to their preferred item.

Then the (competitive) puppet in the light dress came and asked the child for her preference before making its own choice. Now there was a large difference between ages, as the dotted bars in the foreground of figure 8.5 show. Nearly all 3- and 4-year-olds pointed truthfully, but naively, to their preferred item and were quite frustrated when the puppet chose that very item for itself. In contrast, most 5-year-olds pointed to an item they didn't like (a few refused to disclose their first choice). After this first trial children were given four more.* Quite remarkably, 3-year-olds, despite their mounting frustration at seeing their preferred item snatched away each time by the competitive puppet, kept pointing truthfully to their first choice. On the fifth and last trial still only two of them concealed what their choice was (see cross-hatched bars in the background of figure 8.5; one refused to answer and one pointed to a different item). Four-year-olds quickly learned after their first frustration. Already on the second trial half of them concealed their choice (hatched bars).

From this result I want to draw two conclusions. First, by the age of 5 years most children (and even at the age of 4 years many children) understand how to influence a competitor's action by manipulating information. Second, most 3-year-olds find it extremely difficult to do that. Do these conclusions hold up under closer scrutiny?

Let us begin with the oldest children. To establish that Peskin's 5-year-olds concealed their preference because they intended to manipulate the puppet's belief, we have to exclude other possibilities according to my two criteria. The first criterion is easy to satisfy; we may safely claim that there is no innate tendency to be silent or point to a wrong item when asked about one's preferences. The second criterion is somewhat more difficult to satisfy. Ashley's anecdote about his dog makes clear that strategies like, "If I want my master to get up from the chair, then I go to the door and scratch" need to be ruled out. In the case of Peskin's study we have to exclude the existence of a strategy like: "If somebody asks me what I like best and I don't want that person to snatch away what I like, then I point to something else." That children could have used such a rule is excluded by the fact that they truthfully reported their choice to the other (friendly) puppet in the dark dress. So this experiment is one up on Ashley's anecdote about his dog.

Perhaps children have developed a more specific strategy: "If somebody, *who I know takes whatever I like best,* asks me what I like best, then I point to something else." However, such a strategy is unlikely for two reasons. Although the situation where a sibling wants to have exactly what the child wants is more than familiar to even the youngest, the conflict usually occurs after the child has started playing with the desired toy. It is less likely that the other child first asks, "What do you want?"

---

*On two of those trials (order counterbalanced) they had to answer on behalf of a friend of the same age and sex. There was no difference between answers on their own behalf and answers on behalf of their friend.

and then goes for it. This is particularly unlikely to happen when an adult is watching, since adults tend to arbitrate on a "first-want-first-served" rule in disputes over toys. So, one could argue, with an adult present it is usually safest to declare one's choice to stake one's claim; and to keep quiet about it is actually an unusual thing to do. The 5-year-olds in Peskin's study must therefore have arrived at their deceptive strategy by reasoning out its informational effect on the puppet's mind.

In the case of Peskin's 4-year-olds it is more difficult to defend their concealment efforts as genuine acts of deception (informational manipulation) since these acts did not occur spontaneously on the first trial. However, if these children had been trying to explore strategies over trials, then improvement would have been gradual. The fact that almost all 4-year-olds who ever discovered a deceptive strategy did so on the second trial suggests that these children did possess an understanding of belief manipulation.

Finally the 3-year-olds. Peskin's data give no support to the idea that any noteworthy number of them were able to deceive. In fact, their repeated failure to employ deception despite their apparent frustration over losing their favorite item strongly suggests a conceptual deficit.

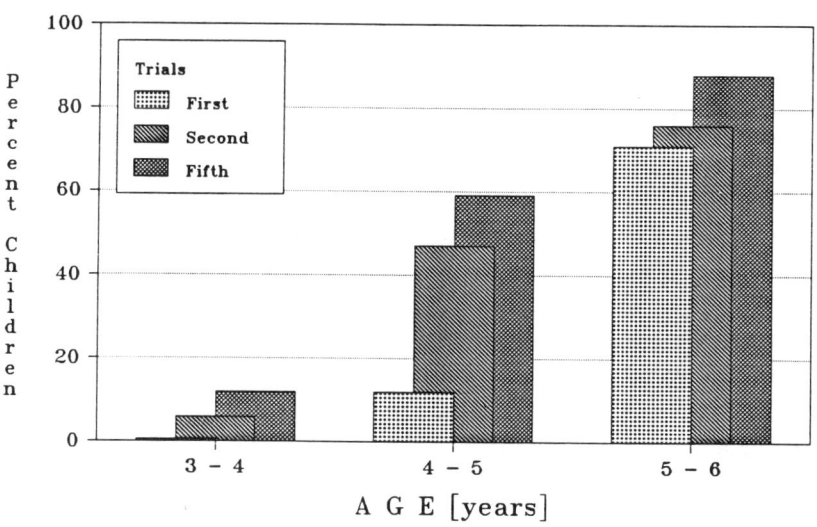

Figure 8.5
Deceptive Responses.
Data from Peskin 1989, study 2.

Furthermore, data from a control condition rule out the possibility that
these children simply failed to appreciate the competitive puppet's
intentions. On these trials children were given a choice between only
two stickers, and they were allowed to decide which of the two puppets
should have first choice before themselves. Of the 17 3-year-olds, 15
chose the (friendly) puppet in dark clothes. This decision stands in stark
contrast to their inability on subsequent regular trials to conceal their
preference from the competitive puppet (figure 8.5). However, 9 of the
3-year-olds spontaneously tried to *physically prevent* that puppet from
taking their favorite item by placing their arm around it, putting it under
the table, refusing to hand it over, and so on.

Young children's failure to deceive or conceal on this task can certainly
not be attributed to a lack of familiarity with the situation, or a lack of
emotional involvement, which Chandler, Fritz, and Hala (1989) have
suggested accounts for children's difficulty under traditional methods of
assessment. [Note 8.7 Claims about experimental evidence for early
deception by children.]

Three-year-olds' inability to deceive can be even better highlighted by
contrasting it with their ability to sabotage a competitor by physical
means. This has been demonstrated by Beate Sodian (in press).

Deceit versus Sabotage   Deceit and sabotage are both cases of what Wilensky (1978)
has called "antiplanning." *Antiplans* are plans about how to
prevent a competitor from executing his plan and reaching his
goal. *Sabotage* achieves this *antigoal* by manipulating the physical world
so that the competitor is deprived of a necessary condition for reaching
his goal. For instance, if the competitor wants to get a treasure from a
box, he first needs to open the box. By locking the box and removing the
key, one makes the necessary step of opening the box more difficult, if
not impossible. *Deceit*, in contrast, achieves the *antigoal* by manipulating the competitor's beliefs about the state of the world so that he will
take the wrong action. For instance, in the case of the treasure one can
misinform the competitor about where the treasure is so that he will go
elsewhere.

Beate Sodian (in press) had children from 3 to 4½ years hide a
treasure of playcoins in one of two boxes. On *competitive* trials in the
sabotage condition a robber came to look for the treasure. Being lazy, he
would look into only one box. It was made clear to the child that the
robber would take the treasure if he found it, but if he didn't the child

could keep the coins. So as the robber was announced the experimenter said,

Inducement to Sabotage
"Now you make it hard for the robber to get the coins. Don't let him get them. Which box do you want to lock?" (and the two response options were pointed out)

As a check on whether some children might suggest locking the box just for the fun of it, a king appeared on *noncompetitive* control trials. The king, equally lazy, was also willing to open just one box. However, when he found the treasure, he would add some more coins for the child. Accordingly, children were instructed, "Now you make it easy for the king to get the coins. Help him find them," and they were asked the same question about which box to lock as on the trials with the robber.

From the viewpoint of a healthy and (in defense against a robber) morally justified self-interest the child's correct answer was to lock the box with the coins for the robber and to lock the empty box for the king. The hatched bars in the background of figure 8.6 show the percentages of children who gave correct answers on the robber trial *and* on the king trial. Even the younger 3-year-olds, although they had their difficulties

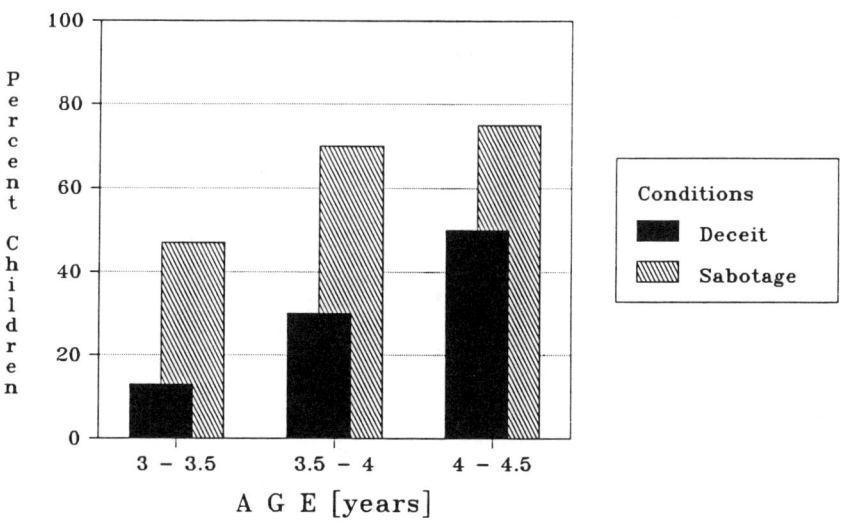

Figure 8.6
Adequate responses for king and robber.
Data from Sodian, in press.

with the task, were far from being incapable saboteurs (most errors consisted in locking the full box for the king).*

This contrasts quite sharply with these children's near inability to think of deception as a way of preventing the robber from getting at the treasure. In the *deception* condition children had the same two trials (robber and king) as in the sabotage condition. But the problem was what to do when the robber or king came to ask where the treasure was:

> Inducement to Deceive
> "Now you make it hard for the robber to get the coins. Don't let him get them." And as the robber asked the child, "Where are the coins?", the child was helped by the experimenter ("Where do you want to point?") and the two options were demonstrated.

As the dark bars in figure 8.6 show, very few 3-year-olds (older or younger) thought of pointing to the empty box in order to make it harder for the robber to find the coins. By the age of 4 years about half of the children thought this a good method.

These results parallel quite closely the developmental trend in Peskin's study, showing that children start to appreciate the expedient effects of deception from about 4 years onward. In addition, the considerable gap between young children's use of sabotage (locking the full box) and their reluctance to rely on a deceptive strategy (pointing to the empty box) suggests a specific difficulty with deception. It is not the demands of the experimental task that make children look incapable of deception, since the cognitive demands of the sabotage task were comparable.

This specific difficulty with deception in most 3- and some 4-year-olds fits the finding in most other studies that children do not conceive of the mind as a representational system before the age of 4 years. Therefore, they cannot understand the point of deception, namely, to manipulate mental representations.

---

*Having to lock the empty box for the king was of course thought of as helping him find the coins in the other box. However, this requirement seems a bit superfluous and made this condition more difficult than it needed to be. The sabotage condition was therefore a somewhat conservative measure of children's ability, which makes the finding that sabotage was understood much earlier than deception even more remarkable.

Onset of Lying:
Adult Intuition
That something important is happening around the age of 4 years in children's understanding of the deceptive use of language is also suggested by adults' intuition. Stouthamer-Loeber (1986) asked 21 teachers at 11 day-care centers and the mothers of 80 4-year-olds at what age they thought children are able to tell a *deliberate lie*. As one would expect, answers varied. One mother thought children able to do so even at 1 year of age; several others thought them still unable to do so by 5½ years. But as figure 8.7 shows, within that span of uncertainty the only point where intuitive judgments made something of a leap was at the age of 4 years.

Thus, mothers and day-care teachers, who are quite intimate with children of this age in their natural environment, tend to agree that 4 is the age when most children become capable of genuine deception. This provides a welcome validation of the experimental data, which are often criticized as having been collected in the unusual situation of children being interviewed by a stranger—a situation in which such young children (some would argue) may not display their full intellectual abilities.

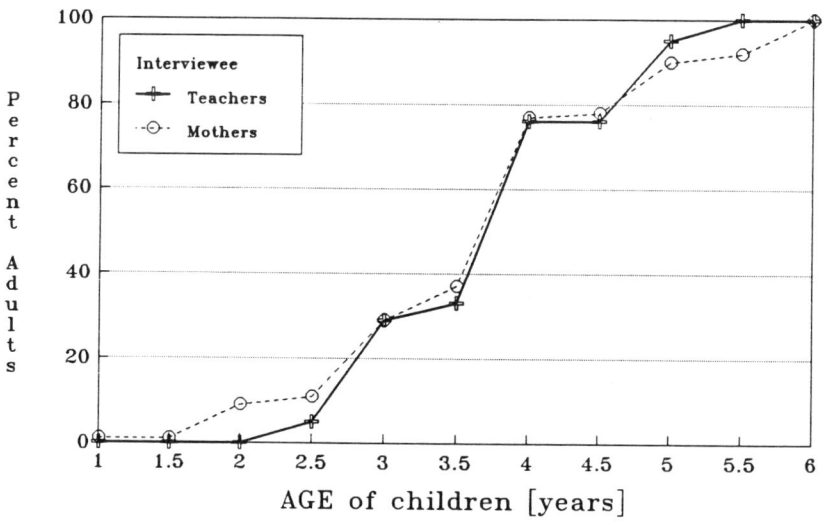

Figure 8.7
Children thought capable of deliberate lies.
Data from Stouthamer-Loeber 1986, table 1.

That our tasks for testing children's understanding of belief and deception are tapping important conceptual changes is further validated by the fact that there is a group of mentally impaired children who show a specific deficit in this respect.

Autism

Autism is a rare but severe developmental disorder. Its main diagnostic criteria are impairment in verbal and nonverbal communication and a general problem in coping with the social environment. This social aloofness and withdrawal led two quite independent researchers to label the disorder "autism" (Asperger 1944; Kanner 1943). Uta Frith's (1989) book gives a good introduction to the syndrome in general and to recent research into autistic children's problem with a "theory of mind."

Although autism is usually paired with severe mental retardation, about 30% of afflicted children are of "normal" intelligence; that is, they have an IQ of 70 or higher. Simon Baron-Cohen, Alan Leslie, and Uta Frith (1985) tested a group of 20 intelligent autistic children on a version of our (Wimmer and Perner 1983) false belief task and assessed them for their verbal and nonverbal IQ. Their performance on all these tasks was

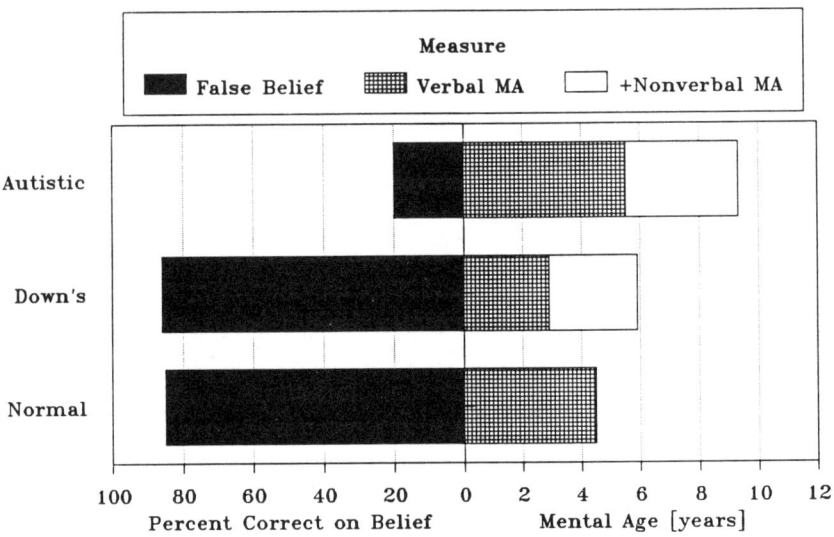

Figure 8.8
Understanding of false belief and mental age.
Data from Baron-Cohen, Leslie, and Frith 1985.

compared to that of 14 children with Down's syndrome and 27 normal children aged 3½ to 6 years. The dark bars in figure 8.8 show a specific inability on the part of the autistic children to understand belief. Only 4 of the 20 autistic children gave correct answers to the belief task, whereas almost all the normal children and children with Down's syndrome were able to do so. This difference cannot be explained by saying that the autistic children were more severely impaired since even their *verbal mental age* (as measured by the British Picture Vocabulary Test), shown by the checkered bars in figure 8.8, and especially their *nonverbal mental age* (white portions in figure 8.8 give non-verbal mental age in excess of verbal mental age), was considerably higher than that of the other groups of children. Thus, autism seems characterized by a rather specific inability to understand belief.

Baron-Cohen, Leslie, and Frith drew the conclusion that *autistic children lack a "theory of mind."* Existing data certainly suggest such a conclusion, but further research is needed to substantiate this claim and what, precisely, it means. In any case, the specific problem that autistic children encounter seems to carry over to their inability to deceive. Beate Sodian and Uta Frith are finding that it is more difficult for autistic children to mislead a competitor by lying about an object's location than it is for a control group of mentally retarded children. However, they tend to be better than the control group in preventing the competitor from interfering with their own goals by physical sabotage.

Jim Russell and his group (Russell, Sharpe, and Mauthner 1989) trained 3- and 4-year-old normal children, children with Down's syndrome, and autistic children in the following task. Children did not know which of two boxes a piece of chocolate was hidden in but were required to point to one box. A confederate of the experimenter then looked inside the indicated box. If the chocolate happened to be there, she ate it; otherwise, the child could keep it. This was repeated 15 times so that children really understood the effects of their pointing. Then the original boxes were replaced by boxes with windows on the child's side so that the child could see where the chocolate was. The question was whether children would spontaneously point to the empty box.

Autistic children and 3-year-olds were hopeless and remained so even when the windowed boxes were presented for another 20 trials. Only 1 of 17 3-year-olds and 2 of 11 autistic children deceived on the first window trial. In contrast, 10 of 16 4-year-olds and 14 of 16 children with Down's syndrome did so (and except for one 4-year-old all of them caught on to the deceptive strategy at some later point). Furthermore, there was a good correspondence between the ability to use a deceptive strategy and the ability to answer our belief task correctly.

Their inability to deceive substantiates the original finding that autistic children have difficulty with false belief. But what about other mental states? There is some evidence that mental states that do not require a representational theory of mind are—at least—not as difficult to attribute as false belief for autistic children. For instance, they can solve level 1 perspective tasks (what a person can and cannot see; Hobson 1984), and their understanding that seeing leads to knowing is somewhat better than their understanding of false belief (Perner, et al. 1989) and in some tasks is almost unimpaired (Leekam and Perner, unpublished research: 13 of 18 correct choices of boy who has looked inside over boy who was not allowed to, as in the task reported by Perner and Ogden 1988). Their understanding of simple emotions is not perfect (Harris and Muncer 1988) but may not be worse than that of other mentally retarded groups (Baron-Cohen 1989b).

At present, then, it may indeed be the case that autism is—at least in part—characterized by a specific lack of a theory of mind. That is, autistic children may be able to some degree to impute mental states as theoretical constructs in explanations of behavior, but they lack insight into the representational nature of mind, which helps in understanding how the mind works. [**Note 8.8** Do autistic children have a metarepresentational deficit?]

Summary

I started by pointing out that children's use and comprehension of the word "think" should not be equated with their understanding of belief, since this word has multiple uses. In particular, as exemplified in the combination *"thinking-of"* it can express "contemplation," "interest," or "preference"—but it cannot express belief, which is instead marked by the combination *"thinking-that."*

This distinction is theoretically important because what a person is thinking-of can be understood by the young situation theorist as a relation between person and thought-of situation. The same is not possible for belief, which cannot be represented as a relation between person and "thought-that" situation. Rather, a *representational theory of mind* is required to understand that *belief* represents something (referent) *as* something (sense).

I suggested that our Maxi-and-the-chocolate story assessed proper understanding of belief, but I warned that attempts to make it easier to avoid underestimation of children's competence might increase the dangers of overestimation. Current evidence suggests that children understand belief between 3½ and 5 years. That belief is understood at this age is also confirmed by findings that children between 3½ and 5 start to manipulate a competitor's belief in acts of *deception* and *lying*.

Finally, I presented evidence that the inability to understand belief and the inability to deceive are hallmarks of *autism*, suggesting that autistic children may *lack a representational theory of mind*. The fact that autistic children have such a specific problem with false belief confirms that normal developmental progress on belief tasks is not due to some common task factor but indeed reflects an important conceptual advance.

Chapter 9

Understanding Desire and Gaining Self-Control

In previous chapters I have said much about those mental states that represent the world as it is *known, believed,* or *assumed* to be. Emphasis on these *epistemic* or *cognitive* states of the mind reflects the research bias in this particular area and also more generally in cognitive science, philosophy of mind, and semantics of mental state reports. However, epistemic states constitute only half of what is needed. Any information-using system of interest needs more than information about the world. It also needs a representation of how the world *should be* (goal states). Even the humble thermostat needs more than just a mechanism for sensing the temperature in a room. It also needs to store the value of the *desired* temperature so that it "knows" to switch the furnace on when the temperature falls below that value.

Commonsense psychology describes human action in even richer terms. It speaks of what we *desire* and of what we *intend* to do. Two levels are involved. At the level of situations and actions there are *goals* and *(goal-directed) actions*. At the mental level there are *desires* and *intentions*. Desires are about desired situations and intentions are about goal-directed action. The developmental question focuses first on when children understand goal-directed action at the level of situations and actions and then on when they understand it at the mental level. They treat desires first as relations to desired situations and then as mental representations of situations. Treating desires as mental representations becomes necessary for understanding how desires change and how they can be controlled. These considerations lead to the interesting speculation that by better understanding their own desires, children gain increasing self-control.

Understanding Goal-Directed Action

From early on infants have goals, since—as Jerry Bruner (1973) has argued on the basis of cybernetic theory—any coordinated action that corrects for deviation from some norm (e.g., hand movement guided by vision) requires representation of that norm (what is intended). But do infants represent *that* they have such a goal and that the purpose of their action is to bring reality closer to that goal? To understand this, a complex model is needed for representing reality as it is and as it is desired to be. I claimed in chapters 3 and 4 that this ability emerges in the second year and that children should therefore start at about this age to understand that they have goals and engage in goal-directed action. To confirm this expectation, we have to look at different indicators of the emergence of such declarative understanding of goals.

Success and Failure   To engage in goal-directed action, one need not be aware of being engaged in it. But without such awareness, what happens when action meets with success or failure? The infant will simply repeat the action or, if the internal motivation changes, go on to some other activity. And such repetition, which Piaget (1936/1953) so aptly described as *circular reactions*, is typical of the first year of life.

> In the evening of [3 months and 13 days] Laurent by chance strikes the chain while sucking his fingers...: he grasps it and slowly displaces it while looking at the rattles. He then begins to swing it very gently which produces a slight movement of the hanging rattles and an as yet faint sound inside them. Laurent then definitely increases by degrees his own movements: he shakes the chain more and more vigorously and laughs uproariously at the result obtained.—On seeing the child's expression it is impossible not to deem this gradation intentional. (Piaget 1936/1953, 185)

As this example shows, at this early age children act intentionally; that is, they intend to make an interesting event last by known means. And although they find the intended result pleasing, there is little indication that they expect a particular action to achieve a particular result, so that they will be disappointed when the result does not occur. Rather, children at this stage simply keep trying and modifying their actions until the pleasing effect occurs or until their interest in the activity wanes.

Repeating behaviors without feeling upset about continuous failure is also characteristic of instinctive behavior in animals, as the following example from Wooldridge (1963, 82) shows. (I borrowed this example from Dennett (1978, 63), who used it for a slightly different purpose.)

> When the time comes for egg laying the wasp *Sphex* builds a burrow for the purpose and seeks out a cricket which she stings in such a way as to paralyze but not kill it. ... The wasp's routine is to bring the paralyzed cricket to the burrow, leave it on the threshold, go inside to see that all is well, emerge, and then drag the cricket in. If, while the wasp is inside making her preliminary inspection the cricket is moved a few inches away, the wasp, on emerging from the burrow, will bring the cricket back to the threshold, but not inside, and will then repeat the preparatory procedure of entering the burrow to see that everything is all right. ... The wasp never thinks of pulling the cricket straight in. On one occasion, this procedure was repeated forty times, always with the same result.

Even very young infants are not that rigid in their repetition. But still the repetitive nature of circular reactions and the absence of objection to repeated failure suggests that specification of the infant's goal does not yet include an expectation about when the desired end state is supposed to be achieved. In other words, young children, at best, *have goals* that enable goal-directed action, but they do not yet *conceive of having goals*. Without this conception children do not expect completion of the planned action to produce the goal. And without this expectation they do not experience failure or success.

This starts to change during the second year. For instance, Merry Bullock and Paul Lütkenhaus (1988) showed toddlers a picture of a three-part block structure like a house and asked them to build that structure from an assortment of the three relevant blocks and three distractor blocks. In a second task children had to cover the body of a clown cutout with four colored wooden squares, and in a third they were asked to clean a blackboard with sponge and water. Children's perfor- mance on these tasks was scored with respect to whether they simply engaged in the offered activity but ignored the requested goal (no outcome orientation), whether they took the goal into account (outcome oriented), and how they reacted when the goal was reached (whether they kept on playing—seemingly oblivious of having achieved their goal—or whether they stopped as a sign of recognizing their accomplish- ment).

At 17 months it was difficult to get children to pursue the suggested goal. At 20 months children did work toward the suggested goal on most occasions, but very few ended up with a correct result (matching the requested standard) and very few showed any sign of stopping their activity after reaching their goal (or the point nearest to the goal). At 26 months outcome orientation became very high, and children stopped on a majority of occasions, even though complete success was still low except in the blackboard-cleaning task.

Another indicator of children's growing appreciation of goals was their ability to correct mistakes in the block construction task, that is, their ability to remove a wrong block, refrain from adding a wrong block, or change the orientation of a block or the order of blocks. Such corrections were made by a considerable number of children (40%) only in the 26-month group.

Finally, children's affective reaction was noted at the end of their building activity. The prototypical reaction consisted of a smile and an abrupt movement of the arms and hands, made just as a tower was completed (as if to say, "Done!"). At 17 months only 36% of children showed such a reaction. This percentage increased sharply to 62% at the age of 20 months, growing further to 75% at 26 months and 90% at 32 months.

This study illustrates that at the end of the second year children become increasingly aware of their goals and goal achievements. Kagan (1981, 47–54) has also reported that at around 20 months infants become aware of their own insufficiency and become distressed when asked to model an adult's actions. A slightly earlier indication of children's emerging awareness of their goals is that children as young as 15 to 18 months start to comment on success (e.g., "There!") and failure ("Uh-oh," "Oh dear," "No!": Gopnik and Meltzoff 1984).

Thus, in the second year of life there are various indications that children become increasingly aware of their goals and that their actions are directed at achieving these goals. They comment on success and failure, they adopt a suggested goal to guide their activity, they start checking the specification of their goal to correct mistakes, and they show emotional recognition of having reached the goal (or something approaching it). Furthermore, this emerging awareness of goals starts to be expressed at this age using words like "want."

Talking about Goals   The words "want" and "need," which adults use to indicate people's goals and how they relate to their actions, appear very early in children's speech. However, the following examples from a manuscript by Bretherton and Fritz and from work by Bretherton, McNew, and Beeghly-Smith (1981) illustrate that not every use of "want" and "need" reflects genuine understanding of goals and goal-directed action:

(1) At 1 year and 7 months: "I love mommy. I want to hold mommy."
                                 (mother had just scolded child)
(2) At 1 year and 8 months: "Want juice."
(3) At 1 year and 10 months: "Want out see wow-wow."

In these examples the word "want" may not denote a mental state of wanting but mark a request (example (2)) or express what is about to happen (examples (1) and (3)). However, uses of "want" that occur slightly later make more plausible reference to a state of wanting or a goal:

(4) At 2 years and 1 month: "Baby Nancy want bottle."
                                 (about baby sister who is crying)
(5) At 2 years and 4 months: "You want it on/you have it on."
                                 (said when mother takes microphone back from child)
(6) At 2 years and 1 month: "I don't have to go." (meaning to bathroom)

That by 2 years of age children start to view others as intentional agents in effecting change in their environment is also shown in their use of different types of verbs. Huttenlocher, Smiley and Charney (1983) differentiate between *no-change verbs* like "have," "hit," "pull," and "push" and *change verbs* like "build," "get," and "give." They then argue that no-change verbs describe the physical characteristics of action, whereas change verbs can be used consistently only if the child has some conception of an actor as an intentional causal agent effecting change in the world. Children's use of these verbs indicated that no-change verbs were used distinctly earlier than change verbs.

Smiley (1987) extended this line of research by showing children from about 1½ to 3 years video films of two children interacting (either two strangers or the subject with a familiar playmate). Children were asked what one of the actors was doing, and their answers were classified according to whether they described the activity with a *no-change* verb, a *change* verb, or a *volitional* expression (the verb "want"). The younger children tended to use only no-change verbs, whereas the older ones (from about 2 years on) also used change verbs. Interestingly, the use of change verbs coincided with the use of volitional expressions, substantiating the idea that from 2 years on children see others as causal agents effecting intentional change on their environment.

Predicting Action

Children's understanding of how action depends on a person's goal and the current state of the world has recently been demonstrated experimentally. Henry Wellman and Jacqui Woolley (1990) told children from 2 years and 7 months to 3 years and 1 month stories in which a protagonist is looking for his rabbit to take it to school. The rabbit, children were told, may be hiding in either one of two depicted locations (the porch or the garage). The protagonist then looks in, say, the garage and, depending on condition, either finds the rabbit (*find wanted*), finds nothing (*find nothing*), or finds his dog (*find other*). At this point children were asked the critical question: "What will Sam do next, will he look under the porch (other possible hiding location) or will he go to school?"

Even at this young age children were quite able to predict that the protagonist would go to school if he had found the desired animal (78%) but that he would continue his search if he found nothing (97%) or some other animal (91%). [**Note 9.1** Difficulties in replicating Wellman and Woolley's results.]

Distinguishing "Intentional" from "Accidental"

For children from 3 years on there is also good evidence that they can distinguish intended actions from accidents on the basis of whether an action does or does not achieve a stated goal. Tom Shultz (1980) and his colleagues have demonstrated this ability in a series of experiments. For instance, Shultz, Wells, and Sarda (1980, experiment 1) investigated children's understanding of situations like the following. In the first situation the child herself or another child had to interlace her fingers. The experimenter then pointed to one of the fingers and gave the instruction to stretch out that finger. In this situation it is easy to move the indicated finger. In the other situation, however, fingers had to be interlaced with hands crossed over, leading to many action errors.* In both situations the child was asked to indicate whether she or the other child *meant to move that finger or not*. The youngest children studied (3-year-olds) were as accurate as the oldest (7-year-olds) on this and several

---

Reader's Guide to Playing the Interlaced Fingers Game: Stretch out your arms with your thumbs pointing upward and put one arm across other. Rotate your thumbs downward so that your palms face each other. Interlace your fingers to a common fist. Move your hands downward by rotating them toward your body, moving your elbows apart until the interlaced fingers are close to your face. Then point with your tongue to one of your fingers, without touching it, and try to stretch out that finger. Good luck!

other, similar error-provoking tasks in judging *correct responses* as *intended* and *mistakes* as *not intended*.

In summary, there is varied evidence that at least by the age of 3 years children understand that people act because they aim at achieving a certain goal. This raises the question whether children understand what kinds of situations can reasonably function as goals. In our commonsense view people tend to strive toward things they consider *desirable*. What is children's view on that?

Understanding Desirability and Simple Emotions

We all know that desires are subjective: what may be desirable to one person may be repugnant to another. There are no satisfactory long-term objective grounds for settling disputes over taste: *"De gustibus non disputandum."* However, that is not how we experience the desirable. If I like beer, then I experience beer as *something good (desirable)*. That is, we experience desirability as something *objective*, inherent in the objects and situations that we, therefore, desire. Kurt Lewin (1931/1935) captured this commonsense view in his topology of life space, where people operate in a field of positive and negative valences.

Of course, our common sense can take a more sophisticated view, but only when necessary. Imagine that you and I are in a Bavarian beer garden, each of us lifting a double pint. You put down your mug: "Dreadful stuff." My first reaction is that your beer must have gone off; that is, it is "objectively" bad. Not until I have taken an exploratory gulp from your mug and found nothing wrong with it do I realize that our standards of desirability must be at odds. I like beer; you don't. Only then do I relinquish my objectivist interpretation of your negative comment and take a relativistic stance: it's not the beer that has gone bad; it's that you don't like beer (not even Bavarian beer).

These considerations are important because they raise a question about children's understanding of desirability: whether they understand it as something *objective* (pertaining to objects or situations), or as something *personal* (that is, as a relationship between a particular person and an object or situation). Children's understanding of desirability has been investigated by assessing their understanding of the emotional consequences of getting what one wants. A person who gets or achieves something desirable will feel *happy* or *pleased*, whereas a person on whom something undesirable is inflicted will feel *sad*. Children understand this connection from an early age.

Nicola Yuill (1984) presented children with a three-picture story. The first picture showed the protagonist holding a red ball and two other children (say, a boy and a girl) standing in the distance. A "wants bubble" (modeled after the "thinks bubbles" in Disney cartoons) above the protagonist's head showed what the protagonist *wanted*; for instance, if he wanted the girl to catch the ball, the bubble showed the girl holding the ball. This was explained to children before the story was told. The second picture showed the ball in mid-flight, having been thrown by the protagonist. Then the excitement heightened for children as they were made to wonder who would catch the ball. The outcome was shown on the last picture. In the *match story* it was the intended person who caught the ball, while in the *mismatch story* it was the other character who ended up catching it. In each story children had to judge how "pleased" the protagonist was with the achieved outcome. Even among the 10 youngest children (2 years and 11 months to 3 years and 5 months) all but 1 rated the protagonist as more pleased when the intended person caught the ball than when the other person caught it. Older 3-year-olds, 5-year-olds, and 7-year-olds all gave the same, correct differential rating.

Julie Hadwin recently replicated this good performance by 3-year-olds (Hadwin and Perner, in press, experiment 1). Wellman and Woolley (1990) also asked children to rate Sam the protagonist in their stories described above. Even at the age of 2½ to 3 years 72% of children said that Sam, who was looking for his rabbit, would feel "happy" when he found it and "sad" when he found a dog instead.

These data provide good experimental evidence that from an early age children have some understanding of *desirability* and its *emotional consequences*. However, these data do not settle the issue of how children conceive of desirability. At first glance it may appear that children must be understanding desirability as a personal relationship between a person and a situation, since it seems natural to adults that it is only the protagonist who desires the ball to be caught by the girl. Other people —in particular, the children themselves—may not find this outcome desirable. Yet it might be that children take a different view. For them, desirability may be an objective (not necessarily permanent) feature of situations. People feel "happy" whenever they find themselves in a desirable situation. Applying this view to Yuill's experiment, the two situations of the boy or the girl catching the ball are initially neutral (neither desirable nor undesirable), but the information that the protagonist "wants" to achieve one rather than the other makes the wanted situation appear somewhat "desirable" for children whereas the other remains neutral in value.

I don't think that decisive data are available yet to determine whether children treat desirability as a *subjective* matter or an *objective* feature. But there are some data that can be nicely explained by the "objective desirability" hypothesis.

Desirability: A Feature of Situations   The 3-year-old children in Nicola Yuill's (1984) experiment showed good understanding of how emotion depends on the satisfaction of one's desires in those stories where possible outcomes were initially neutral. In other stories the protagonist wanted something decidedly bad. He wanted to hit another child, whom he didn't like, on the head with his ball. Again, in one story the protagonist achieved this goal, and in the other story he failed to do so. Now 3- and even 5-year-old children were reluctant to rate the protagonist as more "pleased" when he achieved his (reproachful) goal than when he failed to do so. In Yuill's study only the oldest group of 7-year-olds gave the correct rating difference.

More recent studies indicate that Yuill's original study probably underestimated the 5-year-olds' competence. Gertrud Nunner-Winkler and Beate Sodian (1988, experiment 3) report that 19 of 24 5-year-olds judged a transgressor to be pleased about his misdeed. In a replication attempt Denise Peerbhoy (1990) incorporated story material from both studies and obtained a compromise result. Three-year-olds judged the successful transgressor to be "sad," as Yuill had reported, whereas 5-year-olds judged the transgressor to be "happy," in agreement with the study by Nunner-Winkler and Sodian. The transition occurred in the group of 4-year-olds.

The younger children's failure to understand an actor's satisfaction when bad intentions are involved nicely fits the hypothesis that desirability is considered to be an objective feature. Presumably, children consider being hit on the head as intrinsically "undesirable." The information that the protagonist nevertheless "wants" that "undesirable" result will do little to make it look "desirable." So, even when the protagonist is successful in hitting the other child on the head, he cannot really feel "pleased" since he did not achieve anything "desirable."

Alison Gopnik and William Seager (1988) argue that children until the age of about 4 or 5 treat desirability as an objective fact, on the basis of the following experiment. They presented children with two books, one a typical brightly colored children's picture book and the other a dull-looking textbook for adults. Most children said that the picture book *was for children* and that the other book *was for adults*. Nevertheless, when asked which book the adult experimenter would choose if she could choose just one, only 43% of 3- and 64% of 4- but 89% of 5-year-olds answered that she would choose the textbook. Children's response that the adult would choose the picture book could be explained by the hypothesis that children treat desirability as an objective fact, since for them only the picture book is known to be desirable.[*]

In contrast, a study by Flavell, et al. (1990) speaks more against than for the hypothesis that 3-year-old children treat desirability as an objective fact. Children selected their favorite cookie from a choice of three. The experimenter also took a bite, agreed that the cookie was delicious, and then offered a piece to Ellie, the second experimenter. Ellie took a bite and gave strong behavioral evidence that she did not like that cookie at all. She shook her head, frowned, puckered her mouth, and pushed the cookie away. Children were asked whether they and whether Ellie *liked* the cookie, and whether they and whether Ellie *thought it was a yummy-tasting cookie*. Even though the children were quite young (2 years and 11 months to 3 years and 7 months), 75% answered that *they liked* it and *thought it was yummy* but that *Ellie didn't like* it and *didn't think it was yummy*.

These answers suggest that children understand desire as a personal relationship to things; that is, they understand that someone may dislike something they themselves find very attractive. Yet the position that children do see the cookie as objectively desirable can still be defended. For it is not implausible to assume that children might treat Ellie's "unrealistic" reactions as a case of pretense (at least that possibility would cross my mind if I encountered someone with such aberrant reactions to a perfectly normal cookie).

In my judgment, then, the hypothesis that young children conceive of desirability as an objective fact is still an intriguing and viable possibility surrounded by not quite conclusive evidence. Despite being unable to answer the question "When do children conceive of desirability as personal preference?", I move on to the question "At what age do

---

[*]Of course, this result can also be explained by younger children's incomplete factual knowledge about what adults really desire (the fact that the book *is for adults* does not mean that *adults like it*, since there are many things that are *for children* that children don't necessarily like).

children conceive of goals and desires not just as *subjective* but also as *representational*?"

When Is a Representational View of Desire Necessary?

I have characterized the young child as a situation theorist who is not yet capable of metarepresentation. That is, young children can represent different situations, real and imagined, but have no conception of something representing these situations. It is important to realize, that even without such a conception the young situation theorist can go far in understanding goal-directed action and desirability, because adult commonsense rarely takes a representational view of these matters. To make this clearer let me describe the young situation theorist's capabilities in more concrete terms.

The situation theorist views people as actors in a landscape of possible situations that can be reached by different possible actions, very much as Aristotle viewed the movement of time (Horwich 1987). Among these, one situation is the real one, differentiated from those that could be but aren't. Then there are different possible future situations into which the real situation can develop depending on what action is taken.

For instance, in the experimental material used by Wellman and Woolley several possible situations need to be considered. Even the real situation is not completely specified. Sam is looking for his rabbit, but it is not clear whether the rabbit is under the porch or in the garage. Furthermore, Sam's desire to bring his rabbit to school specifies the possible future situation of Sam being with his rabbit at school. Children understand which sequence of actions will get Sam from his current situation to his goal. There is no point in going to school right away; Sam first needs to pick up his rabbit. And so they understand that if Sam finds either his dog or no animal at all, it will not suffice. He has to keep looking until he finds his rabbit before he can make his way to school and achieve his goal of showing his rabbit to his classmates.

Notice that even my overly explicit description of this reasoning process does not imply that Sam is *mentally representing* what he wants. To accurately predict what Sam will do, it is perfectly sufficient to view Sam as an actor driving toward the situation designated as his goal. The desirability of his goal may be seen as an objective fact (in line with the "objective desirability" hypothesis). However, even if children construed desirability as subjective, by representing that being with his rabbit at school is desirable *to* Sam specifically, that would not imply that they had to conceive of Sam as holding a mental representation of what is desirable for him.

My argument in chapter 8 was that beliefs need to be construed as representational when it becomes essential to understand that a person mentally misrepresents reality as a different situation—in other words, when it is necessary to clearly differentiate belief (thinking-that) from close impostors like pretense and imagination (thinking-of). However, a similar distinction seems unnecessary for understanding desire or goals (Perner, in press). This can be made clear via an experiment by Gopnik and Slaughter (in press) contrasting children's memory of a false belief with their memory of a past desire.

Memory for
Desire and Belief
Alison Gopnik and Virginia Slaughter (in press) tested 3-year-old children for their memory of a previous, now rectified false belief and their memory of a past, now outdated goal. The *belief task* was modeled after a task devised by Gopnik and Astington (1988). Children were shown a familiar box (for instance, a crayon box) and were asked, "What do you *think* is inside this box?" All children answered, "Crayons." Then they were shown that they were wrong: the box contained birthday candles. The box was closed again with the candles inside, and children were asked again what they thought was inside the box. All answered, "Candles." Finally, they were asked the critical test question: "When I first asked you, before we opened it, what did you *think* was inside the box then?" Only 39% of 3- and 78% of 4-year-old children answered correctly that they had thought there were crayons in the box.

In the *desire task* children were offered two books and asked which one they *wanted* read to them. The book chosen was then read to them. Then the two were offered again. All children now chose the other book. Then the test question was asked: "When I first asked you, before we read the first book, what did you *want* then?" To this question 67% of 3-year-olds and 83% of 4-year-olds gave the expected correct answer that they had wanted the first book.

The difference between tasks is slender and statistically reliable only because the same difference was found again in a second experiment. However, it becomes somewhat more impressive when one realizes that the odds were strongly stacked against old desires being remembered better than old beliefs. The main reason why the desire task was unduly "difficult" was that the answer that was scored as "wrong" was not really wrong. It is perfectly plausible that when shown the two books the first time, children wanted to look inside both books, not just the one they indicated. The answer "I wanted the (second) book (the first time around)" was probably perfectly true and should not have been scored as "wrong." The scoring of answers to the desire task may therefore have underestimated children's true memory of their past desire. The fact that children despite this possibility remembered their original choice better than their mistaken belief becomes more impressive since the wrong answers to the belief question ("I thought there were candles in the box") were *definitely wrong* descriptions of their past belief.[*] I thus interpret the results of this experiment as showing hope for an eventual demonstration that desire is easier to remember than belief. And this demonstration is important for my developmental argument.

My argument in chapters 4 and 8 was that 3-year-old children find it hard to remember their mistaken belief or mistaken statement about a fact because they have no concept of misrepresentation. For this, a clear distinction between thinking-of and thinking-that is necessary. The child did not just *think-of* a different situation (crayons in the box) in contrast to what she is thinking-of now (candles in the box), but the child *thought-that* the real situation was different from how (the child now knows that) it actually was. So to properly remember what they thought earlier, children have to be able to understand that they misrepresented the actual content of the box. In the desire task no misrepresentation is involved. There is just a change of desire. The child first *wanted* one book and later *wanted* the other one.

Causal Efficacy   The fact that our commonsense view of the mind gets by without construing goals as represented still leaves open the question that Janet Astington (in press) and I (Perner, in press) asked, namely whether there might not be other aspects of commonsense desire psychology that require an understanding of goals and goal-directed action as being mentally represented in desires and intentions. One such aspect may be the causal efficacy of desires and intentions.

---

[*]Another reason why the desire task was unnecessarily difficult is that it did not assess memory of a plain desire ("I *wanted* that book") but rather an *epistemic desire* ("I *wanted to know* what was in that book"). As we have seen, understanding of knowledge requires a similar understanding of the representational mind as understanding belief, and so it is not wise to test children's understanding of nonrepresentational desire by mixing in problems of knowledge.

One major benefit of a representational view is a systematic understanding that action is governed not by some hypothetical situation but
by something that is part of the real world and merely projects (by
representing) hypothetical situations. Because things that are part of the
real world are subject to the causal laws of real events, a representational
view of mind enables understanding how events in the world influence
the state of the (representational medium) mind, and how the mind
causes action.

Situation theorists can only simulate the behavioral effects of mental
representation by asking, "How would one act *if* the world were different
from how it really is?" or "How would one act *if* one worked towards a
particular goal?" They have no conceptual basis for understanding under
what conditions a person actually starts to engage in acting as-if. As I
have discussed in chapter 8, this understanding is necessary to solve the
puzzle of false belief, namely, to understand that a person aiming to act
appropriately in the real situation nevertheless acts as-if the situation
were a different one. Without a representational view of mind, then,
mistaken action remains a puzzle for situation theorists. This lack also
constrains their understanding that actual desires are formed and that
they drive action.

Situation theorists can understand that *if* a person strives toward a
certain goal, that person will take certain actions (e.g., Wellman and
Woolley's (1990) stories about Sam looking for his rabbit). They also
understand that actions that do not lead to that goal were not intended
(research by Tom Shultz (1980) and his colleagues) and that a person
who reaches that goal will feel pleased (e.g., Nicola Yuill's (1984)
experiment). Astington (in press) points out that in all these demonstrations of early competence children were told what the person's goal was,
and she surmises that children might have greater difficulty understanding
intentionality of action when no goal is explicitly stated.

Knee Jerks   An investigation into children's understanding of reflex action
by Shultz, Wells, and Sarda (1980, experiment 2) may constitute
a relevant test case. In the *intentional movement* condition of this
study children were simply instructed to move their leg. In the *nonintentional movement* condition they were instructed to try not to move their
leg; then their knee was gently tapped just below the disk, reliably
eliciting the familiar "knee-jerk" reflex movement of the lower leg.
Three-year-olds, when asked whether they *had meant to move their leg*,
did not differentiate between their intentional movement and the reflex

movement. In both cases they tended to say that they *had meant* to move it. Only at 5 years did children state that the knee-jerk reflex had not been intended.

As Janet Astington (in press) has pointed out, 3-year-olds' failure to recognize the knee-jerk reflex as involuntary can only be interpreted tentatively and with caution, since 3-year-olds were much better in distinguishing intended from nonintended action in other, very similar conditions used by Shultz and his colleagues. In particular, their ability to differentiate intended action from mistakes in the "interlaced finger game" stands in striking contrast. When observing themselves (or another person) move a different finger than the one designated by the experimenter, they correctly say that they *did not mean* to move that finger. So what causes the difficulty in the nonintentional movement condition of the knee-jerk experiment? Upon observing that they did move their leg, children should have been able to judge that movement as *not intended*. Why the difference?

It is quite plausible that children interpret the instruction to try not to move their leg not as "Try to keep your leg still!" but rather as "Do not initiate a movement of your leg!" Thus, children do not see their involuntary leg movement as contradicting any stated goal of keeping the leg still. Notice that in the interlaced finger game movement of the wrong finger and immobility of the designated finger violate the stipulated goal of moving the designated finger. If this is the correct analysis of 3-year-olds difficulty with the knee-jerk task, it shows how closely their understanding of intentional action is tied to understanding action as being goal directed. Lack of intention is equated with lack of success. The knee-jerk reflex cannot be judged on that basis, since no overt criterion for success (that is, no overt movement) was stated. And without an explicitly stated goal the default judgment is that actions are *intended* (Smith 1978).

To perceive the reflex as lacking intention, the child needs a concept of action being caused by an internal intention. In the situation theorist's view of goal-directed action there is no place for such a thing. There are only goals that are assigned to people and actions that these people undertake to bring about their goal. What kind of situation or action could an internal intention to move one's leg be within such a conceptual framework? There is only room for the intended movement, not for a separate notion of the intention to move the leg.

Intention ≠ Goal + Action   In a representational view of mind these two notions can be separated. The intention to move one's leg can be understood as a mental state representing that one will move one's leg. And since the representation of the leg movement is not an alternative situation but part of the same world as the leg movement itself, the representational mental state can also be understood as causally responsible for that leg movement. [**Note 9.2** The causal self-referentiality of intention.]

Janet Astington (1990) is currently working on a new task for assessing children's understanding of intended and accidental outcomes. In line with my analysis above it is argued that if the judgment between intended and accidental cannot be made by comparing the outcome with what the actor wanted (explicit description of goal), then children need a representational view of mind. Consequently, 3-year-olds are expected to find this judgment as difficult as, say, judgments about another person's mistaken belief.

So, Astington and her colleagues therefore tested 3-, 4-, and 5-year-old children (10 in each age group) on a *false belief task* in which they had to predict what another child would think was inside a crayon box containing a candle instead of crayons (see chapter 8) and on two *intention tasks*. Each intention task consisted of two picture stories that differed only with respect to how the event leading to the final outcome was described. Here is the text for the two "getting wet" stories:

Story 1: Intended	Story 2: Accidental
The boy is standing by the swimming pool.	The boy is standing by the swimming pool.
The boy *jumps* into the water.	The boy *falls* into the water.
The boy is wet.	The boy is wet.

Which boy meant to get wet?

The other pair of stories described a girl *dropping* and another girl *throwing* crumbs to the ground, which were then eaten by birds. Which girl *meant* the birds to eat the crumbs? Percentages of correct answers to the question for each of the two story pairs went up with age (35% – 80% – 100%) in remarkable synchrony with percentages of children passing the false belief test (40% – 80% – 100%).

This synchrony was expected on the assumption that both tasks require a representational understanding of mind: the false belief task for the reasons discussed at length in chapter 8 and the intention task because, since the actor's goal was not explicitly stated, a decision about who meant to get wet could not be based on judging the match/mismatch between desired situation and achieved situation. Without this possibility the task is beyond the young situation theorist. To answer correctly, the child has to understand that one event (jumping into the water) is triggered by an internal representation of being in the water (goal situation). Such a representation, as I have pointed out, has no place in the realm of situations and can only be conceptualized by the metarepresentational child.

So, the contention, which receives some preliminary empirical support from Astington's study, is that from 4 years on children gain a new insight into people not just as actors working their way toward goals but as actors possessing intentions that drive their actions. Furthermore, the knee-jerk reflex study suggests that this insight concerns not only children's understanding of other people but also children's understanding of themselves as intentional actors. This reflective insight into their own mental workings should have important practical consequences for children's self-control, as better understanding of the intentional origin of action provides better ability to control it. In the following section I will speculate more generally on the effect of children's growing understanding of goals, desires, and intention on their ability to control their actions and desires.

Tantrums and Control of Action

The basic idea for this and the following section is a quite general one, namely that one can only want what one knows about.* Thus, very young infants might know only about what is desirable and what is not. Consequently, their actions will be directed at obtaining the desirable and at avoiding the undesirable. I have discussed evidence that children become aware of themselves as goal-directed actors during the second year of life. This awareness should allow them to make their goal-directed action itself a goal.

Wanting to Do It Yourself   Children who can understand that they are doing something in order to achieve a goal can make their effort to reach the goal a goal in itself. That is, whereas before the goal may have been

---

*For this section and the following one I have borrowed heavily from Heinz Wimmer's essay "Common-Sense Mentalism and Emotions" (Wimmer 1989b) though my interpretation of developmental phenomena is somewhat different from his.

Simple Goal
"tall tower"

and the child then stacked blocks to produce that goal, now the goal might be

Do-It-Yourself Goal
"I stack blocks in order to make a tall tower."

The consequences are that children will now want to build by themselves and object to being helped. Indeed, Geppert and Küster (1983) report that from 18 months on children increasingly object to an adult's helpful intervention.

Another consequence is that children begin to feel proud of their success in having built a tall tower and not just pleased about the tower, since pride consists in being pleased about one's own achievement. Around the middle of the third year children show in their bodily and facial expressions clear signs of pride and shame (Heckhausen and Roelofsen 1962). Before that children are pleased when they themselves or someone else finishes a tower, but they show no specific reaction of pride to their own achievement or any negative emotional reaction (like shame) when they fail (Bullock and Lütkenhaus 1988; Lütkenhaus, Bullock, and Geppert 1987).

Tantrums   An important question for children is what to do in case of failure. Very young children who have no concept of a goal will not be disappointed. They will not show a strong negative reaction to failure. They will continue to pursue the goal until distracted and another goal takes over. In contrast, children who know disappointment and understand what or who is the cause of it may get angry at the obstacle or the interfering person. Some of these reactions turn into violent emotional outbursts. Such tantrums start in the second year and culminate at about the second birthday (Goodenough 1931). That period in the child's life has thus earned its nickname, "The Terrible Twos."

Individual children differ in the frequency and strength of their tantrums. According to Leach (1977), more than half of all children in their second year have tantrums at least once or twice a week and very few reach their second birthday without having had any at all. Although their strength varies with the individual, tantrums are a remarkable phenomenon for parents with offspring inclined to violent outbursts. The seemingly exaggerated depiction of emotional outbursts in cartoons of people pounding the floor with their fists, their faces turning an angry purple, can be experienced in real life with a 2-year-old.

Such violent behavior is often the reaction to adults who restrict children in their current activity or who refuse to grant a wish (Kemmler 1957). However, children also react that way toward recalcitrant physical objects or their own physical inability to achieve a certain goal (Leach 1977, 323–324). Yet despite the violent nature of the outburst, as soon as parents give in and let children have their way they will almost instantly be all smiling happiness again (Scupin and Scupin 1907).

Tantrums may have adaptive functions. For one, their sheer violence will often get children what they want, since it takes a cold-blooded parent to endure one of those fits of anger without caving in to the child's demands. Another adaptive function might be the sudden release of energy that has been built up to focus attention and effort on the attainment of a particular goal. The tantrum releases this emotional energy relatively quickly (Kemmler 1957), albeit in an unpleasant way, and enables the motivational system to make way for new and hopefully more acceptable goals.

If tantrums serve such useful functions, why do they not persist into adulthood? In fact, they stop very early in life. As children pass the age of 3 years, their tantrums become less violent and less frequent. When children do throw a tantrum at this age, one cannot help having the impression that the involuntary nature of the outburst is gone and that they use the tantrum intentionally to get their way. What is it that helps children to get their tantrums under control?

I think that these outbursts subside initially because 3-year-olds learn to manipulate their goal-directed action so as to better cope with goal conflict. Later, around 4 years, children become capable of *metavolition*, which enables them to change the content of their goals directly and provides a more radical cure.* They enter what Charlotte Bühler (1928/1967) called the *age of reason*.

---

*It is tempting to suggest that severe tantrums persist in many autistic children for several years because these children are specifically delayed in gaining the necessary insights into the functioning of the mind (see chapter 8).

Control through "Self-Sabotage" By conceiving of themselves as having goals and of their action as being goal directed, children not only create emotional problems for themselves but also lay the foundations for solving these problems. By understanding that action is goal directed, children gain some degree of self control. For instance, they can prevent themselves from obtaining a goal by interfering with the necessary actions—which, following Wilensky's (1978) terminology, we might dub *self-sabotage*. How this ability emerges is nicely demonstrated in the work by Claire Kopp (1982) and her colleagues.

For instance, Vaughn, Kopp, and Krakow (1984) asked children aged 1½ to 3 years to refrain from opening a present while the experimenter was in the room but did not pay any attention to the child. The 1½-year-olds were hardly able to control their impulse at all and soon unwrapped the parcel. Many 3-year-olds, however, could control their natural desire by employing various disabling techniques like sitting on their hands or distracting themselves by looking elsewhere or singing.

I interpret this ability as showing that children are aware of their goals and of the need to take preventive action to keep themselves from pursuing a prohibited goal. There is a subtle difference between this awareness and what older children can do. Although 3-year-olds can prevent themselves from pursuing a particular goal, the goal itself is not abandoned. Older children can do a more permanent job. They can *persuade* themselves to adopt another goal altogether. For this they have to form a *metagoal*, that is, the goal to change their original goal.

Metavolition

Before I continue my description of children's ability to master metavolition, I would like to highlight its broader importance.

Freedom of Action and Will Frankfurt (1971) asks the interesting question how a prisoner's loss of freedom differs from the loss suffered by a drug addict. He answers this question by distinguishing between *freedom of action* and *freedom of the will*. This distinction is relevant to our developmental concerns because Frankfurt proceeds to analyze this distinction in terms of first-order volition (freedom of action = freedom to do what one *wants* to *do*) and (second-order) metavolition (freedom of the will = freedom to want what one *wants* to *want*).

According to Frankfurt most animals and young children have only *first-order volitions*, that is, desires that become effective in governing action. Only humans, after a certain age, have *second-order volitions*, that is, effective desires to change their first-order volitions. The ability to carry out the necessary action to satisfy one's first-order goals is freedom of action. The ability to change one's first-order goals is freedom of will. Jail deprives its inmates of their usual freedom of action, but their freedom of will remains unencumbered, since they are still free to form new desires. In contrast, addiction deprives its victims of their freedom of will. Addicts remain free to act as they please but lose their metavolitional grip on resisting their own desire for drugs.

My question here is when children acquire this metavolitional ability of influencing the formation of their own volitions, the kind of freedom the addict has lost. The ability to want to change what one wants requires an understanding of one's desires as something that one can change. As I have argued, the situation theorist understands desires as desired situations (goals) that a person is affiliated with. The situation theorist's idea of change is limited to actions that transform one situation (the current one) into another situation (the goal). Within this view there is no action that has the effect of changing one's affiliation with a goal (desire), since this affiliation with a desired situation is not itself a situation.

For instance, if Sam wants to bring his rabbit to school but doesn't know where it is, then he needs to first look for it and (if he finds it) carry it to school. That much is clear. But what should Sam do in order not to want to bring his rabbit to school? Or what should someone do to make him change his mind? These questions cannot be sensibly asked by the young situation theorist.

Things change once the mind is understood as representational. This is true for two reasons, one of principle and one practical. As soon as desires are understood as representing goals (desired situations), desires can be seen as part of the real world and hence become manipulable. However, looking at desires as representations only gives the in-principle insight that desires can be changed.* This still leaves the practical question about what kind of action can achieve such a feat. What methods do we employ? The one method I am aware of is to gain more accurate information (or manipulate information) about the true nature

---

*For what it is worth, I recorded the following anecdote a week before Hannah's fourth birthday:

Hannah: "I don't want my peas."
Cosette: "But you asked for them."
Hannah: "I don't want them. I changed my mind when you didn't look."

of the desired goal—which in decision theory is known as the *cost-benefit analysis*.

For instance, Sam may persuade himself to leave the rabbit at home by considering the likely consequences of bringing it to school: the teacher might get angry; the other children might hurt his rabbit. These prospects are so undesirable that they far outweigh the original desire to show off the rabbit. A similar technique can be used by Sam's mother if she doesn't want him to take the rabbit. She may inform (or—I know some mothers who would do such a thing—indeed misinform) him about the consequences—which in fact illustrates the other, practical reason why *metavolition* depends on an understanding of representation, namely, that information and misinformation are intrinsically tied to the concept of representation.

Unfortunately, I know of no evidence of the changes in children's attitudes occasioned by the onset of metavolition except the badly documented intuition that children become "reasonable" (Bühler 1928/1967, 240ff: "vernünftig") at the age of about 4 to 5 years. When thwarted in pursuing their desired goals, they need not throw a tantrum but can choose to negotiate, that is, to agree to give up their intended action if they are given something else in return. As children approach school age, then, not only do they become more "logical" in their reasoning about facts—what Piaget tried to capture in the notion of *concrete operational thinking*—but, more importantly, they become rational about their desires.

In the absence of any systematic investigation into these changes I can only close by relating a personal anecdote. When Hannah was between 4½ and 5½ years, we moved into a new house and I told her to stop sliding down the banisters. I could feel her tantrum brewing when she completely surprised me by calmly stating: "Okay, then I'm gonna do something else." [Note 9.3 Metavolition as a specifically human acquisition.]

Summary

In line with my general view of how mental models develop I argued that it is in their second year that children become able to reflect on their *goals* and *goal-directed action*. This ability emerges at this time because children become able to build complex models that are necessary for representing that a particular situation is desired and how it relates to what has been achieved.

I discussed two possibilities for how children might view *desirability*. They may treat it naively—as adults often do—as an *objective* feature, or they may understand it as a *subjective* matter of personal taste. Existing data do not allow a firm conclusion.

Next I raised a familiar question, namely, whether *desires* need to be understood *as mental representations*. Desire differs from belief in this respect insofar as desires do not misrepresent. However, in order to understand that desires are formed and can be changed, children need to understand them as representations, because only when they conceive of them as representations can children understand that desires have a propositional content (project hypothetical situations) and yet are part of the real world.

This consideration led to the speculation that children become "reasonable" at the age of 4 or 5 years because they become *metavolitional* and can begin to *control* their *desires* (want to want something else), whereas earlier their self-control was limited to the level of action (self-sabotage).

PART III

Developmental Issues

Chapter 10

Representational Change and Theory Change

In chapter 2 I provided an analysis of the concept "representation" from which a sequence of *representational levels* emerged: *primary* (single updating model), *secondary* (multiple or complex models), and *meta* (models of models). In chapter 3 I looked at corresponding representational changes in children's thinking, in particular, how changes from a single mental model to multiple models enable children to break away from current reality to conceive of past and other nonexistent situations. In chapter 4 I asked how these changes affect children's understanding of external representations and appearances. The ability to form *multiple models* allows systematic *use* of representations, and the ability to *metarepresent* gives an understanding of the *concept* of representation and its defining features (reference, interpretation). The better part of chapters 5 through 9 was devoted to the question of how these representational changes affect children's conception of the human mind.

Throughout, I have had little to say about what motivates these representational changes. The easiest way of thinking about this issue is to treat representational levels as *maturing* at a particular age. Their explanatory use lies in imposing order upon an otherwise scattered picture of developing abilities. However, this still leaves the nagging question of what motivates the change between levels. I will use this chapter to speculate on some of these issues.

In general, I view representational changes as opening up new intellectual possibilities that lead to a restructuring (theory change) of the existing body of knowledge. My first speculation concerns the transition from primary to secondary representations. I point out that the observed changes need not be explained by the maturing of a new cognitive architecture; instead, they can be predicted from a necessary delay between the successful functioning of different parts within an existing structure.

My second and somewhat more extensive point is to illustrate the repercussions of new developments on existing knowledge, which I characterize as "theory change." I do this by showing how metarepresentation affects children's understanding of knowledge in a change from a *(mentalistic) theory of behavior* to a *theory of mind*. I argue that this change between "theories" is not one of replacement but one of *extension*, by analogy to some changes in scientific theories.

Representational Change

Alan Leslie (1987), who provided us with the terms "primary" and "secondary representation" to characterize the changes that occur at around 1½ years, views these changes as the result of a new cognitive mechanism maturing at this age. This mechanism is dubbed a "decoupler" and "expression raiser," which—in my terminology—would correspond to mechanisms for building multiple models or complex models partitioned into contexts (see chapter 2). Leslie's view raises the question of why the decoupler does not exist from the beginning. I therefore want to speculate briefly on the possibility that such mechanisms may well be functional from the beginning but that there is some necessary delay before they can operate successfully.

One basic feature of my analysis of representation is that any system of representation must first establish itself as a *causal stand-in* (chapter 2). That is, the representational states must provide adequate guidance for the environment in which the organism has to succeed. It is in this function that the states of the representational medium have meaning in terms of the external world. And they do so in two ways. Mental tokens have meaning because they concur with what they refer to in the external world and because they play an important role in adequately directing behavior in relation to what they denote. Only after this system of meaning has been established can the system start to put multiple models to sensible use, and it will take time until their use becomes recognizably successful. Let me make this clearer by means of a "connectionist" example.

A Connectionist Analogy   Rumelhart, Hinton, and Williams (1986) describe a connectionist network that displays interesting internal features after learning family relationships among a set of individuals. Such a network consists of layers of nodes. Within a layer each node is connected to every node in the previous layer and to every node in the following layer. The input to the network is a question consisting of a name and a family relation—for instance, "Colin's Aunt?", which activates the input node responsible for *Colin* and another input node for the relationship *aunt*. The network has to learn to activate the correct output node(s)—namely, those for *Margaret* and *Jennifer*, who happen to be Colin's aunts. This learning is achieved by feedback, which adjusts the strength of the connections or *associations* between nodes. A schematic of this network is presented twice on the lower level of figure 10.1. On the right-hand side the network is shown as it is responding to the question "Colin's Aunt?". On the left-hand side it is shown at work at the previous point in time where the question was "Lucia's Aunt?" The degree of shading within each circle indicates the amount of activation of each network node caused by the particular input question.

In the beginning the system will make many errors, and the pattern of associations will change from trial to trial until the system *settles down* and associations stabilize. At this point, after many trials, the system not

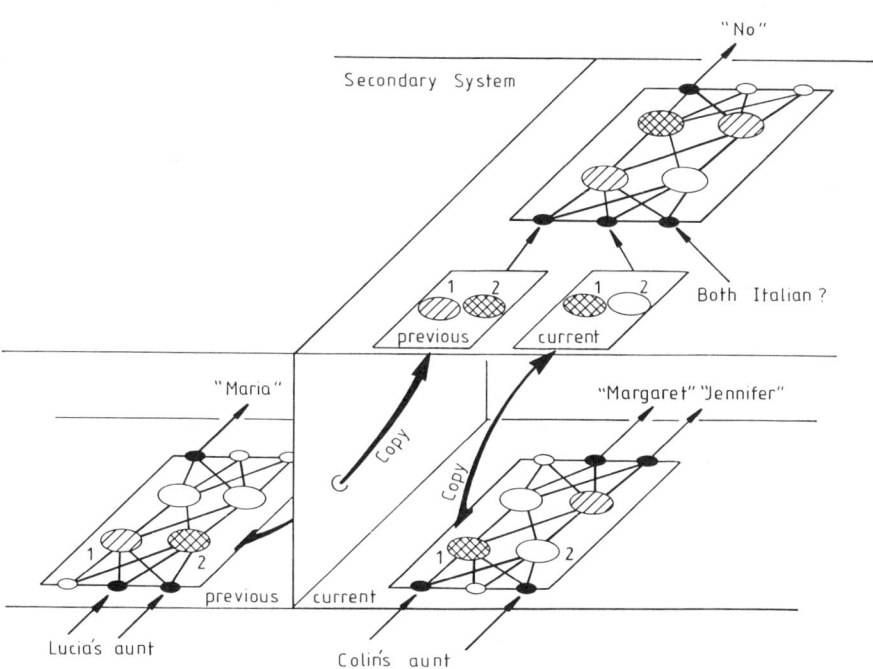

Figure 10.1
An extended connectionist analogy for a system operating at a primary and secondary representational level.

only performs quite accurately but also generalizes correctly to novel pairings of members; that is, it can answer "Jennifer's brother?" even though it has neither been asked this particular question before nor been given feedback about the correct answer.

Most interestingly, activation of particular internal nodes in this system tended to correspond to particular concepts—and not just concepts that were specified in the input. For instance, the individuals in the set happened to come from two unrelated families, an English one and an Italian one, and the system singled out a particular node "representing" that difference; in other words, that node was highly excited when a member of the Italian family was part of the input but kept its cool for members of the English family (e.g., node 2 in figure 10.1). Another node encoded generation; that is, it was not excited about grandparents, it was mildly excited about parents, and it was wildly excited about sons and daughters (e.g., node 1 in figure 10.1).

The analogy between this toy problem and the real-life learning situations of infants is far from perfect. To see any at all, it is useful to slightly redescribe what the network is doing. It is faced with a situation (e.g., Colin asking who his aunt is), and it must learn to give the right response to this situation, just as the infant who is interested in a toy and has information about its location must learn what to do to get it. With this in mind we can say that the *activation pattern* of internal nodes *represents* the *current state* of the world (i.e., Colin asking who his aunt is). And it represents this situation in a conceptually interesting way. It doesn't just activate a node for Colin; it also activates to varying degrees two nodes (node 1 and 2) that describe Colin as "young English." (In the infant case the relevant representation would describe the kind of object and where it is.) Next, the *associations* between nodes *represent* the *general laws* of the world—in this case the family relationships (the laws of successful object retrieval in the case of real-life infancy).

The activation pattern of nodes, one could say, is a primary representation, since its purpose is just to reflect the current state of the world to enable correct responses. Therefore, this system could not answer questions about past states of the world or compare the present state with a past state. Now the real thought experiment starts. Let us assume this system could be extended in the following way to enable it to answer questions like "Were the last two people both Italian?" This hypothetical extension is shown in the upper layer of figure 10.1.

To make a comparison between past and present, possible copies of activation patterns (models) have to be made and stored. An important assumption is that this copy is to some degree *conceptual* (activation pattern of internal nodes) rather than purely *sensory* (activation of input nodes). These copies of primary activation patterns (models of different states of the world) then provide the input for the *secondary system*—that is, a network, perhaps, that learns to compare these stored activation patterns and answer questions about them.

A comparable problem for infants would be the Piagetian invisible displacement problem (chapter 3) where an object disappears in the experimenter's hand, which then goes under a cloth and reemerges empty. To find the object, the infant has to be able to remember that the hand grasping the object had been under the cloth. Only then can the infant figure out that that is the most likely place the object could be.

The important point about this hypothetical extension of the connectionist network is that there is a necessary delay between successful functioning at the primary level and successful functioning at the secondary level even under the assumption that the architecture exists and is functioning from the very beginning. This point could have been made with any learning system; I chose a connectionist example because the notion of *settling down* emphasizes that learning need not be gradual, in particular, that the relationship between input and internal activation patterns does not become gradually more ordered. If improvement were gradual, then the secondary system could start useful learning at the same time as the primary system. Consequently, the delay between success at the primary level and success at the secondary level would be minimal. However, for much of the initial learning period there may be little consistency between internal activation patterns of the primary system and its external input. Hence, the secondary system, which is fed activation patterns of the primary system as its input, can learn little in relation to the external world until its input (primary activation patterns) starts to correspond to the external world. Since this correspondence may emerge only late in the primary system's learning phase, and since the secondary system can start meaningful learning only when the primary system is close to perfection, the delay between success at the primary level and success at the secondary level can be large.

Back to infancy. Successful performance on Piaget's invisible displacement task may not evidence the *maturing* of multiple models (secondary representations; Leslie 1987) for encoding an object's previous location in addition to where it is now. Rather, these models may have been in place earlier but the (secondary) system has not yet learned how to use them meaningfully. That these models exist earlier but on occasion interfere with, rather than assist, correct performance is suggested in the so-called *A-not-B error* observed in infants as young as 8 months.

The A-not-B Error   In one kind of test Piaget (1937/1954) assessed his children's notion of object permanence when an object was first put under one cloth (location A) and then under a second cloth (location B). Although by about 8 months they had no difficulty retrieving the object from under cloth A, they committed a peculiar error when the object was subsequently hidden under cloth B. Instead of looking under cloth B, where they had just seen the object disappear, they tended to search again under cloth A (hence *A-not-B error*).

Subsequent research found that the error occurs even when infants do not retrieve the object from under A on the first trial themselves but simply observe someone else retrieving it (Evans 1973; Sophian and Wellman 1983). Also, it was found that erroneous search under A does not increase with the number of prior successful retrievals from A (see Wellman, Cross, and Bartsch 1987, for a meta-analysis of A-not-B error studies) and that the error is committed not only by infants but also by amnesic patients (Schacter and Moscovitch 1984). These findings suggest that the error is not due to the child egocentrically identifying the location of the object with his own retrieval action (Piaget 1937/1954), or to response perseveration (Gratch et al. 1974) or habit (Diamond 1985). Rather, the child seems to have some memory of the object having been under A, and this memory interferes with searching in the right place (Harris 1973; Sophian 1984; Wellman, Cross, and Bartsch 1987). In other words, even at 8 months infants must have a secondary representation of a past event. However, unlike 1½-year-olds, these young children have not yet figured out how to use this information adequately. If anything, this information about the past interferes with information about the present. [**Note 10.1** Explaining the A-not-B error by fading context markers.]

What emerges in the second year, then, is not a maturing of secondary representations. They may have been functional from the start. Rather, what we may see there is the system mastering proper use of secondary representations. Whereas the A-not-B error evidences the existence of secondary representations in terms of interference, success on invisible displacement tasks nine months later (Piaget 1937/1954; Haake and

Somerville 1985) demonstrates the continued existence of temporal context representations but this time in their more adequate role of helping the child understand temporal change.

The same development may underlie pretense. Long before we see genuine pretense in children, they may possess the cognitive mechanism for *decoupling* representations (Leslie 1987). Decoupled models may, like the secondary models of past events in the A-not-B error, gain behavioral control. However, what we observe then is at best unusual behavior because the relationship between what the decoupled model represents and reality has not yet been worked out. So the child cannot show a *knowing smile* signaling that the unusual behavior is recognized as an intentional distortion of reality-adequate behavior, hence pretense.

To sum up, I want to point out that with my connectionist analogy I did not mean to propose that such systems provide an adequate account for conceptual development.* All I had in mind was to provide a semiconcrete alternative to Leslie's explanation for why various indicators of secondary representation skills emerge in the second year. They may emerge, as Leslie (1987) would say, because the secondary mechanism (decoupler) *matures* at this age. Figure 10.1 was meant to illustrate that a secondary system may be functional from the beginning, yet, because of its hierarchical dependence on the primary system (the primary system's internal structure being the secondary system's input) there is a necessary sequence between successful functioning at the primary level and successful functioning at the secondary level. No maturational assumptions are necessary.

I have used the findings on infants' A-not-B error as possible evidence for early existence of secondary representations. Their effect, however, is one of interference when the infant negotiates present reality. What characterizes development in the second year is that the relationship between secondary models is being understood. This understanding, as I argued in chapters 3 and 4, provides infants with a measured freedom from the here and now by enabling them to understand the past (invisible

---

*Clark and Karmiloff-Smith (1990) suggest that connectionist models may provide a useful way of thinking about the acquisition of implicit knowledge (know how). Further developmental progress is achieved by making this implicit knowledge explicit through a process of *representational redescription*. Only after such redescription onto a higher level does knowledge obtain theoretical status. This process of redescription is actually quite similar to the copying of internal nodes onto a secondary level in figure 10.1, except that the secondary system is thought of not as another connectionist system but as a more traditional symbolic information processor.

displacement), understand counterfactual possibility (pretense), and use representations (e.g., interpreting language, pictures, mirror images).

Development does not stop here. Successful functioning at the secondary level provides a new domain for learning. For instance, types of temporal change and representational relationships (interpretation, reference) now come within reach of conceptualization. Again, it will take some time before these new relationships are understood so that models of them can be built. Let me speculate on these further acquisition processes in the case of the concept of representation.

Toward Modeling Representation   In chapter 4 I argued that the ability to form multiple models (or use them successfully) enables children to interpret symbolic or representational media like language and pictures. For instance, at about 1½ years infants start to recognize themselves in the mirror. In other words, they become able to *interpret* the mirror image. They see an *image of themselves* and not another person—unlike younger children, who often search behind the glassy surface for the presumed playmate. In order to give the mirror image the correct interpretation, children must be able to relate the mirror image with reality, similarly to the way they need to relate the past with the present in the invisible displacement task.

However, the ability to interpret one's image in a mirror as oneself is not the same as understanding that the image is a representation of oneself. I have characterized the young child as a situation theorist for whom the image in the mirror is "myself in a situation that is different from my actual situation." But the mirror is not understood as a *representation*. What is missing is an understanding that something (the reflection in the mirror) *represents* something else (oneself). And understanding "represents" requires appreciating that the mirror image has an *interpretation* and a *reference*. That is, the child has to understand (1) that there is something that isn't me (the reflection in the mirror), (2) that when I look at it, I see myself there (interpretation), and (3) that this thing that isn't me corresponds to me in real life (referent).

To develop a concept of these representational relations is a quite different task from what the child has encountered so far. Understanding reference requires appreciating that something in the real world can correspond to something else (mirror reflections of self), and we have seen from deLoache's (1987, 1989a) data (chapter 4) that children come to understand correspondence just before their third birthday.

To understand interpretation poses another, quite different problem, namely, that something in the real world evokes something *as* something, which need not be how it really is (reflections in a mirror evoke me *as* I may or—in the case of a distorting mirror—may not really be). In pretend play, when treating something as-if it were something else, the child creates a relationship very similar to representing something as something else. And so I do think pretend play is an important stepping stone to understanding representation (though, as I have argued in chapter 3, it is not clear from the child's early pretend action whether the child treats an object as-if it were something else or as representing something else).

So, observing correspondences and engaging in pretense provide important insights into the components of representation. And, of course, the naturally occurring uses of representational means like language, pictures, and even mirrors also contribute to these insights. For instance, by interpreting statements and determining what they refer to, children are constantly exposed to the process of interpretation and reference. And so, helped by pretense and the observation of correspondences in their attempt to understand these instances of representation, children will eventually hit on the *concept of representation* as their common denominator. The indications are, based on various sources of evidence discussed in chapters 4 through 9, that this concept is formed around the age of 4 years.

I have discussed the developmental progression so far as one of opening up new possibilities that simply add to existing knowledge. But development is not that linear. Therefore, I now turn to looking at the repercussions of these new abilities on existing knowledge. I use this as an opportunity for reviewing the revolutionary effects of the emerging concept of representation on children's existing knowledge of the mind. I argue for the view that from about 2 years on—if not considerably earlier—children use mental terms to make sense of human action. They are—one could say—working on a *mentalistic theory of behavior*. At around 4 years this original understanding changes into or is extended by a *representational theory of mind*. Let me start this discussion by asking whether talk of a "theory"—in particular, of a "theory of mind"—is at all justified where such young children are concerned.

Why Call It "Theory"?

The developmental changes in children's understanding of the mind can profitably be viewed as changes in theory, I think, because such a view emphasizes at least the following five important points about intellectual development:

1. Major changes are more than just acquisition of facts but need not be interpreted as changes in representational format or in logical makeup ("operativity") as Piaget argued (Carey 1985b, 190–194).
2. The child's conceptual system is geared to explanation from a very early age, if not from birth (Carey 1985b, 201; Murphy and Medin 1985).
3. The child's concepts acquire meaning not independently of each other but by being part of a network of interrelated concepts just like theoretical terms within a scientific theory (Wellman 1990, chap. 5; Churchland 1984, 50).
4. Something can be learned from looking at theory change in science (Carey 1988; Karmiloff-Smith 1988; Karmiloff-Smith and Inhelder 1974/5).
5. More specifically, the child's understanding of her own mind as well as that of others conforms to the *theory view* in the philosophy of mind as opposed to the *Cartesian* tradition that the mind is transparently observable by itself (Churchland 1984).

However, we should be careful in specifying *what theory* children have at a particular age and *what* it is a *theory of*.

Theory of Mind?   Premack and Woodruff (1978) ask the provocative question "Does the chimpanzee have a theory of mind?" and go on to explain what they mean:

> In saying that an individual has a theory of mind, we mean that the individual imputes mental states to himself and to others.... . A system of inferences of this kind is properly viewed as a theory, first, because such states are not directly observable, and second, because the system can be used to make predictions, specifically, about the behavior of other organisms. (p. 515)

"Theory of mind" was quickly adopted by developmental psychologists (Bretherton, McNew, and Beeghly-Smith 1981; Wellman 1985) as a convenient label for investigations into children's understanding of the mind. It was Henry Wellman (1988) who actually raised the question whether young children, when they start to talk explicitly about mental states, deserve to be described as "having a theory of mind." He suggested that three criteria—on loan from the philosophy of science —must be met to justify the use of the term "theory." A theory must be a *coherent* body of knowledge; it must make an *ontological commitment* about what kinds of things there are in the world; and it must provide a *causal explanatory framework* to account for phenomena in its domain.

My argument is that even though young children's early understanding of mental states may conform to these three criteria,we are still not justified in saying that they have a theory of mind. The reason is that one has a *theory of something* only if one has a deeper explanation for how that something works. In fact, that is Sue Carey's criterion for characterizing older children's understanding of biological processes:

> Asked why people eat, 4-year-olds answer, "because they are hungry" or ... "otherwise they would die"..., but these are not yet biological explanations because the child knows no biological mechanisms by which eating has these consequences. (Carey 1985b, 188–189)

In other words, even though the child uses a biological concept like "death" to give a reason for why people eat (indicative of a causal framework: not eating causes death), we would not want to say that the child has a "biological theory of death," or even less that he has a "theory of biology" on the grounds that he is using a biological term like "dying" in his explanation. Rather, 4-year-olds use "dying" as a hypothetical, negatively motivating state in a *psychological theory of eating*.

We can look in the same way at young children's use of mental terms in justifying their actions (Hood and Bloom 1979). For instance, asked why she took the chocolate from the cupboard, a 3-year-old may answer, "Because I wanted to" or even "Because I knew it was in there," but this is not yet a *theory of mind* because the child knows no *mental mechanism*[*] by which wanting or knowing has this consequence.

Thus, the use of mental terminology even in causal and justificatory statements is not enough for a theory of mind. A mechanism explaining

---

[*]"Understanding the mental mechanism" does not imply understanding the details of some physical mechanism (how the brain works), much as the "understanding the biological mechanism linking lack of food to death" does not imply understanding the chemical details of this process. Rather, it implies only understanding the representational and information-carrying characteristics of the mental mechanism.

the workings of the mind is required. Therefore, young toddlers who start to use mental terminology to make sense of people's behavior may be characterized as having a "mentalistic theory of behavior" but not a "theory of mind" since they have no explanation, yet, for why and how these mental states do their job. This changes at around 4 years, as children start to understand the representational underpinnings of mental states and so acquire an—at least rudimentary—theory of mind.

In the next section I elaborate the difference between using mental terminology and understanding the representational mechanism of the mind by means of an analogy between medical practice and medical theory. I have chosen medicine as an example because it provides a close analogy to the change in children's understanding of what "knowledge" is.

Tuberculosis: A Medical Analogy   The way of thinking characteristic of the natural sciences arrived in medicine with Louis Pasteur's discovery of bacteria (Glaser 1967, chap. 11). Although originally proposed as an explanation for why brewers' beer kept spoiling, within a decade this discovery led to a theory of infectious disease and with it to the first scientific revolution in medical thinking.

In order to gain a useful analogy for children's changing understanding of knowledge, I caricature the contrast between the theoretical understanding of tuberculosis made possible by Pasteur's insights and the medical practitioner's "know-how." This is not to say that there was a direct transition from no theory to Pasteur's theory. In fact, many competing theories flourished, held by their advocates with great conviction.* However, there was an older school of practitioners who deplored the new obsession with discovering the causes of disease in order to understand it, to the detriment (they felt) of the *art of healing* (Glaser 1967, 73).

I first investigate how the practitioner's approach differs from bacteriological theory. I then show that the young child's understanding

---

* For instance, there was Max Pettenkofer's theory about the origin of cholera. Pettenkofer, the public hygienist of Munich, was so convinced that the bacteriological theory was wrong that, to save his own theory from the threat of Robert Koch's discovery of cholera bacteria, he resorted to a "heroic" self-experiment. He swallowed a culture of Koch's cholera bacteria to prove Koch wrong. Apart from minor diarrhea and a slightly heightened temperature, he suffered no ill effects. Unfortunately, his assistant, who repeated the experiment, came close to death (Glaser, 1967, 93–97).

of knowledge is akin to the practitioner's understanding of tuberculosis, whereas the older child seems to subscribe to a "theory of knowledge" based on *transmission of information* that is in some ways similar to a "theory of disease" based on *transmission of bacteria*.

Here is how I characterize the medical practitioner's understanding of tuberculosis vis-à-vis the bacteriologist's theory:

Practitioner's View

1. Tuberculosis is something undesirable to have. Its "nature" cannot be specified further. Its explanatory value consists in how it relates to the following classes of other events (it is thus a theoretical construct).

2. Possible causes: Some events are known to be likely to lead to tuberculosis, such as contact with already afflicted persons, catching a chill. (These causes are neither necessary nor sufficient for the occurrence of tuberculosis.)

3. Typical effects (symptoms): Roaring cough, spitting blood, high fever.

Bacteriological Theory

1. Tuberculosis is the possession (of a critical quantity) of tuberculosis bacteria.

2. Necessary condition: Transmission of tuberculosis bacteria. (No specific condition under which this is achieved—for instance, contact with infected persons, eating contaminated food, or drinking contaminated water—is in itself necessary or sufficient.)

3. Typical effects (symptoms): Bacteria afflict the lungs, leading to roaring cough, spitting blood, high fever.

To differentiate bacteriological theory from the practitioner's understanding of tuberculosis, the two criteria given by Premack and Woodruff (1978), *nonobservability* and *predictive power*, are not sufficient. Even the practitioner cannot directly perceive tuberculosis but has to infer it from the presence of symptoms. Furthermore, predictive power is not the exclusive province of the bacteriologist. The practitioner, too, can predict from diagnosed tuberculosis that the patient will show further, more severe symptoms and is likely to die.

The three criteria advanced by Wellman (1988) do not differentiate the practitioner from the bacteriologist either. Even the practitioner is *ontologically committed* to the notion that "having tuberculosis" is something different from its possible causes and its symptoms ("tuberculosis" is a theoretical term). Even in the practitioner's framework there must be *coherence* among possible causes, disease, and symptoms, for without it the practitioner's knowledge about tuberculosis would be of no use. Finally, the relationship among these elements is interpreted within some sort of *causal framework.** Even early physicians recognized kissing an afflicted person to be a cause of later developing the symptoms of tuberculosis and did not believe that exhibiting the symptoms was responsible for having the disease. And this causal understanding must have played an important role. Doctors' advice for escaping the disease would have included avoiding contact with a diseased person and avoiding cold temperatures but not trying to suppress the coughing.

Yet despite ontological commitment, coherence, and some grasp of a causal framework, we remain reluctant to call the medical practitioner's understanding of tuberculosis a "theory of tuberculosis." Such a theory arrived when scientists tried to find the reasons why kissing an afflicted person leads to tuberculosis and why tuberculosis makes its sufferers spit blood. What precisely is the difference between medical practice of the art of healing and medical theory?

Criteria for a Theory   Causal statements like "kissing an afflicted person caused you to catch tuberculosis" are what Searle (1983, 116) refers to as "causings," that is, chains of events in which one event is responsible for the occurrence of the next. In contrast, a bacteriological theory of tuberculosis *explains why* one event caused the other. It does so by providing a *mechanism* (or model) that *underlies* the observed causal sequence of "kissing → tuberculosis → coughing": when you kiss someone with tuberculosis, it is likely that tuberculosis bacteria get into your respiratory system, where they multiply, and irritate your lungs, causing you to cough and spit blood.

One important consequence of *having a theory* is that it introduces a strict distinction between what is *possible* and what is *impossible*.
For instance, in a bacteriological theory it is necessary to become infected with bacteria in order to catch tuberculosis. Without bacteria, no disease! Lacking such a theory, medical practitioners could say nothing about when it is impossible to catch tuberculosis, because they only knew an open-ended list of possible causes. Of course, the concept of tuberculosis played an important role as a theoretical construct by linking symptoms to possible causes for finding the correct treatment, but

---

*Wellman might rightly object that my use of "causal framework" here is not what philosophers of science, whose term he is using, mean by it. However, I would submit that his demonstration (Wellman 1988) of young children's understanding of the causal relationships that mental states are involved in does not go beyond my use of the term here.

nothing was impossible. The proof lay in the pudding. As Rademacher, one of the last great proponents of the art of healing, put it:

> First of all the treatment, and if it helps, then one has the diagnosis as well. (cited in Glaser 1967, 73)

The fact that under a theory certain courses of events become *impossible* has relevant consequences for deciding whether someone has a theory:

Three Symptoms of Having a Theory:

1. Distinguishing essential causes from facilitatory or indirect causes: A bacteriological theory of tuberculosis makes transmission of bacteria a *necessary* condition for the existence of tuberculosis. Consequently, known conditions of transmission like contact with a diseased person or drinking contaminated water are now seen as *essential* causes, in the sense that one or the other of them must have been present or there could be no disease. In contrast, catching a chill and living in unsanitary conditions are now seen as merely facilitatory. They may facilitate the proliferation of tuberculosis bacteria.

2. Necessary conditions over diagnostic criteria: For real-life diagnosis the classical symptoms of a roaring cough, spitting blood, high fever, and so on, are much more reliable diagnostic indicators for tuberculosis than possible causes. The reason is that usually little useful information about possible causes is available. In particular, it seems impossible to rule out tuberculosis on the basis of the absence of all possible causes: the patient had no contact with afflicted people, did not drink from a dubious water supply, and so on. For real-life diagnosis the situation is not much different even when the diagnostician is armed with a bacteriological theory. However, under controlled conditions in the hospital or laboratory the possibility of bacterial infection can be monitored. And then the possibility of infection takes precedence over classical symptoms in diagnosis. If there was no conceivable way of catching tuberculosis bacteria, then a patient *cannot* have tuberculosis despite all the classical symptoms. It must be some unknown disease with similar symptoms.

3. Being in the grip of a theory: Let us assume that without any conceivable way of having been infected by tuberculosis bacteria, several patients nonetheless develop the classical symptoms of the disease. The medical practitioner will not be puzzled. He will either shrug his shoulders or, if he can find some commonality across these cases, will gratefully make a new entry in the list of already known possible causes of tuberculosis. In contrast, the bacteriologist *ought* to be utterly perplexed, because this event threatens her theory. She should not rest until she finds either that there was a way of contracting tuberculosis bacteria after all, or that there is a new nonbacterial disease with identical symptoms. In practice, however, negative data are often ignored and—at best—only prepare the way for adopting a new theory when one becomes available.

Armed with these "diagnostic criteria" for *having a theory*, we can look again at whether the young child has a theory of mind. My chief examples come from children's acquisition of a theory of knowledge, since it provides a neat parallel to the changes in medical thinking.

Do Children Have a Theory of Knowledge? There is a striking parallel between the medical practitioner's understanding of tuberculosis and the young child's understanding of knowledge before the age of about 4 years, and between the bacteriologist's understanding of tuberculosis and the older child's understanding of knowledge. Children's understanding of knowledge at these two ages can be sketched as follows:

Younger Child's View:

1. Knowledge is something desirable to have (it confers status among peers and elicits praise from adults). Its nature is not specified further. Its explanatory value lies in how it relates to the following other events (it is thus theoretical construct).
2. Possible causes: Some actions and features of a person are likely to lead to knowledge, such as seeing, being told, and so on; age (being an adult).
3. Typical effects (symptoms): People who know are likely to find things, answer correctly, and so on.

Little Information Theorist's View

1. Knowledge is a correct representation of some fact (and it is correct for some good reason).
2. Necessary condition for correctness: A mental representation of a fact can only be correct for good reasons if it is caused by that fact; that is, the mental state contains information about the fact.
3. Typical effects (symptoms): A correct representation can guide behavior so that the person finds things, answers correctly, and so on.

That the child from 4 years on develops such a theory of knowledge is indicated by the presence of the three symptoms of having a theory.

Distinguishing "Essential" from "Facilitating" From the age of 4 children see informational access as the important and necessary condition for the possession of knowledge in distinction to other, indirect factors like age. By contrast, for 3-year-old children age seems to be a very important factor in judging a person's knowledge. They consider other children as largely ignorant and adults as quasi omniscient. This conjecture has not been demonstrated experimentally, but a lovely "experimental" anecdote has been reported. When Jürgen Hogrefe used dolls representing a child in some of our experiments (Wimmer, Hogrefe, and Perner 1988, 393), 3-year-old children tended to answer that the doll did not know what was in a box regardless of whether the doll had looked inside the box or not (and children demonstrably attended to that fact). At least that was so in the first two kindergartens where the study was conducted. Then in the third kindergarten most children tended to do exactly the opposite. They claimed that the doll knew what was in the box regardless of condition. It turned out that the doll happened to be called "Monika" which was also the name of the headmistress in that particular kindergarten. As soon as the doll was given a different name, the children in this kindergarten, too, reverted to denying the doll any knowledge.

Although we know about the importance that 3-year-olds attach to age as a determinant of knowledge only from anecdotes like this, we do have experimental evidence that by the age of 4 children pay little attention to a person's age (facilitatory) but judge knowledge mostly by how much information (essential) that person was given (Taylor, Cartwright, and Bowden 1989).

Necessary Conditions over Diagnostic Criteria   By the age of 4 years children also start to realize just how important informational access is by preferring it as a criterion for judging a person's knowledge over the usually much more reliable diagnostic criterion of the person's success. Whereas 3-year-olds rely predominantly on a person's success for attributing knowledge, between 4 and 5 years children switch to availability or lack of information as their basis for judgment. They correctly distinguish between knowledge and a lucky guess (see figure 7.1).

An important aspect of this change from familiar diagnostic criteria to necessary conditions is that it seems to come from the children themselves. There are no obvious changes in, for instance, how adults talk about or start explaining to children the origin of knowledge. Rather, it is the children themselves who spontaneously begin getting interested in these issues. The spontaneity of this change is reminiscent of the spontaneity in the characteristic-to-defining shift noted by Frank Keil (1987, 179) for many different concept domains.

In the Grip   A person in the grip of a theory either will be perplexed
of a Theory   when faced with seemingly incompatible evidence and
inquire into the case more thoroughly in the hope of
finding a resolution or—the more radical reaction—will simply deny the
evidence or explain it away. That the grip of a theory can be firm not just
on scientists but even on young children has best been demonstrated by
Annette Karmiloff-Smith (e.g., 1984).

For instance, young children have no particular theory for balancing
blocks on a ledge (Karmiloff-Smith and Inhelder 1974/5); they just use
their common sense and so, in fact, manage to get most building blocks
into balance. At about 6 years children seem to trade their common
sense for the simple *theory* that every block balances with respect to its
geometric center. This theory works well for the usual symmetric block
but not for blocks that are heavier on one side. Yet these children adhere
to their theory, try to balance even the most obviously asymmetric block
by centering it on the ledge, and then declare it "unbalanceable." They
do not change their theory even when the experimenter demonstrates
that the block can be balanced, albeit off center.

Somewhat less striking signs that young children are in the grip of an
informational theory of knowledge can be found in their persistent
inquiries into the informational origin of knowledge. Recall 5-year-old
Sybille, for instance, who wanted to know how her friend found out
where she lived, how to get to her street, how to find the right door, ...
(chapter 7).

There are also experimental data suggesting that 4-year-olds are taken
in by a simple information theory of knowledge that leaves no room for
inference based on general background assumptions. For instance, Beate
Sodian (1986, experiment 5) tested children's understanding of inferential
processes in another person (symbolized by a doll) seated next to them.
Children and doll were first asked some general questions like whether
all dogs have four legs. All children said, "Yes," and the doll gave the
same answer with the experimenter's help. It was confirmed that the child
understood that the doll knew that all dogs have four legs. Then the
experimenter took a picture out of her bag, which she did not show to
the children or the doll. She only told them that there was a dog in that
picture. The children were then asked whether they knew how many legs
that dog had. All children answered that it had four legs. Then they were
asked the critical question: whether the doll knew how many legs the dog
had. Now, 11 of 14 4-year-olds thought that the doll would *not* know
(only 4 of the 14 6-year-olds made this error). This is remarkable since

all children had agreed that the doll did know that dogs in general have 4 legs.

When the children were asked why the doll did not know, dialogues of the following kind unfolded:

Child: "She doesn't know because she can't see the picture."
Experimenter: "Can you see the picture?"
Child: "No."
Experimenter: "Then how do you know how many legs the dog has?"
Child: "Because I have seen other dogs before."
Experimenter: "And [name of doll] hasn't seen any dogs before?"
Child: "Oh yes."
Experimenter: "Does she know, then, how many legs dogs have?"
Child: "Yes."
Experimenter: "Does she know, then, how many legs the dog in this picture has?"
Child: "No, 'cause she can't see it." (Sodian 1986, 149; my translation)

This dialogue makes clear that 4-year-olds' judgment of another person's knowledge is in the grip of the simple-minded theory that a person can know how many legs a particular dog has only if that person has direct (visual) information about that particular dog. If their judgment were not dominated by that theory, then they could have used their common sense and realized that the other person, being in the same position they are, should be able to draw the same trivial inference that if all dogs have four legs, then this particular one must have four legs too, even though it is out of sight.

By drawing the analogy between changes in medical thinking and changes in children's understanding of knowledge, my immediate aim was to justify attributing a theory of mind to at least the older children. They can be said to have a theory of mind because they start to understand the representational mechanism underlying mental states. But what about children before the age of 4 years? Do they have a "theory"? If so, what is it a theory of?

Theory Change

One can view the transition in children's understanding of the mind that takes place at about 4 years in two different ways: as a change from *no theory* to a *theory of mind*, or as a change of theory from, perhaps, a *mentalistic theory of behavior* to a *representational theory of mind*. Let me deal first with the view that the younger child has no theory.

Earlier Theory? My analogy between the young child's understanding of mind and the medical practitioner's understanding of tuberculosis may make the no-theory position look plausible. The practitioner—one might say—has no theory. His notion of tuberculosis is an atheoretical concept summarizing observed correlations between different symptoms and potential causes. And when the practitioner answers the question "Why does the patient cough?" by saying, "Because he has tuberculosis," one is reminded of Molière ridiculing the doctors of his time for explaining that opium puts people to sleep because of its *dormative potency*. However, as Thomas Kuhn (1977, 24, 25) has pointed out, there is no logical flaw in explanations of this sort and they have been used from classical Greek science down to modern physics.

So we should say that the medical practitioner does have a "theory." But a theory of what? It is probably best characterized as a "theory of symptoms" in which the concept of tuberculosis plays an important role as a theoretical construct. It is a theory of symptoms because "tuberculosis" provides the explanatory glue for the syndrome and the bridge between causes (contact with an afflicted person) and the later symptoms. It is not a theory of tuberculosis, because the practitioner has no deeper explanation of why contact with afflicted persons causes tuberculosis or why tuberculosis produces its symptoms.

Concerning children's understanding of the mind we should then say that the young child has a "(mentalistic) theory of behavior" but not a "theory of mind." It is a mentalistic theory of behavior (including perceptual action) because mentalistic notions, such as knowledge, play an explanatory role similar to the role tuberculosis plays for the medical practitioner. For instance, the concept of knowledge makes correctness of action symptomatic, provides a focus for seeing individual perceptual actions as belonging together, and builds a bridge between perceptual actions and success.

I have also referred to the young child's understanding of mind (and external representations) as a "situation theory" since they use mental terms to characterize a person's different relationship to real and hypothetical situations. And some of the evidence for this understanding also shows that the child is *in the grip of a situation theory*.

Symptoms of a Situation Theory   One symptom that even 3-year-olds are in the grip of a theory, a situation theory, is their bad memory for mistaken statements (chapter 4). Recall the study in which children were asked about the contents of a matchbox. They all answered, "Matches," and then were shown that the box actually contained chocolate. After having learned the true contents of the box, few 3-year-olds could remember their earlier erroneous answer. In contrast, when they were asked to say "Matches" as a joke, knowing full well that the box contained chocolate, their memory for their jokingly wrong response was considerably better.

If children "objectively" observed their own actions and simply remembered them, there would be no reason why they should have trouble remembering their mistaken statement. Their forgetfulness can be explained by assuming that memory is not retrieval of observed facts but a theoretical reconstruction of what happened. Thus, the child reconstructs her statement as one describing the real contents of the box. Within a situation theory a statement describing the real situation can only describe the true contents (hence children's failure to remember the mistake), but a statement describing the real situation for fun as-if it were a different situation can be remembered as describing that different situation (hence children's good memory for the jokingly false statement). Thus, one could say, it's because they are in the grip of a situation theory that they are blind to their mistakes (misrepresentations).

Having concluded that the change in children's understanding of the mind and of symbolic means (language, pictures) is a change from a situation theory to a representational theory, I should specify in more detail what kind of change it is.

What Kind of Theory Change?   In the most commonly discussed case of theory change the old theory is simply replaced by the new and better theory. For instance, Ptolemaic astronomical calculations were replaced by Kepler's laws of planetary motion (Hanson 1958), and Lavoisier's "oxygen" won out over Priestley's "phlogiston" theory of combustion (Kuhn 1970, chap. 6; Kitcher 1988, 219–221). Unfortunately, I think the change from a situation theory to a representational theory is not like these examples from the history of science. There is no simple replacement since—as I argued in chapter 5—we stay situation theorists at heart. We resort to a representational theory of mind only when we need to. A better analogy from the history of science may therefore be an instance of *theory extension*: for example, the extension of classical genetics by molecular genetics discussed by Philip Kitcher (1984, 365).

Classical genetics assumes the existence of *genes*, which are responsible for producing an organism's phenotype and which *replicate* from one generation to the other. Occasional replication errors (*mutations*) result in new varieties. Classical genetics is a "theory of heredity," that is, of how features are passed on from parents to offspring. It is not a "theory of genes" or a "theory of gene replication." In fact, replication of genes became a problematic presupposition (Kitcher 1984, 362). Since mutations were experimentally produced by bombarding genetic material with X-rays, it was thought that mutation was a result of the rays *damaging* molecules. This posed a problem because it seemed unlikely that anything damaged could still replicate. This foundational problem was eventually solved through the work in molecular genetics by Watson, Crick, and others, which showed that any part of DNA can replicate and that the kind of damage caused by radiation (insertion, deletion, or substitution of nucleotides) did not affect replicability. Thus, a threatening controversy was resolved.

However, although the discovery of DNA provided a model of genetic material, it is difficult to identify any section of DNA with a particular gene as defined by classical genetics. Thus, despite the fact that molecular genetics explains how genes replicate and mutate, it does *not* *replace* classical genetics but only *extends* it. Classical genetics is still needed to explain inheritance. That is, the recombination of genetic features is still dealt with at the cellular level of chromosomal alignment and "not by rehearsing the gory details of the reshuffling of the molecules" (Kitcher 1984, 370).

I take a similar view on the relationship between the young child's situation theory and the later ability to consider the mind as a representational system. The representational view does not supplant the situation theory but only amends it for certain problems. Even as adults we remain situation theorists whenever possible and treat mental states as straight propositional attitudes. However, in contrast to young children, we are able to take a representational view when necessary—to explain cases of misrepresentation, for instance.

Advantages of a Situation Theory   Remaining a situation theorist whenever possible can save many unnecessary complications, or, to paraphrase Kitcher, it saves rehearsing the gory details of reshuffling mental representations. A good illustration is the *mutual* *knowledge problem*. David Lewis (1969, 52–60) points out that any coordination problem, like agreeing on a meeting place, requires not only that you know what has been agreed but also that you know that the other party knows. If one party thought that the other didn't know, then there would be no point in making the effort to show up. Furthermore, knowing that the other knows is not enough. You also need to be sure that he knows you know, because if he doesn't know you know, he'll think you won't show up and therefore won't bother to make the effort himself, and consequently there won't be any point in your showing up either. This kind of reasoning can be repeated forever so that only an infinite series of reciprocal knowings would establish *mutual awareness* of the agreement.

Even worse, since word meaning depends on speakers' intentions to make listeners recognize their intentions (Grice, 1957), every simple act of communication could raise this ugly problem of establishing mutuality (Strawson, 1964). Yet in normal life—I suspect—we do not bother about these problems at all, because we are situation theorists. We simply assume that everyone who is part of an interactive situation is linked to that situation, that is, knows everything about it, including the participants' knowledge. The problem of mutuality arises only when knowledge is conceived of as a representation of the situation that is not part of the represented situation. Therefore, only when the need for taking a representational view of knowledge arises do we encounter the problem and only then might we employ some algorithm (Perner and Garnham 1988) to test whether knowledge is mutual.

Intermixing of Theories That we are at once situation and representation theorists becomes apparent in our different uses of words like "know" and "lie."* For instance, Richards (1982) distinguishes three different senses of "know," one of which is illustrated in this example:

> upon hearing thunder and the first drops of rain, we exclaim (in exasperation), "I just knew it was going to rain today and ruin our picnic!" What is asserted is that a speculation or conjecture turned out to be correct. In this sense, *guess* is a synonym rather than an antonym of *know*. (Richards 1982, 388)

---

*I owe this idea to Beate Sodian.

It is true that we use the word "know" in this way. But one is also left with the sense that this is not its "proper" use, since one can legitimately object, "Yes, but you did *not really* know it, you just guessed." The interesting interpretation of this is that the "not really proper" use of "know" is a leftover from young children's way of using the word as an indication of success (see chapter 7), whereas its "proper" use is the one prescribed by the representational, information-processing theory of knowledge.

A similar analysis applies to our uses of the word "lying." Coleman and Kaye (1981) suggest that the commonsense meaning of "to lie" is a conjunction of three aspects of a statement: (1) its being false, (2) its being thought to be false by the speaker, (3) its being intended to mislead the listener (deceptive intention). The more of these three criteria that apply to a statement, the greater the likelihood that it will be judged a "lie". Again, it is true that many adults will be happy with the situation theorist's definition "a lie is something that's false." And it may be a natural reaction to call anyone a "liar" who says something wrong. However, upon reflection—long before it comes to a libel suit—we are able to entertain more refined, representational considerations of whether the speaker herself thought her statement was false and whether she actually meant us to believe it. In any case, some such refined view must underlie our natural concept "lie"; otherwise, we would not be able to differentiate it from *mistakes* as even young children can do (Gruber 1984; Wimmer, Gruber, and Perner 1984) or from *jokes* and *sarcastic remarks* (Leekam 1988).

Summary

In this chapter I speculated on how representational change comes about and I defended the *theory view* of children's understanding of the mind.

Representational Change. My intention was to point out that the sequence of representational levels around which I organized children's understanding of mind and symbolic means does not depend on assumptions about a particular mechanism or concept maturing at a specific age. Rather, the sequence is inherent in the way any representational system must unfold. I illustrated this point with a connectionist analogy showing that since the secondary system takes internal structures of the primary system as its input, a developmental sequence from successful *primary* functioning to later *secondary* representational functioning results. This sequence obtains because the secondary system can begin to learn sensibly only after the primary system's internal structure already shows some degree of consistency.

Theory View. I defended the view that once children understand the representational function of mental states, their understanding of mind deserves to be called a "theory of mind," because they have some explanation (mental mechanism) of how mental states functionally relate to the world. The younger child's understanding of mind, I suggested, should be characterized as a "mentalistic theory of behavior" in which mental states are employed as theoretical constructs. Since at this stage mental states are construed as relations to situations, I frequently referred to young children as "situation theorists." The representational view of mind does not replace the earlier situation theory but merely extends it, and adults are still situation theorists with the capability of taking a representational view.

In the next chapter I contrast the "theory view" with traditional developmental approaches like egocentrism and role taking, and I discuss how my brand of theory view differs from similar proposals.

Chapter 11

Origins of Commonsense Psychology

In this chapter I evaluate alternative accounts of the origin of children's commonsense psychology. The first account says that children are familiar with mental states from their own inner experience. I argue that this view is implicit in Piaget's notion of *egocentrism*, according to which children take their own point of view as absolute. Recent experimental evidence suggests that egocentrism of this kind is largely a myth. This has implications for *role taking* as the prime method for overcoming egocentrism.*

The alternative view, the *theory view of mind*, is that the mind is a theoretical construction for explaining observable behavior. I opt for a refined view that admits information about inner (privately observable) states as an integral part of the theory. As a convenient means for highlighting some essential features of my account, I contrast it with alternative versions of the theory view.

Whither Egocentrism?

A most important question in the philosophy of mind is how the mental terms in our language obtain their meaning (Churchland 1984). There are two major philosophical positions on that issue, one associated with the *theory view of mind*, the other with *Cartesian introspection*.

---

*My analysis of the relationship between different positions in philosophy of mind and developmental research on *egocentrism* and *role taking* was very much inspired by Heinz Wimmer's (1989; Wimmer and Hartl, in press) thoughts on this topic.

Theoretical Terms versus Inner Ostension   The commonsense answer to the question "How do we know about the mind?" is that we just need to look inside our own mind to find out. This view has a philosophical tradition in the writing of René Descartes:

> the soul acquires all its information by the reflexion which it makes either on itself (in the case of intellectual matters) or (in the case of corporeal matters) on the various dispositions of the brain to which it is joined which may result from the senses or from other causes. (Descartes in a letter of 16 October 1639 to Friar Mersenne; in Kenny 1970, 66)

From this point of view knowledge of one's own mind is direct; that is, the *mind is transparent to itself*. Mental terms like "know" and "want" can be given meaning ostensively by just pointing to particular internally observed states of one's own mind. Although this position may well appeal to our common sense, it does create the *problem of other minds*, that is, "How can we know that other people have similar states of mind when we cannot observe them?"

The competing position is that mental terms do not denote internally observable states but are *theoretical terms*, which get their meaning by being embedded in a coherent body of knowledge or theory. This is the way I have characterized children's approach to the mind. For instance, children come to understand the word "know" in terms of how a person relates to situations in the world, in particular the fact that knowledge results in success.

Siding with the theory view of mind has repercussions, since it does not go well with certain entrenched positions in developmental psychology. It is opposed to the view that children tend to be "egocentric" in their attribution of mental states to others and that this egocentrism is overcome by the ability to "take the other person's perspective or role." In the recent developmental literature this position has been defended by Carl Johnson (1988) and by Paul Harris (1989a, chap. 3; in press). I first clarify what precisely the relationship between *egocentrism* and *inner ostension* is and thereby make clear in what sense *egocentrism* is incompatible with the *theory view of mind*. I then reevaluate traditional evidence for egocentrism to show that this evidence needs to be reinterpreted.

Egocentrism and Inner Ostension

The notion of *egocentrism* forms an important part of Piaget's theory of intellectual development. Its effects are illustrated, for instance, by children's responses on the "three-mountains task" reported by Piaget and Inhelder (1948/1956). Children were seated in front of a model of three Swiss mountains and were shown several photographs taken from different angles around the model. The children's task was to point out the photograph that showed the view seen by a doll looking at the mountains from a different angle. Younger children, it was reported, tended to "egocentrically" choose the picture showing their own view of the mountains.

When looking for definitions of "egocentrism" in Piaget's work, one finds passages like the following, which stipulate that it is an inability to conceive of differences in perspective:

> When we use the term ego-centrism, we mean the inability to differentiate between one's own point of view and other people's or between one's own activity and changes in the object. (Piaget 1959, 267, fn. 1)

It is important to note that egocentrism defined in this way would be fully compatible with the theory view of mind. However, this definition does not capture an implicit but important element of "egocentrism" that is essential for its wide popular appeal. Namely, from this definition it does not follow that children should prefer to choose the picture giving their own view; any error would do.

Although Piaget did not include preference for one's own view as part of his definition of egocentrism, he and Bärbel Inhelder introduced it as a corollary in their explanation of data from the three-mountains task:

> The egocentric attitude tends to encourage him [the subject] to accept it [his own view] without question as the only one possible. ...Consequently he turns it into a kind of "false-absolute." (Piaget and Inhelder 1948/1956, 194)

What is left unexplained in this addendum is why the inability to differentiate between one's own point of view and other people's encourages acceptance of one's own perspective as a false-absolute. One might suspect that Piaget and Inhelder did not see any need for explanation here because they tacitly assumed that mental state terms derive their meaning from *inner ostension*. Indeed, when one accepts the *ostensive definition* of mental states, preference for one's own view becomes clear. Let me illustrate this with reference to the three-mountains task.

The mental state at stake in the three-mountain task is the other person's (doll's) *visual percept* of the model mountains. Let us assume that the meaning of "What does one *see* when looking at something?" is defined by inner ostension to one's own visual percept. Then we would indeed expect young children to give "egocentric" errors, since "what one sees" is by definition given as their own percept. In fact, one prominent researcher of role-taking abilities has interpreted Piaget's notion of egocentrism in exactly this way:

> Egocentric thought, defined here as the relative inability to recognize or take into account the privileged character of one's own private thoughts and feelings. (Chandler 1973, 326)
> Childhood egocentrism is often understood as the expression of an over-embeddedness in, or concentration upon, one's own subjective experience. (Chandler and Helm 1984, 146)

And there is some early evidence in support of this view.

A Scent of Egocentrism   In chapter 6 I mentioned the study by Lempers, Flavell, and Flavell (1977) in which children were asked to show another person a picture glued to the inside of a hollow cube. At the age of 1½ children went to considerable lengths to turn the cube so that both they and the other person could look into it simultaneously. One interpretation of this somewhat curious behavior is that for children at this young age "showing the picture" means obtaining a *visual percept* of the picture and—in Cartesian fashion—that means their *own percept*. Consequently, they take pains to obtain that percept. Even so, these children are not completely egocentric, since their "egocentric" concern for having a percept is already mixed with a concern for getting the picture into the other person's line of sight. Then why should there be evidence for egocentrism as late as 6 or 7 years as reported by Piaget and Inhelder in their three-mountains task?

Reevaluating Old Evidence   Kielgast (1971) suggests that children's choice of picture in the three-mountains task might be, not an "egocentric" preference for their own view, but a preference for selecting a "good picture of the mountains," namely, one that depicts all mountains. In Piaget and Inhelder's task "a good view" and "one's own view" largely coincided since the task demanded that the child had to see all mountains lest it be impossible to figure out what the other observer's view could be.

Paul Light and Carolyn Nix (1983) have provided clear evidence that 4- to 6-year-old children do treat this kind of task primarily as one of choosing a good picture regardless of whether it depicts their own view or not. The setup in their task was much simpler than in Piaget and Inhelder's. A bottle and a glass were standing next to each other on a table. From two sides of the table the view was good; that is, one could see the glass and the bottle side by side. From the two other sides the view was bad, since either the glass partly obscured the bottle or the bottle partly obscured the glass. When children had a good view and the other observer seated at a 90° angle to the child had a bad view, then half of the children tended to pick their own good view (possibly because of a trace of egocentrism or possibly because their own good view seemed even better than the other good view). However, when children were given a bad view, 75% of them picked one of the two good views at even chances, but only 10% "egocentrically" chose their own view.

Lynn Liben (1978) reports comparable data. In another study Liben and Belknap (1981) presented 3- to 5-year-olds with an array of blocks and asked them to "point to the picture that shows exactly what you see from where you are sitting." When children could see nothing but one block and did *not know* what other blocks were behind that obscuring block, practically all chose the picture showing the obscuring block only. However, when children first watched the array being constructed and therefore *knew* what was behind the obscuring block, a majority chose a picture showing the entire array.

Egocentrism or Intellectual Realism?   Liben and Belknap (1981) suggest, therefore, that children's responses on these visual perspective tasks are not so much *egocentric* (preference for their own view) as a sign of *intellectual realism*. This term, coined by Luquet (1927), was used by Piaget and Inhelder (1966/1969, 63–68) to describe children's tendency to show in their drawings as much as possible of what they know is there (for instance, they draw an object inside an opaque cup as if the cup were transparent) rather than what they can see from a particular vantage point (the outside of the cup only).

Traditional evidence for egocentrism remains ambiguous with respect to whether children take their own view (egocentrism) or reality—as they know it—as absolute (intellectual realism). For instance, in the studies by Masangkay, et al. (1974; see my chapter 4) children said that another person seated opposite would see the turtle in the picture as they themselves saw it; that is, if the turtle appeared to them to be standing on its feet, they thought that the other person also saw it standing on its feet. However, this need not be a sign of egocentrism (taking their own view as absolute). Rather, in this case their own view simply determines what they see the turtle (objectively) doing: it's standing on its feet. And so they assume as *realists* (rather than egocentrists) that everyone sees the turtle doing what it is doing right now: standing on its feet.

In this task it is difficult to tease apart what children see from what they think is objectively there, but (as we saw in Liben's task, where what children see does not exhaust what they know is objectively there) the evidence clearly points to realism, rather than egocentrism.

The same methodological problem has affected other areas of study. For instance, under the label of "conceptual perspective taking" it has been claimed that children tend to attribute their *own state of knowledge* to everybody else (Marvin, Greenberg, and Mossler 1976; Mossler, Marvin, and Greenberg 1976).

Is There "Conceptual Egocentrism"?   For instance, Marvin, Greenberg, and Mossler (1976) tested 2- to 6-year-old children for their understanding of knowledge in the context of sharing a secret. Each task involved the child, the child's mother, and the experimenter. On a particular task any two of them shared a secret, excluding the third person. For instance, in one task child and mother agreed on a secret by pointing to one of several toys as the one they would think about together. Meanwhile the experimenter covered his eyes so that he could not see which object mother and child were pointing to. The critical questions were whether each of the participants knew what the secret was. By the age of 4 nearly all children gave correct answers to these questions for themselves and the other participants. The younger children were also fairly accurate on questions about themselves but committed many errors concerning the other participants. Their predominant kind of error was to state that all participants knew the secret.

These errors were interpreted as signs of egocentrism because they occurred when children knew the secret and then wrongly attributing their own knowledge to the other participants. So it came as quite a surprise when more recent results from a very similar investigation by Wimmer, Hogrefe, and Perner (1988) defied that interpretation. In these experiments there were, for instance, two conditions in which the child always had a different perspective from that of the other person (a classmate or a doll representing another child). Either the child was

Table 11.1
Percentage children giving a particular pattern of answers to question about other person's knowledge when the other person had a different perspective.

| Type of response | Response given when other: | | Study | |
	Looks	Doesn't look	Wimmer et al.	Ruffman and Olson
Correct	yes	no	34	40
Yes-bias	yes	yes	9	44
No-bias	no	no	44	9
"Egocentric"	no	yes	13	7

allowed to look inside a box and the doll (other child) was not allowed to do so, or the other way around. Therefore, the correct answer to what the other person knew was always the opposite of what the child knew. Of 16 children in each age group, only 2 3-year-olds, 9 4-year-olds but all 16 5-year-olds gave correct answers, very much in line with the findings by Marvin and his colleagues. However, the pattern of errors left little room for egocentrism.

The correct answer to the question "Does the other person know what is in the box?" is "Yes" when the other person has looked inside and "No" when the other person was not allowed to look. Wrong responses can consist in saying "Yes" or saying "No" in both tasks or in being "egocentric," by attributing one's own knowledge to the other person. This would result in responses exactly opposite to correct attributions. As is clear from the last row in table 11.1, the frequency of "egocentric" responses given by 3- and 4-year-old children in the study by Wimmer, Hogrefe, and Perner (1988) and in a replication of that study by Ruffman and Olson (1989) was minimal.

This lack of egocentric responding seems puzzling at first in light of the previous studies by Marvin, Greenberg, and Mossler (1976). However, on closer analysis their results are quite consistent with the more recent ones. Children's errors in the study by Marvin, Greenberg, and Mossler of wrongly granting knowledge to their mother or the experimenter independent of informational conditions were the same errors children made in the study by Ruffman and Olson (yes-bias). [**Note 11.1**: Remarks on Ruffman and Olson's study.]

But if the data from these studies are compatible, then why did the authors reach such different conclusions? The reason for that is a missing control condition. Had Marvin, Greenberg, and Mossler included a condition in which *both the child and an adult* had been left out of the secret—extrapolating from recent findings—results would have shown the quite *nonegocentric* tendency to attribute knowledge to the ignorant adult.

Thus, we see that refined experimental control has helped unmask previous evidence for egocentrism in visual and conceptual perspective tasks as something different. For instance, Liben (1978) and Light and Nix (1983) found that children do not take their own visual perspective as absolute, as Piaget and Inhelder (1948/1956) suggested. Rather, children understand these tasks as requiring them to pick out a picture that shows as much as possible of reality as they know it (intellectual realism). And they do this whether the objective is to choose a picture showing another person's view or their own. In the case of knowledge attribution Wimmer, Hogrefe, and Perner (1988) discovered that children do not treat their own state of knowledge or ignorance as absolute (hence no "conceptual egocentrism"). Young children simply lack the required understanding of how people, including themselves, acquire knowledge.

An important implication of these findings is that children's own mental states do not take privileged status as a basis for understanding other minds. Rather, children must first develop the conceptual framework (theory of behavior and mind) needed to interpret their own actions and inner sensations as much as another person's actions. This in turn casts doubt on a popular view in developmental psychology that *role taking* is the chief mechanism by which children come to understand other people's minds.

Self-Interpretation and the Limits of Role Taking

I have been arguing against the view that mental state concepts acquire their meaning purely from inner ostension, that is, by pointing to an inner state and saying, "This is an instance of knowledge." In contrast, the theory view of mind states that mental concepts are theoretical constructs in a theory of behavior. However, I also think it would be a mistake to discount "inner life" altogether as a source of useful information. That our concepts of our own inner states integrate information about outer events and inner sensation has been amply demonstrated in attribution theory.

An Example from Attribution Theory There is controversy between attribution theorists and cognitive psychologists over whether we can report on our inner processes by direct introspection (Ericsson and Simon 1980) or whether such reports are sometimes correct not because of direct introspective awareness but because of correct use of causal theories (Nisbett and Wilson 1978). However, this discussion is concerned with only those internal processes for which we have concepts to describe them. For present purposes it is important that many findings about self-understanding in attribution theory (Nisbett and Ross 1980, chap. 9) make a slightly different point, namely, that some of our concepts for "inner" states do not just describe inner states but integrate information about internal and external events. Schachter and Singer (1962) were among the first to demonstrate that emotional experience is not a simple introspection of some internal state but an interpretation of internal processes in light of a causal theory of eliciting stimuli.

As an illustration, consider the following study. Cantor, Zillman and Bryant (1975) asked male subjects to rate the attractiveness of nudes after a vigorous ride on an exercycle that resulted in a high degree of physiological arousal. Immediately after the exercise the men were aware of their arousal and its source. However, a few minutes later this awareness had vanished, even though, by physiological measures, the men were still aroused. They rated the nudes much more attractive while in this state of unaware arousal than earlier on when they were still aware of the true source of their arousal or later when the effects of the physical exercise had dissipated objectively.

This goes to show that men do not judge a woman's sexual attractiveness by simply examining what feelings she arouses in them. Rather, their judgment depends on integrating perception of their inner state (for which we seem not to have a commonsense concept, since "arousal" is the investigator's term) and assumptions about what caused it. If the men in the study assumed the cycling was responsible for their arousal, they found the nudes less attractive than when they thought it was the nudes who caused it. However, it is also worth emphasizing that this internal state (of undifferentiated arousal) is an integral part of the judgment, since without it (at the third point of assessment) the men rated the nudes as less attractive than before. There must be some "introspective" access, then, since the arousal did influence the judgments and since it is not plausible that judgments were made by observing the external effects of the arousal (e.g., the men observed their hands shaking).

To summarize, the following two points can be made about sexual arousal:

1. Feelings of sexual attraction are not completely specified by some internal state, since one and the same internal arousal is sometimes identified as "sexual attraction" and sometimes as "physical arousal," depending on what is thought to have caused it.
2. Feelings of sexual attraction are not determined by externally observable factors alone (the nudes and one's trembling hand), since the internal state of arousal does influence the judgment.

Similar points can be made about children's understanding of knowledge.

Knowledge:
A Refined
View on
Inner
Ostension
The concept of *knowledge* serves as a good example in illustrating how children need to integrate internal information from inside with information about the external world. Take for instance the little pilot study reported by Wimmer, Hogrefe, and Perner (1988). The experimenter either let children see what was put inside a box or prevented them from seeing it. When asked *whether they knew* what was inside, 3-year-olds answered correctly "Yes" when they had seen it and "No" otherwise. However, when asked *how they knew* (or why they didn't know), few 3-year-olds were able to say, "Because you showed me" or "Because I couldn't see it." This result was taken to demonstrate that children lack an understanding of the origin of their own knowledge (Wimmer, Hogrefe, and Sodian (1988). However, on what basis did these children give correct answers to the question about *whether* they knew?

If one wanted to deny introspection any role whatsoever, one would expect children to judge their own knowledge on the basis of some overt behavior, for instance, the ability to name the contents of the box. In this case children should first call out the contents of the box and then say, "Yes, I know." However, most children do not do that. They simply say, "Yes, I know." They must have made their judgment on purely internal grounds; perhaps a check on the internal potential to give an actual response.

However, the ability to give a response does not capture the entire concept of knowledge. Knowledge—some philosophers would hold—is *properly caused true belief*. Hence, to judge whether one knows something, it is not sufficient to introspect whether one can dredge up an internal representation of it; instead, one needs to check whether that representation matches reality (truth) and whether it has been properly caused (by information). Unlike pain or the feeling of hunger, then, "knowledge" does not denote a purely internal state. It denotes an internal state as that state relates to the external world. And as we saw in chapter 7, 3-year-olds do not understand this very well. They do not answer questions about the origin of their knowledge (Wimmer, Hogrefe, and Perner 1988), they cannot differentiate knowledge from a lucky guess (see figure 7.1), and they do not understand which modality (vision or touch) informs them about an object's color or weight (O'Neill and Astington 1989; see my figure 7.2).

The fact that our mental concepts do not describe purely internal states calls into question the view that role taking is the primary means by which children come to understand the mind of others. Let us first look at the attractive side of role taking.

The Appeal of Role Taking (Simulation)   The way out of egocentrism—it has been widely held—is by taking the other person's role or perspective (e.g., Feffer 1959; Flavell et al. 1968; Chandler 1973). Thus, in the three-mountains task the child imagines himself in the spatial position of the other person and asks himself *what he himself would see* in that position. With this trick other people's percepts can be defined in terms of the original ostensive definition: what the other sees is what I would see if I were in her position.*

Gordon (1986) calls this technique *simulation* and suggests that much of commonsense psychology can be based on it. His first and most appealing example is simulation in the service of predicting behavior. When trying to anticipate the next move by an opponent who plays white in a chess game we often ask ourselves what we would do if we played white. This allows us to predict a move our opponent might make, by engaging our own chess-playing mechanism for the opponent's men without any *theory* about how a chess player generates moves. Of course, since we are only simulating in a pretend mode, we won't then move the

---

*It is important to distinguish *role taking*, based on purely hypothetical reasoning ("If I were..., what would I..."), from *role playing*, where one actually takes another person's place (for instance, the place of a company manager in a simulated management problem). I am not denying the usefulness of this exercise, since it brings to light or draws one's attention to the problems faced by a manager, just as in the three-mountains problem it helps to actually walk over to the other person's position and find out what there is to see from that vantage point.

opponent's men; we simply register the result of our simulation as what the opponent is likely to do.

However, even in this compelling example of how to "understand" another person's mind by simulating it on our own, not all of this simulation process can be atheoretical. Even to start simulation we have set ourselves in the mode of *wanting* to win with the opponent's men. This in itself cannot be simulated, because it is the prerequisite for simulation. But it is true that for much of the more intricate planning that follows from that initial step we can take advantage of simulation and do not need a theory of planning.

Another compelling area where simulation plays a role, which motivated Paul Harris (1989a, chap. 3) to suggest it as a major developmental mechanism, is the area of emotions. I am personally convinced that simulation works very well here, because when walking home at night I often find myself toying with the hypothetical possibility that a seedy-looking character is closing in on me from behind. And every time I am surprised at the mixed emotions of fear and defiant anger that my imagination evokes. So, we see that our emotional mechanism can be triggered by imagined situations and therefore can be used to simulate another person's emotion. And that, perhaps, is the reason why children start at such an early age to understand emotions in others and can react empathically (see chapter 6).

Yet even for emotions, simulation cannot be completely atheoretical, at least not when it is supposed to produce an accurate prediction. Assume you learn that your colleague's mother-in-law has just died. How does he feel? It will not do to imagine that your mother-in-law has just died and consider how that makes you feel, because your relationship with your mother-in-law may be quite different from your colleague's relationship with his mother-in-law. Your simulation must be informed by some "theory" about which personal relationships are emotionally relevant. If you love your mother-in-law but your colleague hated his, then your simulation will be more accurate if you imagine the death of one of your foes.

However, this is not to deny that once these parameters of simulation have been set, the simulation can provide the answer to the question about what actual emotion will be generated. But simulation seems less useful when we go back to the classical case of visual perspective and to the case of knowledge.

The Limits of Role Taking (Simulation)

What would simulation involve in the three-mountains problem? I am asked to figure out how the person over there sees the scene. I hypothetically assume that I am standing over there and then wait until my visual mechanism provides an answer (just as my emotional mechanism produces an emotion in response to hypothetically assumed conditions). Still waiting. I have to confess the mechanism fails in my case. I have to do some intellectual work: "Since the big mountain is over there, he will see it on the right side; and of the small mountain farther away from him he will see only half behind the large one,... ." Now, in order to keep track of all these piecemeal results of my explicit (theoretical) considerations, it is helpful to integrate them within a visual image. Yet this image comes not as a result of my visual mechanism running a simulation but as a result of hard intellectual labor.

What about knowledge? Can we simulate what someone knows by imagining what that person sees? Perhaps, but the answer depends on what case we are dealing with. For instance, as a subject in one set of conditions in the experiments by Wimmer, Hogrefe, and Perner (1988) I would have seen that there was a coin in the box. Thus, when I see the other person peek inside the box as well, I might try out the following simulation (although I am not aware of ever using this technique): I imagine myself looking inside the open box with the coin in it and let my knowledge formation mechanism operate on this imagined visual input. Will my thus hypothetically engaged knowledge formation mechanism allow me to tell what is inside? Yes, it does: "A coin." Therefore, the other person knows there is a coin inside.

But now consider the case where I am not allowed to look inside the box. I know that there is something in the box but do not know what it is. Seeing the other person look inside, I might try to simulate her knowledge formation process by imagining myself looking inside the open box. However, since I do not know what is inside, I cannot see anything in it in my simulation. Therefore, I cannot tell what is inside, and my conclusion will be that the other person does not know what's inside. But that is wrong!

Perhaps one could get it right by abstracting one step farther and introducing the notion of an arbitrary content: I don't know what is inside, but let's call it X. Simulating a look inside will tell me that an X is inside, so the other person does know what's inside. Of course, it isn't really an X, but that was assumed for simulation's sake. So even here simulation may be possible, but the point is that it is a blatantly more complicated case than the one where I knew that a coin was inside the box. We would therefore expect children to have many more problems with predictions when they themselves are ignorant than when they themselves are in the know. However, existing data do not bear out this expectation.

The study by Wimmer, Hogrefe, and Perner (1988, experiments 2 and 3) contains the relevant data. This study was—as I remember—designed to show that children would find it more difficult to judge that another person looking inside a box would know what is inside it when they themselves are ignorant of its contents ("difficult to simulate condition") than when they know what is in the box ("easy to simulate"). However, since there was no systematic difference between these two conditions, the original objective of the study got lost in the eventual report. By restructuring the data in table 2 of that study one can recapture that there were, if anything, slightly more (23 of 32) correct "yes, other knows" responses in the "difficult to simulate" condition than in the "easy to simulate" condition (20 of 32 correct). And in their Experiment 3 the respective proportions were 14 of 24 and 15 of 24 correct "yes" responses.

Results like this and the general point that some theoretical understanding of mental phenomena needs to be present before simulation can be productively employed make me doubt that simulation is the route by which children come to understand others' minds. Furthermore, there is increasing evidence that children do not come to understand the relevant aspects of their own mind any earlier than they understand the relevant aspects of other people's minds. For instance, children do not understand the origin of their own knowledge under actual conditions—not to mention under hypothetically assumed conditions (Wimmer, Hogrefe, and Perner 1988; Gopnik and Graf 1988; Poole 1988; and current research on distinguishing "know" from "guess" reported in chapter 7) any earlier than they understand it in the case of other people (Hogrefe, Wimmer, and Perner 1986; Pillow 1989; Pratt and Bryant, 1990; Wimmer, Hogrefe, and Perner 1988). The upshot here is that children cannot figure out what another person knows by imagining themselves in the other person's informational situation since they have no understanding of what they themselves would know in that situation.

The simultaneous emergence of understanding these aspects of one's own and of other people's mental states speaks against egocentrism and against role taking (simulation) as the prime mechanism by which other minds are understood. Rather, this evidence suggests that the theory view has an important role to play in explaining how children develop an understanding of the mind; namely, that they come to understand mental states as theoretical constructs in a theory that integrates internal information with externally observable facts. The question is how this theory or commonsense psychology develops. Recent research on this topic has focused on the age of 3 to 6 years. I outline several alternative accounts of this development to highlight the distinctive features of my own theoretical proposal.

Alternative Theory Accounts: Copy Theory?

I briefly discuss several proposals for characterizing 3- to 6-year-old children's understanding of the mind. Most current researchers think that important developments occur during these years. But I will start with one position that assumes that no significant changes take place during this period.

Chandler's "Copy Theory"   Michael Chandler has refined the role-taking approach within Piaget's theory of egocentrism. He realized that egocentrism cannot be a general characteristic of young children but affects only their understanding of those aspects of other people's minds that they cannot yet adequately comprehend. Chandler and Boyes (1982) characterize the child's epistemological development in three stages, from *presymbolic* (during Piaget's preoperational stage, from about 1½ to 6 years) to *symbolic* (concrete operational stage, from about 6 to 12 years) to *metarepresentational* (formal operational stage). From this they deduce the general role-taking principle that children can adequately account for another person's knowledge only at the level of their epistemological development. Higher levels of functioning are reduced to egocentrism. Therefore, at the presymbolic level, which concerns us here, children's intellectual limitations have—in Chandler and Boyes's vivid description—the following effect:

> The cumulative effect ... is to reduce the functional epistemology of such preoperational children to a kind of "copy theory" of knowledge. ...[S]uch children seem to proceed as though they believe objects to transmit, in a direct-line-of-sight fashion, faint copies of themselves, which actively assault and impress themselves upon anyone who happens in the path of such "objective" knowledge.
>
> Within such a view projectile firings from things themselves bombard and actively victimize individuals who function as passive recorders and simply bear the

scars of information which has been embossed upon them. (Chandler and Boyes 1982, 391)

The problems these young copy theorists encounter are illustrated in a study by Chandler and Helm (1984). Children were shown a line drawing of two elephants sniffing a grapefruit. Then the drawing was covered with a piece of paper from which a small window had been cut out. Through that window the children could see only an uninterpretable part (the so-called *droodle*) of the full drawing, namely, a circle (the grapefruit) between two rectangles (the tips of the elephants' trunks). Children were then asked "to describe how this abbreviated or abridged picture would be seen and understood by one of their classmates." The 4-year-old children obtained an almost perfect *egocentrism* score for their answers because they "entirely collapsed the distinction between what was known by the subject and by their less well-informed role-taking partner" (Chandler and Helm 1984, 151 153).

These results have been discussed by Chandler and Helm as a case of egocentrism but by Chandler and Boyes as a demonstration of the use of a copy theory. Why these findings demonstrate the young child's copy theory is made clear in the following passage:

> When such presymbolic children view a stimulus object, such as the dot and dashes of [the droodle picture], and know, on the basis of previous experience, that these cryptic lines represent the tips of two elephant trunks and a grapefruit, they have no alternative other than to assume that these same drawing fragments would telegraph an identical understanding to anyone else who was exposed to them. To arrive at any other conclusion would require that they appreciate the subjective nature of the knowing process and recognize the essential distinction between symbols and their referents. (Chandler and Boyes 1982, 396)

However, the experimental report (Chandler and Helm 1984), does not specify precisely what children were asked and what their actual answers were. This is unfortunate since much of the proper interpretation of the data may depend on it. So let me describe a more recent study for which this information is available.

After 4: More than a Copy Theory   Marjorie Taylor (Taylor, Cartwright, and Bowden 1989) showed 4-year-olds droodles varying in the size and interpretability of visible parts of animals, ranging from nothing, to an uninterpretable part, to an interpretable part. Her question to the children was whether another person who had never seen the entire picture would know what animal was in the picture from just looking at what was visible in the droodle. When a recognizable part was visible, almost all children (83%) said correctly that the ignorant viewer would know what animal was in the picture.

Is this result to be expected if children were using a "copy theory"? Going back to Chandler and Boyes's vivid characterization of such a theory, children should assume that projectile firings bombarding individuals can only come from what is visible in the droodle. Consequently, only *the animal's head* (recognizable part) will be embossed on the viewer's mind. Strictly speaking, the copy theorist should therefore say "No" to Taylor's question about the animal: the viewer knows only that the animal's head is in the picture, but *not* that the entire animal is in the picture.

Perhaps that is taking things too literally. One shouldn't deny copy theorists their common sense, and the copy-theory position needs to be amended:

Copy Theory Rescue Attempt No. 1
Children are using a copy theory together with the commonsense assumption that *if a part embosses itself on the mind, the whole thing is known.*

If that is how children approach the droodles task, they should grant the other, naive viewer knowledge of the entire animal regardless of whether the visible part is recognizable or nondescript. However, only 53% of children thought the other person would know what the animal was when the visible part was nondescript. And from earlier research (Taylor 1988) we know that this percentage goes even lower when only a tiny speck is visible.* Why is there this difference? The copy theory needs to be amended again:

Copy Theory Rescue Attempt No. 2
Children are using a copy theory together with the commonsense assumption that *the smaller the part that embosses itself on the mind, the less likely it is that the whole thing is known.*

With this amendment in place the copy theorist should be fairly certain that, say, the little circle in Chandler and Helm's original study can be known as a grapefruit since the entire object is visible. Graham Davies

---

*Taylor (1988) devised several conditions that are relevant for the present discussion, but her data presentation makes it difficult to extract the precise percentages of responses.

and I (Perner and Davies, in press) happened to ask a question about the circle in such a droodle, but only 28% of 4-year-olds said that the viewer who hadn't seen the entire picture before would know that the circle was a grapefruit.

This pattern of results becomes increasingly difficult to square with the claim that children after the age of 4 years are copy theorists—even if one makes allowances for the precise form of that theory. On the contrary, the data are quite compatible with the view that 4-year-olds do start to understand the need for *interpretation*. What is lacking is adult accuracy in judging how much and what needs to be visible before the depicted object can be identified.

So, children after 4 years have more than a copy theory. But what about younger children? Do they subscribe to such a theory?

Before 4: Not Even a Copy Theory   In Chandler and Boyes's neo-Piagetian theory children are copy theorists throughout the concrete operational period, from about 1½ years onward. Henry Wellman (1990, chap. 9) lifts the notion of a copy theory out of its original wider theoretical context and uses it descriptively to characterize specifically the 3-year-old's understanding of "reality-oriented" mental states (those that refer to the real situation).

This idea that, in particular, younger children are copy theorists does not go well with the finding that young children have difficulty understanding the simple perceptual origins of knowledge. For instance, 3- and even many 4-year-olds (and in the study by Johnson and Wellman (1980), even some 6- and 7-year-olds) tend to misidentify lucky guesses as instances of knowledge (see chapter 7). They erroneously judge themselves as *having known where an object was* when they successfully retrieved the object, even though they had not seen (or acquired any other information about) where the object had been put. With a copy theory this should not happen because the children's lack of informational access should loom large: *not bombarded* by any information means *no copy* in the mind, and hence *no knowledge*.

This confusion between lucky guesses and knowledge cannot be explained away by assuming that children got their initial lack of knowledge mixed up with their possession of knowledge at the time the question was being asked. This salvage operation fails because in one of the control conditions, where children were unsuccessful in their search, they were still told where the object was before the critical question was asked. Yet they correctly answered that they had merely guessed.

Further evidence against a copy theory at younger ages is provided by children's difficulty in explaining that they know what is in a box *because* they have looked inside (see chapter 7)—a difficulty that cannot be attributed to a reluctance to answer "why"-questions (Perner and Ogden 1988). Even the—for a copy theorist very basic—ability to judge *that* a person knows on the basis that the person had informational access is at best unreliable (see chapter 7). This fact was also demonstrated in Taylor's (1988) droodle study, where children younger than 4 years showed no coherent response pattern indicative of a copy theory.

In sum, there is little sign of a "copy theory" at any age. From 4 years up children have more than a copy theory, and below that age children don't even understand that the mind could form copies. The reason is—I claim—that before about 4 years children do not conceive of knowledge as any sort of representation, not even a copy-like representation. And around 4 years children begin to understand knowledge as representation, with all its essential characteristics. One such characteristic is *interpretation*. Thus, many 4-year-olds understand the need for interpretation of droodles, though they may have inaccurate ideas of how much one needs to see before one can actually interpret a cryptic drawing.

Before leaving the topic of copy theories, I would like to draw attention to an interesting implication of Wellman's conjecture that 3-year-olds hold a copy theory of belief.

Wellman's "Copy Theory of Belief"   Wellman (1990, 257–259) states that 3-year-olds (in particular, younger 3-year-olds) have a direct copy notion of belief.[*] This claim has interesting repercussions for the research by Wellman and Bartsch (1988) where children were tested in a variety of tasks allegedly demonstrating their early understanding of belief.

For instance, in the *not-own belief* task children were told that Sam's puppy might be hiding in the garage or under the porch, and they were asked where they thought the puppy was. If they ventured the guess that it was, say, under the porch, then they were told that Sam thought it was in the garage. At the end they had to predict where Sam would look for

---

[*]This, by the way, raises the question of how belief can differ from knowledge, since both presumably are direct copies of reality created under direct bombardment from reality. However, if there is no difference for the young copy theorist, then it is misleading to talk about the child's understanding of knowledge as distinct from the child's understanding of belief, since it suggests richer distinctions than the child is actually able to make.

his puppy. Even of the children younger than 4 years, 83% answered correctly that he'd look in the garage. Wellman and Bartsch interpreted this as evidence for 3-year-old children's understanding of *belief*, in particular, that the story character's belief (puppy in garage) can be different from their own (puppy under porch).

But now, if children at this age understand belief as a direct copy of reality, they would have to assume that Sam's puppy is in two places simultaneously: *in the garage*, of which Sam's belief is a direct copy, and *under the porch*, of which their own belief is a direct copy. This might be worth testing in an experiment, but I doubt that there is much chance of demonstrating that 3-year-olds genuinely think that the puppy is under the porch *and* in the garage at the same time, as they should if they entertain a copy theory of belief.

To repeat my verdict, closer analysis of existing evidence dispels the notion that young children adhere to a copy theory. After the age of 4 years children quickly develop an understanding of knowledge which surpasses that of a copy theory, and before that age they don't even conceive of knowledge as a copy of reality. Another shortcoming of the copy theory as a general description of children's understanding of mind is that, unlike my situation theory, the copy theory does not yield a uniform explanation for children's understanding of mental states other than knowledge (and perhaps other epistemic states). For instance, it cannot be applied to desire and intentional action, since the whole point of intentional action is that it is motivated by an unfulfilled desire to change the world so that the desire will be fulfilled. Unfulfilled desires, by definition, are not copies of the real world. Hence, more than a copy theory is needed to account for children's early understanding of desire and intentional action, but also for pretense, the ability to distinguish between real and imaginary, and other such abilities that tend to emerge before the age of 4 years.

Cognitive Connections and Simple Desires?

In this section I focus principally on two alternatives to my proposal that young children are situation theorists: John Flavell's notion of *cognitive connections* and Henry Wellman's suggestion of a *simple desire psychology*.

Flavell's "Cognitive Connections" John Flavell and his research group were the first to discover one of the important intellectual changes that take place around the age of 4 years. It is the change from what Flavell (1974) called "level 1 knowledge of visual perspective" to "level 2 knowledge." This distinction was the first to split the monolithic notion that Piagetian egocentrism rules throughout early childhood into a more refined and theoretically interesting view of young children's understanding of the mind. Lempers, Flavell, and Flavell (1977) showed that from very early on children indeed understand what other people can and cannot see. But not much before the age of 4 years can they understand that people viewing the same scene (picture) from different angles may describe (represent) that scene differently (Masangkay et al. 1974).

To integrate this finding with more recent discoveries of similar changes at this age—in particular, children's ability to distinguish appearance from reality (Flavell, Flavell, and Green 1983) and the emergence of understanding false belief (Wimmer and Perner 1983)— Flavell (1988) has redescribed this change as one *"from cognitive connections to mental representations."* I fully agree with his description of what the young child is lacking:

> I am suggesting, then, that young children are cognizant of cognitive connections to things but are relatively ignorant of the mental representations of the things these connections engender. (Flavell 1988, 246)

This sounds very similar to the transition I have proposed (Perner 1988): *"from propositional attitudes to mental representation."* However, we differ substantially, I think, with respect to how the child before 4 years conceives of the mind. Flavell characterizes this period as follows:

> By 2 to 3 years of age children have learned that they and other people can be epistemically related or "cognitively connected" to things in the external world in a variety of different ways. An example of a cognitive connection is seeing something. ... They further ... understand at least roughly what it is to hear or not hear something, ... know it, think of or about it, ... image or imagine it, pretend with it, want it,... (Flavell 1988, 244, 245)

What is missing from this account is best illustrated with mental activities like imagining or pretending. These activities appear to satisfy Flavell's definition of a cognitive connection as a "relation to things in the external world." However, imagining and pretending are not just that. As Wellman and Estes (1986) show 3-year-olds understand not only that they can imagine a balloon but also that they can imagine it as being in different states or situations: blown up, deflated, popped, under the table, and so on. In other words, children understand imagining as a relationship not just to an object (balloon) but to propositions (the balloon has popped). Similarly, when pretending that the cloth was her pillow, Piaget's daughter Jacqueline did not just see herself connected to the cloth (pretend with it) but saw herself as connected to the proposition that the cloth was her pillow (pretend the cloth was her pillow).

A similar problem arises with a recent suggestion by Henry Wellman concerning children's understanding of desire.

Wellman's "Simple Desires" Wellman (1990, chap. 8; Wellman and Woolley, 1990) suggests that 2-year-olds—even before they develop a copy theory of mind—have some understanding of desire. He characterizes this early understanding as a *nonrepresentational conception of simple desire* or as a *"simple" desire psychology*. Wellman contrasts this level of understanding with that of adults:

> In adult understanding as philosophers treat it, a person's desires are typically construed as similar to beliefs. Thus, both desires and beliefs are called propositional attitudes. ... In this construal beliefs are therefore understood as representational. ... Since a person's desires are representational in this sense it is feasible to talk of desires for not-real, non-existent imaginary things. ... It is possible, however, to imagine an alternative conception of desire, ..., in which desires are not representational. ... In this simple conception, desires are not attitudes about a proposition but attitudes about an actual object or state of affairs. (Wellman 1990, 210)

The important feature of this simple conception of desire is that it construes desire not as "attitudes about a proposition" but as "attitudes about an actual object or state of affairs." With this simple conception of desire, it is claimed, children can master the experimental tasks by Wellman and Woolley (1990) that I discussed in chapter 9. Children were told about Sam, who wants to take his rabbit to school to show to his friends. His rabbit might be in the shed or in the garden. He looks first in the garden and either finds the rabbit or finds a dog. Children were then asked what Sam will do next; whether he will look in the shed or go to school. Even as young as 2 years and 7 months to 3 years children gave 88% correct answers by pointing out that Sam will go to school if he finds his rabbit but that he will look in the shed next if he finds the dog in the garden (Wellman and Woolley 1990, experiment 1).

The point I want to make here is that children could not give appropriate responses if they were limited to a simple conception of desire as proposed by Wellman (1990). This simple conception limits children's understanding of what Sam wants to being an "attitude about an actual object or state of affairs." This means that children could only understand "Sam wants the rabbit (which exists)." They could not have encoded "Sam wants to take the rabbit to school" because "taking the rabbit to school" is a nonexistent state of affairs and therefore, according to Wellman, beyond the simple conception of desire. However, without this understanding it is difficult to see how children could have predicted "Sam will go to school" after finding the rabbit. This answer makes sense only if they understood that *he wanted to take the rabbit to school*, a desire that Wellman claims cannot be understood at this early age.

There is a way of making the findings by Wellman and Woolley consonant with Wellman's notion of a simple desire psychology. Children answer that Sam will go to school when finding his rabbit because they got the impression from the information "Sam wants to bring his rabbit to school" that rabbit and school belong together. In this case a "correct" answer can be given without understanding the propositional attitude inherent in Sam's desire. However, if that is the basis for correct responses in the condition where Sam finds his rabbit, then why could responses in the other condition not be based on a similar level of understanding, namely, that Sam and the rabbit belong together? That is, children opt for "shed" in that condition, because they associate Sam with the rabbit and because, at this point, they know that the rabbit must be in there. But if this were the basis for children's "correct" responses, then what would this research tell us about understanding of desire?

We may then conclude either that the good performance by such young children in Wellman and Woolley's (1990, experiment 1) study is a methodological artifact or that it is incompatible with Wellman's (1990) suggestion that these children are restricted to a simple conception of desire.

In contrast, Wellman and Woolley's results are in principle compatible with my proposal that children are situation theorists about desire. Being situation theorists does not preclude children from understanding desire as a propositional attitude, that is, an attitude toward real or nonexisting situations (goal situation). Thus, 2½-year-old children are not precluded from understanding that *Sam wants to take his rabbit to school.*

One should not get the impression that our differences are just a minor haggling over how to best describe the way children view the mind at particular ages. I have chosen to dwell on Wellman's "simple desires" because they highlight the deeper conceptual roots of our differences, which bring us directly back to the theoretical analysis of the concept of representation in chapter 2.

The Deeper Conceptual Issues   I should note that I have singled out the work of Henry Wellman as my prime target in this discussion because it is the richest source of detailed suggestions for how to describe the younger child's commonsense psychology. Moreover, since Wellman and I speak a similar language, that of propositional attitudes, it is relatively easy to pinpoint the source of our divergence. To better understand this source, we have to remember an essential issue about representation: the tendency to conflate representational *medium* (or mental process) with representational *content*. As a consequence of this conflation there is a tendency to equate *propositions* with *representations*, which in turn blurs an important difference between *cognitive psychology* and *commonsense psychology*.

The Medium–Content Confusion   In chapter 2 I presented Lehrer's (1986) reconstruction of Reid's analysis of Hume's faulty argument equivocating representation as process (or medium) and **representation** as the content of that process. If we define representation as *something that stands for something else*, as I have done, then we use the word "representation" to refer to the representational medium (more precisely, the state of the medium). For instance, in the case of a picture it is the picture (medium) that is the representation and not the scene depicted on it (content). However, as Lehrer points out, "representation" is ambiguous; it is also used to refer to the content. In a note to chapter 2 I quoted passages written by Wellman and Estes (1986) showing that they equivocate medium and content in their term "mental entity." They use that term sometimes to refer to the mental process representing, say, a chair (the thought of a chair) and sometimes to refer to the represented object (the thought-of **chair**).

There is less of a temptation to equate representational content with its medium when the represented object (or state of affairs) itself exists, because then one can point to that object when asked what the representation represents. In the case of something nonexistent—a unicorn, for instance—this is impossible. When asked what the picture of a unicorn represents, one can only point to the unicorn by pointing to the picture of the unicorn. Or in the case of a person thinking of a unicorn, when asked where that unicorn is, the best one can do is point to that person's head and state: "It's just in his head." However, as I have discussed at length in chapter 2, this does not mean that the picture (or thought) of the unicorn and the depicted (or thought-of) unicorn are therefore the same. But one can see where the temptation to treat them as identical comes from. The same temptation occurs for nonexisting states of affairs, leading to the equivocation of **proposition** with representation.

The
Proposition –
Representation
Confusion

More often than not we talk about nonexistent states of affairs (situations). Because language is used so commonly in this way, the term *proposition* was coined to cover both existent and nonexistent states of affairs. Following Barwise and Perry (1983), I chose the more commonsense talk about *situations* (which cover roughly the same ground). Here too, propositions are not the same as representations; that is, the sentence (representation) "Sam takes his rabbit to school" *expresses* the proposition *Sam takes his rabbit to school*. In other words, the proposition is the content or meaning of the sentence. In any case, the sentence and its meaning ought not to be equivocated.

As we can gather from the passage in Wellman's book cited above, he equates propositions with representations, insofar as he concludes that when beliefs are construed as *propositional attitudes*, they are therefore understood as *representational*. This is supported by his contrasting "representational desires which are attitudes about propositions" with "simple desires which are attitudes about existing objects or states of affairs." However, as I have discussed in chapter 5, this equation has not been intended by philosophers or semanticists. For instance, Richard Montague (Dowty, Wall, and Peters 1981) gives the meaning of a simple sentence (representation) as a proposition, defined as that set of possible worlds in which the sentence would be true. The meaning of a complex sentence reporting a mental state is given as a relationship (attitude) between a person and a proposition (*not* between a person and a sentence, that is, a representation). To interpret mental state reports as expressing the relationship between a person and a representation (sentence) is a quite distinct proposal put forward by Rudolf Carnap (1947, chap. 13). It is true that Fodor (1978) argues that Carnap's view is the right one for cognitive psychology to adopt. However, we are not concerned here with children becoming cognitive scientists but with how they acquire the adult commonsense view of the mind.

The Blurring of Cognitive and Commonsense Psychology. Fodor (1985) argues that mental states need to be viewed as mental representations by a scientific psychology because that is the only scientifically acceptable way to explicate what it means to *grasp a proposition*. Put another way, propositions do not exist except for being projected by some representation. Thus, propositions cannot be grasped unless they are mentally represented.

However, commonsense psychology—I argued in chapter 5—is typically not bothered by these considerations of scientific respectability. Propositions can be made to exist by being represented by the commonsense psychologist himself. They need not be (metarepresentationally) conceived of as being projected by mental representations in the target person's mind. The commonsense psychologist can afford to think of that person's grasp of a proposition as a direct link between that person and the proposition, where the proposition "exists" by being projected by the psychologist's own mind. So, commonsense psychology can go a long way by remaining a situation theory without taking a representational view of the mind.

A nonrepresentational account of propositional attitudes is, of course, not possible when propositions are equated with representations as Wellman does. Consequently, the development of commonsense psychology is seen as a transition from nonmental behaviorism to a representational, cognitive psychology with little middle ground. It is true that Wellman with his simple desires tries to create such middle ground. However, as they are restricted to being desires for existing objects and states of affairs, they fall short of being *mental*, in Brentano's sense of allowing for intentional inexistence.

In contrast, by clearly separating propositions from representations, I have created a much larger middle ground that allows for a proper *mental* conception of mind. It is this middle ground of a *mentalistic situation theory of behavior* which distinguishes my account of how commonsense psychology develops from most other recent attempts at specifying this development. So let me end this book by summarizing my view on how commonsense psychology develops.

Developing Commonsense Psychology: My View

Sue Carey (1985a) looks at children's intellectual progress as the development of "naive theories." This development consists of gradual unfolding of two innate theories ("physics" and "psychology") into increasingly specialized "theories." The idea that the child should be born with a ready-made psychology, which approximately captures the internal workings of human beings, is strongly favored by Jerry Fodor:

> Here is what I would have done if I had been faced with this problem in designing *Homo sapiens*. I would have made a knowledge of commonsense *Homo sapiens* psychology *innate*; that way nobody would have to spend time learning it. And I would have made this innately apprehended commonsense psychology (at least approximately) *true*. ... The empirical evidence that God did it the way I would have isn't, in fact, unimpressive. (Fodor 1987, 132)

My hunch is that God followed *Fodor's Guide* only with caution (as I would have). Although babies are *innately predisposed to attend to expressions of mental states*, they are *not born with a conception of mental states*.* Virtually from birth infants have a clear preference for looking at faces. Why? Because the face is the locus of important sense organs (the eyes are after all the "windows to the soul") and the principal medium for expressing internal states such as emotions. But this does not mean that the infant has a conception of the mental states that are formed by using one's eyes and that are expressed by the face. Their *understanding* of behavior does move from the outside in—it deepens.

In this book I have tried to outline how the child comes to conceptually grasp the mental states behind the relevant behavior. (If one wanted to characterize infants as "behaviorists," the emphasis should be on behavior as an expression of mental states.) This conceptual advance—I have argued—takes place within the confines of the child's general development of mental representation. I have characterized this general development as a progression from *primary representation* (single model) to *secondary representation* (multiple or complex models) to *metarepresentation* (modeling models). The result is the following series of steps in a developing commonsense psychology:

Three Steps in the Child's Development of Commonsense Psychology
1. Innate sensitivity to behavioral expression of mental states
2. Mental states as relations to situations: "Situation theory of behavior"
3. Mental states as internal representations: "Representational theory of mind"

---

*Innate predisposition to attend to behavioral expression of mental states undercuts Carl Johnson's (1988, 49) question: "Why are children intuitive mentalists and not intuitive behaviorists?" The answer is that there is no real contrast. Behavior is an expression of mentality and children improve their understanding of behavior by building a theory that gets increasingly closer to the heart of the matter, the mind.

To appreciate the nature of this developmental proposal, it is important to understand its theoretical motivation. My intention is not to provide a description of what children can understand about the mind at different ages. Instead, it is to show that developmental levels can be theoretically tied in with my analysis of the concept of representation (chapter 2).

Representational systems have to start at a *primary level* as *causal stand-ins* for the real world so that its elements acquire meaning. The developing mind as a representational system is therefore limited at first to a *single model* of reality. At this stage of development the infant's understanding of the mind is restricted to selective attention to behavior (as an expression of mentality) and perhaps to detecting behavioral regularities reflecting the common mental root of different behaviors.

Only after primary functioning has established stable mental representations can *secondary functioning* develop. That is, *multiple (complex) models* can be formed and be detached from immediate reality to represent past, future and purely hypothetical situations. Not until this point can the child start to understand people as *mentally aiming* at something *nonexistent*. This is the first step in conceiving of the mind as characterized by intentional inexistence, which—according to Brentano's thesis—is the distinguishing feature of the *mental* as distinct from the *physical.*

Formation of secondary representations (multiple, complex models) provides the ground for *metarepresentation* (modeling models). Multiple models allow the child to represent the interpretation of external representations and their referent. But the child still needs to work out the notion that something (referent) is apprehended (represented) as something (sense). Having achieved this, the child can understand cases of misrepresentation by separating sense (interpretation) from referent and thus appreciate two further features of intentional inexistence: *aspectuality* and *misrepresentation.*

Finally, I argued that understanding representation initiates a restructuring of mental concepts such as "knowledge" within a representational theory of mind. The child's appreciation of the importance of "informational access" for knowledge formation over "success" is symptomatic of this restructuring. However, the representational view does not replace the original situation theory (mental states as propositional attitudes) but only *extends* it. Even our adult commonsense psychology is not cognitive at heart, but is capable of taking a cognitive, representational stance when needed.

Notes

Chapter 1

1.1 Semantic concerns in cognitive psychology

Although cognitive psychology has neglected the issue of *what* is represented there are some notable exceptions. Phil Johnson-Laird (1975) introduced the notion of model used in semantics to formalize the meaning of words to explain performance on logical reasoning tasks. The explanatory variable is the number of alternative models necessary to check the validity of a syllogism. The number of models captures the way in which the premises of the syllogism specify (represent) reality by detailing how many different interpretations of the premises are possible. Thus, the theoretically important role of mental models is to specify *what* precisely is represented by premise information. It is worth noting that this is how Johnson-Laird (1983) is using the term "mental model" where the emphasis is on how something (e.g., premises of a syllogism) represents something (the possible states of the world). The term is also widely used simply to specify the particular content of the mind as, for instance, by Gentner and Stevens (1983), without trying to explicate what is represented and why it is a representational relationship.

Workers in artificial intelligence interested in systems that naturally interact with their user have become aware of the necessity to model not only the user's mind but also the user's commonsense theory of the system's mind. With these concerns old logical problems about how the mind relates to reality debated by philosophers of mind and language (Brentano 1874/1955; Frege 1892/1960; Carnap 1947) have resurfaced in the recent literature on knowledge systems (e.g., McCarthy and Hayes 1969; Moore 1980; Konolige 1985), and Bruce and Newman (1978) encountered this problem when trying to represent the contents of the tale about Hänsel and Gretel.

Furthermore, the human mind not only has a theory of people's minds but also reflects upon and interprets itself by means of this theory. This, I think, is the key to understanding the natural language distinction between "know" and "remember" that has recently been rediscovered by memory theorists (Tulving 1985). At the heart of this distinction is the mind's concern about the origin of its own knowledge. See chapter 7 below for further discussion and data.

Chapter 2

2.1   The effects of the medium-content equivocation on the "metarepresentation" controversy in cognitive development

The recent literature on children's theory of mind abounds with instances where "representation" or "mental entity" is used equivocally to refer to <u>representational medium</u> and **representational content**. This equivocation has serious theoretical consequences, since it leads researchers to misinterpret demonstrations of children's ability to mentally <u>represent</u> something nonexistent (a mere **representation**), hence: "<u>representing</u> a **representation**" as cases of genuine *metarepresentation*: "<u>representing</u> a <u>representation</u> (as a representation)."

One instance of this equivocation occurs in Wellman and Estes's (1986) use of the expression "mental entity." For instance, the abstract of their paper starts: "Real physical objects (e.g., a chair) can be distinguished from mental entities (e.g., a thought about a chair)." In this sentence "mental entity" is clearly exemplified by a mental process (<u>the thought of a chair</u>), and not its content (**the thought-of chair**). And this interpretation of "mental entity" is confirmed later: "...mental entities can be *about* physically impossible, nonexisting things (e.g., a dog that flies)" [italics mine], since only a mental process (a thought) can be *about* something. The content of a thought (e.g., a dog that flies) cannot be *about* anything (unless, of course one thinks about a thought, rather than flying dogs). However, this interpretation of "mental entity" as a mental process is contradicted by its use in the preceding sentence: "Even 3-year-olds were able to judge real and mental entities appropriately ..., to sort such entities into real and not real." Keeping to the original meaning of "mental entity" as, for instance, a thought, what Wellman and Estes are saying is that children *appropriately* judge thoughts as not real (e.g., a thought of a dog that flies). But that cannot be appropriate, since why should the <u>thought</u> of a dog that flies not be real? Surely, when I am thinking of a dog that flies, I am *really* thinking. My <u>thought</u> (process) exists. What doesn't exist is **the dog that flies**, but that is the content of my thought and not my thought. It appears that in Wellman and Estes's summary of 3-year-olds' ability "mental entity" must be referring to the mental **content** (a dog that flies), whereas in the other passages cited it refers to the <u>process</u> of thinking (the thought of a flying dog). Voilà, the equivocation.

And with this equivocation Wellman and Estes may have set the stage for misinterpreting their data as demonstrations of metarepresentational abilities. The same equivocation appears in Forguson and Gopnik's (1988) evaluation of Wellman and Estes's demonstration that 3-year-olds can contrast dreams, images, and thoughts with real objects: "The 3-year-olds' achievements require them to contrast real objects or states of affairs with *merely* represented objects or states of affairs. So these children seem to be able to differentiate between real things and desires, dreams, imaginings, thoughts and the like" (p. 235). In this passage Forguson and Gopnik equate the contrast between real objects and **merely represented objects** with the contrast between real things and <u>thoughts</u>. And so it appears that they are treating "<u>thoughts</u>" (representational processes) and "**represented objects**" (the representational content) as interchangeable. Voilà, the equivocation.

Hence, it is not surprising that Forguson and Gopnik refer to the young child's ability to distinguish reality from the hypothetical content of the mind as a case of metarepresentation: "Perhaps the most convincing example of metarepresentation in this early period comes in a recent study by Wellman and Estes (1986) ... a particularly convincing demonstration that even very young children can form second-order representations and can contrast 'mere' representations and 'actual' reality" (p. 234). They do not explain why this is an instance of metarepresentation. However, one can guess. Since contrasting is a representational mental activity (<u>representation</u> as process) and since what is contrasted is a "mere representation" (**representation** as content), one can say that the child must be <u>representing</u> a **representation**, hence, executing an act of metarepresentation. But this follows only if the two meanings of "representation" are equivocated.

My suspicions spread that the equivocation of representation as activity with its content still exerts its tacit influence elsewhere, but I have no demonstrable proof. For instance, Leslie (1987) gives an interesting analysis of pretend play, where he correctly points out that the mental representations of the pretend scenario must be "decoupled" from the causal ties to perceived real situations. Being "decoupled," these representations can represent nonexisting entities, false propositions. He (and I quite agree) terms these representations "secondary," in contrast to the "primary" perceptual states, which are causally tied to reality. However, rather inexplicably, he also equivocates secondary representations with metarepresentations, that is, representations of representations. The question this terminology raises is, What representation does a secondary representation represent? Leslie does not raise or answer this question. That is where my suspicions started, because should he, indeed, have tacitly identified nonexisting (merely represented) entities with the representations necessary to project such entities, then mentally representing such an entity would amount to "<u>representing</u> a **representation**," hence "metarepresentation." It is interesting to note that Leslie evokes the notion of "metarepresentation" only for secondary, decoupled representations, not for primary representations. This supports my suspicion that there is little temptation to equivocate representational activity with representational content when the representation has an external, real referent.

Chapter 3

3.1   Distinguishing meanings of "pretense": *symbolic substitution* and *hypothetical-real substitution*.

Although *"acting as if something were something else,"* is an act quite distinct from *"using something to represent something else,"* the word "pretend" can be used to cover either one. Let me illustrate this using the now familiar military models.

Take first a case where "pretend" clearly marks a representational relationship: A general is bent over the sandbox in his headquarters as a civilian unfamiliar with military models enters. The visitor is somewhat perplexed to see the dignified general playing in a sandbox and asks, "What are you doing with blocks in a sandbox, Sir?" The general, who senses the visitor's perplexity, explains, "I am *pretending* these blocks are tanks on the battlefield." Clearly, with the word "pretend" the general means that the blocks *stand-for* (represent) the real tanks.

Now let us take a very similar situation. Said general is musing over various possibilities, and he wants to see what the situation would be like if the tanks had been placed on the left instead of on the right flank of the infantry. So he moves the tanks over. Just then another general enters who wants to remind himself of the tanks' current position. Seeing his colleague move the blocks around, this general asks with some alarm, "What are you doing to the tanks?" The first general answers, "I am *pretending* the tanks are on this flank of the infantry." In his answer the general is referring with the word "pretend", not to the representational relationship between model and battlefield, but rather to the counterfactual nature of the hypothetical situation that he is projecting by moving the elements in the model. As in pretend play, the projected nonreal situation provides the basis for acting-as-if. The general can now engage in a hypothetical attack as-if the tanks were stationed on the left flank.

To bring the ambiguity of the word "pretend" to a point, consider the following example where green blocks stand for the home country's tanks and blue blocks stand for enemy tanks, and where the same color coding is used for soldiers. Now the general is observed putting a green twig into a blue block. When asked what he is doing, he points to the blue block and says, "I'm *pretending* this is now one of our tanks." Obviously, the general is assuming something out of the ordinary. But what is it? Is he imposing a different mapping relation from model to reality, where the blue block—counter to convention—is now used as a symbol for his own tank, or is he talking about an imagined scenario where an enemy tank has been captured and is now used by his own men? In the latter case, he is not changing the symbolic relationship—the blue block still symbolizes the same old enemy tank—he is only changing the actual situation to a desirable possibility.

This ambiguity in the general's use of "pretend" highlights the developmental psychologist's dilemma in interpreting a child's pretend play. What we observe is deviant behavior, for instance, using a teddy as a pillow. This means nothing much unless the child gives a "knowing smile" or at a later age even says, "Me p'tend pillow." These are clear signs that the child is aware of the discrepancy that makes her behavior noteworthy. The question is still what kind of discrepancy the child is commenting on.

3.2   Other voices against play being symbolic

Vygotsky (1966/1978) also argues against the interpretation of play as a symbolic activity but, I think, for different reasons: "If play is understood as symbolic, there is the danger that it might come to be viewed as an activity akin to algebra; ... The child would be seen as an unsuccessful algebraist who cannot yet write the symbols but can depict them in action. I believe that play is not symbolic action in the proper sense of the term, ..." (p. 94).

Huttenlocher and Higgins (1978, 115) ask the question "When is behavior symbolic?" and present a list of critical arguments against accepting behavior as symbolic. But in the end they agree that when the child explicitly verbalizes the pretense as Piaget's (1945/1962, 124) daughter Jacqueline did at 2 years ("finger walking ... horse trotting"), then we can be sure that the child understands her behavior as symbolizing something else. My interpretation of pretend play is more radically antisymbolic. Even explicit verbalization need be nothing other than an explicit comment on the child's understanding that she is acting as if her fingers were walking or as if her fingers were a horse trotting.

In fact, not even the explicit mention of the word "pretend" need imply that the child has any symbolic relationship in mind. Jacob at 3 years and 3 months asked his mother why she was going to Grandmother's apartment. Her answer was that she was going to get a pot for cooking. "You are *stealing* a pot," was his comment on that. "No, I am just *borrowing* it," explained his mother. "That's *pretend stealing*," was his final verdict. Did he mean that by borrowing the pot his mother was "representing" an act of stealing?

3.3   Background on opacity

Straight reports about the real world are often referred to as "transparent," which is intended to indicate that their meaning could be construed as directly and straightforwardly *referential*. For instance, if a description that is part of such a factual report is replaced by another description that refers to the very same thing, then the (transparent) meaning and the truth of the report do not change. Take a famous example from Frege (1892/1960):

"The Morning Star is a body illuminated by the sun."

"The Morning Star" is simply an old-fashioned name for the planet Venus. And so is the expression "the Evening Star." So, if we replace one name of Venus by the other, the truth of the sentence should not change, which in fact it doesn't in transparent contexts.

"The Evening Star is a body illuminated by the sun."

This fact that substituting one expression in a factual report for another with the same meaning does not affect the truth of statements has been formalized by Leibniz as the logical rule of "substitutability of identicals." However, Frege has noted that Leibniz's rule does not always hold. It only holds in transparent contexts where the meaning of descriptions can be specified by objects they refer to. There are other contexts where this does not hold. One important class of such "opaque" contexts is the class of mental state reports. For instance, the following sentence is true:

"The ancient Greeks did not *know* that the Morning Star is the Evening Star."

If according to Leibniz's law we replace "Evening Star" with "Morning Star," we should get a new *true* sentence. The result is false, however, since the new sentence

"The ancient Greeks did not know that the Morning Star is the Morning Star."

is not an accurate description of the ancient Greeks' ignorance. Whereas the original sentence describes a certain lack of astronomical knowledge, the new sentence doubts the ancient Greeks' fundamental logical ability to recognize that something is itself. From examples like this Frege (1892/1960) drew the conclusion that in certain contexts, like the one created by the word "to know," the meaning of expressions like "Evening Star" is not *transparent*—that is, it does not simply refer to Venus anymore. It is as if an opaque screen had been inserted between linguistic expressions and objects in the real world. In such opaque contexts the meaning of "Morning Star" is therefore not the referent *Venus* but something more opaque, what Frege termed its "sense" (German "Sinn").

It is useful to note that the problem of opacity is not created by mental state reports alone, but also by statements of possibility. Consider the true sentence

"It is *possible* that the Morning Star is not the Evening Star."

If we now replace "Evening Star" with "Morning Star," we again obtain a false sentence:

"It is *possible* that the Morning Star is not the Morning Star."

This sentence is obviously false since it is a logical contradiction that the Morning Star is not itself, and therefore the situation the sentence describes clearly is not possible.

Problems of opacity occur in other domains besides possibility and mental states. Difference in time is another classical problem for semantics (Dowty, Wall, and Peters 1981), and there are many others, such as different geographical regions, plays and their actors, and so on (Fauconnier 1983/1985).

Since Frege there have been many attempts to spell out what this *sense* could be that provides the meaning for expressions. I will consider just two of them. One approach is called "possible-worlds semantics." The most sophisticated system of this kind is Richard Montague's (see Dowty, Wall, and Peters 1981). Montague defined the meaning (sense) of a word as its referents across all possible worlds and times. According to this definition two words are synonymous (have identical meaning) only if they have the same referent in every possible world at all times. One can see how this might solve Frege's problems, or save Leibniz's law in opaque contexts. Consider again the sentence

"It is possible that the Morning Star is not the Evening Star."

Since there is a possible world in which "Morning Star" refers to a different object than "Evening Star," their meaning is not identical. Hence, they cannot be substituted for each other within that sentence without endangering its truth, since Leibniz's law holds only for words of identical meaning.

Although possible-worlds semantics does a fairly good job in solving problems of opacity created by statements about possibility and time, some problems remain. Carnap (1947) noticed that logically equivalent expressions that hold at all times and in all possible worlds still cannot be substituted for each other in mental state reports. For instance, $2+2=4$ must be true at all times in all possible worlds (since "possible" is defined as noncontradictory and since assuming that $2+2$ would be anything other than 4 is logically contradictory). Since (according to possible-worlds semantics) the meaning of "4" is identical to that of "$2+2$," replacing "4" by "$2+2$" should therefore (according to Leibniz's law) have no adverse effects on truth. But this does not work. Consider the following sentence about Johnny, aged 2 years and 6 months:

"Johnny *thinks* he got 4 candies."

If this sentence is true, then (unless Johnny is a mathematical prodigy) substituting "$2+2$" for "4" produces the almost certainly false sentence

"Johnny *thinks* he got $2+2$ candies."

Apart from this technical demonstration, we know anyhow that "4" and "$2+2$" are not identical in meaning. Thus, possible-worlds semantics does not provide a sufficiently fine definition of meaning.

For that reason Carnap (1947, chap. 13) suggested, roughly speaking, something like this. In mental state reports, like the ones above, Johnny is linked by "thinking" not to the proposition "He got 4 candies" but to a representation of that proposition:

"Johnny *thinks* ' he got 4 candies.' "

This takes care of the substitutability of 4 for $2+2$ in mental state reports, since the representation "4" is evidently not the same as "$2+2$." Although 4 and $2+2$ mean the same (refer to the same numerical entity in all possible worlds), they are different representations of that entity and therefore cannot be replaced in mental state reports according to Carnap's suggestion.

Logicians did not take easily to this solution, because introducing representations leaves mental state reports logically intractable. But, as Fodor (1978) points out, it comes close to what cognitive psychologists have always considered mental states to be, namely, mental representations. Lately, Carnap's suggestion has been taken up again under the name of the "syntactic approach" by logicians working in artificial intelligence (e.g., Konolige 1985). But note that Carnap's suggestion was not meant as a solution for opacity problems in general—in particular, not for problems created by statements of possibility or about time. Rather, it was specifically aimed at coping with the particular logical problems created by mental state reports. And we will have to contend with Carnap's suggestion again later, when we discuss commonsense theories of mind.

3.4   Problems with Leslie's isomorphism of opacity between pretense and mental state reports

Leslie (1988, 25, 27) suggests that there is a "deep isomorphism" between pretense and mental state reports because one can line up three types of pretense with three types of logical problems found in mental state reports.

	Type of Pretense	–	Type of Logical Problem
1.	Object substitution	–	Referential opacity
2.	Property attribution	–	Nonentailment of truth
3.	Imaginary objects	–	Nonentailment of existence

This claim seems curious for two reasons. First, the correspondence shown is not between types of pretense and types of mental state reports. Why, then, should it demonstrate an isomorphic relationship between pretense and mental state reports? Second, Leslie is lining up types of pretense and types of logical problem for which there is no particular correspondence, since any one of the three logical problems can be associated with any one of the three types of pretense. Let me give just one example, namely, that *nonentailment of truth* occurs in pretense involving *object substitution*.

Leslie (1988, 26–27) illustrates nonentailment of truth with the following example:

> Compare: "John picked up the cat, *which was ill*" and "John believed that *the cat was ill.*" The first sentence can be true only if the embedded italicized expression is also true, but the second sentence can be true (or false) regardless.

If we now consider as a case of object substitution the sentence "John pretends *the banana is a telephone,*" then this sentence can be true (or false) regardless of whether the embedded italicized expression is true. Clearly, nonentailment of truth occurs in cases of pretend object substitution. This shows that the alignment of a particular case of pretense with a particular type of logical problem in Leslie's "deep isomorphism" is arbitrary. There is no isomorphism.

3.5   Copying a representation does not create a metarepresentation

Leslie's (1987, 417) suggestion that a pretend representation *"decouples* the primary expression from its normal input-output relations" is incorporated in my military example (chapter 2) in which generals are using two models. Their "primary," center model that informs them about the current state of the battlefield has "normal input relations" (built by the scout) and "normal output relations" (it forms the basis for orders to the commanders in the field about where to attack the enemy, etc.). The other, "secondary" model in the corner is *not* built by the scout and is *not* used for giving orders to attack. So it is "decoupled from normal input-output relations." Yet crucially, its component elements still retain *the same meaning* or *reference* as their corresponding elements in the primary model. That is, "stick$_2$" still refers to the *soldier*, "block$_2$" to the *tank*, and so on.

Leslie's idea of decoupling is more radical; it deprives all model elements of their meaning and reference. And there appears to be a good argument for that, if one asks how elements in the primary model acquire their representational powers. Presumably, "stick$_1$" refers to the *soldier* because on, say, the causal view the presence of "stick$_1$" is *caused* by the presence of the soldier where the scout saw him on the battlefield. On that view, elements in the secondary model (e.g., "stick$_2$") indeed do not get their referent in the same way as elements in the primary model (e.g., "stick$_2$"), as Leslie has observed:

> Decoupled expressions no longer have an automatic reference. Indeed, I shall not use the term *reference* in connection with them because they do not relate directly to the world. I shall instead use the term *anchoring*. Decoupled expressions do not refer to objects, then, they are anchored to parts of primary representations. This is not automatic, but needs to be specially stipulated. (Leslie 1987, 418)

That seems a sensible suggestion of how elements in the secondary model obtain their meaning, but one has to beware of interpreting "anchoring" as a kind of representational relationship. It is certainly not so that by being "anchored" to elements in the primary model (e.g., "stick$_2$" is anchored to "stick$_1$") elements in the secondary model come to "represent" primary elements (e.g., "stick$_2$" represents "stick$_1$"). If that were the case, then the secondary model could be called "metarepresentational" since it represents the primary model, which is itself a representation. But "anchoring" does not do that; it simply gives the elements of the secondary model the *same referent* as the elements of the primary model to which they are "anchored." That is, if "stick$_1$" refers to *soldier*, then by being anchored to "stick$_1$," "stick$_2$" acquires the same referent, namely, the *soldier*. In other words, although the way in which the elements of the secondary model acquire their meaning is indirect via the "naturally evolved" meaning of the primary model, the meaning they do acquire is the same as that of the elements in the primary model. That this is so can be seen intuitively from the fact that when the generals play with the secondary model, they are doing it, not because that model represents the primary model, but because that model, too, represents the battlefield, their soldiers, tanks, and so on, although they may be represented as interacting in purely imagined situations.

Chapter 4

4.1   The difference between mental tokens and definite descriptions
To be able to compare different situations at all, it is essential that the tokens used to model these situations refer to the same relations and entities. These tokens are what in Barwise and Perry's (1983, 53) approach form the constituent sequences of situations. So the token "Daddy" in my examples is used as a proper name for a particular person. This name functions as a "rigid designator" (Kripke 1971/1977) that refers to the same person in all possible situations. In this respect the tokens of mental models are different from definite descriptions in natural language (Barwise and Perry 1983, chap. 7), which pick out different referents depending on what discourse situation they are used in. For instance, the definite description "my daddy" refers to the father of the speaker, that is, to different people if it is used by different speakers with different parents.

4.2   Do early assertions imply a concept of truth?
John Macnamara (1986) claims that infants' assertions imply their having a concept of truth. Specifically, he claims that even basic assertion presupposes a grasp of the notion of truth because it presupposes a judgment of truth: "The learner does not need the concept of judgment because he can perform the act of judging without knowing that he is judging. But the learner must have the concept of truth: there is no action that can stand in its place" (p. 106). David Olson (1987) has criticized this claim, arguing (in line with my proposal) that even explicit denial of assertions "are, in fact, judgments of agreement or disagreement with the assertion and not judgments of the truth or falsity of the proposition" (p. 396).
It is often assumed that having a concept of truth implies metarepresentation. However, I do not see that this necessarily follows. If I may gloss "proposition" as "situation described by the assertive statement," then my position about young children's capabilities is compatible with Macnamara's. Macnamara's insistence that the child possesses a "concept of truth" implies no more than that the child be able to represent the difference between the situation described by the assertion and reality. This is not metarepresentation, since only a comparison of situations is required. Metarepresentation becomes necessary for representing how the assertion (as representational medium) embodies the described situation

(representational content) and for representing the fact that the assertion makes a claim about reality (referent). But these "representational" facts need not be represented; rather—to paraphrase Macnamara—they can be performed in the act of judging without knowing that they are being performed.

4.3   Four points about DeLoache's paradigm and data

In this note I would like to make four points about DeLoache's paradigm and data.

Children's awareness of experimenter's intentions. In personal communication Judy DeLoache has pointed out that in more recent experiments some children showed awareness that the arrangement of the furniture in the small room and the arrangement of the furniture in the large room *were supposed to correspond.* In a study (DeLoache, in press) where children were tested on consecutive days and where on the second day the furniture in one of the rooms had been rearranged, many children remarked on this unexpected turn of events and some told the experimenter that "she had made a mistake" or got it "wrong." This would get us closer to an indication that children start to understand the representational function of DeLoache's models. That some children at this age show signs of understanding representation would go well with other evidence for understanding of interpretation and misrepresentation.

What Represents What? DeLoache used the two corresponding rooms in a way that makes it difficult to speak of representation in an unambiguous manner. As noted in chapter 2, *representation* is an asymmetric relationship—for example, the map represents the land but the land does not represent the map, or the sandbox model represents the battlefield but not the other way around. Furthermore, in the case of maps or models it is always the representation that is made to correspond to the represented; that is, the map is made to reflect the land so that interpreters can find their way through the land. It is not the land that is made to correspond to the map so that one can move one's finger on the map correctly. It is difficult to construe the relationship between locations of the two Snoopies in exactly the same way. On the one hand, Baby Snoopy is placed after Daddy Snoopy, suggesting that Baby Snoopy's location is intended to represent that of Daddy Snoopy. On the other hand, it is Daddy Snoopy's location that serves as guide for finding Baby Snoopy, suggesting the opposite—namely, that Daddy Snoopy serves as representation for Baby Snoopy. One is tempted to ask how this experimental paradigm can serve as a test for children's understanding of representation if the setup does not even make clear what represents what. Treating DeLoache's study as an investigation of the child's understanding of correspondence raises no such problems.

The "dual orientation" hypothesis. DeLoache (1987) also found that children more easily locate Snoopy in his room when the experimenter shows them a picture of the room and points out on the picture which piece of furniture he is hiding under. This fact led DeLoache to claim that the model task is difficult because children must represent it both as a real object and as a symbol, whereas the photograph typically has no role other than as a symbolic representation of something else (DeLoache 1987, 1557). Recent findings (DeLoache 1989c) support this hypothesis. For instance, when the 3-D model was put behind a transparent barrier, 2½-year-olds performed better than their counterparts who participated in the original task. In contrast, when the child subjects were allowed to play with the model, even 3-year-olds found it difficult to use the model as a guide to the large room.

I find the dual orientation hypothesis quite plausible but want to point out that the duality also occurs at the level of understanding correspondence. The small room is an interesting structure in its own right, as well as a structure that corresponds to the large room. Therefore, playing down or enhancing interest in the small room in its own right may help or inhibit the child in the task of focusing on its correspondence with the other room. The fact that pictures are easier to use most likely has a quite different explanation. Pictures relate to the depicted large room in a different way than the miniature room does.

Pictures have interpretations! Do miniature rooms? There is an important difference between pictures and models in how correspondence to the large room is established. The difference arises from the fact that the picture is (at this age) already treated as a representation. Let me explain this with a more recent study by DeLoache (personal communication) in which children are shown a picture of Big Bird hiding behind a sofa and have to find Big Bird in his room. To bring out the contrast to the miniature model room, I will speak as though the study had been done with a picture of Daddy Snoopy hiding in his room.

When looking at the picture of the room, the child automatically *sees* Snoopy in his large room in the picture. That is, the child interprets the picture in terms of Daddy Snoopy and his room or, in other words, builds a mental model of Daddy Snoopy in his room. The problem the child has to solve is to realize that the situation shown in the picture (which already has Daddy Snoopy in it) is the *same situation* as the one in the actual room. This ability apparently develops between 2 and 2½ years. The 2-year-old understands that the picture shows Daddy Snoopy (can interpret it) but does not catch on to the fact that this informs about Daddy Snoopy's real location. The timing of the emergence of this ability (understanding that the *depicted situation* is supposed to correspond to the real situation) fits quite well with the finding that children's ability to reject false statements (Pea 1980; Antes 1989), which requires comparing a *described situation* with the real situation, blossoms after the second birthday.

In contrast, understanding the correspondence between Baby Snoopy's room (instead of a picture of Daddy Snoopy's room) and Daddy Snoopy's room has to be drawn at the level of the two physical structures because Baby Snoopy's miniature room is not naturally (maybe after long practice) interpreted in terms of Daddy Snoopy's room. That is, by looking at Baby Snoopy's room, one sees Baby Snoopy's room (builds a mental model of Baby Snoopy's room), but one does not see Daddy Snoopy's room. This makes Baby Snoopy's room essentially different from a picture of Daddy Snoopy's room as a representation of Daddy Snoopy's room.

To summarize, in the case of the picture of Daddy Snoopy's room we have to distinguish three different structures:

1. The picture as a physical entity with its regions corresponding to particular items in Daddy Snoopy's room.
2. The interpretation of the picture in terms of Daddy Snoopy and his room.
3. Daddy Snoopy and his room in reality.
* The problem is to understand and anticipate sameness of situations.

In the case of the miniature (Baby Snoopy's) room two structures have to be considered:

1. Baby Snoopy in his miniature room.
2. Daddy Snoopy in his large room.
* The problem is to understand the correspondence between items in one room and items in the other and to understand that they are arranged in the same way (i.e., Baby Snoopy is in the corresponding place).

To use knowledge of one structure to find one's way in the other is a matter of inference (it is symmetrical since it can be used either way). It only becomes a matter of *representation* once one structure (e.g., the picture) has an *interpretation* in terms of the other.

From DeLoache's data we can describe children's relevant intellectual progression in the following way:

1. Before the age of 2 years: ability to interpret pictures.
2. Between 2 and 2½ years (at the same time as the ability to reject false statements): ability to compare situations or expect similarity of situations.
3. Between 2½ to 3 years: ability to establish correspondence between two systems and to use one to infer the state of the other. This can be made easier or more difficult by playing down or emphasizing that the first structure is an interesting thing in itself, not just a thing to be looked at (dual orientation).

I will argue later that the ability to understand that something (picture) has an interpretation (indicating some understanding of its representational nature) or that the models can be used as representations develops between 3 and 4 years.

4.4   Ruling out embarrassment as a cause of children's refusal to remember their own mistake

There is an alternative explanation for why most 3-year-olds couldn't "remember" their original mistaken answer. They simply refused to admit having been mistaken out of embarrassment and so "pretended" their mistake had never happened. However, this account of the data is implausible for two reasons. First, it leaves unexplained why 4-year-olds should have been less embarrassed by their mistaken answers. Second, Wimmer and Hartl (1989) found that children's memory for their own mistakes was no worse than their memory for observing someone else making that same mistake. It is unlikely that children would find it embarrassing to have to recount someone else's mistake.

4.5   Evidence that children assume that an object's color changes when moved behind a color filter

Flavell, et al. (1987) had 3-year-old children watch an experimenter move a piece of white cardboard behind a colored filter so that it looked blue. Then they watched a piece of the cardboard (still behind the filter) being cut off and disappearing in the experimenter's fist. The experimenter then removed her fist from behind the filter while the main piece of cardboard remained there, looking blue. The experimenter placed two identically sized pieces of cardboard in front of the child: the white piece cut off from the card behind the blue screen and a blue piece of the same size and shape. The child had to decide which piece was the one that had been cut off from the cardboard behind the screen (actually white but looking blue). The 3-year-olds who in the original test answered that the piece of white cardboard when viewed through the blue filter was really blue also pointed to the newly added blue piece as the one that had been cut off from the (actually white) card behind the blue filter. It does seem as though 3-year-olds assume not only that the cardboard changes its color while being viewed through the screen but also that it remains so when it is removed, as in the case of the cut-off piece.

Slightly older children, however, may assume that the cardboard changes back to its usual color when being removed from behind the filter. The following finding can be interpreted in this way. Flavell, Flavell, and Green (1983) found that by 4 years children answer the question "Is this really, really white or really, really, blue?" correctly with "White." However, this may be because they interpret "really" to mean something like "usually." When the words "right now" were added to this question (Flavell, Flavell and Green 1989) even some 5-year-olds gave the wrong answer "Blue."

4.6   Controlling for performance difficulties on the appearance-reality task: temperature sensation

I have been arguing that young children's difficulty with appearance-reality questions stems from their problem in understanding that appearances can misspecify reality. However, one could argue that children's answers just reflect "task-generated confusion." Therefore, it helps to sustain the original claim if one can show that children can respond correctly when the same questions can be answered without having to understand appearance as misrepresentation.

Flavell, Green, and Flavell (1989, experiment 2) provide the needed data. They asked children to put an insulated (rubber) miniglove on a finger of one hand and a noninsulated (aluminum) one on a finger of the other hand and to touch an ice cube with both their gloved fingers. The two questions were (first) "*Really* and *truly*, is this a cold ice cube?" and (second) "Right now, does this ice cube *feel* cold to this finger?" (pointing to each of the two fingers in turn). Almost all (91%) 3-year-olds (2 years and 11 months to 4 years) gave correct answers to these questions, whereas only 53% passed the deceptive-appearance task, which this time involved a pen that looked like a tube of toothpaste. The children were asked very similar questions: *"Really* and *truly*, is this a pen?" and "Right now, does this *look* like a pen to your eyes?"

To make clear my explanation of this difference, I must point out a crucial difference in how we phenomenally experience visual perception and haptic temperature sensations (hypothesis 2 by Flavell, Green, and Flavell 1989). The difference is that our phenomenal awareness of temperature sensations can be *(intentionally) directed* toward the sense organ. For instance, I can say, "My finger feels cold," when touching an ice cube. With vision this is not the case. I cannot say, "My eyes feel like a pen," when looking at a pen.

This difference in the structure of experience between haptic temperature sensation and vision makes it possible for the young child to gloss the appearance question "Right now, does this ice cube *feel* cold to this finger?" as "..., does this ice cube *make* your finger *feel* cold?" The child can therefore give the correct answer "No" for the finger with the insulated glove and maintain the truism that "Really and truly, this is a cold ice cube." This is possible because the feeling of the finger is not an *appearance* of the ice cube but a causal effect of the ice cube that can be blocked by the particular kind of glove one is wearing.

A comparable interpretation is not possible for the visual task since the question "Right now, does this *look* like a pen to your eyes?" cannot be glossed as, say, "..., does this *make* your eyes *look (feel)* like a pen?" Eyes, unlike fingers, don't feel their sensations. They only detect properties of the external world. And so the "toothpasty" sensation created by the pen cannot be understood as an effect on one's eyes but can only be understood as what that object actually is. The older, metarepresentational child can understand it as the object's *appearance*. For 3-year-olds this conceptual trick is not possible and so they wrongly answer that the object (pen looking like a tube of toothpaste) looks like a pen.

Chapter 5

5.1   George Herbert Mead's notion of role taking
Paul Light (1987) points out that the post-Piagetian view on the purpose of role/perspective taking is different from that envisaged by George Herbert Mead (1934). Mead saw role taking as a means of developing greater self-awareness by taking the role of others toward oneself, whereas in the Piagetian tradition it is a means of understanding others via understanding oneself.

5.2   *Intentionality* of sensations
If "thinking of an apple" is a typical example of Intentionality because the apple "intentionally inexists" in the thought, then one might wonder how sensations (see table 5.1) or feelings, like "feeling pain," can have Intentionality.

The question is, When I am in pain, what is my pain *about*? What is the "intentionally inexisting" object? Brentano (pp. 126–127) defended Intentionality of feelings by pointing out that we are feeling *something* when we feel pain. We are not just making it up but feel pain as something objectively existing. However, Brentano also admitted that pain—unlike the apple—exists only insofar as it is felt, whereas the apple exists whether it is thought about or not. So one could say that sensations/feelings are *about* themselves, whereas the attitudes are *about* something "external" (other than themselves). In other words, as Colin McGinn (1982) has pointed out, sensations are intrinsically tied up with inner awareness.

5.3   The intensionality of causality

Causal effectiveness of objects, though not a mental process, is also aspect specific. For instance, if I put a rock on a scale, it is only the weight of the rock that produces the desired causal effects on the balance of the scale, not the color of the rock. Dretske (1981, 76, 77) therefore speaks of the "intensionality of nomic regularities." This is also an important idea behind Fodor's (1987, 1990) causal theory of representational content. Dretske's observation still leaves mental relations different from simple physical relations, but it brings the mental within the reach of eventual physical explanation, as intended by philosophers aiming at a *natural* account of intentional phenomena.

5.4   Relating people to nonexisting situations as a scientific problem

Scruples about interpreting statements about goals (e.g., "Sue *wants* to be in Australia") as relations between a person and a nonexisting situation are specifically scientific worries. Our current scientific view of causality allows only presently existing states of affairs to exert any real influence. Therefore, it does not make sense to explicate "Sue is buying a ticket from Qantas because she wants to go to Australia" by saying "Sue's purchase is caused by her wanting the nonexisting situation of being in Australia," since nonexisting situations cannot—in our scientific view—be part of any causal effect. In contrast, "Teleological" explanations of past eras did not have to contend with the worries of the modern scientific outlook on what is in principle possible and on what is a permissible explanation. Commonsense psychology does not share these scientific scruples either, as long as it yields some sensible predictions.

But the scientific psychologist cannot go along with common sense. So the question arises how such a directed desire can be implemented in the mind in a way that is compatible with current scientific views. Behaviorism and drive psychology solved the problem by denying the existence of internal states that are *intentionally directed at* or *about* something. The question then becomes, How can aboutness become part of a scientific psychology? Fodor (1985, 84–85) has this to say:

> ...the current ("Naturalistic") consensus is that if you've gone this far [i.e., talking of relations to propositions] you will have to go further. Something has to be said about the place of the semantic and the intentional in the

natural order; it won't do to have unexplicated 'relations to propositions' at the foundations of the philosophy of mind.

Just why it won't do ... is, to be sure, not very clear. ... A plausible scruple—one I am inclined to take seriously—objects to unreduced *epistemic* relations like *grasping* propositions. One really doesn't want psychology to presuppose any of *those*; first because epistemic relations are pre-eminently what psychology is supposed to *explain*, and second for fear of 'ontological danglers'. It's not that there aren't propositions, and it's not that there aren't graspings of them; it's rather that grasping of propositions aren't plausible candidates for ultimate stuff. If they are real, they must be really something else.

The way out for cognitive psychology was to treat mental states as *representations*. Representations exist and thus can exert causal influence on behavior. Their causal (Fodor 1987, 1990) or functional analysis (Dretske 1988; Millikan 1984) preserves aboutness.

5.5   The representational view of mental state reports in situation semantics

In their chapter 9 Barwise and Perry (1983) interpreted mental state (attitude) reports as relating a person to a situation (be it actual, factual, or nonfactual). This analysis seemed satisfactory for nonepistemic seeing (their chapter 8) and for accounting for some of the logical (opacity) properties of seeing-that, knowing-that, believing-that, and so on. But some limitations remained. To overcome these, the authors sketch in their chapter 10 an interpretation in terms of represented mental states to capture *visual percepts* and *misconceptions* about reality. Instead of relating the person to an event, mental state reports relate the person to an *event-type*, which is like an event but with one or more indeterminates (variables) that need to be *anchored* to particulars. The interpretation of a mental state report then consists of two parts (e.g., 234). One part relates the person to an event-type. Barwise and Perry call this the "frame of mind" (sense). The other part stipulates how the event-type is anchored to the real world, and it is called the "setting" (the referent of the mental representation).

A mistaken belief report can then be interpreted in the following way. Let's say that Sarah does not recognize her golf ball, so she thinks the object she is looking at is not her ball. In the analysis Sarah stands in a belief relation to the event-type "THIS is not my ball," where "THIS" is an indeterminate anchored to "*this* (object Sarah is looking at)" which figures in the real situation: "*this* is Sarah's ball."

Chapter 6

6.1   Learning the meaning of emotional expressions by imitation

A third quite interesting possibility for how children acquire an understanding of their mother's facial expression is mentioned by Paul Harris (1989a, 24)—namely, that they experience her expressed emotion via a process of imitation. Infants initially just observe their mother's fearful face without emotional consequence. They then start imitating her face, which by an innate mechanism elicits fear in themselves. After a few imitations the child starts to associate mother's fearful face with his own reaction of fear. The child avoids the cliff because mother's facial expression induces fear in the child which makes the child avoid the cliff. (By the way, the four babies in the study by Sorce et al. (1985) who crossed the midline in the no-cliff control condition despite seeing their mother's fearful expression pose some difficulty for this account. That is, children's fear reaction must be triggered by their mother's facial expression in conjunction with a dubious environmental stimulus (semiperilous visual cliff) but not by her facial expression alone (no cliff).) However, in this case, too, we cannot say that the internal processes engendered by children's imitation of their mother's facial expression implicitly represent fear, hence that they form part of an "implicit theory of mind." These processes constitute fear; they do not represent it.

6.2   Children's projections of their own visual experience onto others

The only direct evidence that I know of about children's ability to project their own inner experience onto others comes from a study by Novey (1975). He studied 12 boys and 12 girls at the ages of 1½ years, 2 years and 3 months, and 3 years in the following situation. During a brief home visit children were given experience in wearing different types of goggles. Half the children had goggles made with opaque glass, which they naturally found somewhat scary. The other half had goggles made with transparent glass, which they could comfortably see through. Importantly, this difference was noticeable only to the person wearing the goggles—to an onlooker these goggles appeared identical.

Some weeks after this brief experience both child and parent came for a visit to the lab, where the parent was given goggles with opaque glasses to wear. Since the opaque and transparent goggles were identical in appearance, the onlooking child could not tell which kind of goggles the parent was wearing but could only assume that they were the same kind that she had experienced at home. So it is interesting that the children's reactions to this situation differed markedly, depending on which group they were in. Children who had been acquainted with the opaque goggles at home readily objected to their parent wearing these goggles and immediately tried to remove them from the parent's eyes. In contrast, the children who had been acquainted with the transparent goggles found it much less urgent to free their parent from the goggles. This difference in reaction shows that children projected their own negative experience with opaque goggles onto their parent when they saw their parent wearing what appeared to be the same goggles. Unfortunately, reliable evidence for a systematic difference between conditions was obtained only for 3-year-olds, which seems a bit late.

Furthermore, although Novey investigated children's understanding of visual experience, which is so important for gaining information about the external world, his results speak to children's understanding of nonpropositional emotional experience only. There is no indication in the data that these children understood anything about the information (propositional content) transmitted by vision, for instance, that the user of transparent glasses can obtain visual information about the surroundings whereas opaque glasses prevent this flow of information.

6.3   Understanding other *deictic expressions*

Expressions like "in front" and "behind" are known to linguists as "deictic expressions" because they serve the function of *deixis*, which is the Greek word for *indicating* or *pointing* (e.g., Wales 1979). I want to emphasize here that the classification of these expressions as deictic is not the reason why I think their correct use is an indication of the child's understanding of representation. This can be seen by contrasting them with other deictic expressions.

Typical instances of deictic expressions are pronouns like "I" and "you," demonstratives like "here," "there," "this," "that," and the definite article "the." These words serve the function of pointing out a particular referent. For instance, when you say, "I am right and you are wrong" (Barwise and Perry 1983, 5), then "I" points to *you*; but when I utter the very same sentence, then "I" points to *me*. Correct use and comprehension of these personal pronouns requires context-dependent rules for determining their referent in the discourse situation. I don't think that an explicit understanding of representation is needed for that. It lies within the capabilities of the younger child who can *use* language (chapter 4).

Although "in front of" and "behind" are context-dependent in a way similar to "I" and "you," the two sets of words differ in other important ways. Their context dependence is similar because if one of us describes the scene between us as "The doll is *in front of* the glass," it matters very much who says it. If you (sitting nearest to the glass) say it, it is correct, but if I (sitting opposite) say it, it is wrong. I should describe the scene as "The doll is *behind* the glass." However, if one asks what in the discourse situation "in front of" and "behind" *point* at, one can see that these expressions are different from "I" or "you." They don't point in a simple way to the spatial relationship between doll and glass out there; rather, they "point"—if one wants to use that metaphor here at all—to that spatial relationship in a *view-specific description* of the real scene. It is understanding that view-specific description, I claim, that requires a concept of representation. And it is *that*—and not the fact that they are deictic expressions—that makes correct use of these spatial terms indicative of a representational view of mind.

Chapter 7

7.1   Remarks on the concept of knowledge in philosophy
Dating back to Plato (Gettier 1963) knowledge has been characterized as *justified true belief*. Correctness alone (true belief) is not sufficient because an accidentally true assumption is not the same as knowledge. There needs to be good reason for why the belief is true. However, exactly what a good reason or justification of a true belief *is* still controversial. Gettier (1963) started a search for counterexamples to the notion of knowledge as justified true belief. Take the fuel gauge as one of Dretske's favorite examples of an informational device. The fuel gauge in my car is broken. It constantly points to "full." After I filled up the tank, a thief drove off with my car. He looked at the gauge and concluded that the tank is full. His belief is *justified* and *true*. It's true because the tank is indeed full, and it's justified because when the indicator on the gauge points to "full"—and there are no discernible signs of its malfunctioning—it is reasonable to assume that the tank is full. Yet his justified and true belief is not real *knowledge*. Evidently, in order to know it is not enough to have subjectively convincing evidence. The causal theory of knowledge (Dretske 1981; Dretske and Enc 1984) stipulates that a true representation has to be caused by the fact to be known. This condition is, of course, violated in the stolen car example. There, the full tank did not cause the gauge to point to "full." The indicator was in that position, but for different reasons.

7.2   The possibility that correct responses on know-see tasks are due to common association with success
The fact that 3-year-old children make some connection between seeing and knowing can be interpreted to mean that they understand that knowledge (as a theoretical construct) coordinates seeing with successful action. However, this need not be so—an idea I owe to Gerhard Schurz at the University of Salzburg. From a much earlier age onward children see a link between looking and successful action: they not only point to an object they want their mother to hand to them but also explicitly check whether their pointing achieves its goal of getting her to look at the object. This develops as early as 14 months (see chapter 6). Thus, the fact that 3-year-olds link looking inside a box to knowing what is inside may not indicate an understanding that seeing results in knowing. Rather, their meaning of "knowing" may exhaust itself in "leading to successful action." But since they know that "looking" is also related to success, they prefer to point to the person who has looked inside the box when asked who knows what is inside it. This contention is compatible with the fact that children tend to give, if anything, more correct answers when asked directly about the link between looking and the ability to respond correctly. In the study by Pratt and Bryant (1990) children gave over 90% and children in the study by Pillow (1989) gave 75% correct answers, saying that the one who had looked inside could tell what was in the box.

7.3   Early studies of the know-guess distinction

Findings by Miscione et al. (1978) agree with the conclusion from our study that by 5 years most children can judge that a person who correctly guessed the location of an object did *"not know"* where the object was (table 1: −PSAC condition). However, interpretation of performance by their younger children is less clear since these children failed to give correct answers not only on the critical *lucky guess* condition but also on the obvious conditions. Their youngest group of 3½- to 4½-year-old children were not able to decide between "guess" and "know" even when they had seen where the object was put and when they were shown that they were pointing to the correct box when asked where the object was (+PSA condition). Richards (1982, 388) argues that in natural discourse "know" is occasionally treated as a synonym for "correct guessing"—for instance, when it starts to rain during a picnic and someone exclaims, "I just knew it was going to rain today!" However, this cannot account for young children's difficulty in Miscione et al.'s study, because even when children received no feedback about their response (+PAS condition), their performance was hardly better than chance. This failure by 4-year-olds to attribute knowledge when informational access and successful action coincide suggests a basic methodological problem. Quite possibly the study overstepped the children's attention span, since they were subjected to 25 test situations in a row.

Results from two other studies suggest that children acquire an understanding of the "know"-"guess" distinction at a much later age than our study does. But again I think this is due to methodological problems in the earlier studies.

Johnson and Wellman (1980) did not ask children to choose between "know" and "guess." They asked children three independent "yes-no" questions about whether the children knew, guessed, or remembered where the object was. From their table 2 it appears that up to the age of 6 most children chose to say "yes" regardless of question and condition. In particular, 4- to 5-year-olds said 87% of the time that "Yes," they knew where the object was, regardless of whether they had seen it put there or not. This result is totally incompatible with all recent studies, even those with the most conservative results and not to mention those that found near ceiling performance in children a year younger. Again, some fundamental methodological problems must be the reason. As Sodian and Wimmer (1987, 431–432) point out, asking a series of three "yes-no" questions may have induced a strong bias toward mindlessly answering "yes."

Richards (1982) asked 5-, 7-, and 9-year-olds rather complicated questions about two people who either looked or didn't look when an object was put away—for instance, "Was either of them guessing where to find the ball?" and "Did either of them know where to find the ball?" (pp. 390–391). Given such complicated questions, it is not surprising that there was no sign in this study that 5-year-olds can correctly differentiate between "know" and "guess."

7.4   Substitutability of co-referential expressions as a test of understanding aspectuality

Among formal semanticists the classical demonstration that knowledge is aspect specific is to show that "to know" creates a *logically opaque* context. Jim Russell (1987) investigated children's understanding of this logical property. For instance, in one story George's house was burglarized by a man with curly red hair. George found out about the burglary when he woke up and discovered that his new wristwatch had disappeared. Presumably, since George knew that the thief stole his watch, it is legitimate to say, "George was thinking: 'I must find the thief who stole my watch.'" However, since George had no way of knowing that the thief had curly red hair, it is not logically legitimate to say, "George was thinking: 'I must find the man with the curly red hair who stole my watch.'" Children at 5 years were hopeless at this task, and even relatively few 7-year-olds realized that one could not say that George was thinking of the burglar as having red hair.

I don't think this finding contradicts the claim I have made on the basis of other data that children understand aspectuality much earlier, at about 5 years. I say this because a linguistic problem is mixed in. In normal conversation we continually violate this "logical" principle by using *transparent* expressions inside *opaque contexts*. That is, it is conversationally legitimate to use the expression "man with red hair" if it is clear from the context (or not crucial) that this expression does not describe how George sees matters but that it is used as a (transparent reference) aid for the listener to identify the person being talked about (e.g., Barwise and Perry 1983, chap. 9).

Chapter 8

8.1   On thinking influencing action and feeling

It is also important to point out that both kinds of "thinking" can—depending on the context—influence your actions and your well-being. Imagine yourself as my colleague next door. A mutual friend comes by: "Haven't seen Josef for some time, what is he doing?" Now your answer will depend on the state of your knowledge. If you mistakenly *think that* I am on a Mediterranean beach, you will answer, "Oh, he is lying on a beach in France or Spain." If, however, you know that I am in my office but you are just *thinking of* me on a beach, you will answer, "He is next door working on his book."

This does, however, not mean that only "thinking-that" can have any bearing on your answer, because there are contexts in which your answer will depend on what you are thinking-of. Imagine our friend coming in: "Just saw Josef. He said he might be going to France soon. What are you doing?" You answer, "I am thinking of Josef in France." Our friend probes further: "What is Josef doing?" You answer, "He is lying on a beach." In this conversational context, then, your response is determined by what you are thinking-of me doing and not what you know or think-that I am really doing.

Also, mere thoughts can cause profound affective reactions. For instance, if you are of an envious disposition, you might feel discomfort at the mere thought of me lying on a beach even when you know that I am safely chained to my desk.

8.2   Anecdotal evidence for early reference to belief as misrepresentation
Bloom et al. (1989) report one example from a child before the age of 3 years:

Kathryn: "I thought *that was a snacktime.*"

However, in this case it is not clear whether Kathryn might not have expressed possibility or uncertainty: "That was snacktime, wasn't it?"

Shatz, et al. analyzed the utterances of a child named Abe from 2 years and 4 months to 4 years. Abe produced several utterances that suggest understanding of misconceptions before the age of 4 years. For instance:

"I *thought* this was a crocodile; now I *know* it's an alligator."
"The people *thought* Dracula was mean, but he was nice."
"I *thought* there wasn't any socks, but when I looked I saw them."

These are rather convincing cases of Abe expressing his earlier misconceptions; they cannot easily be rephrased as statements of possibility. However, the suspicion is that Abe's statements are due to his precocity and are not to be expected from the average 2- or 3-year-old. This impression is strengthened by experimental findings that in general children at this age fail to remember their own or others' mistaken beliefs. Yet a very small number show signs of understanding belief even in experimental situations at the age of 3 years. Abe may have been one of them.

8.3   Basic problems with Wellman and Bartsch's study
There is the possibility that in the study by Wellman and Bartsch (1988) children did not take in any information about "thinking" but were swayed by a simple positive association between Jane and the bananas in the cupboard because of the affirmative nature of the "think" sentence about the cupboard and by a negative association between Jane and the refrigerated bananas because of the negative nature of the "think" sentence about the refrigerator. This possibility applies to most of the tasks employed by Wellman and Bartsch (Perner 1989).

8.4   The research tradition of "Piaget Bashing"
Starting in the 1960s, "Piaget Bashing" was a popular sport among researchers in cognitive development. The rules were to take one of Piaget's many claims about what "preoperational" children before the age of about 6 to 8 years were supposed to be unable to do, then devise a more child-adequate research method and demonstrate that children did understand the concept (at least to some degree) some years before that. Early works in this tradition were Rochel Gelman's (1968) study of children's early ability to solve problems involving

conservation of quantity and Peter Bryant and Tom Trabasso's (1971) critique of Piagetian transitive inference studies.

In his earlier work Heinz Wimmer (1982) was able to show that Piaget's claims about young children's difficulty with integrating story material into a coherent whole could not be right. Provided the story was told well, at an age-adequate level, even 4-year-olds could remember the causal structure of stories. Our false belief story extends that research by demonstrating that 4-year-olds not only understand stories about the external world but also spontaneously infer story characters' inner worlds (beliefs).

8.5   Paul Harris's proposal that the false-belief task can be solved without understanding representation

My argument has always been (Perner 1986, 1988) that belief (and all of Flavell's Level 2 problems) does require a representational view, since there is no single situation to which the believing person is linked "as believing." In fact, "believing" links people to two situations in different ways, to one as the belief's referent and to the other as its sense. Since this double association is created by the representational properties of belief, I have always thought that understanding belief requires understanding of representation—that is, as something materially existent (though not necessarily specified in its material form, only assumed as something serving the particular representational function) that has sense and reference.

Paul Harris (in press) attempts to introduce a step in between. He thinks that the child who succeeds on our belief task might still fall short of understanding representation but does understand "standing-in-for." Instead of a materially existing representation standing-in-for the real situation the child assumes that the old situation (which the protagonist thinks is still the case) stands-in-for the real situation. An interesting idea, but the important question is whether this proposal leads to different testable consequences than my assumption that passing our false belief task indicates an understanding of representation.

For preliminary support Harris (1989a, 63–64; personal communication) appeals to findings by Kuczaj and Daly (1979) on children's ability to engage in counterfactual discourse about past events, which emerges between 4 and 5 years (Kuczaj and Daly 1979, table 7; Kuczaj 1981, table 1), at the same age as belief understanding. Furthermore, development at this age is specific to counterfactual talk about *past* events, whereas even at 3 children engage quite proficiently in hypothetical considerations about the *future*. Harris points out that unlike talk about the future, counterfactual assumptions about the past (e.g., "If you had eated all the turkey, your tummy would have exploded") must be understood as suspending (substituting for, standing in for) what actually happened ("You didn't eat all the turkey and so you didn't explode"). However, this standing-in-for is not the same as representation. And so, he suggests, it is the understanding of this nonrepresentational standing-in-for that enables children to pass the false belief test.

Provided the natural language data are a reflection of counterfactual reasoning ability rather than some purely linguistic development (and this is not clear, since some of the intricate pretend play at 2½ years seems to require the same counterfactual reasoning ability; for example, Dunn and Dale (1984) describe a 2-year-old boy acting according to the following counterfactual reasoning chain: "If this toy tractor were a train, then it would need gasoline"), then this would have an important implication for the development of belief understanding—but not the implication Harris wants it to have.

The implication it does have is that the difficulty with the belief task may stem not from a lack of the concept of representation but from a lack of the prerequisite counterfactual reasoning ability. So, it could be that 3-year-olds have a perfect understanding of representation but still fail the belief task. But that is not what Harris wants to argue. His argument is that even children who pass the false belief test need not have a concept of representation. But this would not follow even if his analysis of the counterfactual reasoning data were correct, because belief reasoning is more than mere counterfactual reasoning.

Counterfactual reasoning goes from some counterfactual assumption to some counterfactual consequence (you neither ate the whole turkey nor exploded). False belief is different. Although its content is counterfactual ("The chocolate is in the old location" when it really is in the new one), the belief itself is real and is supposed to act as a guide for the real world (its referent). And this fact needs to be understood in the traditional false belief task for two reasons: to understand that lack of information creates a false belief and to understand that the belief with counterfactual content still has real consequences for real behavior aimed at success in the real world. And I contend that understanding of belief in this role is what requires the concept of representation.

Despite Paul Harris's endeavors, then, I still think that understanding belief as measured by the false belief task implies understanding of representation. That the concept of representation is involved in children's changing view of the mind between 3 and 5 years (and not just counterfactual reasoning ability) is also suggested by the changes in their understanding of "knowledge" documented in chapter 7, where no counterfactual assumptions are involved in the same way as they are in understanding false belief.

8.6   Three-year-old children's belief-explanation of mistaken action

Bartsch and Wellman (1989, experiment 2) report that 3-year-old children find it easier to explain a person's mistaken action by inferring that the person had a false belief than to predict how a person would act on the basis of false belief. For instance, they showed children two boxes. One box was marked like a Band-Aid box but was empty, and the other box was plain but full of Band-Aids. Then a hand puppet with a minor injury came looking for Band-Aids. In the prediction task children were asked where the puppet would look for Band-Aids. In the explanation task children observed the puppet look in the marked but empty container and were asked, "Why do you think he is looking in there?" Of 24 children (mean age 3 years and 9 months), only 6 made a correct prediction (on at least 3 of 4 tasks), yet 16 referred to the puppet's thinking (or not knowing) in their explanations (on at least 4 of 5 tasks). This result was interpreted as showing that 3-year-olds have a greater understanding of belief than was hitherto thought on the basis of the traditionally used prediction task. However, two arguments can be made against this conclusion.

One concerns the interpretation of the data, the other their validity. The question about interpretation is the problem of overinterpretation that I raised earlier in the context of the prediction task. I argued that correct predictions can only be interpreted safely as signs of understanding belief (as a misconception about reality) if the task does not lead children to assume that (for some reason) the puppet would act as-if the Band-Aids were in the empty box. This assumption is of course manifestly suggested in the explanation task since the child observes the puppet act as-if the Band-Aids were in the empty box. In other words, so-called belief-explanations do not make clear whether children used the word "think" to refer to the puppet's misrepresentation of the true situation (belief) or whether they used it to mark the situation according to which the puppet appeared to direct its actions (in other words, whether they used it in the sense of either "thinking-of" or "pretend"). It might be possible to sort out which interpretation children had in mind by asking something like, "Why did the puppet look in there? Did it *think* they were in there or did it just *pretend* they were in there?" But this experiment has not yet been done.

The possibility that children gave correct explanations based on an understanding of what the protagonist thought-of (had in mind) is particularly plausible when subjects failed to spontaneously answer the original question, "Why did the puppet look in there?", and had to be prompted by asking, "What does the puppet think?" (which accounts for 2/3 of the successful cases). If subjects interpreted this prompting question as, say, "What did the puppet think of (have in mind)?", they would have answered, for instance, "Band-Aids in there"—an answer scored as "understanding belief."

Another problem with Bartsch and Wellman's data is their replicability and generality. Moses and Flavell (1990) tried to replicate the relatively high frequency of belief-explanations in Bartsch and Wellman's study by showing children videotapes of mistaken actions like the ones Bartsch and Wellman used. Surprisingly, belief-explanations accounted for only 6% of explanations by 3-year-olds (mean age = 3 years 6 months) even though great effort was made not only to show the mistaken action but also to emphasize the actor's surprise and remind children of what the actor was actually looking for.

For these reasons, I think it would be premature to accept Bartsch and Wellman's data as a valid demonstration of 3-year-old children's understanding of belief.

8.7 Claims about experimental evidence for early deception by children

Chandler, Fritz, and Hala (1989) claim to have demonstrated genuine deceptive behavior in children as young as 2½ years. The task was to make it difficult for another person to find a treasure in one of four boxes. As the treasure was hidden by a puppet that left visible tracks leading to the hiding place, one obvious strategy was to wipe out these tracks. Several 2½-year-old children apparently resorted to this method. Paul Harris and Catherine Taylor replicated this finding with a truck in a sand pit. Even 2-year-olds could indeed be brought to wipe out the truck's tracks, but only after massive cuing: "What about the lorry [truck] tracks? Can you do something to the tracks so that [name] won't find the ball?" Three-year-olds also needed to be alerted to the truck tracks as a potential aid in finding the ball before they thought of wiping them out. Only at 4 did children eliminate the tracks without their attention being drawn to them.

Beate Sodian and I investigated Chandler, Fritz, and Hala's interpretation of their finding by checking whether children eliminate tracks in order to make the other person's task difficult or merely because they enjoy the idea of wiping out tracks. To test this, we devised two conditions. In one condition the objective was to make it easy for another friendly person to find the treasure. In the other condition the point was to make it difficult for the person because that person would keep the treasure if she found it. In both conditions children were given the option of either wiping out the tracks or reinforcing their clarity by adding an extra line. Most 3-year-olds preferred to reinforce the existing tracks, though some liked to wipe them out. However, whatever their preference, their choice of action seemed to be made independently of the objective of the game, even though they were acutely aware that the competitive person would keep the treasure at their own expense.

Chandler, Fritz, and Hala also report that 3-year-old children, after some prompting, also thought of laying false tracks to empty locations and of pointing to wrong locations. Harris and Taylor found very little evidence of this among the 2- and 3-year-olds in their study. Beate Sodian, however, noticed that on some trials when children had to be prevented from prematurely uncovering the treasure at its true location, they then pointed "diffusely" to other locations. However, this kind of pointing gave a quite different phenomenal impression from the deceptive pointing by 4-year-old children, who pointed quite decisively to an empty location.

I conclude that young children's wiping out of telltale tracks is the result of massive prompting and has been misinterpreted as a sign of deception because of a lack of necessary control conditions. The other supposed signs of early deception, like misleading pointing and the laying of false tracks, are probably the result of practically making an overt suggestion to do so (e.g., "Wouldn't this [demonstrate false tracks] be a good idea?") or misinterpreting as deceptive something that is actually a sign of uncertainty and confusion (diffuse pointing). For details of our replication attempts see Sodian et al. (in press).

8.8   Do autistic children have a metarepresentational deficit?

Baron-Cohen, Leslie, and Frith (1985) and Leslie (1987) attribute autistic children's problems on the false belief task to a *metarepresentational deficit*. In that case, the problem of autistic children should go beyond a problem with "theory of mind" and should affect their understanding of nonmental representation. To test this hypothesis, Sue Leekam and I (1990) tested 16 autistic children on our version of Deborah Zaitchik's photo task (see chapter 4) and a matching false belief task. Children took a picture of a doll in blue dress. While the picture was developing, the doll changed into a yellow dress. Before they were shown the picture, children were asked what color the doll's dress was in the picture. For the false belief task the doll's friend saw her in blue, and while the friend was away to get a belt for the blue dress, the doll changed into a yellow dress. The question was what color the friend thought the doll's dress was now. As in Zaitchik's experiment, normal 4-year-olds found the photo task slightly more difficult than the false belief task. Also as expected, only 4 of the 16 autistic children gave correct answers to the belief task, but—quite surprisingly—all but 1 gave the correct answer in the photo task. This suggests that autism is not characterized by a general metarepresentational deficit.

Chapter 9

9.1   Difficulties in replicating Wellman and Woolley's results

The finding that children younger than 3 years performed so well on the tasks by Wellman and Woolley (1990) may have been a fortuitous result of a small sample of 16 children. Sue Leekam and I tried to replicate this result with 3-year-olds in the hope of using this elegant test to demonstrate similar abilities in autistic children. However, our subjects gave less impressive results. The best we got was on our third attempt after communication with the authors about procedural details. We tested a sample of 11 younger 3-year-olds (3 years and 2 months to 3 years and 5 months) on two pairs of stories. In each pair there was one story in which the protagonist finds what he wants and one in which he finds something different. Only 4 children got all four stories right. One child gave correct responses on one story pair. That means that 45% at this age showed understanding of how goals and current situation determine further action within this story paradigm. This result is better than what these children do on comparable tests of false belief, but it falls far short of the impressive performance by the even younger group of children in Wellman and Woolley's study.

Note. 9.2   The causal self-referentiality of intention

John Searle (1980) points out that an intention not only has to represent (stipulate conditions of satisfaction) and cause the intended action but also has to *represent that it be the cause of that action* (causal self-referentiality). To make his point, Searle tells the story of the man who wants to kill his uncle by running him over with his car. Preoccupied with his murderous thoughts, he fails to notice a person crossing in front of him, who (it turns out after the collision) was his uncle—now dead. So, Searle argues, even though the man represented the fatal act in his attention-absorbing thoughts and even though these thoughts played a causally vital part in the accident, we can indict the man only for manslaughter, not for murder. It was an accident, not an intentional act, since the man *did not represent that his desire be the cause of what happened.*

9.3   Metavolition as a specifically human acquisition
Norbert Bischof (1985, 541–542) claims that animals' imagination, and therefore their ability to plan are limited by their present motivational state. Chimpanzees, for instance, can achieve remarkable feats within that limitation. On the Ivory Coast bands of chimps journey for miles to an area full of particularly delicious but very hard-shelled nuts. Unfortunately, there are no rocks in that area to crack the nuts with; but the animals have enough foresight to bring suitable rocks with them. However, Bischof argues, this planning feat still remains within the dominant motivation of wanting to get the desirable nuts.

Only humans, he claims, can do more—namely, imagine the motivation itself and therefore plan for changes in desire. For instance, humans would not just plan the actions needed to consume the desired nuts but would also plan for the eventuality that they might become thirsty and bring a supply of water, even though at the moment of planning they feel no desire to drink.

Chapter 10

10.1   Explaining the A-not-B error by fading context markers
Ever since Piaget's first observations of the A-not-B error in his own children, many experimental investigations have cast doubt on his original interpretation of this phenomenon. In particular, Paul Harris (1973) found that infants did not show the error reported by Piaget but searched correctly under B unless they were prevented from searching for some time. Only when a delay was imposed did they search under A. Adele Diamond (1985) discovered that there was a very orderly developmental increase in how long this delay needed to be. A delay of 2 seconds was sufficient to produce search at A at 7½ months whereas a delay of about 10 seconds was required at 12 months.

These findings suggest that infants may initially know where to search but then forget where the object actually is. Several such *memory explanations* have been advanced most of which are based on the idea that the memory for the object's current location fades and then a more long-term memory of the object's previous location takes over (e.g., Harris 1989b; see Wellman, Cross, and Bartsch 1987, for a discussion of several proposals).

My proposal is a variant of these earlier memory explanations and is most closely related to the proposal made by Wellman, Cross, and Bartsch. The basic assumption is that the memory traces for the object's prior location ("object in A") and current location ("object in B") are firmly established but that the internal context markers that, for instance, mark the object's previous location as "past" fade. Perhaps these markers do not fade but are not strong enough to contain the content of their context in safe quarantine when that content attracts too much attention or activation and spills over the context boundary. For simplicity's sake, let us assume that they simply fade with time and that how fast they fade is prescribed by Diamond's (1985) developmental curve: about 2 seconds at 7½ months up to 10 seconds at 12 months. More specifically, when the infant is prohibited from searching immediately mental attention starts to wander and is likely to activate the context marked "past," giving the information "object in A." As long as the marker "past" is in place, this information does not take command of the infant's action. However, should attention be focused on that information after the marker has faded, the infant will search at A.

This explanation can account for quite a few experimental findings that have posed problems for traditional memory accounts that focused on forgetting the object's current location; see discussion by Wellman, Cross, and Bartsch (1987) and Harris (1989b).

1. If the problem were remembering the object's actual location at B, it is difficult to see why children should search under A when B is a transparent cover beneath which the object remains visible (Butterworth 1977). This is not problematic for my account since interference from a past context can occur whether the object's current location is visible or just remembered.
2. Forgetting the object's actual location could not explain why children can correct themselves after unsuccessful search at A and return to B without ever searching at a third location C (Webb, Massar, and Nadolny 1972). My explanation eliminates this problem since the trace "object in B" still exists, guiding search back to B, whereas a trace "object in C," necessary for inducing search at C, has never been formed.
3. It is a natural extension of my explanation to assume that after the context *marker* has faded, the context *boundaries* dissolve as well. Dissolution of boundaries results in a contradictory statement about the object's location: "Object is under A and object is under B." The resulting cognitive confusion can explain the finding by Diamond (1985) that when infants are delayed in their search for another 3 seconds beyond the point where they would show the A-not-B error, they then search randomly and show signs of frustration.
4. One problem for my explanation is to account for the fact that erroneous search under A becomes the predominant response after a certain amount of delay. If all that happened was a weakening of context markers, then search at A should never become more frequent than search at B. However, as Harris (1989b) suggests, the delay imposed on infants may lead them to look away from B, thereby actively increasing the likelihood that location A will capture their attention. This additional assumption can explain why correct retrieval from under B stays higher when A is visually distant from B (Horobin and Acredolo 1986) and when several possible hiding locations are present (an important factor shown in the meta-analysis by Wellman, Cross, and Bartsch (1987)). Under these conditions infants are less likely to focus their gaze on A

because it is less likely that their eyes will wander over a long distance than over a short one and because when several other hiding places are present it becomes more likely that one of these will capture their attention instead of A. Focusing attention on any of these neutral locations—say C—has no effect on where infants will search since there is no memory context showing "object at C." Hence, the likelihood is that "object at B" will gain control of the infant's search action.

I think these predictions make the *fading-context-marker* hypothesis a serious contender for explaining the A-not-B error.

Chapter 11

11.1   Remarks on Ruffman and Olson's study

The following remarks are in order concerning the study by Ruffman and Olson (1989).

Difference in Data. Whereas Wimmer, Hogrefe, and Perner (1988) report that the predominant error was to deny the other person knowledge (no-bias), Ruffman and Olson (1989) found the same predominance of yes-bias as did Marvin, Greenberg, and Mossler (1976). One possible explanation for this difference is that in the study by Wimmer, Hogrefe, and Perner the other person was either another child or a doll representing another child, whereas in the study by Marvin, Greenberg, and Mossler the other person was always an adult. (Ruffman and Olson did not specify whether their doll represented an adult or a young child.) And there is anecdotal evidence from the study by Wimmer, Hogrefe, and Perner that children's no-bias can be turned into a yes-bias by giving the doll the name of an adult.

Interpretation of Data. Although Ruffman and Olson (1989, 605) largely agree with Wimmer, Hogrefe, and Perner (1988) that young children lack a theory of how seeing leads to knowing, they also claim that their results do show some sign of egocentrism. This claim is based on the finding that in two additional conditions where the subject and the other person *shared* the *same perspective* (when the other person looked inside, the subject did too, and when the other person could not look inside, the subject couldn't either) some subjects tended to attribute their own knowledge to the other person (hence a trace of "egocentrism"). However, when perspectives are the same, the correct response is to attribute one's own knowledge or ignorance to the other person. Rather than egocentrism, then, children's responses in these conditions may demonstrate incipient understanding that sameness of perspective suggests sameness of knowledge. In any case, in the different-perspective conditions where egocentrism and correct understanding result in different response patterns, there was no trace of egocentrism, as shown in table 11.1.

Bibliography

Aksu-Koç, A. A. (1988). *The acquisition of aspects and modality.* Cambridge: Cambridge University Press.

Amsterdam, B. K. (1972). Mirror self-image reactions before age two. *Developmental Psychology,* **5**, 297–305.

Anderson, J. R., and Bower, G. H. (1974). *Human associative memory.* Washington, DC: Hemisphere Publishing Co.

Antes, G. (1989). Zur Entwicklung der Konstatierenden Negation in der Kindersprache. Unpublished Doctoral dissertation, Institute of Psychology, University of Salzburg.

Asperger, H. (1944). Die autistischen Psychopathen im Kindesalter. *Archiv für Psychiatrie und Nervenkrankheiten,* **117**, 76–136.

Astington, J. W. (1990). Wishes and plans: Children's understanding of intentional causation. Paper presented at 20th Anniversary Symposium of the Jean Piaget Society, Philadelphia, PA, May 1990.

Astington, J. W. (in press). Intention in the child's theory of mind. In C. Moore and D. Frye (Eds.), *Children's theories of mind.* Hillsdale, NJ: Lawrence Erlbaum Associates.

Astington, J. W., Harris, P. L., and Olson, D. R. (Eds.) (1988). *Developing theories of mind.* New York: Cambridge University Press.

Baillargeon, R. (1987). Object permanence in 3½- and 4½-month old infants. *Developmental Psychology,* **23**, 655–664.

Baron-Cohen, S. (1989a). Perceptual role taking and protodeclarative pointing in autism. *British Journal of Developmental Psychology,* **7**, 113–127.

Baron-Cohen, S. (1989b). Autistic children's understanding of "simple" and "cognitive" emotions. Unpublished manuscript, Department of Psychology and Child Psychiatry, Institute of Psychiatry, London.

Baron-Cohen, S. (in press). Precursors to a theory of mind: Understanding attention in others. In A. Whiten (Ed.), *Natural theories of mind: The evolution, development and simulation of everyday mindreading.* Hillsdale, NJ: Lawrence Erlbaum Associates.

Baron-Cohen, S., Leslie, A. M., and Frith, U. (1985). Does the autistic child have a "theory of mind"? *Cognition*, 21, 37–46.

Bartlett, F. C. (1932). *Remembering: An experimental and social study.* Cambridge: Cambridge University Press.

Bartsch, K., and Wellman, H. M. (1989). Young children's attribution of action to beliefs and desires. *Child Development*, 60, 946–964.

Barwise, J., and Perry, J. (1983). *Situations and attitudes.* Cambridge, MA: MIT Press. A Bradford book.

Bates, E. (1979). Intentions, conventions, and symbols. In E. Bates (Ed.), *The emergence of symbols*, 33–68. New York: Academic Press.

Bates, E., Camaioni, L., and Volterra, V. (1975). The acquisition of performatives prior to speech. *Merrill-Palmer Quarterly*, 21, 205–226.

Bedford, E. (1957/1984). Emotion. *Proceedings of the Aristotelian Society*, 57, 281–304. Extract reprinted in C. Calhoun and R. C. Solomon (Eds.), *What is an emotion?* Oxford: Oxford University Press.

Bennett, J. (in press). How to read minds in behavior: A suggestion from a philosopher. In A. Whiten (Ed.), *Natural theories of mind: The evolution, development and simulation of everyday mindreading.* Hillsdale, NJ: Lawrence Erlbaum Associates.

Bierwisch, M. (1967). Some semantic universals of German adjectivals. *Foundations of Language*, 3, 1–36.

Bischof, N. (1985). *Das Rätsel Ödipus.* München: Piper.

Bischof-Köhler, D. (1988). Über den Zusammenhang von Empathie und der Fähigkeit, sich im Spiegel zu erkennen. *Schweizerische Zeitschrift für Psychologie*, 47, 147–159.

Blackburn, S. (1984). *Spreading the word.* Oxford: Clarendon Press.

Bloom, L., Rispoli, M., Gartner, B., and Hafitz, J. (1989). Acquisition of complementation. *Journal of Child Language*, 16, 101–120.

Bower, T. G. R., and Wishart, J. G. (1972). The effects of motor skill on object permanence. *Cognition*, 1, 28–35.

Braine, M. D. S., and Shanks, B. L. (1965). The development of conservation of size. *Journal of Verbal Learning and Verbal Behavior*, 4, 227–242.

Brand, M. (1984). *Intending and acting.* Cambridge, MA: MIT Press. A Bradford book.

Bremner, G. (1988). *Infancy.* Oxford: Blackwell.

Brentano, F. von (1874/1955). *Psychologie vom empirischen Standpunkt*, Band 1. (Herausgegeben von O. Kraus.) Hamburg: Felix Meiner.

Brentano, F. von (1874/1970). Psychology from an empirical standpoint. (Edited by O. Kraus, translated by L. L. McAllister.) London: Routledge and Kegan Paul.

Bretherton, I. (1984). Representing the social world in symbolic play: Reality and fantasy. In I. Bretherton (Ed.), *Symbolic play*, 1–41. New York: Academic Press.

Bretherton, I., and Beeghly, M. (1982). Talking about internal states: The acquisition of an explicit theory of mind. *Developmental Psychology*, **18**, 906–921.

Bretherton, I., and Fritz, J. (manuscript). Talking about emotions: Early conceptual development and the acquisition of word meaning. Unpublished manuscript, Department of Human Development and Family Studies, Colorado State University.

Bretherton, I., McNew, S., and Beeghly-Smith, M. (1981). Early person knowledge as expressed in gestural and verbal communication: When do infants acquire a "Theory of Mind"? In M. E. Lamb and L. R. Sherrod (Eds.), *Infant social cognition*, 333–373. Hillsdale, NJ: Lawrence Erlbaum Associates.

Bruce, B., and Newman, D. (1978). Interacting plans. *Cognitive Science*, **2**, 195–233.

Bruner, J. S. (1973) Organization of early skilled action. *Child Development*, **44**, 1–11.

Bruner, J.S. (1983). *Child's talk: Learning to use language*. Oxford: Oxford University Press.

Bryant, P. E., and Trabasso, T. (1971). Transitive inference and memory in young children. *Nature*, **232**, 456–458.

Bühler, Ch. (1928/1967). *Kindheit und Jugend*. Göttingen: Hogrefe.

Bullock, M., and Lütkenhaus, P. (1988). The development of volitional behavior in the toddler years. *Child Development*, **59**, 664–674.

Butterworth, G. E. (1977). Object disappearance and error in Piaget's stage IV task. *Journal of Experimental Child Psychology*, **23**, 391–401.

Butterworth, G. E. (in press). The ontogeny and phylogeny of joint visual attention. In A. Whiten (Ed.), *Natural theories of mind: The evolution, development and simulation of everyday mindreading*. Hillsdale, NJ: Lawrence Erlbaum Associates.

Byrne, R. W., and Whiten, A. (1988). *Machiavellian intelligence: Social expertise and the evolution of intellect in monkeys, apes, and humans*. Oxford: Clarendon Press.

Calhoun, C., and Solomon, R. C. (Eds.) (1984). *What is an emotion?* Oxford: Oxford University Press.

Campos, J., and Stenberg, C. (1981). Perception, appraisal and emotion: The onset of social referencing. In M. E. Lamb and L. R. Sherrod (Eds.), *Infant social cognition* (pp. 273–314). Hillsdale, NJ: Lawrence Erlbaum Associates.

Cantor, J. R., Zillman, D., and Bryant, J. (1975). Enhancement of experienced arousal in response to erotic stimuli through misattribution of unrelated residual arousal. *Journal of Personality and Social Psychology*, **32**, 69–75.

Carey, S. (1985a). *Conceptual change in childhood.* Cambridge, MA: MIT Press. A Bradford book.

Carey, S. (1985b). Are children fundamentally different kinds of thinkers and learners than adults? In S. F. Chipman, J. W. Segal, and R. Glaser (Eds.), *Thinking and learning skills,* Vol. 2 485–517. Hillsdale, NJ: Lawrence Erlbaum Associates.

Carey, S. (1988). Conceptual differences between children and adults. *Mind and Language*, **3**, 167–181.

Carnap, R. (1947). *Meaning and necessity.* Chicago: University of Chicago Press.

Chandler, M. J. (1973). Egocentrism and antisocial behavior: The assessment and training of social perspective-taking skills. *Developmental Psychology*, **9**, 326–332.

Chandler, M. J. (1977). Social cognition: A selective review of current research. In W. F. Overton and J. M. Gallagher (Eds.), *Knowledge and development.* New York: Plenum.

Chandler, M. J., and Boyes, M. (1982). Social-cognitive development. In B. B. Wolman (Ed.), *Handbook of developmental psychology*, 387–402. Englewood-Cliffs, NJ: Prentice-Hall.

Chandler, M. J., Fritz, A. S., and Hala, S. M. (1989). Small scale deceit: Deception as a marker of 2-, 3- and 4-year-olds' early theories of mind. *Child Development*, **60**, 1263–1277.

Chandler, M. J., and Helm, D. (1984). Developmental changes in the contribution of shared experience to social role-taking competence. *International Journal of Behavioral Development*, **7**, 145–156.

Church, J. (1961). *Language and the discovery of reality.* New York: Random House.

Churchland, P. M. (1984). *Matter and consciousness: A contemporary introduction to the philosophy of mind.* Cambridge, MA: MIT Press. A Bradford book.

Clark, A., and Karmiloff-Smith, A. (1990). The cognizer's innards: A psychological and philosophical perspective on the development of thought. Unpublished manuscript, School of Cognitive and Computing Sciences, University of Sussex.

Coleman, L., and Kaye, P. (1981). Prototype semantics: The English word *lie. Language*, **57**, 26–44.

Cummins, R. (1989). *Meaning and mental representation.* Cambridge, MA: MIT Press. A Bradford book.

Davidson, D. (1963). Actions, reasons, and causes. *Journal of Philosophy*, **60**, 685–700.

DeLoache, J. S. (1987). Rapid change in the symbolic functioning of very young children. *Science,* **238**, 1556–1557.

DeLoache, J. S. (1989a). The development of representation in young children. In W. H. Reese (Ed.), *Advances in child development and behavior,* Vol. 22 1–39. New York: Academic Press.

DeLoache, J. S. (1989b). Young children's understanding of the correspondence between a scale model and a large scale space. *Cognitive Development,* **4**, 121–139.

DeLoache, J. S. (1989c). The effect of perceptual similarity on young children's understanding of scale models. Paper presented at the Biennial Meeting of the Society for Research in Child Development, Kansas City, MO, April 1989.

DeLoache, J. S (in press). Young children's understanding of models. In R. Fivush and J. Hudson (Eds.), *What children remember and why.* New York: Cambridge University Press.

Dennett, D. C. (1978). *Brainstorms.* Montgomery, VT: Bradford.

Dennett, D. C. (1987). *The intentional stance.* Cambridge, MA: MIT Press. A Bradford book.

Descartes, R. (1970). *Philosophical letters.* Ed. and trans. A. Kenny. Oxford: Clarendon Press.

DeVries, R. (1969). Constancy of generic identity in the years three to six. *Monographs of the Society for Research in Child Development,* **34**, No. 3 (Serial No. 127).

DeVries, R. (1970). The development of role-taking as reflected by behavior of bright, average, and retarded children in a social guessing game. *Child Development,* **41**, 759–770.

DeWaal, F. (1982). *Chimpanzee politics.* London: Unwin.

Diamond, A. (1985). Development of the ability to use recall to guide action, as indicated by infants' performance on AB. *Child Development,* **56**, 868–883.

Dirks, J., and Gibson, E. (1977). Infants' perception of similarity between live people and their photographs. *Child Development,* **48**, 124–130.

Dixon, J. C. (1957). Development of self recognition. *Journal of Genetic Psychology,* **91**, 251–256.

Donaldson, M. (1978). *Children's minds.* London: Fontana.

Dowty, D. R., Wall, R. E., and Peters, S. (1981). *Introduction to Montague semantics.* Dordrecht: D. Reidel.

Dretske, F. (1969). *Seeing and knowing.* Chicago: University of Chicago Press.

Dretske, F. (1981). *Knowledge and the flow of information.* Cambridge, MA: MIT Press. A Bradford book.

Dretske, F. (1986a). Aspects of cognitive representation. In M. Brand and R. M. Harnish (Eds.), *The representation of knowledge and belief*, 101–115. Tucson, AZ: The University of Arizona Press.

Dretske, F. (1986b). Misrepresentation. In R. J. Bogdan (Ed.), *Belief*, 17–36. Oxford: Oxford University Press.

Dretske, F. (1988). *Explaining behavior: Reasons in a world of causes*. Cambridge, MA: MIT Press. A Bradford book.

Dretske, F., and Enc, B. (1984). Causal theories of knowledge. In P. A. French, T. E. Uhling, and H. K. Wettstein (Eds.), *Midwest studies in philosophy*, Vol. 9, 517–528. *Causation and causal theories*. Minneapolis, MN: University of Minnesota Press.

Dunn, J. (1987). Understanding feelings: The early stages. In J. Bruner and H. Haste (Eds.), *Making sense: The child's construction of the world*, 26–40. London and New York: Methuen.

Dunn, J., Bretherton, I., and Munn, P. (1987). Conversations about feeling states between mothers and their young children. *Developmental Psychology*, **23**, 1–8.

Dunn, J., and Dale, N. (1984). I a daddy: 2-year-olds' collaboration in joint pretend with sibling and with mother. In I. Bretherton (Ed.), *Symbolic play*, 131–158. New York: Academic Press.

Ericsson, K. A., and Simon, H. A. (1980). Verbal reports as data. *Psychological Review*, **87**, 215–251.

Estes, D., Wellman, H. M., and Woolley, J. D. (1989). Children's understanding of mental phenomena. In H. Reese (Ed.), *Advances in child development and behavior*, Vol 22, 41–87. New York: Academic Press.

Evans, W. F. (1973). The stage IV error in Piaget's theory of object concept development: An investigation of the role of activity. Unpublished dissertation proposal, University of Houston.

Fantz, R. L. (1961). The origin of form perception. *Scientific American*, **204**, 66–72.

Fauconnier, G. (1983/1985). *Mental spaces: Aspects of meaning construction in natural language*. Cambridge, MA: MIT Press.

Feffer, M. H. (1959). The cognitive implications of role-taking behavior. *Journal of Personality*, **27**, 152–168.

Fein, G. G. (1981). Pretend play: An integrative review. *Cognitive Development*, **52**, 1095–1118.

Fivush, R., Gray, J. T., and Fromhoff, F. A. (1987). Two-year-olds' talk about the past. *Cognitive Development*, **2**, 393–409.

Flavell, J. H. (1974). The development of inferences about others. In T. Mischel (Ed.), *Understanding other persons*, 66–116. Oxford: Basil Blackwell.

Flavell, J. H. (1988). The development of children's knowledge about the mind: From cognitive connections to mental representations. In J. W. Astington, P.

L. Harris, and D. R. Olson (Eds.), *Developing theories of mind*, 244–267. New York: Cambridge University Press.

Flavell, J. H., Everett, B. A., Croft, K., and Flavell, E. R. (1981). Young children's knowledge about visual perception: Further evidence for the Level 1 - Level 2 distinction. *Developmental Psychology*, 17, 99–103.

Flavell, J., Botkin, P., Fry, C., Wright, J., and Jarvis, D. (1968). *The development of role-taking and communication skills in children.* New York: Wiley.

Flavell, J. H., Flavell, E. R., and Green, F. L. (1983). Development of the appearance-reality distinction. *Cognitive Psychology*, 15, 95–120.

Flavell, J. H., Flavell, E. R., and Green, F. L. (1989). Transitional period in the development of the appearance-reality distinction. *International Journal of Behavioral Development*, 12, 509–526.

Flavell, J. H., Flavell, E. R., Green, F. L., and Moses, L. J. (1990). Young children's understanding of fact beliefs versus value beliefs. *Child Development*, 61, 915–928.

Flavell, J. H., Green, F. L., and Flavell, E. R. (1989). Young children's ability to differentiate appearance-reality and level 2 perspective in the tactile modality. *Child Development*, 60, 201–213.

Flavell, J. H., Green, F. L., Wahl, K. E., and Flavell, E. R. (1987). The effects of question clarification and memory aids on young children's performance on appearance-reality tasks. *Cognitive Development*, 2, 127–144.

Fodor, J. A. (1978). Propositional attitudes. *The Monist*, 61, 501–523.

Fodor, J. A. (1984). Semantics, Wisconsin style. *Synthese*, 59, 231–250.

Fodor, J. A. (1985). Fodor's guide to mental representation: The intelligent auntie's vade-mecum. *Mind*, 94, 76–100.

Fodor, J. A. (1987). *Psychosemantics: The problem of meaning in the philosophy of mind.* Cambridge, MA: MIT Press. A Bradford book.

Fodor, J. A. (1990). *A theory of content.* Cambridge, MA: MIT Press. A Bradford book.

Fodor, J. A., and Pylyshyn, Z. W. (1988). Connectionism and cognitive architecture: A critical analysis. *Cognition*, 28, 3–71.

Ford, W. G. (1976). The language of disjunction. Unpublished Doctoral dissertation. Ontario Institute of Studies in Education. Toronto, Ontario. *(Dissertation Abstracts International*, 1977(Dec), 38 (6-B), 2833.)

Forguson, L. (1990). *The book of common sense.* London: Routledge, Chapman, and Hall.

Forguson, L., and Gopnik, A. (1988). The ontogeny of common sense. In J. W. Astington, P. L. Harris, and D. R. Olson (Eds.), *Developing theories of mind*, 226–243. New York: Cambridge University Press.

Franco, F., and Butterworth, G. (1989). Is pointing an intrinsically social gesture? Paper presented at the Annual Conference of the Developmental Section of the British Psychological Society, University of Surrey, September 1989.

Frankfurt, H. (1971). Freedom of the will and the concept of a person. *Journal of Philosophy*, **68**, 5–20.

Frege, G. (1892/1960). On sense and reference. In P. Geach and M. Black (Eds.), *Philosophical writings of Gottlob Frege*, 56–78. Oxford: Basil Blackwell.

Freud, S. (1905/1953). Three essays on the theory of sexuality. In J. Strachey (Ed.), *The standard edition of the complete psychological works of Sigmund Freud*, Vol. 7, 135–243. London: Hogarth Press.

Frith, U. (1989). *Autism: Explaining the enigma*. Oxford: Basil Blackwell.

Gallup, G. G. (1968). Mirror image stimulation. *Psychological Bulletin*, **70**, 782–793.

Gallup, G. G. (1970). Chimpanzees: Self-recognition. *Science*, **167**, 86–87.

Gardiner, J. (1988). Functional aspects of recollective experience. *Memory and Cognition*, **16**, 309–313.

Gelman, R. S. (1968). Conservation acquisition: A problem of learning to attend to relevant attributes. *Journal of Experimental Child Psychology*, **7**, 167–187.

Gentner, D., and Stevens, A. L. (Eds.) (1983). *Mental models*. Hillsdale, NJ: Lawrence Erlbaum Associates.

Geppert, U., and Küster, U. (1983). The emergence of "wanting to do it oneself." A precursor of achievement motivation. *International Journal of Behavioral Development*, **6**, 355–369.

Gettier, E. (1963). Is justified true belief knowledge? *Analysis*, **23**, 121–123.

Gibson, J. J. (1950). *The perception of the visual world*. Boston: Houghton Mifflin.

Gibson, J. J. (1960). The concept of the stimulus in psychology. *American Psychologist*, **15**, 694–705.

Gibson, J. J. (1979). *The ecological approach to visual perception*. Boston: Houghton Mifflin.

Glaser, H. (1967). *Das Denken in der Medizin*. Berlin: Duncker und Humblot.

Goodall, J. (1968). The behavior of free-living chimpanzees in Gombe Stream Reserve. *Animal Behavior Monographs*, **1**, 161–311.

Goodenough, F. (1931). Anger in young children. *University of Minnesota, Institute of Child Welfare Monographs*, **9**.

Goodman, N. (1976). *Languages of art*. Indianapolis, IN: Hackett Publishing Co.

Gopnik, A., and Astington, J. W. (1988). Children's understanding of representational change and its relation to the understanding of false belief and the appearance-reality distinction. *Child Development*, **59**, 26–37.

Gopnik, A., and Graf, P. (1988). Knowing how you know: Young children's ability to identify and remember the sources of their beliefs. *Child Development*, **59**, 1366–1371.

Gopnik, A., and Meltzoff, A. N. (1984). Semantic and cognitive development in 15- to 21-month-old children. *Journal of Child Language*, **11**, 495–513.

Gopnik, A., and Seager, W. (1988). Young children's understanding of desires. Unpublished manuscript, Department of Psychology, University of California at Berkeley.

Gopnik, A., and Slaughter, V. (in press). Young children's understanding of changes in their mental states. *Child Development*.

Gordon, R. M. (1986). Folk psychology as simulation. *Mind and Language*, **1**, 158–171.

Gratch, G. (1964). Response alternation in children: A developmental study of orientations to uncertainty. *Vita Humana*, **7**, 49–60.

Gratch, G., Appel, K. J., Evans, W. F., LeCompte, G. K., and Wright, N. A. (1974). Piaget's stage IV object concept error: Evidence of forgetting or object conception. *Child Development*, **45**, 71–77.

Grice, H. P. (1957). Meaning. *Philosophical Review*, **66**, 377–388.

Gruber, S. (1984). Zur Lügenauffassung des Kindes: Das Verhältnis von moralischem Denken und der Bedeutung des Wortes "Lüge." Unpublished Doctoral dissertation, Faculty of Natural Sciences, University of Salzburg.

Haake, R. J., and Somerville, S. C. (1985). Development of logical search skills in infancy. *Developmental Psychology*, **21**, 176–186.

Hadwin, J., and Perner, J. (in press). Pleased and surprised: Children's cognitive theory of emotion. *British Journal of Developmental Psychology*.

Hanson, N. R. (1958). *Patterns of discovery*. Cambridge: Cambridge University Press.

Harris, P. L. (1973). Perseverative errors in search by young infants. *Child Development*, **44**, 28–33.

Harris, P. L. (1989a). *Children and emotion: The development of psychological understanding*. Oxford: Basil Blackwell.

Harris, P. L. (1989b). Object permanence in infancy. In A. Slater and G. Bremner (Eds.), *Infant development*, 103–121. Hove and London: Lawrence Erlbaum Associates.

Harris, P. L. (in press). The work of the imagination. In A. Whiten (Ed.), *Natural theories of mind: The evolution, development and simulation of everyday mindreading* (ch. 19). Hillsdale, NJ: Lawrence Erlbaum Associates.

Harris, P. L., Johnson, C. N., Hutton, D., Andrews, G., and Cook, T. (1989). Young children's theory of mind and emotion. *Cognition and Emotion*, **3**, 379–400.

Harris, P. L., and Muncer, A. (1988). Autistic children's understanding of beliefs and desires. Paper presented at the Annual Conference of the Developmental Section of the British Psychological Society, Coleg Harlech, Wales, September 1988.

Heckhausen, H., and Roelofsen, I. (1962). Anfänge und Entwicklung der Leistungsmotivation, I: Im Wetteifer des Kleinkindes. *Psychologische Forschung,* **26**, 313–397.

Helmholtz, H. von (1896). *Handbuch der physiologischen Optik.* Leipzig: Voss.

Hobson, R. P. (1984). Early childhood autism and the question of egocentrism. *Journal of Autism and Developmental Disorders,* **14**, 85–104.

Hobson, R. P. (1990). On acquiring knowledge about people and the capacity to pretend: Response to Leslie (1987). *Psychological Review,* **97**, 114–121.

Hochberg, J. E., and Brooks, V. (1962). Pictorial recognition as an unlearned ability: A study of one child's performance. *American Journal of Psychology,* **75**, 624–628.

Hoffman, M. L. (1977). Empathy, its development and prosocial implications. In C. B. Keasey (Ed.), *Nebraska Symposium on Motivation,* Vol. 25, 169–217. University of Nebraska Press.

Hogrefe, G. J., Wimmer, H., and Perner, J. (1986). Ignorance versus false belief: A developmental lag in attribution of epistemic states. *Child Development,* **57**, 567–582.

Hood, B., and Willats, P. (1986). Reaching in the dark to an object's remembered position: Evidence for object permanence in 5-month-old infants. *British Journal of Developmental Psychology,* **4**, 57–65.

Hood, L., and Bloom, L. (1979). What, when, and how about why: A longitudinal study of early expressions of causality. *Monographs of the Society for Research in Child Development.* Serial No. 181.

Hornik, R., Risenhoover, N., and Gunnar, M. (1987). The effects of maternal positive, neutral, and negative affective communications on infant responses to new toys. *Child Development,* **58**, 937–944.

Horobin, K. M., and Acredolo, L. P. (1986). The role of attentiveness, mobility history, and separation of hiding sites on stage IV search behavior. *Journal of Experimental Child Psychology,* **41**, 114–127.

Horwich, P. (1987) *Asymmetries in time.* Cambridge MA: MIT Press. A Bradford book.

Hume, D. (1748/1962). In A. Flew (Ed.), *On human nature and the understanding.* London: Collier Macmillan.

Huttenlocher, J., and Higgins, E. T. (1978). Issues in the study of symbolic development. In W. A. Collins (Ed.), *Minnesota Symposia on Child Psychology,* Vol. 11. Hillsdale, NJ: Lawrence Erlbaum Associates.

Huttenlocher, J., Smiley, P., and Charney, R. (1983). Emergence of action categories in the child: Evidence for verb meanings. *Psychological Review*, **90**, 72–93.

Ives, W. (1983). The development of strategies for coordinating spatial perspectives of an array. In D. R. Olson and E. Bialystok (Eds.), *Spatial cognition: The structure and development of mental representations of spatial relations*. Hillsdale, NJ: Lawrence Erlbaum Associates.

James, W., and Lange, C. (1885/1922). *The emotions*. Baltimore: Williams and Wilkins.

Johnson, C. N. (1988). Theory of mind and the structure of conscious experience. In J. W. Astington, P. L. Harris, and D. R. Olson (Eds.), *Developing theories of mind*, 47–63. New York: Cambridge University Press.

Johnson, C. N., and Maratsos, M. P. (1977). Early comprehension of mental verbs: Think and know. *Child Development*, **48**, 1743–1747.

Johnson, C. N., and Wellman, H. M. (1980). Children's developing understanding of mental verbs: Remember, know, and guess. *Child Development*, **51**, 1095–1102.

Johnson-Laird, P. N. (1975). Models of deduction. In R. J. Falmagne (Ed.), *Reasoning: Representation and process in children and adults*, 7–54. Hillsdale, NJ: Lawrence Erlbaum Associates.

Johnson-Laird, P. N. (1983). *Mental models*. Cambridge: Cambridge University Press.

Kagan, J. (1981). *The second year*. Cambridge, MA: Harvard University Press.

Kanner, L. (1943). Autistic disturbances of affective contact. *Nervous Child*, **2**, 217–250.

Karmiloff-Smith, A. (1984). Children's problem solving. In M. E. Lamb, A. L. Brown, and B. Rogoff (Eds.), *Advances in developmental psychology*, Vol. 3 39–90. Hillsdale, NJ: Lawrence Erlbaum Associates.

Karmiloff-Smith, A. (1988). The child is a theoretician, not an inductivist. *Mind and Language*, **3**, 182–195.

Karmiloff-Smith, A., and Inhelder, B. (1974/5). If you want to get ahead, get a theory. *Cognition*, **3**, 195–212.

Keil, F. C. (1987). Conceptual development and category structure. In U. Neisser (Ed.), *Concepts and conceptual development: Ecological and intellectual factors in categorization*, 175–200. Cambridge: Cambridge University Press.

Keil, F. C. (1989). *Concepts, kinds, and cognitive development*. Cambridge, MA: MIT Press. A Bradford book.

Kemmler, L. (1957). Untersuchungen zum frühkindlichen Trotz. *Psychologische Forschung*, **25**, 279–338.

Kenny, A. (1963). *Action, emotion and will*. London: Routledge and Kegan Paul.

Kenny, A. (Ed.) (Transl.) (1970). *Descartes: Philosophical letters.* Oxford: Clarendon Press.

Kielgast, K. (1971). Piaget's concept of spatial egocentrism: A re-evaluation. *Scandinavian Journal of Psychology,* **12,** 179–191.

Kitcher, P. (1984). 1953 and all that. A tale of two sciences. *The Philosophical Review,* **93,** 335–373.

Kitcher, P. (1988). The child as parent of the scientist. *Mind and Language,* **3,** 217–228.

Konolige, K. (1985). Belief and incompleteness. In J. R. Hobbs and R. C. Moore (Eds.), *Formal theories of the commonsense world.* Norwood, NJ: Ablex.

Kopp, C. B. (1982). Antecedents of self regulation: a developmental perspective. *Developmental Psychology,* **18,** 199–214.

Kripke, S. (1971/1977). Identity and necessity. In S. P. Schwartz (Ed.), *Naming, necessity, and natural kinds,* 66–101. Ithaca, NY: Cornell University Press.

Kuczaj, S. A. (1981). Factors influencing children's hypothetical reference. *Journal of Child Language,* **8,** 131–137.

Kuczaj, S. A., and Daly, M. J. (1979). The development of hypothetical reference in the speech of young children. *Journal of Child Language,* **6,** 563–579.

Kuczaj, S. A., and Maratsos, M. (1975). On the acquisition of front, back and side. *Cognitive Development,* **46,** 202–210.

Kuhn, T. S. (1970). *The structure of scientific revolutions,* 2nd ed. Chicago: University of Chicago Press.

Kuhn, T. S. (1977). *The essential tension.* Chicago: University of Chicago Press.

Leach, P. (1977). *Baby and child.* London: Harmondsworth.

Leekam, S. R. (1988). Children's understanding of intentional falsehood. Unpublished Doctoral dissertation, Laboratory of Experimental Psychology, University of Sussex.

Leekam, S. R., and Perner, J. (1990). Does the autistic child have a "metarepresentational" deficit? Unpublished manuscript, Laboratory of Experimental Psychology, University of Sussex.

Lehrer, K. (1986). Metamind: Belief, consciousness and intentionality. In R. J. Bogdan (Ed.), *Belief,* 37–59. Oxford: Oxford University Press.

Lempers, J. D., Flavell, E. R., and Flavell, J. H. (1977). The development in very young children of tacit knowledge concerning visual perception. *Genetic Psychology Monographs,* **95,** 3–53.

Leslie, A. M. (1987). Pretense and representation: The origins of "Theory of Mind." *Psychological Review,* **94,** 412–426.

Leslie, A. M. (1988). Some implications of pretense for mechanisms underlying the child's theory of mind. In J. W. Astington, P. L. Harris, and D. R. Olson

(Eds.), *Developing theories of mind,* 19–46. New York: Cambridge University Press.

Lewin, K. (1931/1935). The psychological situations of reward and punishment. In *A dynamic theory of personality: Selected papers,* 114–170. New York and London: McGraw-Hill.

Lewis, C., and Osborne, A. (1990). Three-year-olds' problems with false belief: Conceptual deficit or linguistic artefact? *Child Development,* **61,** 1514-1519.

Lewis, D. (1969). *Convention: A philosophical study.* Cambridge, MA: Harvard University Press.

Lewis, M., and Brooks-Gunn, J. (1979). *Social cognition and the acquisition of self.* New York: Plenum.

Lewis, M., Stanger, C., and Sullivan, M. (1989). Deception in 3-year-olds. *Developmental Psychology,* **25,** 439–443.

Liben, L. S. (1978). Performance on Piagetian spatial tasks as a function of sex, field dependence, and training. *Merrill-Palmer Quarterly,* **24,** 97–110.

Liben, L. S., and Belknap, B. (1981). Intellectual Realism: Implications for investigations of perceptual perspective taking in young children. *Cognitive Development,* **52,** 921–924.

Light, P. (1987). Taking roles. In J. Bruner and H. Haste (Eds.), *Making sense: The child's construction of the world,* 41–61. London and New York: Methuen.

Light, P., and Nix, C. (1983). "Own view" versus "good view" in a perspective-taking task. *Child Development,* **54,** 480–483.

Luquet, G. H. (1927). *Le Dessin enfantin.* Paris: Alcan.

Lütkenhaus, P., Bullock, M., and Geppert, U. (1987). Toddlers' action: Knowledge, control, and the self. In F. Halisch and J. Kuhl (Eds.), *Motivation, intention, and volition.* Berlin: Springer Verlag.

McCarthy, J., and Hayes, P. J. (1969). Some philosophical problems from the standpoint of artificial intelligence. In B. Mehler and D. Michie (Eds.), *Machine intelligence,* Vol 4. Edinburgh: Edinburgh University Press.

McCune-Nicholich, L. (1981). Toward symbolic functioning: Structures of early pretend games and potential parallels with language. *Cognitive Development,* **52,** 785–797.

McGinn, C. (1982). *The character of mind.* Oxford: Oxford University Press.

Macnamara, J. (1986). *A border dispute: The place of logic in psychology.* Cambridge, MA: MIT Press. A Bradford book.

Macnamara, J., Baker, E., and Olson, C. (1976). Four-year-olds' understanding of pretend, forget, and know: Evidence for propositional operations. *Child Development,* **47,** 62–70.

McNeill, D., and McNeill, N. (1968). What does a child mean when he says "no"? In E. M. Zale (Ed.), *Language and language behavior.* New York: Appleton Century Crofts.

Marvin, R. S., Greenberg, M. T., and Mossler, D. G. (1976). The early development of conceptual perspective taking: Distinguishing among multiple perspectives. *Child Development,* **47**, 511–514.

Masangkay, Z. S., McCluskey, K. A., McIntyre, C. W., Sims-Knight, J., Vaughn, B. E., and Flavell, J. H. (1974). The early development of inferences about the visual percepts of others. *Child Development,* **45**, 357–366.

Mead, G. H. (1934). *Mind, self and society.* Chicago: University of Chicago Press.

Meltzoff, A. N., and Gopnik, A. (1989). On linking nonverbal imitation, representation, and language learning in the first two years of life. In G. E. Speidel and K. E. Nelson (Eds.), *The many faces of imitation in language learning,* 23–51. New York, Berlin: Springer Verlag.

Meltzoff, A., and Moore, K. (1977). Imitation of facial and manual gestures by human neonates. *Science,* **198**, 75–78.

Menig-Peterson, C. L. (1975). The modification of communicative behavior in preschool-aged children as a function of the listener's perspective. *Child Development,* **46**, 1015–1018.

Millikan, R. (1984). *Language, thought and other biological categories.* Cambridge, MA: MIT Press. A Bradford book.

Miscione, J. L., Marvin, R. S., O'Brien, R. G., and Greenberg, M. T. (1978). A developmental study of preschool children's understanding of the words "know" and "guess." *Child Development,* **49**, 1107–1113.

Mitchell, R. W. (1986). A framework for discussing deception. In R. W. Mitchell and N. S. Thompson (Eds.), *Deception: Perspectives on human and non-human deceit,* 3–40. Albany, NY: State University of New York Press.

Moore, R. C. (1980). Reasoning about knowledge and action. Technical Note 191, Artificial Intelligence Center, Computer Science and Technology Division, SRI International.

Morgan, C. L. (1894/1977). *An introduction to comparative psychology.* Washington, DC: University Publications of America.

Moses, L. J., and Flavell, J. H. (1990). Inferring false beliefs from actions and reactions. *Child Development,* **61**, 929–945.

Mossler, D. G., Marvin, R. S., and Greenberg, M. T. (1976). Conceptual perspective taking in 2- to 6-year-old children. *Developmental Psychology,* **12**, 85–86.

Murphy, C. M. (1978). Pointing in the context of a shared activity. *Child Development,* **49**, 371–380.

Murphy, C. M., and Messer, D. J. (1977). Mothers, infants and pointing: A study of a gesture. In H. R. Schaffer (Ed.), *Studies of mother-infant interaction*, 325–354. London: Academic Press.

Murphy, G. L., and Medin, D. (1985). The role of theories in conceptual coherence. *Psychological Review*, **92**, 289–316.

Murray, L., and Trevarthen, C. (1985). Emotional regulation of interactions between 2-month-olds and their mothers. In T. M. Field and N. A. Fox (Eds.), *Social perception in infants*, 177–197. Norwood, NJ: Ablex.

Neisser, U. (1967). *Cognitive psychology*. New York: Meredith.

Neisser, U. (1988). Five kinds of self-knowledge. *Philosophical Psychology*, **1**, 35–59.

Newman, D. (1986). The role of mutual knowledge in the development of perspective taking. *Developmental Review*, **6**, 122–145.

Ninio, A., and Bruner, J. (1978). The achievement and antecedents of labelling. *Journal of Child Language*, **5**, 1–15.

Nisbett, R. E., and Ross, L. (1980). *Human inference: Strategies and shortcomings of social judgment*. Englewood Cliffs, NJ: Prentice-Hall.

Nisbett, R. E., and Wilson, T. D. (1978). Telling more than we can know: Verbal reports on mental processes. *Psychological Review*, **84**, 231–259.

Novey, M. S. (1975). The development of knowledge of other's ability to see. Unpublished Doctoral dissertation, Department of Psychology and Social Relations, Harvard University.

Nunner-Winkler, G., and Sodian, B. (1988). Children's understanding of moral emotions. *Child Development*, **59**, 1323–1338.

Olson, D. R. (1987). Thinking about logic. A review of J. Macnamara's *A border dispute: The place of logic in psychology*. *Canadian Journal of Psychology*, **41**, 392–398.

Olson, D. R. (1988). On the origins of beliefs and other intentional states in children. In J. W. Astington, P. L. Harris, and D. R. Olson (Eds.), *Developing theories of mind*, 414–426. New York: Cambridge University Press.

Olson, D. R., Astington, J. W., and Harris, P. L. (1988). Introduction. In J. W. Astington, P. L. Harris, and D. R. Olson (Eds.), *Developing theories of mind*, 1–15. New York: Cambridge University Press.

O'Neill, D. K., and Astington, J. W. (1989). Young children's understanding of the role sensory experiences play in knowledge acquisition. Unpublished manuscript, Center for Applied Cognitive Science, Ontario Institute for Studies in Education, Toronto, Ontario.

Pea, R. D. (1980). The development of negation in early child language. In D. R. Olson (Ed.), *The social foundations of language and thought: Essays in honor of Jerome S. Bruner*, 156–186. New York: W. W. Norton.

Pearlman, E. G. (1989). Iconic realism: Understanding the relationship between photographs and reality. Unpublished Doctoral dissertation, Graduate Faculty in Psychology, City University of New York.

Peerbhoy, D. (1990). Do children use intentionality in assessment of neutral and bad moral situations? Unpublished third-year experimental project, Laboratory of Experimental Psychology, University of Sussex.

Perner, J. (1986). Developing semantics for theories of mind: Connecting mental spaces. Paper presented at the International Conference on Developing Theories of Mind, McLuhan Program, University of Toronto, May 1986.

Perner, J. (1988). Developing semantics for theories of mind: From propositional attitudes to mental representation. In J. W. Astington, P. L. Harris, and D. R. Olson (Eds.), *Developing theories of mind,* 141–172. New York: Cambridge University Press.

Perner, J. (1989). Is "thinking" belief? Reply to Wellman and Bartsch. *Cognition,* 33, 315–319.

Perner, J. (1990). Experiential awareness and children's episodic memory. In W. Schneider and F. E. Weinert (Eds.), *Interactions among aptitudes, strategies, and knowledge in cognitive performance,* 3–11. New York, Berlin, Heidelberg: Springer Verlag.

Perner, J. (in press). On representing **that**: The asymmetry between belief and intention in children's theory of mind. In C. Moore and D. Frye (Eds.), *Children's theories of mind.* Hillsdale, NJ: Lawrence Erlbaum Associates.

Perner, J., and Davies, G. (in press). Understanding the mind as an active information processor: Do young children have a "copy theory of mind"? *Cognition.*

Perner, J., Frith, U., Leslie, A. M., and Leekam, S. R. (1989). Exploration of the autistic child's theory of mind: Knowledge, belief and communication. *Child Development,* 60, 689–700.

Perner, J., and Garnham, A. (1988). Conditions for mutuality. *Journal of Semantics,* 6, 369–385.

Perner, J., and Leekam, R. S. (1986). Belief and quantity: Three-year olds' adaptation to listener's knowledge. *Journal of Child Language,* 13, 305–315.

Perner, J., and Leekam, S. R. (1990). Children's difficulty with photography versus colour transmission: Zooming in on representation. Unpublished manuscript, Laboratory of Experimental Psychology, University of Sussex.

Perner, J., Leekam, S. R., and Wimmer, H. (1987). Three-year olds' difficulty with false belief: The case for a conceptual deficit. *British Journal of Developmental Psychology,* 5, 125–137.

Perner, J., and Ogden, J. (1988). Knowledge for hunger: Children's problem of representation in imputing mental states. *Cognition,* 29, 47–61.

Peskin, J. (1989). Concealing one's intentions: The development of deceit. Unpublished manuscript, Center for Applied Cognitive Science, Ontario Institute for Studies in Education, Toronto, Ontario.

Piaget, J. (1936/1953). *The origin of intelligence in the child.* London: Routledge and Kegan Paul.

Piaget, J. (1937/1954). *The construction of reality in the child.* New York: Basic Books.

Piaget, J. (1945/1962). *Play, dreams, and imitation in childhood.* New York: W. W. Norton.

Piaget, J. (1959). *The language and thought of the child,* 3rd ed. London: Routledge and Kegan Paul.

Piaget, J., and Inhelder, B. (1941/1974). The child's construction of quantities: Conservation and atomism. (A. J. Pomerans, transl.) New York: Basic Books.

Piaget, J., and Inhelder, B. (1948/1956). *The child's conception of space.* (F. J. Langdon and J. L. Lunzer, transl.) London: Routledge and Kegan Paul.

Piaget, J., and Inhelder, B. (1966/1969). *The psychology of the child.* London: Routledge and Kegan Paul.

Pillow, B. H. (1989). Early understanding of perception as a source of knowledge. *Journal of Experimental Child Psychology,* **47**, 116–129.

Poole, S. (1988). The relation between memory and consciousness shown by the retrieval of knowledge. Unpublished third-year experimental project, Laboratory of Experimental Psychology, University of Sussex.

Pratt, C., and Bryant, P. (1990). Young children understand that looking leads to knowing (so long as they are looking into a single barrel). *Child Development,* **61**, 973–982.

Premack, D. (1988). "Does the chimpanzee have a theory of mind?" revisited. In R. W. Byrne and A. Whiten (Eds.), *Machiavellian intelligence: Social expertise and the evolution of intellect in monkeys, apes, and humans,* 160–179. Oxford: Clarendon Press.

Premack, D., and Woodruff, G. (1978). Does the chimpanzee have a theory of mind? *The Behavioral and Brain Sciences,* **1**, 516–526.

Pylyshyn, Z. W. (1978). When is attribution of beliefs justified? *The Behavioral and Brain Sciences,* **1**, 592–593.

Richards, M. M. (1982). Empiricism and learning to mean. In S. A. Kuczaj (Ed.), *Language development,* Vol. 1: *Syntax and semantics,* 365–395. Hillsdale, NJ: Lawrence Erlbaum Associates.

Ristau, C. A. (in press). Before mindreading: Attention, purposes and deception in birds. In A. Whiten (Ed.), *Natural theories of mind: The evolution, development and simulation of everyday mindreading.* Hillsdale, NJ: Lawrence Erlbaum Associates.

Ruffman, T. K., and Olson, D. R. (1989). Children's ascriptions of knowledge to others. *Developmental Psychology*, **25**, 601–606.

Rumelhart, D. E., Hinton, G. E., and Williams, R. J. (1986). Learning representations by back-propagating errors. *Nature*, **323**, 533–536.

Russell, J. (1987). "Can we say ...?": Children's understanding of intensionality. *Cognition*, **25**, 289–308.

Russell, J., and Mitchell, P. (1985). Things are not always as they seem: The appearance-reality distinction and conservation. *Educational Psychology*, **5**, 227–238.

Russell, J., Sharpe, S., and Mauthner, N. (1989). *Strategic deception in a competitive game.* Paper presented at the Annual Conference of the Developmental Section of the British Psychological Society, University of Surrey, Guildford, England, September 1989.

Sachs, J. S. (1967). Recognition memory for syntactic and semantic aspects of connected discourse. *Perception and Psychophysics*, **2**, 437–442.

Scaife, M., and Bruner, J. S. (1975). The capacity for joint visual attention in the infant. *Nature*, **253**, 265–266.

Schachter, S., and Singer, J. E. (1962). Cognitive, social and physiological determinants of emotional state. *Psychological Review*, **69**, 379–399.

Schacter, D. L., and Moscovitch, M. (1984). Infants, amnesics, and dissociable memory systems. In M. Moscovitch (Ed.), *Infant memory*, 173–216. New York: New Plenum Press.

Schaffer, R. (1984). *The child's entry into a social world.* New York: Academic Press.

Schreibmüller, M. (1989). Über die Entwicklung eines Konzepts der Glaubensentstehung im *Vorschulalter*. Unpublished *Diplomarbeit*, Institute of Psychology, University of Salzburg.

Scupin, E., and Scupin, G. (1907). *Bubis erste Kindheit.* Leipzig: Grieben.

Searle, J. (1980) The intentionality of intention and action. *Cognitive Science*, **4**, 47–70.

Searle, J. (1983). *Intentionality.* Cambridge: Cambridge University Press.

Shatz, M., Wellman, H. M., and Silber, S. (1983). The acquisition of mental verbs: A systematic investigation of the first reference to mental state. *Cognition*, **14**, 301–321.

Sheingold, K., and Tenney, Y. J. (1982). Memory for a salient childhood event. In U. Neisser (Ed.), *Memory observed*, 201–212. San Francisco: W. H. Freeman.

Shorter Oxford English Dictionary (1973). Revised and edited by C. T. Onions. Oxford: Clarendon Press.

Shultz, T. R. (1980). Development of the concept of intention. In W. A. Collins (Ed.), *Development of cognition, affect, and social relations*, 131–164. The Minnesota Symposia on Child Psychology, Vol. 13. Hillsdale, NJ: Lawrence Erlbaum Associates.

Shultz, T. R., and Cloghesy, K. (1981). Development of recursive awareness of intention. *Developmental Psychology*, 17, 465–471.

Shultz, T. R., Wells, D., and Sarda, M. (1980). The development of the ability to distinguish intended actions from mistakes, reflexes, and passive movements. *The British Journal of Social and Clinical Psychology*, 19, 301–310.

Smiley, P. A. (1987). The development of the concept of person: The young child's view of the other in action and in interaction. Unpublished Doctoral dissertation, Department of Education, University of Chicago.

Smith, M. C. (1978). Cognizing the behavior stream: The recognition of intentional action. *Child Development*, 49, 736–743.

Sodian, B. (1986). *Wissen durch Denken? Über den naiven Empirismus im Denken von Vorschulkindern*. Münster: Aschendorf.

Sodian, B. (in press). The development of deception in young children. *British Journal of Developmental Psychology*.

Sodian, B., Taylor, C., Harris, P. L., and Perner, J. (in press). Early deception and the child's theory of mind: False trails and genuine markers. *Child Development*.

Sodian, B., and Wimmer, H. (1987). Children's understanding of inference as a source of knowledge. *Child Development*, 58, 424–433.

Somerville, S. C., and Haake, R. J. (1985). The logical search skills of infants and young children. In H. M. Wellman (Ed.), *Children's searching: The development of search skills and spatial representation*, 73–104. Hillsdale, NJ: Lawrence Erlbaum Associates.

Sophian, C. (1984). Developing search skills in infancy and early childhood. In C. Sophian (Ed.), *Origins of cognitive skills*, 27–56. Hillsdale, NJ: Lawrence Erlbaum Associates.

Sophian, C., and Wellman, H. M. (1983). Selective information use and perseveration in the search behavior of infants and young children. *Journal of Experimental Child Psychology*, 35, 369–390.

Sorce, J. F., Emde, R. N., Campos, J., and Klinnert, M. D. (1985). Maternal emotional signalling: Its effect on the visual cliff behavior of 1-year-olds. *Developmental Psychology*, 21, 195–200.

Stampe, D. (1979). Towards a causal theory of linguistic representation. In P. French, T. Uhling, and H. Wettstein (Eds.), *Midwest studies in philosophy*, Vol. 2, 81–102. Minneapolis: University of Minnesota Press.

Stern, D. (1977). *The first relationship: Infant and mother*. London: Fontana Open Books.

Stern, C., and Stern, W. (1909/1931). *Monographien über die seelische Entwick-lung des Kindes.* 2. Band: *Erinnerung, Aussage und Lüge in der ersten Kindheit.* Leipzig: Barth.

Stouthamer-Loeber, M. (1986). Adults' perception of verbal misrepresentation of reality in four-year-olds. Unpublished manuscript, Western Psychiatric Institute and Clinic, University of Pittsburgh.

Strawson, P. F. (1964). Intention and convention in speech acts. *Philosophical Review,* 73, 439–460.

Tanz, C. (1980). *Studies in the acquisition of deictic terms.* Cambridge: Cambridge University Press.

Taylor, M. (1988). Conceptual perspective taking: Children's ability to distinguish what they know from what they see. *Child Development,* 59, 703–718.

Taylor, M., Cartwright, B. S., and Bowden, T. (1989). Perspective taking and theory of mind: Do children predict interpretive diversity as a function of differences in observers' knowledge? Unpublished manuscript, Department of Psychology, University of Oregon.

Trevarthen, C. (1979). Instincts for human understanding and for cultural cooperation: Their development in infancy. In M. von Cranach, et al. (Eds.), *Human ethology,* 530–594. Cambridge: Cambridge University Press.

Tulving, E. (1985). Memory and consciousness. *Canadian Psychology,* 26, 1–12.

Vaughn, B. E., Kopp, C. B., and Krakow, J. B. (1984). The emergence and consolidation of self-control from eighteen to thirty moths of age: Normative trends and individual differences. *Child Development,* 55, 990–1004.

Vygotsky, L. S. (1966/1978). The role of play in development. In *Mind in society,* 92–104. Cambridge, MA: Harvard University Press.

Wales, R. (1979). Deixis. In P. Fletcher and M. Garman (Eds.), *Language acquisition,* 241–260. Cambridge: Cambridge University Press.

Waldvogel, S. (1948). The frequency and affective character of childhood memories. *Psychological Monographs,* 62 (Whole No. 291). Reprinted in U. Neisser (Ed.) (1982). *Memory observed,* 73–76. San Francisco: W. H. Freeman.

Walk, R. D., and Gibson, E. J. (1961). A comparative and analytical study of visual depth perception. *Psychological Monographs,* 75 (Whole No. 519).

Walton, K. L. (1974). Are representations symbols? *The Monist,* 58, 236–254.

Webb, R. A., Massar, B., and Nadolny, R. (1972). Information and strategy in young children's search for hidden objects. *Child Development,* 43, 91–104.

Wellman, H. M. (1985). A child's theory of mind: The development of conceptions of cognition. In S. R. Yussen (Ed.), *The growth of reflection in children,* 169–206. New York: Academic Press.

Wellman, H. M. (1988). First steps in the child's theorizing about the mind. In J. W. Astington, P. L. Harris, and D. R. Olson (Eds.), *Developing theories of mind,* 64–92. New York: Cambridge University Press.

Wellman, H. M. (1990). *The child's theory of mind.* Cambridge, MA: MIT Press. A Bradford book.

Wellman, H. M., and Bartsch, K. (1988). Young children's reasoning about beliefs. *Cognition,* **30**, 239–277.

Wellman, H. M., Cross, D., and Bartsch, K. (1987). Infant search and object permanence: A meta-analysis of the A-not-B error. *Monographs of the Society for Research in Child Development,* **51** (Serial No. 214).

Wellman, H. M., and Estes, D. (1986). Early understanding of mental entities: A reexamination of childhood realism. *Child Development,* **57**, 910–923.

Wellman, H. M., and Woolley, J. D. (1990). From simple desires to ordinary beliefs: The early development of everyday psychology. *Cognition,* **35**, 245–275.

White, S. H., and Pillemer, D. B. (1979). Childhood amnesia and the development of a socially accessible memory system. In J. F. Kihlstrom and F. J. Evans (Eds.), *Functional disorders of memory,* 29–73. Hillsdale, NJ: Lawrence Erlbaum Associates.

Whiten, A., and Byrne, R. W. (1988). The manipulation of attention in primate tactical deception. In R. W. Byrne and A. Whiten (Eds.), *Machiavellian intelligence: Social expertise and the evolution of intellect in monkeys, apes, and humans,* 211–223. Oxford: Clarendon Press.

Wilensky, R. (1978). Understanding goal-based stories. Research Report No. 140, Department of Computer Science, Yale University.

Wimmer, H. (1982). *Zur Entwicklung des Verstehens von Erzählungen.* Bern: Hans Huber.

Wimmer, H. (1989a). The Cartesian versus the theory view of mind: Developmental evidence. Paper presented at the Biennial Meeting of the Society for Research in Child Development, Kansas City, MO, April 1989.

Wimmer, H. (1989b). Common-Sense Mentalismus und Emotion: Einige entwicklungspsychologische Implikationen. In E. Roth (Ed.), *Denken und Fühlen.* Berlin: Springer Verlag.

Wimmer, H., Gruber, S., and Perner, J. (1984). Young children's conception of lying: Lexical realism - moral subjectivism. *Journal of Experimental Child Psychology,* **37**, 1–30.

Wimmer, H., and Hartl, M. (in press). The Cartesian view and theory view of mind: Developmental evidence from understanding false belief in self and other. *British Journal of Developmental Psychology.*

Wimmer, H., Hogrefe, G.-J., and Perner, J. (1988). Children's understanding of informational access as source of knowledge. *Child Development,* **59**, 386–396.

Wimmer, H., Hogrefe, G.-J., and Sodian, B. (1988). A second stage in children's conception of mental life: Understanding sources of information. In J. W. Astington, P. L. Harris, and D. R. Olson (Eds.), *Developing theories of mind,* 173–192. New York: Cambridge University Press.

Wimmer, H., and Perner, J. (1983). Beliefs about beliefs: Representation and constraining function of wrong beliefs in young children's understanding of deception. *Cognition,* 13, 103–128.

Wimmer, H., and Perner, J. (1990). Unpublished manuscript, Laboratory of Experimental Psychology, University of Sussex.

Wolf, D., and Gardner, H. (1979). Style and sequence in early symbolic play. In N. R. Smith and M. B. Franklin (Eds.), *Symbolic functioning in childhood,* 117–138. Hillsdale, NJ: Lawrence Erlbaum Associates.

Woodruff, G., and Premack, D. (1979). Intentional communication in the chimpanzee: The development of deception. *Cognition,* 7, 333–362.

Wooldridge, D. (1963). *The machinery of the brain.* New York: McGraw Hill.

Yarrow, M. R., and Waxler, C. Z. (1975). The emergence and functions of prosocial behavior in young children. Paper presented at the Biennial Meeting of the Society for Research in Child Development, Denver, CO, 1975.

Yuill, N. (1984). Young children's coordination of motive and outcome in judgments of satisfaction and morality. *British Journal of Developmental Psychology,* 2, 73–81.

Zaitchik, D. (1990). When representations conflict with reality: The preschooler's problem with false beliefs and "false" photographs. *Cognition,* 35, 41–68.

Index